Foundation Rails 2

Eldon Alameda

friendsof

DESIGNER TO DESIGNER™

an Apress® company

Foundation Rails 2

ISBN-13 (pbk): 978-1-4302-1039-9

ISBN-13 (electronic): 978-1-4302-1040-5

Printed and bound in the United States of America 9 8 7 6 5 4 3 2 1

Distributed to the book trade worldwide by Springer-Verlag New York, Inc., 233 Spring Street, 6th Floor, New York, NY 10013. Phone 1-800-SPRINGER, fax 201-348-4505, e-mail orders-ny@springer-sbm.com, or visit www.springeronline.com.

For information on translations, please contact Apress directly at 2855 Telegraph Avenue, Suite 600, Berkeley, CA 94705. Phone 510-549-5930, fax 510-549-5939, e-mail info@apress.com, or visit www.apress.com.

Apress and friends of ED books may be purchased in bulk for academic, corporate, or promotional use. eBook versions and licenses are also available for most titles. For more information, reference our Special Bulk Sales–eBook Licensing web page at http://www.apress.com/info/bulksales.

The source code for this book is freely available to readers at www.friendsofed.com in the Downloads section.

Credits

Lead Editor Ben Renow-Clarke	**Production Editor** Ellie Fountain
Technical Reviewer Sean Cribbs	**Compositor** Dina Quan
Editorial Board Clay Andres, Steve Anglin, Ewan Buckingham, Tony Campbell, Gary Cornell, Jonathan Gennick, Matthew Moodie, Joseph Ottinger, Jeffrey Pepper, Frank Pohlmann, Ben Renow-Clarke, Dominic Shakeshaft, Matt Wade, Tom Welsh	**Proofreader** Patrick Vincent **Indexer** Ron Strauss **Artist** April Milne
Project Manager Kylie Johnston	**Cover Image Designer** Corné van Dooren
Copy Editor Heather Lang	**Interior and Cover Designer** Kurt Krames
Associate Production Director Kari Brooks-Copony	**Manufacturing Director** Tom Debolski

For my daughter Kaylee

"As you wish . . ."

CONTENTS AT A GLANCE

CONTENTS

Chapter 5 **Advanced ActiveRecord** **115**

Chapter 6 **Presenting the Views**. **139**

ABOUT THE AUTHOR

 Originally hailing from Northern California, **Eldon Alameda** is currently trapped in the harsh climates of Kansas City and is a web developer with over 8 years of experience building web applications and over 15 years in I.T. He is the author of an intermediate-level Rails book named *Practical Rails Projects* (ISBN: 978-1-59059-781-1) and is currently working for a start-up looking to revolutionize the digital coupon industry.

Eldon discovered Ruby and Rails in September of 2005 after a period of questioning whether he had made the wrong career choice as a web developer and quickly found his passion for development reignited. He has been fortunate enough to have been working professionally with Ruby ever since.

Eldon is also an active member of his local Ruby Users Group and strives to give presentations on a semiregular basis. When not coding, Eldon can be found writing at his personal blog, www.simplifi.es and as a contributor to the Ruby Inside and Rails Inside web sites, spending time with his daughter, or planning their next Walt Disney World vacation.

ABOUT THE TECHNICAL REVIEWER

Sean Cribbs wrote his first web page in high school over ten years ago and has been involved in the Web ever since, having built applications in Java, ASP, PHP, and more recently Ruby. He found Ruby on Rails in early 2006, shortly after version 1.0 appeared, and fell in love with its beauty and simplicity. Sean is the lead developer of Radiant, the popular Rails-based content management system, author of several Rails plug-ins, the former organizer of the Kansas City Ruby User Group, and a member of as many tech meet-ups as he can manage to attend.

Sean now lives in Chapel Hill, NC, with his wife and two cats. He likes to spend his free time playing the piano, reading, and keeping up with current events.

ABOUT THE COVER IMAGE DESIGNER

Corné van Dooren designed the front cover image for this book. Having been given a brief by friends of ED to create a new design for the Foundation series, he was inspired to create this new setup combining technology and organic forms.

With a colorful background as an avid cartoonist, Corné discovered the infinite world of multimedia at the age of 17—a journey of discovery that hasn't stopped since. His mantra has always been "The only limit to multimedia is the imagination," a mantra that is keeping him moving forward constantly.

After enjoying success after success over the past years—working for many international clients, as well as being featured in multimedia magazines, testing software, and working on many other friends of ED books—Corné decided it was time to take another step in his career by launching his own company, *Project 79*, in March 2005.

You can see more of his work and contact him through www.cornevandooren.com or www.project79.com.

If you like his work, be sure to check out his chapter in *New Masters of Photoshop: Volume 2*, also by friends of ED (ISBN: 1590593154).

ACKNOWLEDGMENTS

First and foremost, from a personal standpoint, I must take a moment to truly thank my wife Dori, who has now endured two years with a part-time husband, who's also been a part-time author. She truly has gone above and beyond what any wife should be expected to do to support me. She took on many of my household responsibilities while I was writing, did everything possible to give me the extra space I needed to write, and resisted the desire to complain for all the nights that I fell asleep at my desk writing.

Second, from the standpoint of this book, if I had any doubts after my first book, this book confirmed just how hard it truly is to write a book. While my name is the one that graces the cover, this book could not have existed without the hard work, inspiration, contributions, sacrifice, and understanding of many other people.

Writing a book is always a struggle against time. Publishers have hard deadlines for when they want the book completed, and thus it's critical for an author to have a good team of people to provide the insight and guidance necessary to steer the book correctly in such a short period of time. Fortunately, I feel as if I have had a world-class team supporting this book.

Ben Renow-Clarke was my editor again for this book, and as I anticipated, he has been invaluable. This was my second time working with Ben: his insights and direction in identifying weak areas of the book have made the book what it is today. I truly appreciated all of his comments, suggestions (even when they meant I suddenly had a lot more work to do), and criticisms.

Sean Cribbs has been a friend of mine from the Kansas City Ruby Users Group for several years, and I was very excited to have him provide technical editing for this book. Sean is a great guy with a wonderful sense of a humor, and he is a solid Ruby programmer. Working with him on this book has been a real treat, as he always provided good criticisms and corrected many mistakes that someone else might have missed. He's also served as the perfect counter-balance to my sense of humor, helping to reel me in when I would have gone too far.

Kylie Johnston has been the project manager for this project, which means that she has had the unenviable task of trying to keep us all on schedule. However, she has done the job with such grace and tact that, even when she was holding everyone's feet to the fire on the schedule, she was always likable and fun. She was a joy to work with, and if I ever write for friends of Ed or Apress again, I'll be sure to request her as my project manager.

The copy editor Heather Lang deserves thanks for the tireless work that she endured cleaning up my writing, correcting my grammar, and ensuring that the book remained consistent throughout. I'm sure that she probably doesn't get paid enough for the work that she does, but I can certainly guarantee that without her contribution to this project, the final book would have been more tedious to read.

Thanks also go out to Ellie Fountain for her work as the production editor on the book. She made the entire production review a smooth and painless process for me. She's truly professional, and I was impressed with her concern about the quality of the book.

Finally, a quick thanks to the following people who, over the years, have taught or inspired me in my own development as a Rails programmer: David Heinemeier Hansson, Dave Thomas, Chad Fowler, Marcel Molina, Jamis Buck, Michael Koziarski, Geoffrey Grosenbach, Rick Olsen, Ben Curtis, Nick Kallen, John Nunemaker, Obie Fernandez, Venkat Subramaniam, Andy Hunt, Ryan Bates, Chris Wanstrath, PJ Hyett, Peter Cooper, Zed Shaw, Maik Schmidt, Assaf Arkin, David A. Black, Thomas Fuchs, Amy Hoy, Russ Olsen, Ryan Daigle, Shashank Date, Scotty Moon, and Sean Cribbs

INTRODUCTION

As an introduction to this book, I thought I'd start out by telling you my own story of how I came to Ruby and Rails. In the summer of 2005, I had been doing web development for a number of years. At that point in my career, the primary language that I used was PHP, but occasionally, I would venture into the Java and .NET programming realms for projects.

I remember the time clearly, because it was just before my first trip to Disney World, a trip I wanted to take to get away from web development for a little while. You see, at that point, I had really begun to question if I had made a mistake when I chose to be a web developer. Building web applications was just no longer fun and had actually become monotonous and boring to me. All my projects had blurred together to the point that I felt that I was simply reimplementing the same things again and again.

I had grown tired of feeling like I was merely spinning my wheels as a developer and tired of fighting against the limitations of the programming language when I was building large-scale applications. I knew I needed a change, as I could not see myself living with this lifestyle for 10 to 20 years. So even though I was on vacation, I had a hard time relaxing while I contemplated my future: should I go back to doing something more generic in I.T., such as database administration, or could I find a solution to my dilemmas as a web developer?

When I came back from vacation, I went by my local bookstore and purchased a number of new books to help me make a decision. During that period, I read several books on server administration, database design, and even refamiliarized myself with a few other programming languages. Unfortunately, nothing seemed to fit with what I was looking for. Around this time, I discovered a web site that was doing a few cool JavaScript effects in the page that caught my eye. Being the inquisitive type that I am, I went to the page's source code and discovered that it was using a JavaScript library by the name of script.aculo.us.

As I began to learn about script.aculo.us, I noticed that its documentation kept making reference to the Ruby on Rails framework and was constantly giving examples of how several lines of script.aculo.us code were often reduced to a single line of Rails code to produce the same effect. I had read about Ruby a few times over the years but had passed it off as too niche for me to learn. But the ease with which advanced visual effects could be implemented in Ruby on Rails really caught my eye, so I decided to do a little research on the subject.

Fortunately for me, the Pragmatic Programmers had recently released a beta version of the first Rails book named *Agile Web Development with Rails* (ISBN: 978-0-9776166-3-3). I purchased the PDF thinking it would make for some light reading, yet found myself absolutely enthralled by what I read. While it may sound like an exaggeration, I probably read that PDF a good 20 times before the print version of the book was available, and I wore out my copy of that as well.

What I found in Rails was a solution to my dilemma. Rails could free me from much of my daily monotony in web development, allowing me to focus more on the areas that were fun and interesting. In addition, Rails also provided me with many advanced features out of the box to make my applications better than they would normally be. Best of all, Rails worked in a way that felt natural and was *fun* to use. So I immediately went and obtained a new job that would let me develop in Ruby and Rails, and I've been fortunate enough to be able to work with both ever since. Rails has not only saved my career, but I believe that it has made me a far better programmer than I would have been otherwise.

I agreed to write this Foundation book for the simple fact that I truly believe in Rails as one of the ideal solutions for building web applications, and I wanted to help others in their process of learning Rails and capturing the same passion that I have for the framework.

Who this book is for

I wrote this book with the goal of providing an introduction to Rails for people who have some passing familiarity with other scripting languages such as JavaScript or PHP. That being said, the main requirement for success with this book is simply going to be motivation and curiosity. Readers with an abundance of both, who are willing to go beyond simply reading the words on the pages by trying out all the code themselves, will be able to learn the lessons contained in this book the most effectively (regardless of previous experience).

How this book is structured

My goal in this book is to get you not just to follow along with the words on the pages but to also play with Ruby on Rails. So at every turn, I'm constantly trying to introduce you to tools that you can use to experiment and examples that you can play around with. I'm a big believer in the fact that you learn the most by doing, and that you learn even more when things go wrong, because understanding why that result occurred engages your mind.

Please, as you're going through this book, try out everything that I show you (even when I don't explicitly tell you to) and play around with the code—see what happens when you pass in different values or if you try to expand the scope of a solution. You'll learn more that way.

With that said, within this book, you're going to be taking a guided tour of Rails. We'll start simply enough with some introductory chapters that talk about why you should care about Rails and a brief introduction to the Ruby programming language. Afterward, we'll do our first drive through some Rails code, exploring the request-response cycle and how to build some simple pages within the framework.

Once you have your bearings on what Rails is and what it looks like, we'll spend several chapters digging deeper into the core components of Rails, such as how Rails interacts with the database and how we add dynamic content to our pages using Ruby. These lessons are meant to build on each other, so that when we move into building a full Rails application together near the end of the book, you'll be able to easily follow along without fear of getting lost.

For that full example project, we'll be building a Rails application with dynamic features such as user registration, geocoding, AJAX filtering of results, RSS feeds, and an XML interface.

After that, we'll close out our time together with some discussions of important topics such as testing your application's code, securing your application from hackers, optimizing your code for the best performance, and finally, deploying your applications to a production web server.

Layout conventions

To keep this book as clear and easy to follow as possible, the following text conventions are used throughout.

Important words or concepts are normally highlighted on the first appearance in **bold type**.

Code is presented in fixed-width font.

New or changed code is normally presented in **bold fixed-width font**.

Pseudo-code and variable input are written in *italic fixed-width font*.

Menu commands are written in the form Menu ➤ Submenu ➤ Submenu.

Where I want to draw your attention to something, I've highlighted it like this:

> *Ahem, don't say I didn't warn you.*

Sometimes code won't fit on a single line in a book. Where this happens, I use an arrow like this: ➡.

```
This is a very, very long section of code that should be written all on ➡
the same line without a break.
```

Downloading the code

The source code for this book is available to readers at www.friendsofED.com in the Downloads section of this book's home page. Please feel free to visit the friends of ED web site and download all the code there. You can also check for errata and find related titles from friends of ED and Apress.

Contacting the author

I have set up a basic support site for this book at www.foundationrails.com. There, you will be able to find additional links that I feel are relevant, and of course, you'll be able to contact me directly if you have any questions about the book.

Chapter 1

WHY RAILS?

Let me be the first to welcome you to the wonderful world of developing web applications with Ruby on Rails. Ruby on Rails is an absolutely wonderful web development framework that I have a lot of passion for, and by the end of this book, I hope to have infected you with that same passion. Developing web applications in Ruby on Rails has not only made me more productive, but I believe that it has also made me a better programmer.

However, before we start our journey of learning Ruby on Rails, I thought it would be good to pause for a moment and talk about what makes Ruby on Rails special and why you should want to learn it.

What makes Rails so special?

There's no denying that Ruby on Rails has gotten more than a little attention these last few years. The mere mention of its name can cause pretty extreme reactions of love or hate from many web developers. If you've ever read Kathy Sierra's blog about passion (http://headrush.typepad.com/creating_passionate_users/2005/08/physics_of_pass.html), you'll know that it is often the most popular and well-loved products or companies that also have the strongest opponents and that this isn't a bad thing. Anything that generates feelings this strong is bound to attract a significant amount of anti-passion as well. As a great example, just look at the reaction people have to Apple computer products.

But what is it about Rails that causes such extreme reactions? There have been plenty of other web frameworks before Rails and many since that have never received anywhere near the attention that has been lavished onto Rails. So what are some of the things that make Rails so special?

That's a harder question to answer definitively than you might think, but I've put together some of my own thoughts about the features and philosophies behind Ruby on Rails that helped make it such a revolutionary force in the realm of web development.

Extracted from a real application

Perhaps one of my favorite things about the Ruby on Rails framework is that it was extracted from real web applications, unlike many other frameworks and technologies where some unknown group (who may not even use their own technology) decided on the features based on what they thought might be popular. Contrast that development model with Rails, where every single feature was first used in production in a real web application before it was extracted and added to the core framework.

Because Rails came from real applications, as users of the Rails framework, we're not stuck in the role of guinea pigs testing the new features with each release. No, each one of Rails' features has already been battle-tested and proven to be useful by real developers in the real work of building modern web applications.

Uses convention over configuration

There's an urban legend surrounding Albert Einstein that states that he maintained a closet full of copies of the exact same suit, so that he wouldn't have to waste any mental energy deciding which outfit to wear on a given day. Unfortunately, while many believe this legend to be true, historical fact shows us that much of it is actually highly exaggerated.

Regardless, I believe that the reason that so many people accept this myth as fact is because innately we recognize that there is a powerful principle hidden within. The less energy we spend on things that don't matter, the more energy we have to spend on the things that do.

Within Ruby on Rails, there is a standard set of conventions that the framework expects you to follow. For example, when it comes to your database, Rails expects that all database field names are lower-cased, database table names are pluralized, and every database table has a primary key named id. In essence, these conventions gently nudge you down the path of following best practice advice.

Better yet, as long as you follow these conventions, you'll find that you'll be able to build web applications faster and with much less fuss. For example, Rails uses a standard naming convention for the relationship between classes and database tables (classes are singular, and tables are plural). So if for some strange reason, we needed to model dolphins in a Rails application, we would name our class dolphin and our database table dolphins. As long as we followed that naming convention, we would be rewarded in our development time by not having to perform any additional configuration to link that class and that table together.

At first, adopting these new conventions might seem like a lot to remember, but trust me, before long, they will become second nature to you.

80 / 20 rule

One of the primary goals of any web framework is to provide solutions for that 80 percent of code that will typically remain the same between applications, thus freeing you to focus on the remaining 20 percent that will be unique to your application. Rails does this very well by focusing its attention on providing web developers with a superior infrastructure and using extreme restraint (and the all-important willingness to say no) to keep business logic features out of Rails.

So in Rails, you'll find that you've been provided solutions for such things as database abstraction, logging, XML / JSON communication, web services, caching, and testing. But you won't find solutions for things that should belong in the business logic for each individual application such as content management, user authentication, or prebuilt administration systems (although Rails makes building many of these things a trivial matter, and often, you can even find plug-ins to help jumpstart building these components as well).

Model-View-Controller pattern

Ruby on Rails also helps to keep your web applications organized through its implementation of the Model-View-Controller (MVC) pattern. The MVC pattern was originally designed as a means of structuring code for applications that have a graphical user interface. Though it's often implemented in slightly different ways, the core idea of MVC is to separate your code into three distinct areas of responsibility.

Code that controls or manipulates the data associated with your application (most commonly from the database) or stores business logic for validating or formatting of data will be stored in the model layer. Some examples of code that would be stored at the model layer would be any methods that read or write data to the database, interact with a payment processor, or resize and store image uploads.

Meanwhile, your HTML templates that are eventually displayed to the end user in response to a web request would be stored within the view layer. This is where you will find the HTML or XML building templates used by your web application.

Finally, the controller layer is where we store the code that responds to users' requests by interacting with models to obtain the correct data and choosing which view to render in response. Controllers are where you store code that evaluates incoming parameters, receives POST submissions, and handles user authentication.

In a Rails request-response cycle, the different parts of the MVC pattern will be used as shown in Figure 1-1.

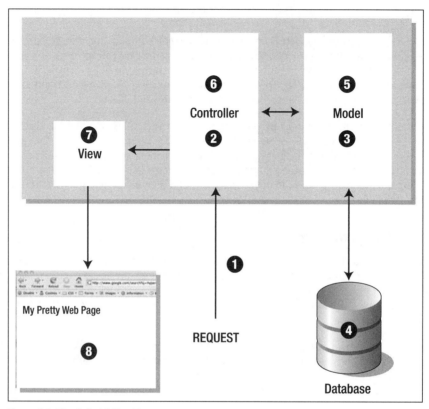

Figure 1-1. The Rails MVC pattern

In Figure 1-1, the following steps occur in response to a request for a page:

1. We receive a new request for a page to our Rails application.
2. Rails routes this request to a controller for processing.
3. Our controller interacts with the models in our application to gather the necessary data.
4. Our model classes may retrieve or insert data into our database.
5. Once our models have generated or retrieved the correct information, they return the data back to the controller.
6. The controller collects all of the data it's received from the models and selects a view template to render.
7. The view template is rendered using the data that the controller gathered and handed to the web server.
8. An HTML page is returned to the user.

DRY (Don't Repeat Yourself)

Adopting the Don't Repeat Yourself (DRY) principle from the book *The Pragmatic Programmer* (Addison-Wesley, ISBN: 020161622X), Rails provides a number of tools to help keep your code DRY (or free from duplication). The basic mantra is that, as developers, we should strive to refactor the same (or similar) code out of multiple locations in our code base into a single location. This allows us to make a change in a single location and see those changes across the application. Doing this not only keeps our code base smaller but results in code that's less buggy and easier to maintain over the long term.

Rails provides a number tools that allow us to easily abstract duplicated elements out of our code and into a shared resource. Some examples include partials (which allow us to reuse common HTML fragments multiple times), layouts (which allow us to define a common header and footer template that will be automatically applied to our HTML templates), and helper methods (which allow us to move snippets of Ruby code to a common place so they can be reused again and again). We'll take a deeper look at these in Chapter 6.

Opinionated software

One challenge that many find when first coming to Rails is the discovery that Rails was designed to be highly opinionated software. Rails attempts to impose many best practice techniques and conventions on the developer in order to create web applications that are composed both elegantly and correctly. It enforces these opinions in a very light-handed way—meaning that Rails provides enough flexibility that you can choose to eschew these opinions—but you will find you'll be much more productive if you choose to follow the golden path that Rails has laid before you.

Uses Ruby for (almost) everything

Another way that Rails speeds up your web development efforts is that it uses Ruby for just about everything that you need to do. Building web applications in other languages, such as PHP, often means that you need to understand of a variety of languages in order to be effective. To interact with your database, you might find yourself writing hundreds of SQL queries. Within your web pages you could write large amounts of duplicated HTML for common elements such as forms, links, and so on. Finally, if you need advanced client interactions, such as AJAX, you might also have to write large chunks of custom JavaScript functions.

Ruby on Rails simplifies much of this by using the power of Ruby.

For database interactions, Rails provides methods that allow you to interact with your database in extremely advanced ways without having to write a single SQL query. We'll be talking about how to use these methods in great detail in Chapter 4. Additionally, Rails provides a solution named "migrations" that allows you to easily create and modify your databases.

For AJAX functionality, Rails provides you with helper methods that make adding advanced AJAX functionality to a page a simple matter of adding a line or two of Ruby code. In addition, Rails also features a complete server-side solution that you can use to automate dynamic changes to a page in response to an AJAX request.

Now, using Ruby for all these extra tasks may seem a bit gimmicky at first glance. After all, if you're already used to writing your own custom SQL queries and JavaScript functions, why would you want to give up that control? I know that I certainly felt that way when these features were first added to Rails. However, after having used them for several years, I can certainly testify that not switching language contexts is a truly powerful practice that really does speed up development.

Plus, using those features is optional; you're always free to write your own SQL or JavaScript by hand if you want to fine-tune things or you just enjoy writing those things.

Emphasis on beauty

Much like programming in the Ruby language that Rails is built with, Rails developers place a special emphasis on their code being both functional and beautiful. The creator of Rails, David Heinemeier Hansson, gave a wonderful presentation on the pursuit of beauty in code in which he stated, "Beauty leads to happiness; happiness leads to productivity; thus beauty leads to productivity." And Rails delivers productivity in spades with the ability to write code that is extremely expressive and beautiful with examples such as this:

```
Debt.transaction do
  peter.borrow(100)
  paul.pay(100)
end
```

In this example, you can see that by wrapping our method calls in a transaction we ensure that we don't pay Paul unless we first successfully borrowed money from Peter.

```
class Post < ActiveRecord::Base
  has_many :comments
end
```

Here, you can see that Rails allows us to easily express a relationship between blog posts and comments in that each blog post is allowed to have many comments associated to it.

```
Book.find_by_author 'Eldon Alameda'
```

In this slightly vain example, you can see that we are able to express complex database searches in a highly readable form.

```
class Rockstar < Person
  belongs_to :band
  has_one :agent
  has_many :sexual_encounters
  has_many :children, :through => :sexual_encounters
end
```

In our final and slightly risqué example, we show how expressive Rails is, as we use it to model very complex (or should they be called complicated?) relationships to try to represent the various types of relationships that a rock star may have.

Testing

Another wonderful thing about Ruby on Rails is the emphasis that the framework places on automated testing. As you build your Rails applications, you'll find that Rails automatically adds test stubs and sample test scripts for each of your models and controllers that Rails generates. In this regard, Rails moves testing from being one of those things that we should do to one of those things that's easy to do. As we progress through this book, we'll be discussing testing in general as well as the practice of test-first development. However, in order to keep current, we'll be focusing our time and energy on a relatively new testing framework by the name of RSpec. Although RSpec isn't the default testing framework included with Rails, it has made huge inroads into the community and has quickly become the testing framework of choice for a massive number of Ruby and Rails developers. We'll cover testing our code with RSpec in Chapter 10, where we'll also discuss how to install and apply it to our applications since RSpec isn't (currently) included with the Rails framework. But don't worry, because even though we'll have to do a small amount of additional work, we'll be rewarded with a far more descriptive, easier-to-read, and—dare I say it—prettier testing language that I believe will help you *want* to test your code.

Development tools

Another beautiful thing about developing in Ruby and Rails is that it comes with a number of tools that make getting up and running quick and easy. For example, rather than making you go through the pain of building and configuring a development web server environment, Rails includes a built-in development web server that you can run for each project.

Of course, as you're starting out with new language, another challenge that comes up often is the need to understand what specific lines of code are doing. Rails provides a couple of powerful tools to aid in your learning. First off, an interactive command line shell allows to you type raw Rails code in to see and interact with the result of each method you call. You can also set breakpoints within your Rails application that will allow you to send the current application environment and variables into the interactive console at any point, so you can explore why something isn't working.

Rich community and plug-ins

Perhaps because of the focus on creating reusable, beautiful code, the Rails community also provides a wealth of shared code through the use of Rails plug-ins. From connecting your Rails application to LDAP systems to generating generic authentication systems or even having your application e-mail you whenever an error occurs in production, plug-ins are available for a large portion of the needs that you might have while developing in Rails. Even better is the fact that extending your applications with these additional functionalities is often as simple as running a single command and sometimes adding a single line to a model—thanks to the wonderful flexibility of the Ruby language.

In addition, the Rails community is a joy to work with (for the most part). That doesn't mean that there aren't some less savory people within the community, but that's going to be true of any community. Overall, though, I always enjoy the time I get to spend talking with other Rails developers, and you'll find that most are more than willing to share their knowledge to help others learn how to code in Rails as well.

One caveat, though, is that a large number of people have attempted to take advantage of the community members' willingness to help each other by pushing too hard and even trying to get people to do their work for them. Don't become one of those people. As the name of this book implies, my purpose is to provide you a solid foundation of how to build applications in Rails and provide you with the knowledge to take advantage of the wealth of information available online. Obviously, no one book could cover every nuance of a framework like Rails, but with a good foundation of the basics, you'll be able to easily take advantage of the Rails API documents, Rails blogs, and numerous other online resources available to you from a few simple Google searches. So all that being said, while you can easily find people who are willing to help you within the community, it's very important that you do go through the effort of looking for the answers yourself in this book and in those other resources before simply posting your question to the nearest Rails mailing group or IRC channel—otherwise, you run the risk of being labeled a help vampire.

Support for different environments

Another point of pain that most web developers deal with is the issue of reconfiguring their application code to move between development and production environments. For example, in development, you'll typically be using a local database, and you might want the application to display verbose errors when things go wrong. However, in production, you typically will use a relational database that's hosted on a different server (with different connection settings, usernames, passwords, etc.), and you'd want to hide most errors from the end user with graceful error messages. In most web programming, reconfiguring these parameters means hacking a number of configuration files, but Rails comes with support out of the box for development, production, and test environments. Each environment has its database connection settings, logging levels, and so on, so you can make these configuration items once and then merely activate your application using the correct environment.

Advanced web services support

While Rails has traditionally provided support for SOAP and XML-RPC web services, it was in Rails 2.0 that the framework took a hard stance of favoring RESTful web services as the preferred format. With Rails 2.0, adding a REST-based API to our application is so easy now that it's almost silly to not consider it.

In addition, Rails 2 added a new library to the framework by the name of ActiveResource that makes consuming external REST services as easy as querying a database.

Making it easy to both build and consume REST services with your Rails applications means that building web applications that communicate with each other and share data is a now a near trivial matter with Rails.

Common directory structure

When I was a child, one area that caused my mother great distress was my inability to keep my bedroom clean. Now, contrary to what my wife may say about me, I don't believe that the problem was that I was inherently lazy or unorganized. Rather, I think it was more an issue of not having enough structure. In my room, I had one large toy chest and eight extra-large bedside drawers in which to store everything I owned, so at any time, these drawers would be filled with toys, clothes, books, and all sorts of miscellaneous junk. Unfortunately when it came time to clean my room, I would often shove whatever items were out into the nearest large container that still had room. So open any of the drawers in my bed, and you might have found stacks of comic books, socks, miscellaneous Star Wars figures, and occasionally something gross like an uneaten sandwich.

Sadly, I've come across far too many web applications that are much like my childhood room. They lack any form of preplanned structure. When a new piece of functionality was needed, the new code was merely shoved into the closest file or directory without much thought for keeping things organized.

Contrast this with my daughter's room, which is kept in a much more orderly fashion. In her room, we've created a system where each of her toys has a specific container it belongs in, so when she goes to clean, it's a simple matter of putting each thing back into its proper place. As a result, her room remains much more orderly and easier to maintain, as evidenced in Figure 1-2.

Figure 1-2. In my daughter's room, each item has a place, just like in a well-built web application.

In much the same way, every Rails application provides a common directory structure that dictates where each bit of code goes. While this organization may sound like a trivial matter, in practice, it's exceptionally powerful, as it not only eliminates any question about where to place the different parts of your application but also makes it extremely easy for another developer to pick up your application and quickly understand what's happening in the code.

Fast to develop in

By allowing you to simply focus on the things that make your application unique, such as the business logic and the user interface, Ruby on Rails allows you to get your web application up and running in a minimal amount of time. In fact, I've personally had a lot of fun over the last few years blowing the minds of clients or non-Rails developers with just how fast I can transform a rough idea into an actual working prototype. In fact, a few times, I've been at an initial meeting with a client in a restaurant, and I've been able to bang out a rough working prototype of what they were describing while they were talking!

Fun

Finally, although it's impossible to quantify this, I believe that Rails is just more fun to develop in. Not only am I able to get my applications up and running faster than with any other technology, but when I'm finished, I enjoy reading the code that I've written because of both its aesthetics and its clearness of expression.

Why not Rails?

There's no doubt that I feel that Ruby on Rails web development is by far the best approach to building modern web applications. For me, it truly has brought the fun back to the Web. Of course, nothing is perfect, and Rails is no exception, so let's close out this chapter with a quick tour of some of the uglier issues of Rails development.

Not a silver bullet

With all the praises I've heaped on Rails, I should mention that Rails is not the solution for every web application. If all you need is a simple brochure site, a web page that can accept a form submission, or simply a way to output a tiny bit of dynamic content onto a page, Rails is almost certainly overkill for those simple needs. However, if you want to build a modern database-driven web application, Rails is the way to go.

In addition, because of the magic of many of the early screen casts and hype surrounding Rails, some people came to the framework thinking of it as some sort of magical solution that would automate the entire business of creating web applications. In reality, while developers of all levels can take advantage of the power Rails and Ruby provide, the best results will still come from developers who invest the time to gain a solid foundation. In this book, I'm striving to help you gain that foundation, and along the way, I'll even show you some of my earliest Rails code as proof that it's possible to create a spaghetti mess in Rails.

Slower benchmarks

One sad truth is that if you were to compare the benchmarks of a Ruby on Rails application with many other web technologies, you'd find that Rails does perform a bit slower. Does this mean that Rails is inferior or unsuitable? Absolutely not! Ruby on Rails is more than fast enough to suit the needs of most web applications. In addition, Rails also provides built-in support for four levels of advanced caching (query, page, action, and fragment), so that you can easily remove any expensive page-generating cycles out of your application's response, massively increasing the scalability and speed of your application. And these advanced caching systems can be enabled with just a few short lines.

So while Rails may never win any benchmark contests (although there is some really fascinating work going on currently to provide faster implementations of Ruby that may change this in the near future), it really is a nonissue for anyone working with Rails.

Deployment difficulties

Although developing web applications in Rails is a pure joy, historically, deploying those same Rails applications to a production web server could be a challenge—especially for people who have never done any server administration. By its nature, Rails is a bit more demanding to deploy when compared to a solution such as PHP. I could tell you horror stories about my first attempts to deploy Rails applications running FastCGI.

Now, before you go running for the hills, let me assure you that deploying Rails applications has gotten tremendously easier over the years. Even while I have been writing this book, the process of deploying Rails applications has become infinitely easier with the release of solutions such as mod_rails. There are also a growing number of service providers who have created applications that eliminate most (if not all) the pain of deploying your Rails application. We'll talk about some of the options for deploying your Rails application in Chapter 14.

Rapidly changing

Another area that I should make you aware of is the fact that development techniques and best practices within Rails can often change at a fairly rapid pace. Because Rails is constantly evolving, it isn't the kind of technology that you can learn one year and come back to it a year later without updating your knowledge. This rapid development is really an indication of the passion behind Rails developers to continuously improve both the framework and the development practices that we use to create web applications.

At the end of this book, I'll share a few of my favorite resources for keeping current with new and upcoming changes to the Rails framework.

Not understanding the code

One final danger of developing in Rails is that there can be a risk of becoming too dependent on the tools that Rails provides and the wealth of plug-ins available. Using Rails scaffolding tools and plug-ins that build authentication systems, administrative back ends, and a wealth of other functionality, you may be able to build a mostly functional application without any understanding of the underlying code that controls it. That quickly becomes a problem when something goes wrong with the application or you need to modify the code to handle a special circumstance. From my own observations, copy-and-paste code jobs always result in pain.

Summary

In this chapter, we discussed some of the highs and lows of developing applications in Ruby on Rails. We also discussed some of the core philosophies behind Ruby on Rails that have made it such a revolutionary force. In our next chapter, we'll start our tour of building a web application in Ruby on Rails by taking a high-level tour of Ruby, the language that Rails is built in.

Chapter 2

A SHORT INTRODUCTION TO RUBY

After spending the last chapter talking about how fun and exciting it is to build web applications in Rails, let's get something out of the way; you're going to need to learn some Ruby.

Not only was Rails built using Ruby but creating a Rails application means that you'll also be coding in Ruby. Because of that, I don't think it would be a good idea for us to rush directly into building our first Rails application without first taking a few minutes to go over some basics of the Ruby language.

What is Ruby?

Ruby is a general-purpose object-oriented scripting language that originated in Japan in the mid-1990s. While it had made some inroads in other countries with its flexible and powerful syntax, it really wasn't until Ruby on Rails came onto the scene that it exploded in popularity and prominence in the United States (sometimes to its own detriment, as the hype surrounding it became almost deafening at times).

But was that hype undeserved? I would say no, but admittedly, I'm also a bit biased. It's been said that Ruby is like programming in English for computers, but I think that programming in Ruby is more like developing a drug problem because it's incredibly addictive. There's such freedom, expressiveness, and yes, beauty to Ruby code that I find myself yearning to get back to it anytime I'm forced to program in another language. In fact, I often joke that Rails is the entry-level drug that starts you down the path to becoming a Ruby programmer.

Leaving my drug hyperbole aside, Ruby is an incredibly powerful language to learn and immensely useful for a large variety of applications beyond the web. You should learn Ruby not only to make you a better Rails programmer but also because, once you do, you'll find it to be a powerful ally for more tasks than you can imagine. To learn Ruby, though, is going to require more then we'll be able to cover in this short chapter, so I've also listed a few recommendations of my favorite Ruby books and resources at the end of the book for you to use to expand your knowledge. In the meantime, let's take a look at what makes Ruby so special.

Ruby is object oriented

Of the variety of programming paradigms within programming languages, object orientation is the one that's gained the most attention over the last 20 years. In object-oriented programming (OOP), programmers use the language to describe and model real-world things, calling these representations "objects." So an OOP program might consist of a number of represented concepts with objects with names like "vehicles," "furniture," "users," or "dogs."

Within OOP, each of these objects that we create is aware of its own unique attributes, and each object is able to interact and communicate with other objects.

Creating an object requires that we first define a class. A class can be thought of as the general template or blueprint for an object. We use that class to create new instances of an object.

Each class defines some generic properties and methods that will be shared among all instances of that class. We use properties to represent the things that the object will know about itself (its state, unique values, etc.), and we use methods to represent the things that an object can do.

To make that clearer, let's use a simple example where we imagine that we want to represent dogs within our application. Thinking about the things that all dogs can do, we might define methods within our class such as bark or wag_tail. Thinking about the attributes of a specific dog, we might create properties in our dog class such as name and breed.

Within our application, we could then use this dog class to create representations of several different dogs. So we might create one dog object with its name set to "Butch" and its breed as an English Bulldog. Meanwhile, a second dog object might have properties of "Tiffany" and "Golden Retriever." Even though you won't understand all of it just yet, let's see what this would look like in Ruby:

```ruby
class Dog
  attr_accessor :name, :breed

  def bark
    puts "Woof"
  end

  def wag_tail
    puts "Wagging Tail"
  end
end
```

So with our new Dog class, we could create a new instance of it in Ruby using the new keyword:

```
dog1 = Dog.new
```

The attr_accessor method we used in our Dog class is a Ruby shortcut that creates both the instance variables of name and breed for us within our class as well as creating the getter and setter methods, which allow us to read or change the values of those variables at any time. We can use the setter methods that were created to set dog1's unique properties:

```
dog1.name = "Butch"
dog1.breed = "English Bulldog"
```

From here, we can also call the methods that we've created to interact with our new dog:

```
dog1.bark       #  woof
dog1.name       #  "Butch"
dog1.wag_tail   #  wagging tail
```

> Technically, we don't really call methods on objects in Ruby; instead we pass messages to the object. The object accepts those messages and invokes the method with the matching name. It may sound like a trivial difference, but it sets the stage for us to do some pretty amazing things, such as responding to method calls that don't exist.

We need to move on, even though we've just barely touched on the concepts behind object orientation. It's important to note, however, that unlike many other languages where object orientation was an afterthought tacked onto the language with some duct tape and superglue, Ruby brings forth a completely unified vision of how object orientation within a programming language should be. In Ruby, everything (and I do mean *everything*) is an object. You'll see what this means and the power it brings as we begin exploring some actual Ruby code.

Ruby is interpreted

With Ruby, there is no compiler like you would find in languages such as C or Pascal. In compiled languages such as those, you write your code in your development environment and then must run that code through a compiler, which converts your code directly into machine code for a specific operating system.

When writing code in interpreted languages such as Ruby, PHP, or Python, however, we simply pass our plain text script into an interpreter that processes it on the fly.

Being an interpreted language does mean that Ruby scripts will always execute slower when compared against a compiled language. It also means that Ruby scripts are far more portable, and they have more flexibility, as they can perform incredible feats of agility that leave compiled languages sitting on the sidelines staring openmouthed in disbelief. Compiled languages are fairly static things once they've been compiled, whereas Ruby code is able to be far more dynamic and even enhance itself at runtime.

15

Ruby is dynamically typed

Within most programming languages, there are two standards for how variables are typed, which is a fancy way of describing how the computer knows whether the number 42 that you just entered is a string ("42"), a whole number (42), or even a decimal (42.0).

Many languages get around this question by using static typing, which requires that you declare the type of data that will be allowed in a variable when you create it, like this:

```
integer mynumber = 42;
string knock_knock = "Aren't you glad I didn't say banana?";
```

In addition, with a statically typed language, if we attempt to store a type of data into a variable other than the one it was defined for (such as putting a string into our mynumber variable), the program will not allow it and raise an error.

Ruby, on the other hand, uses dynamic typing, where variables are generic buckets and the computer will do its best to figure out what type of data is in the variable based on the data that you assign to it:

```
mynumber = 42
            # creates the mynumber variable to hold integer values
my_other_number = "42"
                # creates the my_other_number variable to hold string values
```

Not only does this free up our code of a lot of noise but, since our variables aren't tied to a specific data type, it allows us to store different types of data in a single variable. So we're not limited to only storing strings into the my_other_number variable; we could use it to store integer, decimal, or even array values.

Ruby is reflective

While saying that Ruby is reflective may conjure up an image of some mystic wanderer contemplating the meaning of existence while sitting yoga-style on the top of a remote mountain, "being reflective" means, in computer science terms, that Ruby is aware of its own structure and is able to not only observe what it's doing at any moment in time but also modify its own structure and behavior on the fly in response to events.

What this means in human terms is that our Ruby objects aren't locked down and can be modified at any time. This makes our Ruby code exceptionally flexible, as we can do amazing things such as asking an object if it supports a method and then dynamically create the missing method on the fly if the response is no. While our program is running, we can even use Ruby's dynamic nature to completely redefine and modify an existing method to support our current needs. You'll see this in action in the section called "The Anarchy of Ruby."

Interacting with Ruby

Enough theory—an important thing about this book is that, while I certainly want to give you the high-level knowledge (so you can understand the "whys"), I'm much more interested in getting you to a place where you can get your hands dirty and begin playing around with real code. So now that we've talked about some of the philosophies behind the Ruby language, let's start playing with some real Ruby.

Introducing irb

One of my favorite tools for experimenting with Ruby is the Interactive Ruby (irb) shell. irb is a powerful tool for allowing you to not only interact with Ruby commands and their return values line by line but also inspect objects in real time. We'll be using irb for the rest of this chapter as a means to play around with the Ruby syntax and get some hands-on experience with the language.

Please don't short-change your own learning by simply reading this chapter. You can't learn to program by reading about it anymore than you could learn ballroom dancing from a book. You're going to get the most of this chapter if you follow along with the discussion by typing the example code into your own irb session and experimenting beyond the simple code examples I provide. Plus, doing so helps you prepare for later chapters when we'll be using a Rails-specific version of irb to explore some important Rails concepts.

Using irb is simple. Once you have Ruby installed on your system (see Appendix B for assistance if you don't have Ruby installed yet), you can simply open up a command prompt and type irb to begin your session; see Figure 2-1.

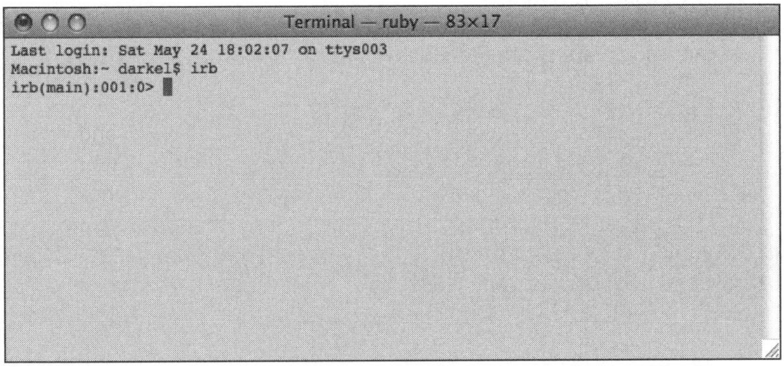

```
Last login: Sat May 24 18:02:07 on ttys003
Macintosh:~ darkel$ irb
irb(main):001:0>
```

Figure 2-1. Starting our first irb session

Now that we have an irb session started, we can simply type Ruby code, and irb will execute it and display the return value for each expression that we enter, as shown in Figure 2-2.

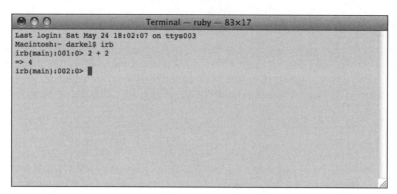

Figure 2-2. Using irb to turn your computer into a large, expensive calculator

Literals

As you saw in our previous example, you can simply type expressions directly into irb. Let's try a few more:

```
4 + 7        #  11
8 * 5        #  40
34 - 12       #  22
60 / 15       #  4
```

All right, so now that we've proven that we can use Ruby as a simple calculator, let's get back to the discussion of what we're actually doing. When we use numbers or strings directly in our code that is not assigned to a variable, we're using them as literals. And as I just indicated, we're not limited to just literal numbers, we can also create string literals that simply repeat back what we just typed.

```
"Stewie is Cool!"        #  "Stewie is Cool!"
```

Yay!

> *Admittedly, you'd have to be a pretty huge fan of Family Guy to get that reference. Let's just say it involves Stewie using a Mac.*

There is always a returned value

Another important distinction about Ruby is that every Ruby literal, variable, statement, method, and so on (in other words, anything we could enter) always has a returned value. You'll notice that irb is extra helpful because it always shows you the returned value of your statement, as you can see in these examples:

```
irb(main):001:0> "Stewie is Cool"
=> "Stewie is Cool"
```

So on the first line we entered our string of "Stewie is Cool", and irb showed us the return value of that statement on the next line preceded by an arrow (=>). This is an extremely helpful feature of irb, as it can help you to troubleshoot blocks of code that are behaving differently than you might expect.

Of course, while every statement does return a value, there are some occasions when that returned value is nil, which is Ruby's term for the absence of a value (similar to NULL in other languages). To see that in action, we can use a method that returns a nil value such as Ruby's puts method, which is used to output a value to the screen:

```
irb(main):004:0> puts "I return nil and yet I exist"
I return nil and yet I exist
=> nil
```

You can see that, after our call to the puts method, Ruby printed out our string, yet the return value of the puts method call was a nil value.

Everything is an object

Recall that earlier I said everything in Ruby is an object. Well, this might be a good time to take a quick peek under the covers and reveal that when we create a literal in Ruby, we are actually creating an object. This is quite different from many other programming languages where language primitives are outside the developer's control for storing values such as numbers and characters.

In Ruby, because we're dealing with objects, we've opened a door to a substantial amount of power. Our objects have values and a collection of cool methods that we can use to do all sorts of fun things.

As an example, let's take a closer examination of our previous string literal by asking it what type of class it is:

```
"Stewie is Cool!".class          #  String
```

So we called a method named class on our "Stewie is Cool!" string, and you can see that this method returned the name of the class, confirming that we are in fact dealing with a String object.

There are a couple things that you should notice. First is the fact that in order to call a method on our object, we used what's called dot notation (i.e., we typed a period and then the name of the method). This should be fairly familiar to you if you've done programming in languages such as JavaScript or ActionScript, but it might be a bit strange if you're used to programming in languages such as PHP.

Second, you should notice that we weren't required to place any sort of line termination symbol like a semicolon (;) at the end of our line. That's a flexibility feature that you'll love about Ruby if you've ever had a script die in other languages because of one stupid missing semicolon.

Let's take a look at a few more methods we can call on our string:

```
"Stewie is Cool!".upcase         #  "STEWIE IS COOL! "
"Stewie is Cool!".length         #  15
"Stewie is Cool!".reverse        #  "!looC si eiwetS"
```

We can also get a full list of all the available methods for an object by asking the object to list its methods; see Figure 2-3.

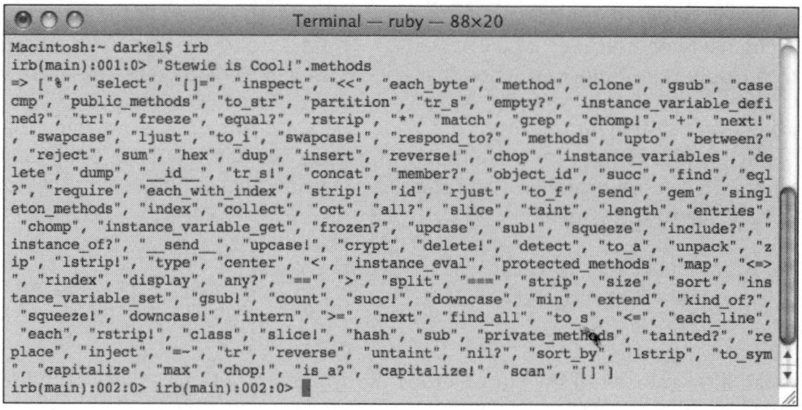

Figure 2-3. Listing the available methods on a string object

Well, that's informative but also kind of hard to deal with if we're looking for anything specific. Fortunately, we can also chain method calls, with each method next in the chain being called on the returned value of the previous (executed from left to right). So when we're calling the methods method on a string, what are we getting in return?

```
"Stewie is Cool!".methods.class       # Array
```

The methods method is returning an array of the available methods for our string object. The Array class includes a method named sort, which will return a new array with the previous array values now sorted alphabetically. So let's enhance our last call to methods by also calling sort on the returned list of methods to alphabetize that list for us (see Figure 2-4):

```
"Stewie is Cool!".methods.sort
```

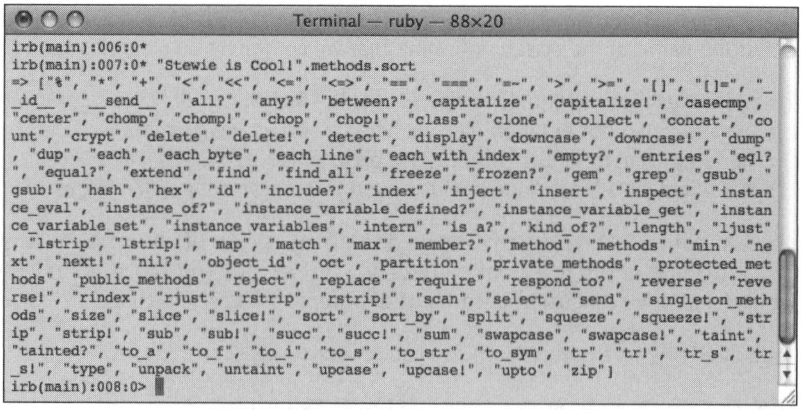

Figure 2-4. Getting an alphabetized listing of our string methods

Ahh, that's much better. Because of the simple fact that we're dealing with a String object, all of these methods have been created on that object, and we can call any of them on it.

By the way, did you notice that the first few methods in that list looked strangely like mathematic operators or comparison checks (*, +, <, ==, >=, etc.). Yep, that's right; even simple things like adding or comparing are actually methods defined on objects. Let's see what happens when we use addition or multiplication on a string:

```
"Eldon " + "Alameda"          #  "Eldon Alameda"
"Eldon " * 5            #  "Eldon Eldon Eldon Eldon Eldon "
```

We can call mathematic operations on strings, but what do you think will happen if we attempt to call a string manipulation method like reverse on a number? Take a look at Figure 2-5.

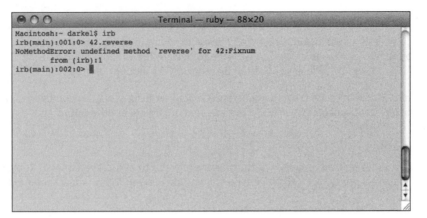

Figure 2-5. Calling reverse on the number 42

D'oh—that method doesn't exist on a number object. When you think about it, this limitation sort of makes sense. After all, you can't *actually* reverse a real number, can you?

But we could reverse a string representation of a number! With that knowledge, we can convert our number to a string using the to_s method:

```
42.to_s          #  "42"
```

And once we've converted our number to a string, we can reverse it by simply chaining the reverse method to the end:

```
42.to_s.reverse          #  "24"
```

We can even convert our reversed string back into an integer by adding the to_i method:

```
42.to_s.reverse.to_i          #  24
```

OK, even I have to admit that this is a bit of a convoluted example for converting objects to different formats, but now you know, and knowing is half the battle.

> *Most objects have a variety of methods to make converting them from one format to another easy. In addition to* to_s, *we also have useful methods like* to_i *(to convert to an integer),* to_f *(to convert to a float), and* to_a *(to convert to an array).*

Variables and constants

Of course, simply entering literal values into our code isn't going to be all that useful on its own. We need a means of storing them into variables that can hold those values while we manipulate and change them. Variables are like nicknames we can use to reference the same value without having to type it out literally each and every time—sort of like how, in geometry, we would use the word "pi" to refer to the mathematical constant of 3.14159. We can create variables very easily in Ruby with a simple assignment, like so:

```
x = 4
y = 6
sum = x + y
```

You'll notice that, as we discussed earlier, Ruby doesn't require us to declare the type of data that we plan on storing into our variables, nor do we have to declare the variable prior to using it. Those two small facts help make our code easier to read by reducing the amount of noise.

Of course, not all variables are created equal, especially in terms of scope. To combat this, we actually have several different variable types available to us that are visible at different levels.

Local variables

The simple variables that we've looked at thus far are referred to as local variables in Ruby. Local variables can be named pretty much whatever you want as long as you follow a few simple rules.

- Variable names cannot contain a space.
- Variable names are case sensitive.
- Variable names *must* start with a lowercase letter or an underscore.
- Variable names can contain only letters, numbers, or underscores.

Local variables are typically short lived and are only accessible within the current block or method (i.e., in the same place that they were defined). You can see their scope limitation with a quick test by typing the following lines into irb:

```
def test_scope
    x = 25
    puts x
end

x = 10

test_scope  #  outputs 25
puts x       # outputs 10
```

So you can see that even though the variable x is used both inside and outside of the method, it contains different values in each location, because the variable instances live in different scopes.

Instance variables

Within an object, we also have instance variables that are easily identified because they are preceded by an @ sign. Examples would be @user, @params, and @lassie. Instance variables have an expanded scope in that they are visible (and shared) among all methods within the object. Instance variables will be the most common variable type that we'll use in Ruby on Rails, as they are one of the key ways that we share data from the controllers to the views.

We can see how this variable is shared among all the methods of an object in this example:

```
class Scope
  def set_variable(x)
    @my_variable = x
  end

  def get_variable
    puts @my_variable
  end
end

s = Scope.new
s.get_variable    # outputs nil (as we haven't set this variable yet)
s.set_variable('test')
s.get_variable   # outputs 'test'
```

Class variables

Less commonly used in Ruby on Rails is the class variable, which follows the same naming conventions but is preceded by two @ signs, so class variables will look like @@name, @@database, and @@administrator. Class variables are used to set a variable within the class so that it will be available to all instances of that class.

For a simple example, let's create a class that keeps a running count of the total number of puppies:

```
class Puppy
  def initialize
    if defined?(@@total_puppies)
      @@total_puppies += 1
    else
      @@total_puppies = 1
    end
  end

  def how_many
    puts @@total_puppies
  end
end
```

In this example, we introduced a couple new things. First, we added a new method named initialize. This is a specially named method, and it is called every time a new object is created from this class. Second, before we could use this class variable we first had to test that it had been defined. Once a class variable has been defined, it will be available for subsequent instances of the class. Now that we have our puppy class, we can see that his variable type is shared between all instances of a class by creating a few instances of the Puppy class and checking the return value of the how_many method.

```
p1 = Puppy.new
p1.how_many     # 1

p2 = Puppy.new
p3 = Puppy.new

p1.how_many   # 3
p3.how_many   # 3
```

Global variables

The final variable type we'll cover here is the global variable, which I'm including merely for completeness as I believe there are very few legitimate uses for global variables. Global variables are easily identified, because they are preceded with a dollar sign like $global, $dbh, and $logfile. As their name indicates, these variable types are accessible from anywhere in the program. You can see the effect of global variables in the following code snippet:

```
def test_scope
   $x = 25
   puts $x
end

$x = 10

puts $x          # outputs 10
test_scope     # outputs 25
puts $x          # outputs 25
```

Constants

In addition, Ruby also supports the use of constants, which are pretty much the same as variables except for the fact that a constant's name *must* begin with an uppercase letter:

```
Answer = 42
```

> *Although constants are meant to be variables whose value will never change, Ruby does, in fact, allow you to change the value of a constant (although it will complain like a creaky old floor board if you do).*

Numbers

We've already seen how we can use numbers within Ruby but it's also worth noting that there are actually a few different number classes that might give you some unexpected results if you're not careful.

Take, for example, this simple division problem:

```
7 / 3          #  2
```

At first glance, it might look like Ruby failed elementary school math, but believe it or not, this is actually the expected behavior, because we're dealing with whole numbers. Whole numbers will always return whole numbers as a result (dropping off any remainder).

> *To be technically accurate, we're actually using integers, which consist of the natural numbers, zero, and their negative values. I chose the term "whole number" here simply because it's more universally understood as not having a decimal or fraction component.*

Fixnums

When we create a whole number in Ruby, it will actually be created as class Fixnum, which can hold numbers up to 2 to the power of 30.

```
-1234567.class          #  Fixnum
((2 **30)-1).class       #  Fixnum
```

> *The value 2 to the power of 30 is the most common limitation of Fixnum classes, but technically, the actual maximum Fixnum size is determined by the highest value that the host operating system can hold in a native machine word (minus 1 bit), which should either be 2 to the thirtieth power or on some higher end systems 2 to the sixty-fourth power.*

Bignum

What happens when we need to create or use a number bigger than 2 to the thirtieth power? In these cases, Ruby will automatically convert our number to the Bignum class, which is pretty much the same as Fixnum except it was designed specifically to hold extremely large numbers. Ruby will automatically convert back and forth between Fixnum and Bignum depending on the value that is stored.

```
my_value = 2**30        #  1073741824
my_value.class          #  Bignum
my_value -= 1           #  1073741823
my_value.class          #  Fixnum
```

> *This ease of converting values from one type to another is a major benefit of Ruby using objects for everything rather than having language primitives to represent items such as numbers.*

Floats

But we still haven't solved our earlier dilemma with the messed up division result, have we? Fixing this is actually very easy, as Ruby has another number type that we haven't covered yet—the Float. We use floats when we want to calculate a value with more precision than a whole number (such as decimals).

So we can correct our earlier division problem by simply creating one of the numbers as a float (i.e., with a decimal), and we'll get a float value returned that's more accurate.

```
x = 7.0 / 3.0          #  2.33333333333333
x.class        #  Float
```

Nil

Ruby also has a special construct named nil for representing the lack of any value:

```
nil          # nil
nil.class          #  NilClass
```

Most objects have a nil? method defined on them to make it easy to determine if its value is nil:

```
nil.nil?        #  true
42.nil?        #  false
```

Of course, you can always use our standard equality comparison operators as well:

```
nil == nil        #  true
nil == false        #  false
```

So you can see that one nil is equivalent to another nil, but that nil and false are separate values and thus not equal to each other.

Comparisons

Calling methods and converting our data between different formats is only going to get us so far, eventually we'll need to have the ability to check our data or compare it against another value. Fortunately, we'll find all of our favorites from high school math are available here in Ruby such as the greater-than and the less-than-or-equal-to conditional statements.

Whenever Ruby performs a comparison between two objects it will return either true or false.

> *It's a good time to mention that, in Ruby comparisons, there are only two values that are equal to* false—false *and* nil. *This can come as a shock if you're used to other languages where a zero can also be equivalent to* false.

We can check if one value is greater than another:

```
12 > 24            # false
```

or less than the other

```
12 < 24            # true
```

We can modify it to check for greater than or equal to:

```
12 >= 24           # false
```

We can test for equality too:

```
12 == 12           # true
'A' == 'a'         # false
'A' == 'a'.upcase          # true
```

> *It's important to note that, when we test for equality, we're using the double equal sign (==) as the comparison operator. A single equal sign (=) is an assignment operator and could actually change the value of one of our variables. Many hard-to-identify bugs have been caused by accidentally using the assignment operator when the developer meant to use the equality operator.*

We can also test that values are not equal using the != operator

```
12 != 13           # true
```

Or we can get a bit extra tricky and use the comparison operator, which will return 0 if the two values are equal, 1 if the left side is higher, or −1 if the right side is higher.

```
12 <=> 24          # -1
```

We also have the ability to string multiple comparisons together with the careful use of parentheses and the && (AND) and || (OR) operators:

```
(1 == 1) && (7 == 7)       # true
(1 == 1) && (3 == 4)       # false

(1 == 1) || (7 == 7)       # true
(1 == 1) || (3 == 4)       # true
```

Conditionals

And what good are comparisons unless we can use them to control our code? Not much indeed.

In most languages, conditional statements are typically represented with the `if` and `if-else` constructs and Ruby is no different. In Ruby, `if` statements look like these:

```
if true
  do this
end

if (false)
  this line won't be executed
  neither will this line
end
```

In Ruby, our `if` statements will have a matching end statement to know what lines of code should be executed (or skipped) in response to the conditional. Like many things in Ruby, parentheses around the condition are optional.

As an example of using the `if` statement, imagine that we were tasked with automating the minimum height checker for a new roller coaster named the Ruby Express at a local amusement park. Because of the particular thrill capacity of this new coaster, it's been determined that all passengers must be at least 42 inches tall to ride. We'll capture that in a variable:

```
min_height = 42
```

Next, as each guest walks up to the gate, we'll capture his or her height in inches and check it against our minimum height before allowing access to board our new roller coaster:

```
guest= 71
if guest > min_height
  puts "You're allowed on"
end
```

That's OK, but it does take up several lines of code for such a simple check. Fortunately, Ruby supports placing the conditional at the end of the statement such as this

```
puts "You're allowed on" if guest > min_height
```

This evaluates exactly the same but is lot nicer to read when we only need to execute a single line in response to a conditional check. Plus, using a single line gives us the slight additional advantage of not needing to add an end onto our condition.

> *Any method that returns a* true/false *value (typically those that end with a question mark such as* .empty? *) can be used for the conditional statement.*

In our current implementation, we compare the height of a guest against the minimum height for the ride and print out a message if the guest is tall enough to ride. But what happens if we also want to provide a message to the customers who are too short to ride the Ruby Express? To do that, we'll modify our code to also include an else statement that will execute when the conditional evaluates to false:

```
if guest > min_height
  puts "You're allowed on"
else
  puts "Come back when you're taller."
end
```

Even in situations like these, there are always going to be exceptions. For our roller coaster ride, we've been instructed to deny access to anyone who doesn't meet the minimum height requirements *except* for the owner's sister-in-law who is exceptionally short for her age and would make life miserable for everyone involved if denied access to any ride. Fortunately, we also have a construct we can use called the elsif command, which allows us to run a secondary check if the first one evaluates to false:

```
if guest > min_height
  puts "You're allowed on"
elsif guest_related_to_boss == true
  puts "You're allowed on"
else
  puts "Come back when you're taller"
end
```

Of course, we would rarely write our elsif conditional so verbosely, as we can simplify that statement by removing the explicit guest_related_to_boss == true check. Instead, we could write it as

```
elsif guest_related_to_boss
```

which works the same, since if this variable is either false or simply not set (nil), it will return false to that conditional.

As a final bit of sugar for our code, Ruby also provides a reverse if statement that goes by the name of the unless command, which is used to test if the statement is false in a cleaner more readable format than an if ! (if not) clause.

```
puts "You're allowed on" if !(guest < min_height)
```

However, that is both ugly and hard to read, especially when compared to this:

```
puts "You're allowed on" unless guest < min_height
```

Ahh, it evaluates the same but is much easier on the old eyes.

Arrays

No language worth its salt would lack everyone's favorite all-purpose container, the array. Ruby arrays have an incredible amount of useful methods available and are a joy to work with overall.

Like most things in Ruby, there is more than one way to create an array. However, the easiest way is to simply use the [ ] characters:

```
my_array = []              #  []
my_array = [1,2,3,4,5]           #  [1, 2, 3, 4, 5]
```

Or we could always define it as a new instance of the Array class:

```
another_array = Array.new          #  []
```

Using that method, we can specify our array to be of a certain size:

```
my_dozen = Array.new(12)
        # [nil, nil, nil, nil, nil, nil, nil, nil, nil, nil, nil, nil]
```

And we can prefill our array with a specific value:

```
my_dozen = Array.new(12, "c")
        # ["c", "c", "c", "c", "c", "c", "c", "c", "c", "c", "c", "c"]
```

Once our array is built, we can start doing all kinds of fun things with it, such as adding elements to it using the << operator:

```
my_array << "f"          #  [1, 2, 3, 4, 5, "f"]
```

> *As this example shows, Ruby arrays aren't limited to holding a single data type; you're free to store as many different data types as you can think of in an array.*

We can reference the individual elements by their index numbers (note that arrays always start with index 0):

```
my_array[0]          #  1
my_array[1]          #  2
```

or even get tricky and use a negative index number to start at the end of the array:

```
my_array[-1]          #  "f"
my_array[-2]          #  5
```

Of course, we could also use some useful methods to access the first or last values in an array:

```
my_array.first          #  "f"
my_array.last          #  5
```

To remove a value from an array, we can use the delete method:

```
my_array << "boo"          #  [1, 2, 3, 4, 5, "f", "boo"]
my_array.delete("boo")
```

We can also remove the last value from an array using the pop method:

```
my_array.pop     #  "f"
my_array          #  [1, 2, 3, 4, 5]
```

We can grab the largest value from the array:

```
my_array.max        #  5
```

We can ask for the length (or its aliased name size) of the array:

```
my_array.length     #  5
my_array.size       #  5
```

We can even change a specific element of an array:

```
my_array[2] = 10    #  10
my_array            #  [1, 2, 10, 4, 5]
```

Here's another useful tip: We often want to build an array of a list of words. However, going through all the work of adding quotes around each word can often be kind of a pain. Fortunately, we have a shortcut method named %w that removes this pain. We use it like so:

```
new_array = %w(this is my list)   # ["this", "is", "my", "list"]
```

And that's just scratching the surface of all the useful and fun methods for working with arrays. Some other methods you should experiment with follow:

```
my_array.sort       #  sorts arrays in alphabetic or numeric order
my.array.reverse    #  reverses the array
my_array.min        #  returns smallest value in array
my_array.shift      #  returns first element, removing it from array
my_array.unshift("A") # Prepends the new element to the front of array
```

And, of course, you already know that you can always use the methods method to gain a list of other methods that you can play around with.

Hashes

Hashes are constructs that are very similar to arrays except for the fact that you must specify the index key for each element in a hash (whereas arrays maintain an integer-based index). In this way, hashes are similar to dictionaries, where each value has a given definition associated to it.

Hashes are most often created using the {} characters like so:

```
me = {'name' => 'Eldon', 'title' => 'Web Developer'}
                    #  {"name"=>"Eldon", "title"=>"Web Developer"}
me.class            #  Hash
```

Just like an array, we can retrieve a value from our hash by specifying the index we're interested in:

```
me['name']          #  "Eldon"
```

And we can obtain the number of values in the hash the same way as well:

```
me.length           #  2
```

To add a new value to our hash, we simply specify the key we want and the value that should be populated in it:

```
me['quote'] = 'skillz to pay the billz'
                        # "skillz to pay the billz"
me.length          # 3
me                 # {"name"=>"Eldon", "title"=>"Web Developer", …
```

We can extract a list of the index keys used in our hash with the keys method:

```
me.keys            # ["name", "title", "quote"]
```

We can extract a list of the hash values with (you guessed it) the values method:

```
me.values    # ["Eldon", "Web Developer", "skillz to pay the billz"]
```

> *One final comment about hashes is that they are completely unordered—if you were to loop over the values of a hash, you have no guarantee in which order they would come out. I forgot this once in my early days of programming in Ruby and spent half a day trying to figure out why my data was coming back in a random order.*

Symbols

You'll see a ton of hashes used while programming in Rails, but you'll very rarely see them used with strings as the index keys. Instead, you'll see a unique kind of string that's called a symbol. You can easily identify a symbol, because it is represented by text preceded by a colon like so:

```
:name          # :name
```

Describing the benefits of using symbols is a bit more complex. If it helps, you can think of them as a special type of string that you can't modify and that uses fewer system resources. They're best used in situations, like the keys of a hash, where we're only interested in using them for identification not for manipulation.

So our previous hash example would most often be created like so:

```
me = {:name => 'Eldon', :title => 'Web Developer'}
                  # {:title=>"Web Developer", :name=>"Eldon"}
me[:name]         # "Eldon"
```

Loops

Ruby provides several ways to repeat a block of code or to iterate over the data in an array or hash.

The while loop

The first loop that we'll look at is the while loop, which does a conditional check and then executes the code within the loop until that condition evaluates to false:

```
i = 0
while i < 10
  puts "Iteration #{i}"
  i += 1
end
```

When executed, the preceding code will print out this:

```
Iteration 0
Iteration 1
Iteration 2
Iteration 3
Iteration 4
Iteration 5
Iteration 6
Iteration 7
Iteration 8
Iteration 9
```

The for loop

For iterating over a collection, Ruby also has the for loop:

```
heroes = ['Superman', 'Batman', 'Hulk', 'Iron Man']

for hero in heroes
  puts hero
end
```

which will print out this:

```
Superman
Batman
Hulk
Iron Man
```

Considering the travesty that was the previous Hulk movie, perhaps we no longer want to keep the Hulk in our list of favorite heroes (at the time of this writing, the 2008 remake with Edward Norton is still forthcoming, so perhaps there's still hope). We can bypass an iteration of our loop using the next command:

```
heroes = ['Superman', 'Batman', 'Hulk', 'Iron Man']

for hero in heroes
  next if hero == 'Hulk'
  puts hero
end
```

Of course, we could also get this same result a little cleaner using the unless statement:

```
for hero in heroes
  puts hero unless hero == 'Hulk'
end
```

The each command

Another way to loop over a collection is to call the collection's each method, which will iterate over every element in the collection:

```
heroes = ['Superman', 'Batman', 'Hulk', 'Iron Man']

heroes.each do |hero|
  puts hero unless hero == 'Hulk'
end
```

You probably notice that the syntax is a little strange after the each method; this syntax is called a block, and we'll discuss how they work next.

Blocks

If you've ever used closures in JavaScript, you might be familiar with the idea of creating anonymous functions (which allow you define a function that's never bound to a name). This same idea is the core concept behind blocks in Ruby—the ability to group together a set of instructions that can then be passed around your program to simplify your code.

If you're coming from a language where you didn't have exposure to anonymous functions or blocks, the concept can feel rather alien at first. But in reality, blocks are fairly natural, and once you make that small mental jump, you'll see why blocks are one of the most popular features in Ruby.

Blocks can come in two basic formats, depending on whether they need to execute a single line or multiple lines of code:

```
#  Single Line
1.upto(10) {|count| puts count}

#  Multiple Lines
10.downto(1) do |x|
  puts "#{x} little monkeys jumping on the bed"
  puts "one fell off and bumped his head"
  puts "momma called the doctor, the doctor said"
  puts "no more monkeys jumping on the bed"
  puts ""
end
```

You'll notice that in both examples we have an odd little variable named count that's wrapped in | | being used to pass the current value from the collection into the code block. I once read a description of this syntax that said to imagine those | | as being a little slide that each value in the collection uses to slide down into the code block while assuming the name that's specified. So in our code samples, with each iteration of the block, the next number passes into the block as count.

Of course, in the preceding examples, some might argue that we're simply creating an overly glorified loop. So let's look at some other common examples of blocks.

```
me = {'name' => 'Eldon', 'title' => 'Web Developer'}
me.each_value {|x| x.upcase!}
me         #   {"name"=>"ELDON", "title"=>"WEB DEVELOPER"}
```

In this example, we created a block to change each value in a hash to its uppercase version using the strings upcase! method.

```
%w(first second third).each do |count|
  puts count
end
```

In this example, we've created a new array using the %w operator that we discussed earlier, and then we use a block to iterate over each element in that array—outputting it to the screen using the puts method.

```
File.open('myfile.txt', 'w') do |f|
  f.puts 'New line added to the file'
end
```

In this final example, we use a block to open a file in the current directory named myfile.txt for writing, we then pass the result of that File.open method into a block as f. From there, we can write to the file using the puts command on our f object in the block. As some extra sweetness, when we open a file into a block like this, Ruby automatically closes the file at the end of the block for us.

Methods

Now that you've learned how to define anonymous functions, you're probably long overdue to learn how to define standard Ruby methods. They're really not very hard, as they follow the same basic structure as most other languages:

```
def method_name(arguments)
  lines of code
end
```

> *Is there a difference between functions and methods? Technically, yes—in traditional object-oriented programming, a method is a function that is bound to or defined on an object. Since everything in Ruby is an object, this means that there are no functions in Ruby.*

Instance methods

The traditional method type that we'll create is called an instance method, because it will be built on an instance of an object. Let's define our first method:

```
class Song
  def my_name_is(name)
    3.times {puts "My name is..."}
    puts name
  end
end
```

With our new method defined, we can call it just like this:

```
mysong = Song.new
mysong.my_name_is "SLIM SHADY"
```

> *Note that the parentheses are still optional even on methods that we create.*

Our method call will output the following song lyrics and reveal my rather poor taste in music:

```
My name is...
My name is...
My name is...
SLIM SHADY
```

Accessor methods

A common need within object-oriented languages is the need to build accessor methods (sometimes referred to as getter and setter methods), and Ruby has us covered with some extra syntactic sugar here as well. It'll be a lot easier to understand the accessors when you see them, so let's modify the Song class that we created in the last example to use accessor methods. Imagine that, for our song class, we decided that we wanted to store the name variable in an instance variable (so it could be used in other methods) and then merely reference it in the my_name_is method. To do that, our class might look like this:

```
class Song
  def my_name_is
    3.times {puts "My name is..."}
    puts @name
  end
end
```

What we need to build now are the methods that will allow us to get and set that @name instance variable. Adding a getter method to return the current value of the @name instance variable is easy enough:

```ruby
class Song

  def name
    @name
  end

  def my_name_is
    3.times {puts "My name is..."}
    puts @name
  end
end
```

But where it gets extra nice is with the setter method, which we could define as follows:

```ruby
class Song

  def name
    @name
  end

  def name=(name)
    @name = name
  end

  def my_name_is
    3.times {puts "My name is..."}
    puts @name
  end
end
```

What's beautiful about that setter method is that, even though it was defined as name=(name), we can use it like this:

```ruby
name = "SLIM SHADY"
```

So Ruby allows us to add an extra space into the method call to make it look exactly like a normal assignment rather than the custom method that it is. Sweet, huh?

Methods with punctuation

Another cool method feature in Ruby is that method names are allowed to have punctuation such as question and exclamation marks in their names to help make the code more readable.

For example, Ruby allows us to end a method name with a question mark to indicate that we're asking a question. Common practice is that if we end a method name in a question mark, that method should return either a true or a false value. Here are some examples of standard Ruby methods that use the question mark:

```
my_array = %w(this is my rifle this is my gun)
my_array.include? "fighting"  #   false
my_array.include? "gun"       #   true
my_array.empty?       #   false
```

Ruby also supported the use of exclamation marks, but rather than just indicating that we're trying to yell, the exclamation mark is used to indicate that this method is more destructive than its non-exclamation-mark sibling. What this typically means is that we'll have one version of a method such as this:

```
my_name = "Eldon Alameda"
my_name.swapcase    #  "eLDON aLAMEDA"
my_name      #  "Eldon Alameda"
```

Here, you can see that while our call to swapcase returned a modified version of my_name, it didn't actually change the my_name variable (when we checked its value, it was still the original value). Let's see what happens when we use the variant with an exclamation mark:

```
my_name = "Eldon Alameda"
my_name.swapcase!       #   "eLDON aLAMEDA"
my_name      #  "eLDON aLAMEDA"
```

The exclamation variant (often referred to as the bang method) modified the variable in place. So best practice is that if your method will not change the original, you should use a nonbang method name, but if your method will modify the existing value in place, you should write it with an exclamation mark to warn any users of the method.

Class methods

The final method type that we'll look at in our primer is the class method. Up until this point, all of our methods have been what would we call instance methods (i.e., they can only be called on an instantiated object). Class methods are different in that they are called on the class without the need to first instantiate the class into a new object. Creating a class method is a simple matter of preceding our method name within the class with either self. or the name of the class, as you can see in this examples:

```
class Song

  def say_hi
    puts "hello from an instance method"
  end

  def Song.say_hi
    puts "hello from the class method"
  end
end
```

In our example, we've created two method names with the same name (say_hi). However, one is an instance method, and the other is a class name. We could also have defined the class method version like this:

```
def self.say_hi
```

Which way you choose is really a matter of personal preference. Let's go ahead and play with our new class to see the difference between calling the instance and class methods:

```
s = Song.new
s.say_hi        #   hello from an instance method

Song.say_hi     #   hello from the class method
```

Within Rails, you'll typically build more instance methods, but an understanding of class methods is important and can be of great help for building custom methods for querying your database from your models.

Classes

Being an object-oriented language, of course, Ruby also has to allow us to define our own classes so we can build our own objects. The best way to learn how they work is to build one, so let's build a basic class:

```
class Book
  def initialize(title)
    @title = title
  end
end
```

Classes are defined by calling class and the name of the class (note that the class name must begin with a capital letter). Then, we define any methods we want within the class, and finally, we complete the class definition with the end statement.

The initialize method is automatically called whenever we create a new instance of this class, so in this case, we're using it to allow us to set the name of the book as we create a new instance of a book object.

Now that we have defined a basic class (albeit a fairly anemic one), we can use it like this:

```
this_book = Book.new('Foundation Rails 2.0')
this_book.class         #   Book
this_book.title         #   NoMethodError: undefined method `title'
```

So we built a basic class, but we don't seem to be able to get much useful information out about our book— that's because we haven't defined any accessor methods yet. In most developer circles, you'll hear of these accessor methods referred to as the getter and setter methods because that's exactly what they do: they allow us to get and/or set the values of our object. We can add getter and setter methods for the title of our book like this:

```
class Book
  def initialize(title)
    @title = title
  end
```

```
    def title
      @title
    end

    def title=(title)
      @title = title
    end
  end
```

Let's discuss what we just built. We created a new class named Book that currently has three methods (initialize, title, and title=). When we instantiate a new instance of this class we'll need to pass it a title which will be used in the initialize method to set the @title instance variable.

Our other two methods simply interact with that same instance variable with the title method used to either set or return the current value of the @title instance variable.

Now let's see how we can use the methods in this class:

```
my_book = Book.new('Foundation Rails 2.0')
my_book.title          #  "Foundation Rails 2.0"

my_book.title = "Practical Rails Projects"
my_book.title          #  "Practical Rails Projects"
```

Groovy—now we actually can get a little use out of our Book class. However if we have a lot of variables that we want to model about a book, such as page count, author, publisher, and so on, writing all those getter and setter methods is going to get really old, really fast, isn't it? Fortunately, we don't need to build them all by hand, as Ruby provides a single method called attr_accessor that will handle the creation of all of those getter and setter methods. Using attr_accessor, we could rewrite our class like this:

```
class Book
  attr_accessor :title, :pagecount, :author, :publisher

  def initialize(title)
    @title = title
  end
end

my_book = Book.new('Foundation Rails 2.0')
my_book.title          #  "Foundation Rails 2.0"
my_book.author         #  nil
my_book.author = 'Eldon Alameda'
my_book.author         #  "Eldon Alameda"
```

One final class concept that we should cover is the issue of how Ruby handles inheritance between classes. Ruby supports single inheritance, which basically means that each class you create can only have one parent class.

If you don't explicitly state a parent class, the class inherits from Object. You can see this by calling parent on the base Book class:

```
my_book.class            #  Book
my_book.class.parent          #  Object
```

But now we want to model a new type of book, an e-book. An e-book will need pretty much the exact same functionality as our existing Book class, except it may also need to define a few additional methods of its own. In Ruby, we can represent this through inheritance like this:

```
class Ebook < Book
  attr_accessor :downloadable

  def initialize(title)
    super(title)
  end
end

my_ebook = Ebook.new('Practical Rails Projects')
my_ebook.title          #  "Practical Rails Projects"
my_ebook.author = 'Eldon Alameda'
my_ebook.downloadable = true
```

In this example, we defined a new child class of our Book class named Ebook. Our new Ebook class inherited all the methods that were already defined in the Book class, which is why we're able to get and set values such as title and author. In addition, we were able to define a custom downloadable value (with its own getter and setter methods) within our subclass.

You might have noticed, though, that we wrote our initialize method a bit differently in this subclass. This was because we didn't want to have to duplicate the initialize method to set the title in our subclass, so we used the super method instead. The super method basically tells Ruby to look up its inheritance chain and call the method with the same name as the method that called it.

Modules

The last construct that we'll look at in this introduction to Ruby chapter is the module. In some ways modules are similar to classes in that they are used as containers for a collection methods, constants, and so on. However, modules can also contain classes and even other modules.

The major difference between classes and modules is that a module can never be instantiated into an object (in other words you can never call new on a module). So while a class can be defined as a blueprint or template for an object, a module really only lives to be a giant container of code.

The usefulness of modules goes far beyond being a simple code container though. To explore that, let's create a sample module named MyModule, which will contain a method and a simple class:

```
module MyModule
  def MyModule.hello
    puts "Hello"
  end
```

```
        class Puppy
          def bark
            puts "Bark"
          end
        end
      end
```

First off, modules are often used as a form of name spacing within Ruby. By using modules, we can avoid name conflicts because the only way to access the data in a module is through the module name, as you can see in these examples:

```
MyModule.hello     #   Hello

pup = MyModule::Puppy.new
pup.bark   #  Bark
```

The second functionality of modules is that they can be used to share functionality across multiple classes. As you'll recall from the last section, Ruby classes do not support multiple inheritance (the ability to inherit from multiple classes at the same time). When a module is included into another class, all of the methods that were defined within that module are suddenly made available to the class.

We can see that in the following example:

```
module MyMixin
  def hello
    puts "hello from Mixin"
  end
end

class MyClass
  include MyMixin
end
```

With our module included (or mixed in, as it's commonly called) to our class we can instantiate an object and call our module method directly:

```
m = MyClass.new
m.hello   #  hello from Mixin
```

If you ever look around the source of Rails, you'll see that Rails makes fairly extensive use of modules.

The Anarchy of Ruby

One final topic that I wanted to share with you about Ruby is the fact that no classes or methods are locked down in Ruby. This means that you're able to reopen a class at any time to add additional methods or to redefine existing ones. Say, for example, that you've reread *The Hitchhikers Guide to the Galaxy* and decided the ultimate answer truly is 42, and you want to change your programs so that every addition always equals 42. You could do so like this:

```
class Fixnum
  def +(*args)
    42
  end
end
```

Now all of our addition calls involving whole numbers will no longer be correct (in a mathematical sense):

```
2+2          #  42
5 + 10       #  42
```

Hopefully, you recognize the sheer madness that would be associated with doing something like this, but the concept of keeping our classes open like this provides a powerful door for our programs to enhance the core of Ruby for our own needs. In fact, Rails does this quite extensively, enhancing many built-in Ruby classes with a wide array of useful methods such as these:

```
"dolphin".pluralize        # "dolphins"
1.ordinalize        # "1st"
640.megabytes        # 671088640
2.weeks.ago        # Sun Mar 16 01:08:46 -0500 2008
```

Summary

In this chapter, we took a whirlwind tour through some of the high level features of the Ruby programming language. Yet, we've barely skimmed the surface of the power and beauty of Ruby. While what we've discussed here should carry you through your needs to create basic Ruby scripts and Rails applications, you'll be best served if you don't end your Ruby education here. In Appendix A, I list a few other books and resources that I recommend for learning Ruby.

Chapter 3

TOURING A RAILS APPLICATION

I sure hope that you had some fun exploring the basics of the Ruby language in the last chapter (and if you didn't, you should go back and keep typing until it is fun).

But as great as that was, I'm sure that you've been just itching to start playing around with Rails. After all, that is why you bought this book, isn't it?

> *If by some chance you didn't buy this book but stole it instead, my point still stands, but I do recommend that you go make amends for your crime before karma gets you back.*

One of the challenges with learning (and teaching) Rails is the classic chicken-and-egg syndrome: you see, Rails is composed of a number of distinct libraries that work together as a cohesive whole. To understand Rails, you need to gain knowledge of each of those pieces. However, understanding Rails by looking at those libraries in isolation is difficult (and near impossible in some circumstances). You need to be able to see both. So that introduces the challenge of determining the best way for you to learn in this book.

We could plunge headfirst into building a Rails application and hope that you'll be able to learn as we go along as many other books have done. While that would be easier on me, my concern is that it would become too easy for you to become overwhelmed or lost as we chugged through theory and code at the rapid pace of Rails development.

However, if instead we focused all of our attention on the individual components without looking at the big picture, we might just as easily fall into the trap of missing the forest for the trees with long discussions of every option and feature that even reading through this book would become so tedious that we'd lose sight of the joy that Rails brings back to the process of building web applications.

To further complicate the learning process is the fact that Rails has been in a state of constant evolution since its initial release. This means that many of the current processes that you need to learn are actually evolutions from previous ways of solving the same problem. And it's much harder to understand the current process without first understanding the history of how Rails previously solved the same problem, what the limitations with that previous solution were, and how the new process solves those limitations.

Because of all these issues, I struggled to determine which approach I thought would be the best to help you gain the strongest footing as you step into the exciting and fun world of Rails development before finally settling on a process that attempts to give us all of these considerations. Let's take a moment to discuss the roadmap to learning Rails that I've laid before us in this book.

Our roadmap

In order to meet the needs of letting you view both the forest and trees, the road that we'll travel together will be a winding one.

We'll start out in this chapter by starting a simple Rails application, and using it to tour what a Rails application looks like as we gain an appreciation of the big picture. During our tour, we'll look at some of the nice features that every Rails application includes, how Rails maps to the MVC architecture, and discuss the basics of how Rails responds to requests. This will give you a 50,000-foot view of Rails, which should help us keep our bearings in the next few chapters as we dig deeper into some of the individual components that make up Rails.

After this chapter, we're going to spend the next several chapters with an ultra-fast tour of many of the individual components of Rails, starting with the Rails libraries that provide us with our MVC (model-view-controller) architecture. We'll spend time discussing how we connect our Rails application to a database using models, how we add dynamic content to our HTML content using Ruby, and how we use the Action Controller library to build controllers that we use to respond to users requests, along with a few others.

Once we've completed that investigation into some of the Rails components, we'll then bring what you've learned back together again as we work to utilize everything you've learned to build a complete Rails application together.

By the end of this book, you'll have gained the solid foundation that you'll need to begin building your own Rails applications, learned as many tips and tricks as I can slip in without overwhelming you, and have a list of additional resources to use to continue your learning into intermediate-level Rails development topics.

Creating a sample application

As I said earlier in this chapter, we're going to start our journey by looking at the 50,000-foot view of Rails applications through a whirlwind tour of creating our first Rails project and taking a deeper look at what it looks like.

So this first Rails project isn't going to be anything complex; it will just be a simple little application for us to get our feet wet and to examine and feel what a Ruby on Rails application is. Assuming that you have Rails installed (and if you don't, I've placed some instructions in Appendix B), we'll start our first application together by generating a new Ruby on Rails project using the `rails` command.

The first thing we need to do is to open a new command prompt window and navigate to the directory that you want to use to store your Rails applications.

> I recommend putting your Rails applications into a folder where they can be separated from other files in order to keep things clean. I typically create all my new applications within a folder named projects that resides in my home directory.

Once you're at that command prompt, we'll create a new Ruby on Rails application named demo by executing the following command, as shown in Figure 3-1:

```
rails demo
```

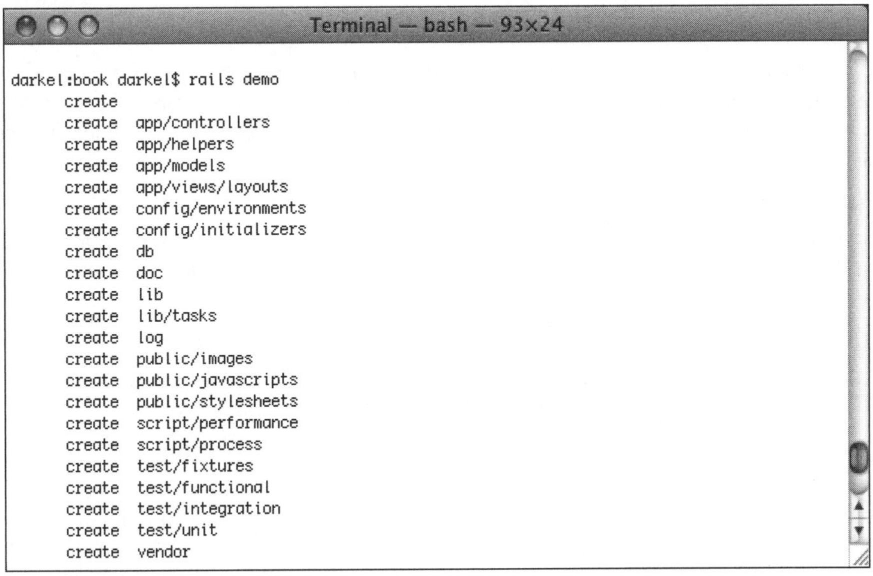

Figure 3-1. Creating our demo Rails application

Quite a lot of text just flew by, didn't it? Well, that's because that `rails` command just created the folder structure and all the configuration files that we need for our application. In other words, it just created the starting template for a Rails application, and now we just need to add our own code to make it work. But before we add anything, let's take a moment to examine some of the things that were provided to us out of the box.

Common directory structure

Go ahead and change directories into the demo directory that our `rails` command built, and lets start by looking at the directory structure that Rails has created for us. You can see the directory structure as displayed in my code editor (TextMate) in Figure 3-2.

What we have here is another example of the power of using conventions. The fact that every Rails application comes with this standard directory structure means that there are very few questions about where we need to place each component of our application code. In addition, this common directory structure in every Rails application means that another developer could pick up our application and quickly be able to find their way around.

Figure 3-2. The Rails directory structure

Of course, to take advantage of the benefits of a standard directory structure, it would help if we first understood what each of those folders is used for, so let's a take a look at them, shall we?

app/

The app directory is where you will spend most of your time when building Rails applications. Within this directory, you'll discover several subdirectories that are named for the type of code that belongs in each. Here, you'll find folders to contain controllers, helpers, models, and even your view code.

app/controllers

Your controller classes will be stored here; Controllers are the classes that we will build for responding to user requests by interacting with models and choosing the correct view to render back.

app/models

The models directory is used to store our model classes; models contain the business logic of our applications and will typically be used to interact with our database tables.

app/views

Our view template files will be stored within this directory. The easiest way to think of these for now is that they are the HTML files that our end users will see when interacting with our application. Assuming we use the Rails generators to create our controllers, Rails will automatically create subfolders in this directory whose names will match each of our controllers.

app/helpers

Helpers are small methods that we can build and use to simplify our HTML views, among other things, and we store these methods in modules that are stored in this directory. When building advanced web applications, our HTML view files can often very easily become cluttered with duplicated code or large blocks of complex code embedded into the HTML. When that happens, helper methods are a wonderful tool that we use to move that code out of the views and into these helpers to simplify the code that's present within your view templates and maximize reuse, thus making our view templates easier to maintain over time.

config

While Rails favors convention over configuration, there will still always be a small amount of custom configuration that we need to perform in our Rails applications. Those configuration settings will be stored in files within this directory. The three most important ones that we'll touch in every Rails application are database.yml, routes.rb, and environment.rb. We'll look at each of these in detail in just a few pages.

db

This directory stores database-specific files such as schema.rb, which is an automatically generated file that documents the current schema for our application's database. This folder also contains a subdirectory named migrate that will hold our database migration files. Migration files are used to progressively build our database, and they provide a simplified form of version control to our database schema; we'll discuss these in detail in Chapter 4.

doc

This directory isn't always used, but if you ever plan to share your application with others, you could place documentation for your application within this directory. In addition, a more advanced trick is to place specially formatted comments in our applications code that we can use to generate RDoc documentation for our application (that would be stored in this directory) by running the rake doc command.

lib

Occasionally, we need to build functionality for our application that doesn't quite fit into any of the existing directories in /app—for example, modules and classes that cross boundaries among multiple branches of the MVC architecture or modules that extend core Rails classes. In these advanced cases, the common convention is to store these types of files within the /lib directory. In fact, you'll even see this directory used when we build our final project, as we will have an authentication library that will be stored in this directory.

log

Rails generates detailed log files for our application that captures information about the requests that it received, how the application responded to each request, the response time of each response, and any errors that were raised during the processing of the request. Those log files are stored in this directory.

public

From the web server's perspective, the public directory is the document root of our Rails applications. This directory contains several subdirectories that are used for storing the images, style sheets, and JavaScript files used by our application.

script

This directory is where many important Rails scripts live, such as the command line generator scripts that we'll use to create controllers, models, migrations, and so forth. So while you will probably never have a need to place anything in this directory, at least you know what it's used for.

test

Our scripts for running unit, integration, and functional tests are stored in this directory.

tmp

This is another directory that we'll never use, but Rails uses this directory to store temporary files such as cached files and session data files.

vendor

Third-party or external libraries that our applications will use, such as plug-ins, are stored in this directory.

In addition, this directory is used to solve another common problem with web applications by providing a solution for the fact that our applications are dependent on the version of the language or tools that are installed on the server. Before switching to Rails for web development, I can remember the fun of doing frantic midnight upgrades to an applications code base after a hosting provider did an unannounced upgrade to a new version of PHP (yes, I fired that provider afterward). Since the Rails framework is installed systemwide, we could have a similar risk of an unknowing system administrator upgrading the Rails framework, and that upgrade might introduce some incompatibilities with our existing application. To combat this, Rails provides a feature that we call "freezing Rails," where the existing Rails framework is copied into the applications /vendor directory and once there, the application will use that local copy when the application is running instead of the version that is installed on the server.

Multiple environments

In addition to solving the issues of code organization by providing a common directory structure, Rails also provides us with the ability to support multiple environments within the same application code base. If you've developed web applications in any other language, you might have experienced issues such as needing to connect the application to one database in development but use completely different database settings once it rolls out into production. Or you might have encountered the issue where you want to display verbose debugging information on any errors while in development to aide in troubleshooting, yet want to hide those error messages behind something more graceful in production. Rails allows us to support these needs easily from the same code base with its support for multiple environments and comes with three environments configured by default—development, production, and testing). If you look in /config/environments, you can see that there are custom configuration settings for each of these default environments. For example, let's take a look at some of the configuration settings for the development environment (/config/environments/development.rb):

```
# Settings specified here will take precedence over those in
config/environment.rb

# In the development environment your application's code is reloaded on
# every request.  This slows down response time but is perfect for development
# since you don't have to restart the webserver when you make code changes.
config.cache_classes = false

# Log error messages when you accidentally call methods on nil.
config.whiny_nils = true

# Show full error reports and disable caching
config.action_controller.consider_all_requests_local = true
config.action_view.debug_rjs                          = true
config.action_controller.perform_caching              = false

# Don't care if the mailer can't send
config.action_mailer.raise_delivery_errors = false
```

You can see that these configurations settings are fairly well documented, with comments above each configuration line explaining what each line is doing. In summary, one of the most important things to understand about the development environment is that first configuration line which sets our application to reload any changes to the code on the next request. This is great for development, as it means we don't have to keep stopping and restarting our application every time that we modify a file. However, it also means that we take a substantial performance hit while running our application in development, as our application code has to be reloaded from the file system with every request rather than remaining cached in memory.

In addition to the continual reloading of our application's code with each request, the development environment is also configured so that any issues that occur while running in development will output the full error reports to make it easier for us to debug the code. Compare these settings to the ones that are set in the production configuration which are set just the opposite.

Standard configuration files

Another cool feature of our standard Rails application is that there are only a few key configuration files that we ever have to deal with. This is especially valuable when you compare it to other web frameworks where it's possible for you to spend as much time building configuration files as you do writing actual code. In fact, within most Rails applications, you'll only have to worry about touching three configuration files.

Database configuration

The most commonly handled configuration file is the file where we configure our various database connection settings. If you look in the /config directory, you'll find a file named database.yml that stores the database connection settings that our Rails application will use in the YAML format.

> YAML is a popular format for data serialization that is intended to remain exceptionally human-readable (unlike XML). Originally, YAML stood for "Yet Another Markup Language," but over time, the name has changed to distance YAML from being used for markup; it currently stands for "YAML Ain't Markup Language."

Currently, the database.yml file looks like this:

```
# SQLite version 3.x
#   gem install sqlite3-ruby (not necessary on OS X Leopard)
development:
  adapter: sqlite3
  database: db/development.sqlite3
  timeout: 5000

# Warning: The database defined as "test" will be erased and
# re-generated from your development database when you run "rake".
# Do not set this db to the same as development or production.
test:
  adapter: sqlite3
  database: db/test.sqlite3
  timeout: 5000

production:
  adapter: sqlite3
  database: db/production.sqlite3
  timeout: 5000
```

You should note a few things about the contents of this file.

First off, you'll notice that there are three top-level elements named development, test, and production, and underneath each is a group of different database configuration options. These three headings are references to the three default environments, which we just discussed. Having separate configuration options for each environment means that we can have database-connection settings for use while doing development on our local machine and a completely different set of settings that are used when the application is deployed onto a production server.

The second thing you should notice is that, even though we didn't provide Rails with any information about what type of database that we wanted, Rails built our application with a default configuration that uses SQLite 3.

Here's an interesting tidbit: Prior to Rails version 2.0.2, the default database for new Rails applications was actually MySQL. It changed to SQLite 3 as a response to the release of Mac OS Leopard, which included full Ruby, Rails, and SQLite 3 libraries out of the box—but not MySQL.

Personally, I think it's awesome that SQLite 3 is the default database that Rails now uses for all projects, as I've long been a proponent of using it in development. Some of the reasons why I think SQLite 3 is the best choice for development work are:

- **Speed**: SQLite 3 is quite often just as fast (and in some cases faster) than MySQL.
- **Size**: SQLite 3 databases are typically very small and easy to maintain.
- **Maintenance**: For a development database, I can't begin to express how much I enjoy not having to deal with the boring database administration tasks such as creating the database, adding users, or even setting permissions for tables and users.
- **Portability**: I love how easy it is to share my development database with other developers. All the examples in this book include the SQLite database, so when you download the source archive you will have full access to the same data that I used without any extra work. During my day-to-day work, it's also extremely nice to be able to check my development database into the version control system so that other developers I work with don't have to do a data load every time they check out the application.

Since our database connection settings are stored in this single file, we can easily change our application from one database solution to another by simply adding the new connection information here. For example, if we wanted to suddenly change our production database to connect to a MySQL database, we could simply replace the current production settings to reflect connecting to a MySQL database like this:

```
production:
  adapter: mysql
  database: mysql_database_name
  username: root
  password: my_root_password
  #socket: /tmp/mysql.sock
```

In addition to SQLite 3 and MySQL, ActiveRecord can also connect to most common database solutions including PostGreSQL Server, Microsoft SQL Server, Oracle, and Firebird—all through simply changing the relevant connection settings in this file.

But of course, what if we know off the bat that we don't want to use SQLite? Perhaps we work in an environment where we will always be using a MySQL database for our development. Are we going to be stuck having to always edit this file manually to change it from SQLite to our database of choice? Nope, as we can simply specify the database that we want when we create our new Rails application, and the Rails command will generate our `database.yml` file with sample settings for the database we specified.

If we wanted to create our demo application using MySQL instead, we would have created the project with this command:

```
rails demo --database=mysql
```

or better yet, using this shorthand version:

```
rails demo -d mysql
```

> *Other valid database options to pass to the rails command include* oracle, postgresql, *and* sqlite2.

Environment configuration

Another configuration that you might occasionally edit is the environment configuration file that lives at /config/environment.rb. Previously, we talked about and looked at the specific environment files created for each of the default environments that Rails supports. However, those files are meant to enhance the configuration within the /config/environment.rb, which focuses on applicationwide configuration settings that would be used across all environments.

In the olden days of Rails development (i.e., more than ten months ago), the most common changes we might make to this configuration file would be to add a few additional lines at the very bottom of this file to do tasks such as adding additional gems that we want Rails to include or to configure our mailer settings if we wanted our application to be able to send e-mail. However, with Rails 2.0, the environment configuration has changed so that we no longer need to add any configuration elements to this file. Instead, there's a new subdirectory within /config named initializers. Any Ruby file that is placed within this /config/initializers directory will automatically be included into our environment configuration. So now, we simply add any additional configuration elements into files within the initializers directory.

Routes configuration

The final configuration file that we will normally have to edit during development of our Rails application is the configuration of our routing rules, which is found in /config/routes.rb. In this file, we define how Rails will map URLs to the actions in our controllers. We'll discuss how to configure this file in more detail in Chapter 8.

Starting our application

Let's go ahead and fire up our application and see what it looks like before we make any changes. Within the /script directory, there is a script named server that we can use to start up our Rails application on our local machine. By default, this script will first look to see if we have Mongrel installed on our development system and, if so, use it to run our Rails application. If Mongrel is not available, script/server will default to using a pure Ruby web server named WEBrick. My personal recommendation is that you have Mongrel installed, as it will run faster and (in my opinion) a bit more accurately. We'll start the server from a command prompt in the root of our application with the command (see Figure 3-3):

```
ruby script/server
```

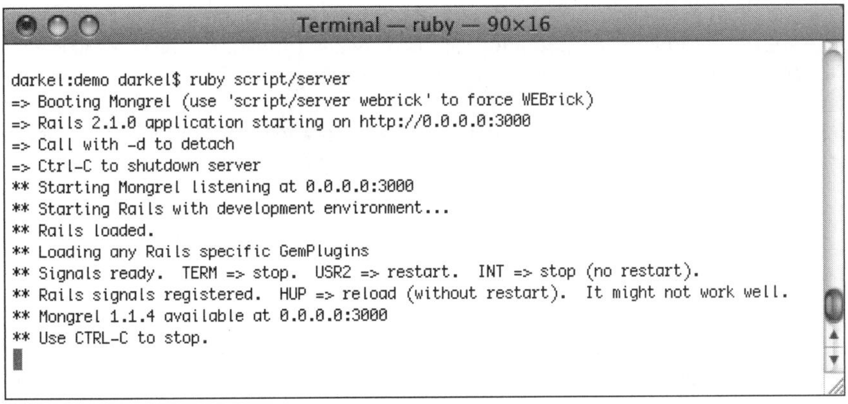

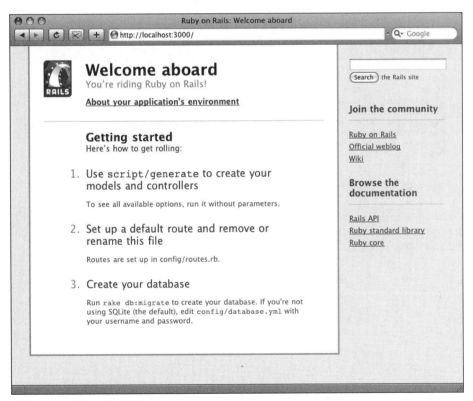

Figure 3-3. Staring our development web server

If you read the output from the command, you should see it report that it was starting our Rails application on http://0.0.0.0:3000. This is a special address that will allow us to access our web application at this URL and at 127.0.0.1 or localhost.

Let's go ahead and open a web browser and point it to http://localhost:3000. You should be rewarded with a web page like the one in Figure 3-4.

Figure 3-4. The Rails Getting Started page

Right off the bat, Rails provides us with some useful information about how to get started and links to many online sources of documentation and help. If you click the About your application's environment link, you'll get some useful information about your versions of Ruby, Rails, and the various libraries that make up Rails. Does it sound strange that I referred to Rails as actually being made up of a group of libraries? Well, let's take a quick look at the different libraries that compose Rails and what they each do before we continue on with our demonstration application.

A tour of the Rails framework

A good first step toward understanding the libraries that compose Rails is to copy them locally into our demonstration Rails application. In Rails circles, this is called freezing Rails, and doing so is generally considered to be a best practice. After we perform this task of freezing Rails, when our Rails application starts up, it will use this frozen version instead of the version that is installed on the server. The main benefit of freezing Rails in our application is that it guarantees that no matter what happens to the version of Rails on the server, our application will always use the version of Rails that it was created with. Pretty nice feature, huh?

To freeze the Rails gems, we simply need to issue another command from the root of our application (obviously, though, if your `script/server` is still running, you'll need to stop it first):

```
rake rails:freeze:gems
```

The result of running the command is shown in Figure 3-5.

```
darkel:demo darkel$ rake rails:freeze:gems
(in /Users/darkel/book/testing/book/demo)
Freezing to the gems for Rails 2.1.0
Unpacked gem: '/Users/darkel/book/testing/book/demo/vendor/rails/activesupport-2.1.0'
Unpacked gem: '/Users/darkel/book/testing/book/demo/vendor/rails/activerecord-2.1.0'
Unpacked gem: '/Users/darkel/book/testing/book/demo/vendor/rails/actionpack-2.1.0'
Unpacked gem: '/Users/darkel/book/testing/book/demo/vendor/rails/actionmailer-2.1.0'
Unpacked gem: '/Users/darkel/book/testing/book/demo/vendor/rails/activeresource-2.1.0'
Unpacked gem: '/Users/darkel/book/testing/book/demo/vendor/rails/rails-2.1.0'
darkel:demo darkel$
```

Figure 3-5. Freezing the Rails Gems

A few short lines later, this script will have copied the different Rails libraries into our application into /vendor/rails. If you open that directory in a file browser window, you should see the six subdirectories shown in Figure 3-6.

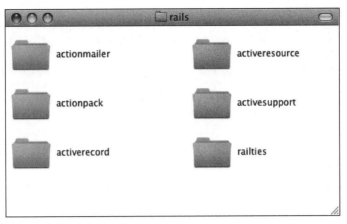

Figure 3-6. The Rails libraries

If you ever wanted to remove this frozen version of Rails from your application, you could do so with a simple unfreeze task like so:

```
rake rails:unfreeze
```

Components of Rails

Each of these libraries serves a different role and provides a different component of Rails that we'll be using as we build our web applications, so let's do a quick overview of each.

Action Mailer

Action Mailer is a library that we use for the creation and transmission of e-mail. It provides support for both plain text and HTML-formatted e-mails.

Action Pack

The Action Pack libraries are responsible for providing Rails with its support for the controller and view components of the MVC pattern.

ActiveRecord

Providing the "M" in our MVC is ActiveRecord, an absolutely fantastic library that provides a clean system for mapping our database tables to the models in our application. It provides a wealth of useful methods for doing all of our database interactions and will be the subject of our next few chapters.

ActiveResource

New to Rails in version 2.0 is the ActiveResource library, which is used to provide the ability to easily consume RESTful web services. Previous versions of Rails included Action WebService instead, which provided support for SOAP and XML-RPC web services. Being opinionated software, Rails has chosen to side with REST in the web services war as its default web service implementation.

> *Representational State Transfer (REST) is a style of software architecture for distributed systems. The terms "Representational State Transfer" and "REST" were introduced by Roy Fielding (who was also one of the authors of the HTTP specification) in his doctoral dissertation. It refers to a collection of network architecture principles that outline how resources are defined and addressed and is often used to describe a web interface that doesn't require an additional messaging layer such as SOAP. Systems that follow the REST principles are often referred to as being "RESTful."*

Active Support

Active Support is a fun library that many intermediate and advanced Rails developers invest their spare time reading through as a great resource for learning how to code the Rails way. Active Support provides many of the enhancements to standard Ruby objects that we talked about in the last chapter. Gaining an understanding of the methods that have been made available by Active Support will amaze you with the impact that it can make on your code.

Railties

Finally, we have the Railties library, which provides many of the scripts and tools that we use within Rails to build our applications. It's also within the library that you'll find many of the static resources, such as the Prototype JavaScript libraries that are included with Rails for AJAX support.

Teaching Rails to say hello

Going back to our demonstration application, you're probably wondering where this default page came from. Well, to answer that let's take a look inside /public; in there, you'll find a variety of files and subdirectories, as you can see in Figure 3-7.

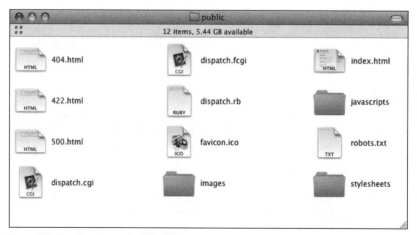

Figure 3-7. The files in our /public folder

As we discussed earlier, this folder functions as the document root to the Rails application, so all of these files are accessible at the root of our application. You'll notice that one of these files is named index.html, and if you were to look at the source of this file, you would discover that this is the file that we displayed when we accessed http://localhost:3000 in our web browser.

While this file provides some nice information, it's not useful in production, and we wouldn't want to display this page as the home page of our application. Let's go ahead and delete it now:

```
rm public/index.html
```

Afterward, open the site again in your web browser (restarting script/server if you happened to stop it), and you should see the error message shown in Figure 3-8 in your web browser.

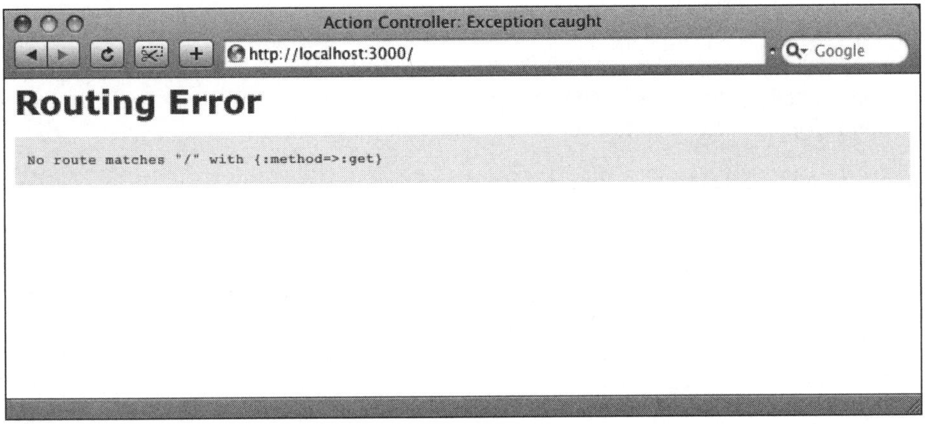

Figure 3-8. Our application now generates a routing error.

Nothing to worry about though, it's just Rails informing us that now that we've removed the index.html file, we need to add something within Rails to respond to this request. You should recall from our previous discussions about the MVC pattern in Rails that the first thing that we'll need to build is a controller that will respond our request.

Fortunately for us, we don't have to build this by hand, because Rails provides a number of generator scripts that we can use to build the basic components of our Rails application. There are generators available to build controllers, models, and many other things as we'll see as we work though this book. Let's start by building a basic controller that we can use to respond to this request. We'll start simple by building a basic "hello world" page, so let's build a new controller named hello using the rails generator (if script/server is still running, you'll want to stop it first so that you can use the command prompt):

```
ruby script/generate controller hello
```

Figure 3-9 shows the output as we build our first controller.

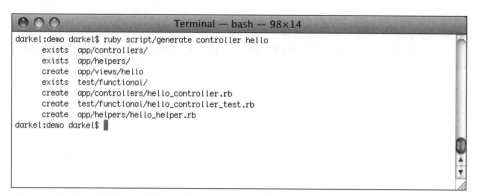

Figure 3-9. Using script/generate to create our first controller

You'll notice that this generator created several new files and a couple directories. The file that we're the most interested in, though, is the hello_controller.rb that was created in /app/controllers. If you open this file in your text editor, you'll see that it currently contains this:

```
class HelloController < ApplicationController
end
```

Now that we have our controller ready, we need to define a method inside it that will be used to respond to a specific request. For some extra kicks, we'll go ahead and define two methods. The default method that every controller will respond to is index, so let's add the index method to our controller. Second, we'll add another new method named world, which we'll use to say "hello" to the world. Afterward, your controller should look like this:

```
class HelloController < ApplicationController
  def index
  end

  def world
    render :text => "Hello World!"
  end
end
```

Just like in the previous chapter when we defined methods within a class, we've simply added two methods to our HelloController class (however, within controllers they're typically referred to as actions instead of methods, even though they're the same).

Here, we've added an index action that is empty, and an action named world that makes a call to a render method specifying that it should render the text Hello World! back to the requestor. After saving these changes to our controller, opening our web browser again, and navigating to http://localhost:3000/hello/world, we'll be greeted with Rails sending us that Hello World! message, as you can see in Figure 3-10.

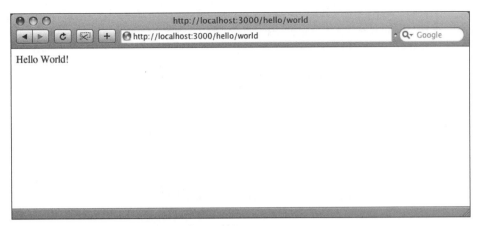

Figure 3-10. Oh goodie, yet another "Hello World!"

But how did we get that response? To answer that question, we'll need to first look at one of our configuration files. The one in particular we need is named routes.rb in /config. You can see what it looks like at this point in Figure 3-11.

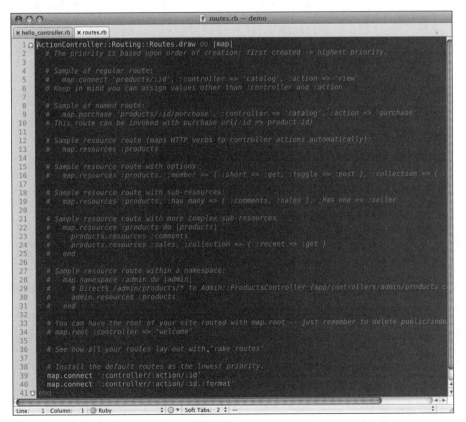

Figure 3-11. The default routes configuration file

We use this routes configuration file to map URLs to methods in controllers. You'll notice that most of the file consists of comments that provide instructions on a variety of routes you can create, but down at the bottom, there are two active statements:

```
# Install the default routes as the lowest priority.
  map.connect ':controller/:action/:id'
  map.connect ':controller/:action/:id.:format'
```

You'll notice that the default route is composed of a group of symbols that represent the controller and action for a specific route. You can see in Figure 3-12 how our URL maps into this format.

Figure 3-12. How URLs map to the default route

So this URL told Rails to look inside our hello_controller for a method named world. Since we created this method in the last step to render Hello World! back as a text response, that's exactly what happened. Now, let's see what happens if we attempt to access the index method we also created by loading either http://localhost:3000/hello/index or just simply http://localhost:3000/hello in our web browser (see Figure 3-13).

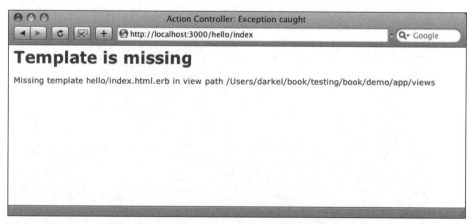

Figure 3-13. Our method is working, but we're missing a template to render.

And we're back to an error again. However, this is a different one than before. It's telling us that it found the method, but there was no template (or explicitly rendered content) to send back to the user. Let's fix that now. If you look in /app/views, you'll see that when we created the hello controller, the generator also created a subdirectory named hello under the views directory. This is the location where we'll store any view templates that are related to the hello controller. Let's create a new file within /app/views/hello/ named index.html.erb (you might notice that this is the name of the template that Rails was looking for in the error message in Figure 3-13).

> You'll notice that our template files are probably named a little differently than you might have expected. There are actually reasons for the way that they're named, and each piece of that name has special meaning. We'll cover those meanings in detail in Chapter 6.

Let's go ahead and populate this new file with the following HTML code:

```
<!DOCTYPE HTML PUBLIC "-//W3C//DTD HTML 4.01 Transitional//EN"
  "http://www.w3.org/TR/html4/loose.dtd">
<html>
  <head>
    <meta http-equiv="Content-type" content="text/html; charset=utf-8">
    <title>My Hello Application</title>
    <style type="text/css" media="screen">
      h1 {font-family: Arial, "MS Trebuchet", sans-serif;}
      h2 {color: red; font-style: italic;}
    </style>
  </head>
  <body>
    <h1>Welcome to the World of Tomorrow!!</h1>
    <h2>Why do always have to say it that way?</h2>
    <h1>Haven't you ever heard of a little thing called showmanship? </h1>
    <h1>Come, your destiny awaits!</h1>
  </body>
</html>
```

Now when we refresh our browser at http://localhost:3000/hello, we'll be greeted with a much more grandiose welcome (and quote from the pilot episode of *Futurama*), which you can see in Figure 3-14.

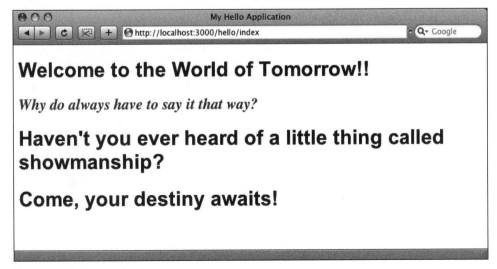

Figure 3-14. An improved welcome message

Summary

With that, we'll end our first introduction to building Rails applications. In this chapter, you were exposed to quite a lot, but we have a lot more to cover in the coming chapters. Here, you learned how to start a new Rails application using the built-in `rails` command. You learned how to freeze your Rails application to the version of Rails that it was created with.

We also discussed the different libraries that make up the Rails framework and talked about what each library is used for. We then used the Rails generator scripts to build our first controller and learned the basics of how Rails routing allows us to map URLs to the methods in our controllers. Finally, we built two basic pages to respond to user requests: a simple "hello world" page and a more traditional HTML page that included yet another obscure pop culture quote. While we played around with the views and controllers in this chapter, things will get more interesting (and slightly more technical) in the next chapter as we'll dive headfirst into models, and learn how we use ActiveRecord to connect our Rails application to our database.

Chapter 4

INTRODUCING ACTIVERECORD

In the last chapter, we took a high-level tour of not only creating our first Rails application but also of using the controller and view components to render some static text in response to a request. The application that we put together was intentionally incredibly simple. I wanted you to start out your Rails learning experience by first learning what a Rails application looks like and to get a hands-on feel for the process we use to send a request to a Rails application and to receive a response back from it. That request-response cycle is key to understanding the big picture of how Rails works. Everything else we learn about in Rails is simply to enhance that process through actions such as pulling data from a database, formatting data for display, and inserting the dynamic data into the response that's returned. That's why our previous application focused on letting you see exactly how we were able to send requests to a Rails application and how Rails is able to send back different responses.

The downfall of that application though was that the responses we sent back were very static, and that's certainly not what Rails was created for. Rails was designed to make building modern *database-driven* web applications easy, so in this chapter, we're going to turn things up a notch as we focus our attention on the tools that Rails provides for connecting our applications to a database. You'll learn about how we can both store and retrieve data from our database that can then be used by Rails.

The very nature of the topic at hand means that things are going to have to get a bit more technical in this chapter. But don't worry; Rails removes much of the complexity from this process, and if we do come across something in this chapter that you don't fully understand the first time we go over it, just keep moving forward. As I said in the last chapter, some features and topics in Rails might not make sense when viewed in isolation, but once you see them used in a real application later in the book, they should all come together for you. In the meantime, just think of these next two chapters as an introduction or overview for how we can use Rails to interact with the data in our database while eliminating most of the pain that's normally associated with the task. Groovy?

What Is ActiveRecord?

As I mentioned in our tour of the Rails libraries in the last chapter, Rails provides a library named ActiveRecord that serves as the means through which we interface to our database. The ActiveRecord library is an implementation of a design pattern created by Martin Fowler that was named Active Record (note the space between the words). This pattern defined a way to bridge objects within a programming language to data in a database.

But what does that mean in human terms?

You see, one of the core issues that we encounter when we want to link our object-oriented applications to a database is the fact that the two technologies speak very different languages. Within our application, we're using objects, methods, and attributes to manipulate data like so:

```
if post.comments?
  for comment in post.comments
    puts comment
  end
end
```

Meanwhile, our database solution is using its own SQL language for interacting with data like so:

```
select * from comments where post_id = '123'
```

What we need is a way to bridge the language gap between these two. Many web technologies and frameworks simply go around this by forcing developers to embed SQL into their application code, such as in this excerpt from a legacy PHP application a friend of mine once worked on:

```php
<?php
class Users
{
  private $site_id;
  public $firstname;
  public $lastname;
  public $email;
  private $password;
```

```php
    const ADMIN = 0;
    const MANAGER = 1;
    const AUTHOR = 3;

    function __construct(){
      global $sql, $site;
      $user_id = $_SESSION['user_id'];
      $query = "SELECT * from users where id = '$user_id' LIMIT 1";
      $row = $sql->_query($query);
      $user = $sql->_fetch_object($row);
      if($user) {
        $this->site_id     = $user->site_id;
        $this->firstname   = $user->firstname;
        $this->lastname    = $user->lastname;
        $this->email       = $user->email;
        $this->password    = $user->password;
      } else {
        return FALSE;
      }
    }

    function updatePassword($userid, $password)
    {
      global $sql;
      $updateQuery = "UPDATE users set password = AES_ENCRYPT ➥
        ('$password', 'password') where id = '". $userid."'";
      $row = $sql->_query($updateQuery);
    }
  }
?>
```

Even if you're not familiar with PHP, you should be able to look over that code and see what a royal pain it would be to build an entire application in this manner. Having to manually map all of our table columns to object attributes and manually write large chunks of SQL for any method that we want our objects to be able to call would not be a lot of fun. And this is just a simple example; imagine all the SQL you would have to write to build methods that could be used to update other user attributes back to the database or to search the database for a user based on last name.

Instead, the Active Record pattern provides a solution for us to easily map each table in our database to objects that exist in our application. This mapping of database row to objects is called object-relational mapping (ORM).

Using the ActiveRecord library means that, for any table in our database, we can simply create a class in our application, and ActiveRecord will tie the two together: whenever we create a new object of that class in our application, we're automatically creating a new record in that table. In fact, it simplifies the process so much that virtually anything we do to the object in the application is transformed in the background for us into the relevant SQL commands.

> *While there are other ORM implementations available, in my opinion, ActiveRecord is certainly one of the best due to its minimal configuration requirements and extensive flexibility.*

Don't worry if all that doesn't make perfect sense just yet; I promise that once we start working with ActiveRecord in the next few pages it will become crystal clear.

The demonstration application

Before you can play with ActiveRecord though, it would help out if you had some data to interact with. For this section, you'll be using a sample project named `clients` that I've provided in the source archive for this chapter. Let's have some fun with it.

This project is a simplified application that allows a user to maintain and display contact listings for a collection of companies, as you can see in Figure 4-1.

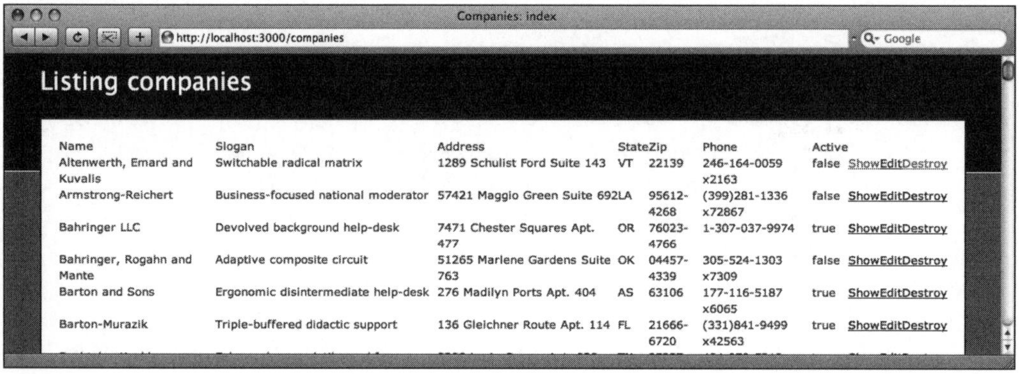

Figure 4-1. A simple client listing

However, in its current state, the application will not run if you attempt to start it, because it's missing the necessary ActiveRecord model class it needs to interact with the database. In this section, you're going to fix this shortcoming by building the ActiveRecord model yourself, and then this application will provide you the tools to explore ActiveRecord fundamentals. I've already built everything else the application needs (i.e., the necessary controllers and views), and I've provided a prepopulated SQLite 3 database with the application.

You'll recall from our discussion in the last chapter that in order to configure the database our application will use, we edit a single configuration file named `database.yml` that resides in `/config`. You can see the current configuration of the database in our sample application in Figure 4-2.

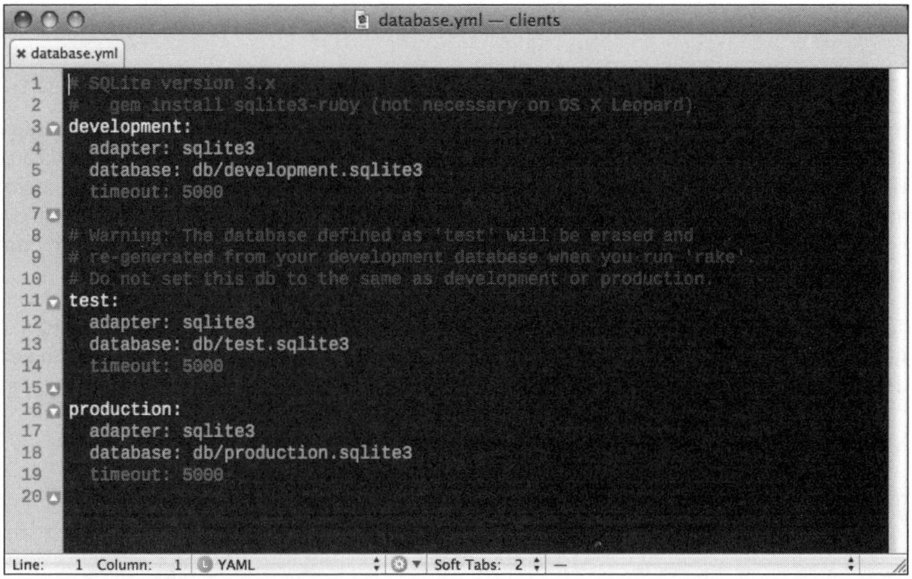

Figure 4-2. Default database.yml file

Within this file, you can see that we're configured to use a set of SQLite 3 databases that are stored in /db. Throughout this chapter, we'll be using the database that's defined in the development environment.

At this point, our application is almost ready to go; all that's left is for you to build the necessary ActiveRecord model to interact with the data that's in the database. So let's do that now.

Creating your first model

As I've said before (and it's worth repeating to help seal it in your memory), the basic principle of ActiveRecord is that database tables map directly to Ruby classes, each row in that database table maps to an object instance of that class, and each column in that row is mapped to an attribute of that object. While that all sounds fine in theory, let's put rubber to the road and see it in action.

The first step in mapping database tables to ActiveRecord objects is to check that our database is following a standard set of conventions for how we build and name database tables, columns, etc. So let's start by first looking at the raw SQL schema definition of the database that I provided:

```
CREATE TABLE companies (
"id" INTEGER PRIMARY KEY AUTOINCREMENT NOT NULL,
"name" varchar(255) DEFAULT NULL,
"slogan" varchar(255) DEFAULT NULL,
"address" varchar(255) DEFAULT NULL,
"state" varchar(255) DEFAULT NULL,
"zip" varchar(255) DEFAULT NULL,
"phone" varchar(255) DEFAULT NULL,
```

```
"active" boolean DEFAULT NULL,
"created_at" datetime DEFAULT NULL,
"updated_at" datetime DEFAULT NULL);
```

Now, of course, I built this database to follow along with the Rails conventions, so you'll notice that the database table is named in a plural form (companies), that we have a primary key that's a unique integer, and that it's named id. You'll also notice that the table name and all of our column names are using lowercase. Those simple rules make up the majority of the Rails conventions for database tables, and by following them, we're going to be rewarded with an amazing amount of functionality once we build our model.

In order to connect our Rails application to this companies table, we simply need to build a special class (called a model) in our Rails application that matches it. This model will be named using the singular form of our table name, so in this example it will be named Company, as shown in Figure 4-3.

Model Conventions	
Model Name	*Company*
Table Name	*companies*
File System Name	*app/model/company.rb*

Figure 4-3. Model naming conventions

To simplify the common process of creating a model, Rails provides a generator command that we can use from the command line to create a new model. Open a command line window, and navigate to the root level of our sample application. Once there, go ahead and run the following generator command to create our Company model:

```
ruby script/generate model Company
      exists  app/models/
      exists  test/unit/
      exists  test/fixtures/
      create  app/models/company.rb
      create  test/unit/company_test.rb
      create  test/fixtures/companies.yml
      exists  db/migrate
      create  db/migrate/20080503181343_create_companies.rb
```

As you can see, this generator created four new files for us within our Rails application:

- company.rb: Our new model, which resides in /app/models

- company_test.rb: A unit test file for our new model (We'll talk about unit tests in chapter 10.)

- companies.yml: A fixture that allows us to load sample data for testing (We'll talk about these briefly in chapter 10 as well.)

- xxxxxxxxxxxxxx_create_companies.rb: A time-stamped migration file that is used to help us create and manage our database schema (We'll go over these later in this chapter.)

Now if you go into the /app/models folders of our application and open the company.rb file that was created by the generator, you should see that it currently looks like this:

```
class Company < ActiveRecord::Base
end
```

Here, we have a simple class named Company that inherits from the ActiveRecord::Base class. Believe it or not, with this simple class, we now have all the functionality we need to interact directly with anything in our database table.

In fact, if we were to fire up our Rails application right now, you could see that by simply adding this one missing model our application is now fully functional, as shown in Figure 4-4.

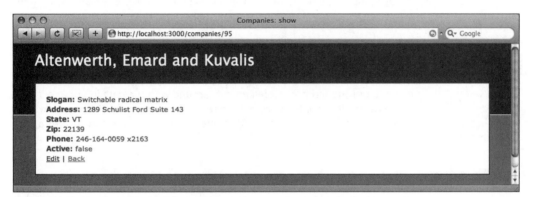

Figure 4-4. Viewing an individual company record

You can now use the application to view, add, and edit client records, and while I want you to feel free to play around with the web application and poke around in the code that's being used to power it, you'll need to do that on your own time. That's because to gain a better understanding of how an ActiveRecord model interacts with our database we're not going to be using this web application; instead, we'll be using a special interactive command line tool—the console.

Do you remember back in Chapter 2 when we used the Interactive Ruby (irb) shell to explore how Ruby worked interactively? Well, the console is a special version of the irb shell that's been extended to also load our Rails application so that we can do exactly the same thing with Rails code. We fire up the console from the root of our application using the command line like so:

```
ruby script/console
```

Once you do, you should be seeing a prompt with >>, as shown in Figure 4-5.

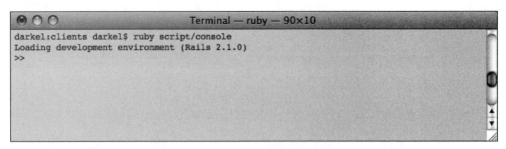

Figure 4-5. The Rails console

So now that we have a way to interact directly with our model via the console, let's start having some fun with it.

CRUD interaction using our model

In this section, we're going to use the script/console and play around with the data in our application using our new ActiveRecord model. You'll be able to directly (and interactively) see how easy ActiveRecord makes each of the standard database CRUD (create, read, update, and delete) operations that we will need.

Tailing the log

Before we begin, one step that you might want to do is to open a separate command prompt window and start a tail on the development.log file in the /log directory of our application. By doing so, you'll be able to view some detailed information about what's occurring with each of the commands that we'll issue in the script/console, and best of all, you'll be able to see the SQL that was generated by each command and sent to the database. From the root of your application, you can begin a tail session using the following command:

```
tail -f log/development.log
```

While this command will only work out of the box for Linux and Mac users, it should work for Windows users running the command in a Cygwin window.

Finding your first company

To begin with, let's take a look at how easy it is to retrieve a record from our database using our Company model. Within the script/console, enter the following command to load the first record from our table:

```
client = Company.find :first
```

The script/console immediately responds with a company object that contains all of the data from the first record in our database, as shown in Figure 4-6.

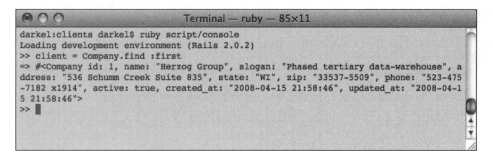

Figure 4-6. Loading our first record

If you happened to be tailing your log file, you would also have seen something similar to the following line appear:

```
Company Load (0.101209)    SELECT * FROM companies LIMIT 1
```

You can see that ActiveRecord has converted our interactions with the Company class directly into SQL, sparing us from both typing the more verbose SQL statement and leaving Ruby.

You'll notice that we maintained a reference to this result by storing it in a new variable named client, so we can use that variable to continue to work with the results of that find operation. For example, we can access any of the individual attributes of that record:

```
client.name      #  "Herzog Group"

client.state     #  "WI"

client.phone     #  "523-475-7182 x1914"
```

Changing the value of any attribute is equally easy:

```
client.state = 'CA'
client.save    # true
```

Once we called save on that object, you might have noticed that an update statement was recorded in the log as being sent to the database.

```
UPDATE companies SET "created_at" = '2008-04-15 21:58:46', ➥
"phone" = '523-475-7182 x1914', "zip" = '33537-5509', "name" = ➥
'Herzog Group', "active" = 't', "slogan" = 'Phased tertiary ➥
data-warehouse', "state" = 'CA', "address" = '536 Schumm Creek➥
 Suite 835', "updated_at" = '2008-08-18 02:21:23' WHERE "id" = 1
```

Hopefully, you can immediately see the benefit of using ActiveRecord to interface to our database. Over the next few sections, we'll take a deeper look at the main interactions we might have with the database using ActiveRecord: creating, finding, updating, and deleting records.

Creating a new company

The first operation we'll explore deeper is the process for creating a new record in our database. We actually have two different methods we can use in our Company class to create a new record: the new method and the create method.

Using the new method is actually fairly simple; we simply assign a variable a new instance of a Company object:

```
c = Company.new
```

Once we have a reference to a Company record, we can now assign values to each of this object's attributes one at a time:

```
c.name = 'My name'
c.address = '123 Test Lane'
c.zip = '66062'
```

When we're finished, we just need to call the save method to create the record in our database:

```
c.save
```

Easy as pie, huh?

> Don't forget to check the logs to view the SQL that was generated for this insert.

The create method is very similar to the save method, except that it both instantiates the new object and saves it all in one fell swoop. So obviously, in order to use the create method, we need to pass all of our data values as parameters into the create method.

```
Company.create(:name => 'My Name', :address => '123 Test Lane', ➥
:zip => '66062')
```

The generated SQL is exactly the same between the two methods; which you use is just a matter of personal preference.

ActiveRecord's new method in our application

To see how our existing Rails application uses this functionality to create new records, it's a simple matter of looking at the create action in the companies controller (/app/controllers/companies_controller.rb):

```
def create
  @company = Company.new(params[:company])
  if @company.save
    flash[:notice] = 'Company was successfully created.'
    redirect_to(@company)
  else
```

```
        render :action => "new"
    end
end
```

I know there are a fair number of things in this action that we haven't discussed yet, so don't get too hung up on everything that's occurring in this action—I've made the important lines bold for you.

As you can see, in the first line we create a new instance variable named @company using the Company.new method that we just played with. In this application, we're passing into this method all of the form variables that were submitted with this request using a special method named params (which we'll discuss more in Chapter 7 when we talk about controllers). Then on the next line, you can see that we're calling the save method on this instance.

Reading and finding company records

Now that you understand how easy it to create new records in our database using ActiveRecord, let's take a closer look at how we can retrieve records. You've already seen how we can use the find method to easily access data, but we barely touched the tip of the iceberg in that early example.

You see, the find method equates to a SELECT statement in SQL, and when it comes to interacting with databases, the SELECT statement is the most powerful and the most frequently used SQL command. Any method that tries to map to a SELECT statement must also feature a considerable amount of power and flexibility in order to be useful, and our little find method meets that requirement in spades. Let's take a deeper look at the ways we can retrieve data using ActiveRecord including some of the powerful options we can use to enhance those method calls.

find

As you saw earlier, to retrieve a record, we use the find method. However, the most common approach is to simply pass the id of the record that we're interested in directly to the find method like so:

```
c = Company.find 61
=> #<Company id: 61, name: "Davis, Tremblay and Reichel", slogan: ➥
"Robust intermediate toolset", address: "4589 Benny Forks Suite 124" ➥
, state: "AP", zip: "67784-2937", phone: "(545)073-1148 x9519", ➥
active: false, created_at: "2008-04-15 21:58:47", updated_at: ➥
"2008-04-15 21:58:47">
```

So just as before, our find method has returned a Company object that is now loaded with all of the data from our database record with the primary key of 61.

And just like before, we can also read the individual attributes directly:

```
c.name      #   "Davis, Tremblay and Reichel"
c.slogan    #    "Robust intermediate toolset"
c.active    #    false
```

We can also get an array of multiple Company objects by simply passing more than one id to our find method:

```
Company.find 61, 62
  => [#<Company id: 61, name: "Davis, Tremblay and Reichel", slogan: ➥
  "Robust intermediate toolset", address: "4589 Benny Forks Suite 124"➥
  , state: "AP", zip: "67784-2937", phone: "(545)073-1148 x9519", ➥
  active: false, created_at: "2008-04-15 21:58:47", updated_at: ➥
  "2008-04-15 21:58:47">, #<Company id: 62, name: "Hauck, Hilll and ➥
  O'Keefe", slogan: "Persevering bifurcated open system", address: ➥
  "827 Veronica Valleys Apt. 849", state: "CO", zip: "61950-6292", ➥
  phone: "208-292-3424 x784", active: true, created_at: "2008-04-15 ➥
  21:58:47", updated_at: "2008-04-15 21:58:47">]
```

which generated a SQL select that looks like this:

```
SELECT * FROM companies WHERE (companies."id" IN (61,62))
```

In addition, the find method also supports a number of special Ruby symbols that we can use when we don't have a specific ID that we want to load. You've already seen that we can use a symbol named :first to retrieve the first record from the database, but the find method also supports the :last and :all symbols:

```
Company.find :first
  => #<Company id: 1, name: "Herzog Group", slogan: "Phased tertiary➥
  data-warehouse", address: "536 Schumm Creek Suite 835", state: ➥
  "WI", zip: "33537-5509", phone: "523-475-7182 x1914", active: true,➥
  created_at: "2008-04-15 21:58:46", updated_at: "2008-04-15 21:58:46">
```

The preceding :first symbol generates a SQL statement like SELECT * FROM "companies" LIMIT 1.

```
Company.find :last
  => #<Company id: 100, name: "Schroeder-Fahey", slogan: "Cloned➥
  24/7 hierarchy", address: "51325 Corine Lane Apt. 902", state: "PW"➥
  , zip: "32083-4540", phone: "1-446-917-8519", active: true, ➥
  created_at: "2008-04-15 21:58:47", updated_at: "2008-04-15 21:58:47">
```

The preceding :last symbol generates a SQL statement like SELECT * FROM "companies" ORDER BY companies.id DESC LIMIT 1.

```
Company.find :all
  => [#<Company id: 1, name: "Herzog Group", slogan: "Phased
  tertiary data-warehouse", address: "536 Schumm Creek Suite 835",
  state: "WI", zip: "33537-5509", phone: "523-475-7182 x1914", active:
   true, created_at: "2008-04-15 21:58:46", updated_at: "2008-04-15
  21:58:46">, #<Company id: 2, name: "Berge Group", slogan:
  "Configurable national hierarchy", address: "332 Gerlach Circle
  Apt. 223", state: "AA", zip: "26579", phone: "354.381.7810",
  active: true, created_at: "2008-04-15 21:58:46", updated_at:
  "2008-04-15 21:58:46">, #<Company id: 3, name: "Barton and Sons",
  slogan: "Ergonomic disintermediate help-desk", address: "276 Madilyn
```

```
      Ports Apt. 404", state: "AS", zip: "63106", phone: "177-116-5187
      x6065", active: true, created_at: "2008-04-15 21:58:46", updated_at:
      -- excerpt --
```

And the preceding :all symbol generates a SQL statement like SELECT * FROM "companies".

I'm sure I know what you're thinking, "How often am I going to be searching my database when I already know the ID of the record I want?" Most times, we're going to be looking for a record based on something a little easier to remember, such as a company name. You might wonder if we can do that by simply passing the name to the find method like so:

```
Company.find "Schroeder-Fahey"
ActiveRecord::RecordNotFound: Couldn't find Company with ID=➡
Schroeder-Fahey
```

Nope, that doesn't work. It seems Rails hasn't figured out how to read our minds for what we want just yet. But all is not lost, as Rails does provide a pretty interesting solution to this problem—the ability to generate dynamic find_by_* methods.

find_by_*

Since querying a database based on one or a few columns is such a common need for web developers, Rails uses some fancy metaprogramming magic to provide us with dynamic methods that we can use to search by any set of columns in our database. Imagine that we wanted to find the record for a company named Schroeder-Fahey, but we didn't know the ID of that record. In that situation, we can simply make a call like this:

```
Company.find_by_name "Schroeder-Fahey"
=> #<Company id: 100, name: "Schroeder-Fahey", slogan: "Cloned 24/7➡
  hierarchy", address: "51325 Corine Lane Apt. 902", state: "PW", ➡
  zip: "32083-4540", phone: "1-446-917-8519", active: true, ➡
  created_at: "2008-04-15 21:58:47", updated_at: "2008-04-15 21:58:47">
```

Looking at the log, we can see that this method generated a SQL query that looks like this:

```
SELECT * FROM "companies" WHERE ("companies"."name" = ➡
'Schroeder-Fahey') LIMIT 1
```

That's right; that was a completely dynamic method. In other words, that method didn't exist before we called it. Rails recognized that we called a method that started with find_by and used whatever words followed that to dynamically generate a query using those column names. We could have used any of the column names as part of the method name. In fact, we could also query for more than one column by appending and_* onto the end of our method like so:

```
Company.find_by_name_and_state("Schroeder-Fahey", "PW")
=> #<Company id: 100, name: "Schroeder-Fahey", slogan: "Cloned 24/7➡
  hierarchy", address: "51325 Corine Lane Apt. 902", state: "PW", ➡
  zip: "32083-4540", phone: "1-446-917-8519", active: true, ➡
  created_at: "2008-04-15 21:58:47", updated_at: "2008-04-15 21:58:47">
```

This call, of course, generated a query to the database on both the company and the state columns like this:

```
SELECT * FROM "companies" WHERE ("companies"."name" = '➥
Schroeder-Fahey' AND "companies"."state" = 'PW') LIMIT 1
```

Since these methods are dynamic, there really is no limit to how many columns we could potentially use in the method name:

```
Company.find_by_name_and_state_and_zip_and_active("Schroeder-Fahey",➥
"PW", "32083-4540", true)
=> #<Company id: 100, name: "Schroeder-Fahey", slogan: "Cloned 24/7➥
  hierarchy", address: "51325 Corine Lane Apt. 902", state: "PW", zip:➥
  "32083-4540", phone: "1-446-917-8519", active: true, created_at: ➥
  "2008-04-15 21:58:47", updated_at: "2008-04-15 21:58:47">
```

The find_by_* construct is pretty cool, right? But there is an important gotcha to keep track of.

Watch what happens when we do a query for all of our clients that live in a specific state:

```
Company.find_by_state "MO"
=> #<Company id: 20, name: "Mueller-Gerlach", slogan: ➥
"Multi-channelled national productivity", address: "35302 Larson ➥
Crest Apt. 515", state: "MO", zip: "95195", phone: "1-818-212-2936 ➥
x9420", active: true, created_at: "2008-04-15 21:58:46", updated_at:➥
  "2008-04-15 21:58:46">
```

Hmm, that doesn't seem right. Surely we have more than a single client in the entire state of Missouri. The problem lies in the fact that the find_by_* method will always return only a single value (the first one that it finds). Looking at the generated query in the log it's easy to see the issue:

```
SELECT * FROM "companies" WHERE ("companies"."state" = 'MO') LIMIT 1
```

It's that limit 1 clause at the end of the query. How do we get around this? Surprisingly easily. If we want to get the full collection back, we'll need to use the find_by_* method's close relative—the find_all_by_* method:

```
Company.find_all_by_state "MO"
=> [#<Company id: 20, name: "Mueller-Gerlach", slogan: "Multi-➥
channelled national productivity", address: "35302 Larson Crest ➥
Apt. 515", state: "MO", zip: "95195", phone: "1-818-212-2936 x9420",➥
 active: true, created_at: "2008-04-15 21:58:46", updated_at: ➥
"2008-04-15 21:58:46">, #<Company id: 84, name: "Kiehn-Tromp", ➥
slogan: "Optional global benchmark", address: "28434 Carroll Dale ➥
Suite 993", state: "MO", zip: "54840", phone: "077-484-6164", ➥
active: false, created_at: "2008-04-15 21:58:47", updated_at: ➥
"2008-04-15 21:58:47">]
```

Ahh, much better—that find_all_by_state method issued a query of SELECT * FROM "companies" WHERE ("companies"."state" = 'MO') to our database so that we could get the full result set.

And just as we can with the find_by_* methods, we can append additional search columns onto the find_all_by_* method:

```
Company.find_all_by_state_and_active('OR', true)
=> [#<Company id: 55, name: "Bahringer LLC", slogan: "Devolved➡
background help-desk", address: "7471 Chester Squares Apt. 477", ➡
state: "OR", zip: "76023-4766", phone: "1-307-037-9974", active: ➡
true, created_at: "2008-04-15 21:58:47", updated_at: "2008-04-15 ➡
21:58:47">, #<Company id: 76, name: "Dicki-Boyle", slogan: ➡
"Open-architected zero defect info-mediaries", address: "4707 Kyra ➡
Loop Suite 967", state: "OR", zip: "65133-1056", phone: ➡
"(441)661-3113", active: true, created_at: "2008-04-15 21:58:47",➡
 updated_at: "2008-04-15 21:58:47">]
```

Optional parameters for find methods

While those dynamic finders are amazingly powerful, one challenge that comes up with them is that, while great for the simple queries when we're only searching against a single column or two, they do tend to become a bit unwieldy as we add more columns or as our queries become more complex. For example, keeping track of the order parameters in relation to the names in the method can become a bit hard when you start adding more and more columns to query on.

For those cases, switching back to our standard find method is often better: that way, we can begin to use the variety of powerful options that it supports to enhance the queries that we generate. You should enter all of the examples in the following sections into your script/console to get a hands-on feel for how they work.

:conditions When the number of columns that we're querying against grows beyond the point where it makes sense to use the dynamic finders, try switching to using the :conditions parameter. The conditions parameter allows us to pass the query arguments into our find method in a more straightforward manner.

We can pass our parameters to the conditions parameter in several ways:

```
Company.find :all, :conditions => {:state => "OR", :active => true }
Company.find :all, :conditions => ["state = ? and active = ?", ➡
                                               "OR", true ]
Company.find :all, :conditions => "state = 'OR' AND active = t"
```

:order This parameter allows you to set a string that is used in the generated query to specify the sort order of the returned data:

```
Company.find :first, :order => 'created_at DESC'
```

:limit This option allows you to set an integer that limits the number of results returned:

```
c = Company.find :all, :limit => 12
c.size   # 12
```

:offset Using the offset parameter allows you to specify a number of rows to skip before the first result that will be returned. Often used for creating pagination in lists of results, it should be used with the limit parameter:

```
c = Company.find :all, :limit => 12
c.first.id    # 1

Company.find :all, :offset => 12, :limit => 12
c.first.id     # 13
```

:joins This parameter allows you to specify a string that is added to the FROM statement in the SQL query to manually create JOIN associations. With ActiveRecord associations (which we'll discuss in the next chapter), this option is rarely needed. However, it is nice to know it's there in the event that we do need it.

```
Company.find :all, :joins => "LEFT JOIN contracts on ➥
                     contracts.company_id = company.id"
```

> Note that this query won't work in our console, since we don't acutally have a contracts table. However if we did, it would be valid.

:select The default behavior of our find methods is to return all columns, but in some situations, we only need a small selection of the available columns, or more likely, for performance reasons, we want to avoid returning a large BLOB column when we know we're not going to be using it. The :select parameter allows us to specify the columns that we're interested in:

```
Company.find :all, :select => "name, phone, address"
```

> A BLOB (binary large object) is a database term for a field that can hold a variable amount of data. They are usually used for holding large values of data such as text fields or fields that hold raw data such as image uploads for the database.

:readonly Sometimes, for security purposes, you want to ensure that an ActiveRecord result cannot be used to update a record. In these situations, you can simply set :readonly to true, so that the returned object will return an error if someone attempts to modify it:

```
c = Company.find :first, :conditions => ["state = ?", 'KS'], ➥
                                              :readonly => true
c.name = "My Data"
c.save      # ActiveRecord::ReadOnlyRecord: ActiveRecord::ReadOnlyRecord
```

:from The from option allows you to override the tables used in the SQL query. This option is rarely used, however, as it's often easier to simply use the find_by_sql method (which we'll discuss shortly):

```
Company.find :all, :from => "companies WHERE state = 'CO'"
```

:group Another lower level SQL option, this option allows you to manually specify a GROUP BY option that will be used in the SQL query. The group option as the name implies allows you to group results together based on one or more fields:

```
Company.find :all, :select => "state, count(*) as total",
                                        :group => 'state'
```

> *As a side note, ActiveRecord also features a number of summary methods and this previous example could be written more succinctly by replacing* find *with the* count *method:*
>
> ```
> Company.count :all, :group => 'state'
> ```

find_by_sql

As you can see, our standard find method is extremely powerful and able to adapt to just about any need you could possibly have. But there's always that small percentage of time when you need to be able to write the SQL yourself. Perhaps you really want to use some database-specific function that you can't access through the dynamic finders, or perhaps you've already been given a specific query to execute and just don't want to go through the work of converting it into an ActiveRecord find method call.

Whatever the reason, it's nice to know that Rails recognizes the fact that you might occasionally need to bypass the Rails magic and send your SQL queries to the database directly. Rails enables us to do this through the use of a method named find_by_sql. This method simply accepts a raw SQL statement as a string that it executes directly against the database.

Perhaps a little nicer, though, is the fact that even though we're no longer using the Rails way of accessing the data, Rails still bundles up the response as ActiveRecord objects for us so that we don't lose any functionality in the rest of our application when dealing with these records.

```
Company.find_by_sql("select * from companies where state = 'KS'")
[#<Company id: 51, name: "Runolfsson, Ondricka and Ferry", slogan:➡
 "Enhanced solution-oriented knowledge user", address: "151 Solon ➡
Mount Apt. 437", state: "KS", zip: "26827-2113", phone: "1-059-036-➡
0317 x782", active: true, created_at: "2008-04-15 21:58:47", ➡
updated_at: "2008-04-15 21:58:47">]
```

ActiveRecord's find method in our application

Let's take a quick look at how our Rails application uses the find method. Once again, we'll look in the companies controller (recall that I said that it's the controller that interacts with our models). In here, you'll see that most of our methods such as show, edit, update, and destroy all start out by first using the find method to look up a record from our companies table based on the id that was specified in the URL. For an example, look at the following show method:

```
def show
  @company = Company.find(params[:id])
end
```

In addition to those examples, we have the index method that uses the find method with the special :all symbol and an :order clause:

```
def index
  @companies = Company.find(:all, :order => :name)
end
```

When that find method is executed, it generates a SQL query that pulls back all records in alphabetical order by name (SELECT * FROM "companies" ORDER BY name) and the results of that find are then used in the index template to display a list of all companies.

Moving finds to our model

After talking about all those options that we can use on our find methods and looking at how we can use those find methods in our controller, I wanted to draw your attention to a best practice when working with Rails, and that is the process of moving complexity out of our controllers and into our models.

Anytime that you find yourself writing some complex find method in your controller, you should be asking yourself if it makes more sense to place this method in your model so that it could be easily reused in multiple places.

For example, assume we had a blog application and we were doing a find in our controller that was looking for active posts and returning them in order of newest to oldest like this:

```
def index
  @posts = Post.find(:all, :condtions =>{:active => true },
                            :order => "created_at DESC")
end
```

It would make sense to define this find as a class method in your Post model like this:

```
class Post
  validates_presence_of :headline, :body

  def self.find_recent
    find(:all, :conditions => {:active => true}, :order => ➥
                                          "created_at DESC")
  end
end
```

In this way, we could then change the index action back in our controller like so:

```
def index
  @posts = Post.find_recent
end
```

Not only is that a much cleaner (and more DRY) approach, but it's using your model in the most effective way possible—as the location for all of our business logic.

Updating a company record

Now that you've experienced both creating new records and retrieving existing records, updating a record should seem like a walk in the park. In fact, doing so is just as simple as creating a new record using the new method:

```
c = Company.find 1
c.name = "My Awesome Company"
c.save
```

This, of course, would generate a SQL update statement like the following:

```
UPDATE "companies" SET "name" = 'My Awesome Company', "updated_at"➥
= '2008-08-18 04:44:47' WHERE "id" = 1
```

So you can see that not only did Rails update the name of our company, but it also updated one of our fields named updated_at with the current date and time. We call these magic fields in Rails, and we'll come back to those near the end of this chapter.

Of course, sometimes we don't want to go through all of the extra steps of specifying each changed attribute one at a time; to save us from that monotony, ActiveRecord provides an alternative method that enables us to update the attributes and save the record in a single line named update_attributes that acts much the same as the create method did earlier:

```
c.name    # "My Awesome Company"
c.update_attributes(:name => "Boom Shack a lack a", :active => true)
c.name    #  "Boom Shack a lack a"
```

This update_attributes method issued the exact same type of update SQL statement in our database, with the added bonus of being able to execute in a single step.

ActiveRecord's update method in our application

We can see ActiveRecord updating in effect in our companies controller within the update method.

```
def update
  @company = Company.find(params[:id])

  if @company.update_attributes(params[:company])
    flash[:notice] = 'Company was successfully updated.'
    redirect_to(@company)
  else
    render :action => "edit"
  end
end
```

Here, you can see in the update action in our controller that we start out by first doing a find to load the specific company record from the database. Next, we're using the update_attributes method to update that existing record with any changes that were submitted. If that update was successful, we redirect to another page. If not, we'll redisplay the edit action again. Again, you may not understand everything that's occurring here; the key is to focus on the ActiveRecord calls that are occurring in this action.

Of course, in the same way that it was a best practice to move complex find methods out of the controller, it's also a good idea to consider moving special update methods to your model as well. For example, if we had code in our controller to activate or deactivate a blog post by setting an active field in the database to true or false, we might place those in our model as well:

```ruby
class Post
  validates_presence_of :headline, :body

  def self.recent
    find(:all, :conditions => {:active => true}, :order => ➥
                                                "created_at DESC")
  end

  def activate!
    self.update_attribute(:active, true)
  end

  def deactivate!
    self.update_attribute(:active, false)
  end
end
```

In this way, you could put code in your controller that looked like this:

```ruby
def activate_post
  @post = Post.find(params[:id])
  @post.activate!
end
```

Little tricks like this can go a long way to making all of your code far more expressive and intuitive to other developers.

Deleting a company

Finally, there will always be those few sad (or with some clients, joyous) times when we have to say goodbye to a client forever. In that case, we'll want to remove that record from our database.

If we have an instantiated ActiveRecord object, we can remove the record like this:

```ruby
company = Company.find 12
company.destroy
```

This destroy method issued a SQL query to remove this specific record from the database using a query that looks like this:

```sql
DELETE FROM "companies"  WHERE "id" = 12
```

Alternatively, we could use a class method to delete the record without first having to load it:

```
Company.delete(12)
```

Both are valid options for removing the record, and which you use is typically a matter of personal preference rather than necessity.

ActiveRecord's delete method in our application

Of course, we can see this within the delete method of the companies controller:

```
def destroy
  @company = Company.find(params[:id])
  @company.destroy
  redirect_to(companies_url)
end
```

Here, you can see that we're simply loading a record and then calling the destroy method on that record—easy as pie.

CRUD recap

With that final step, we've covered all of the major operations that we might need to use in the inter-actions from our Rails applications to the database. Along the way, we also took a small bunny trail and explored how we could use those standard ActiveRecord methods in our controllers to provide the core functionality that we need to build a web application.

Validations

Everything that we've done so far has been accomplished with nothing more than just a single empty class, but we can add a lot more power to our model by adding a few additional lines to our code. Our previous examples showed you how easy it is to create new records in our database using ActiveRecord, but what if we wanted to ensure that we didn't just save any weird thing that got sub-mitted to us?

For example, would it really make sense for us to be able to create a record of a company with no name, no address, or with nothing more than a state?

```
c = Company.new
c.state = 'CA'
c.save       # true
```

That doesn't make any sense does it? Well, that's exactly where Rails validation methods will come to the rescue.

You can think of validations as a series of rules that we define for our model that must be followed in order for a record to be created. If our application attempts to save a record that doesn't pass these rules, the record will not be saved and a series of error messages are generated to inform us which rules were violated.

For this section, I've provided another sample application in the source archive that you can use to experiment with these validations. The application is appropriately named "validations" and is very similar in functionality to our previous application (with pages to view, edit, create, and delete a resource). The key difference here is that this application will be used to manage a list of members (users). However, it's the page to create a new member (http://localhost:3000/members/new) that will be the most important for our purposes; this page will work as a simple sign up form to which we will establish a number of validation rules. You can see the form in Figure 4-7.

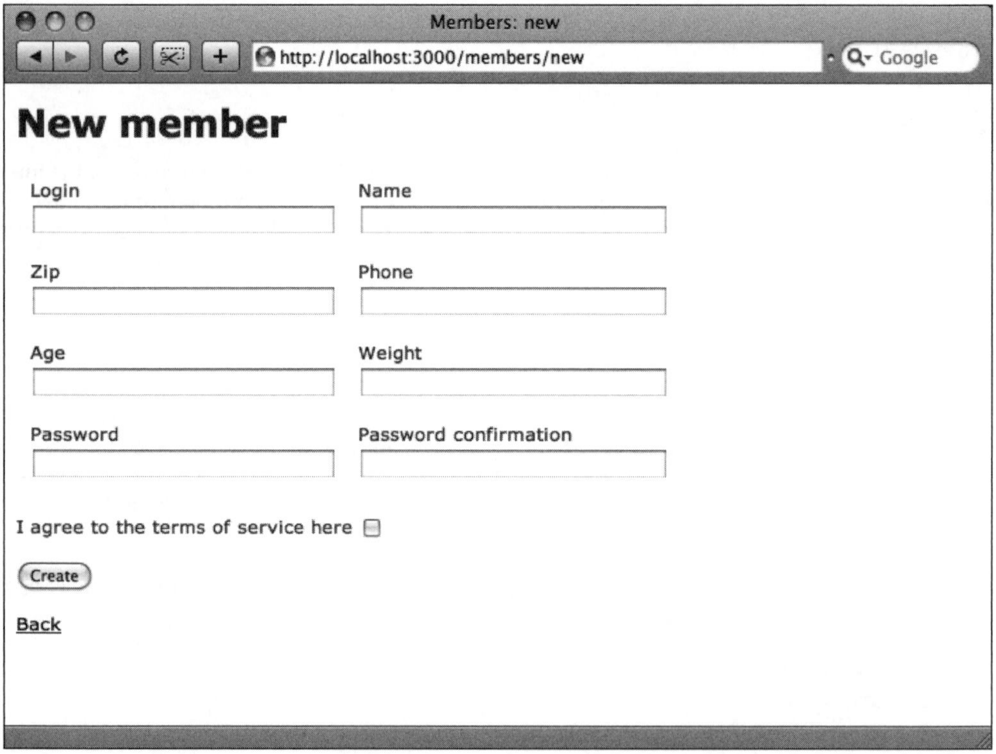

Figure 4-7. The sign up form

As you can see in the form in Figure 4-7, we're capturing a variety of data about any user that wants to sign up in our demonstration application. Including a login name, the user's real name, current ZIP code, and phone number, as well as the user's age and weight. We close out the sign up form by asking the user to type in a password twice (to confirm that it's been typed correctly) and to mark an agreement to our terms of service. Thus we have many of the common building blocks that you would need to create your sign-up form.

At a database level, the table definition is going to look like this:

```
CREATE TABLE members
("id" INTEGER PRIMARY KEY AUTOINCREMENT NOT NULL,
"login" varchar(255) DEFAULT NULL,
"name" varchar(255) DEFAULT NULL,
"password" varchar(255) DEFAULT NULL,
"address" varchar(255) DEFAULT NULL,
"city" varchar(255) DEFAULT NULL,
"state" varchar(255) DEFAULT NULL,
"zip" varchar(255) DEFAULT NULL,
"phone" varchar(255) DEFAULT NULL,
"age" integer DEFAULT NULL,
"weight" integer DEFAULT NULL,
"created_at" datetime DEFAULT NULL,
"updated_at" datetime DEFAULT NULL);
```

Thus you can see that most of our fields (login, name, password, address, city, state, zip, and phone) are simply strings (stored as varchars in the database). We also have age and weight, which are stored as integers and created_at and updated_at fields stored as datetimes.

Ensuring values are set

Let's take a look at the most basic validation, where we want to require that certain fields are populated with data and are not empty. For example, we don't want to allow a member to be created that doesn't have a login or a name set. To enforce that, we can add a validation rule by the name of validates_presence_of to our Member model (/app/models/member.rb) like so:

```
class Member < ActiveRecord::Base
  validates_presence_of :login, :name

  validates_acceptance_of :accepted
  validates_confirmation_of :password
end
```

Because of the special nature of our form—the password confirmation and terms of service agreement fields—we need to have the validates_acceptance_of *and* validates_confirmation_of *validation rules in the model now. Just add them and ignore them for now; we'll discuss what they mean shortly.*

With that simple line added to our model, ActiveRecord will now generate an error anytime we attempt to save a record with a blank login or name, as shown in Figure 4-8.

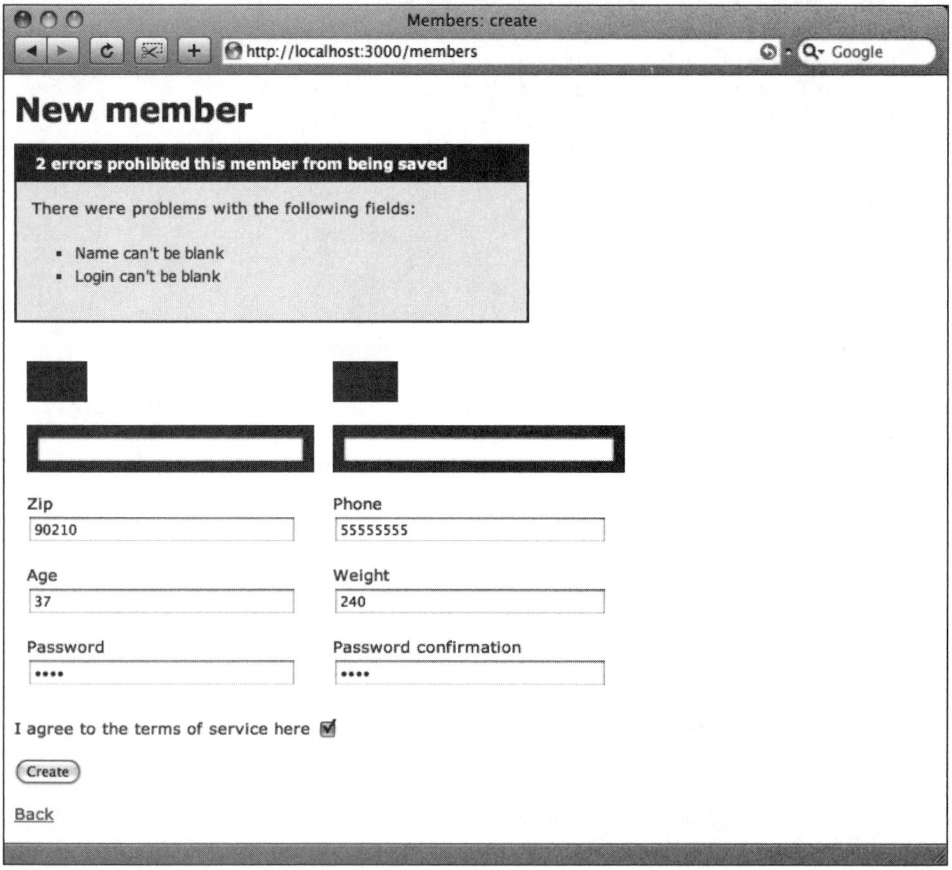

Figure 4-8. Displaying errors for a failed sign-up

> *Were you curious about how the sign-up form in /app/views/members/new.html.erb was able to display those error messages? It actually came from a small helper method that will display any errors that are generated for an ActiveRecord model and looks like this in our view template:*
>
> ```
> <%= error_messages_for :member %>
> ```
>
> *We'll talk more about this method in Chapter 6, but I thought I'd highlight it here, since you just encountered it.*

The validates_presence_of method also accepts a number of options that enable us to further specify the rules around it such as these:

- :message: This allows you to customize the error message that's returned if this validation fails and defaults to "can't be blank":

  ```
  validatates_presence_of :name, :message => "needs to be provided, moron! "
  ```

- :on: This allows you to determine when the validation should be executed. It defaults to :save (so that the validation is run anytime the object is saved), and other options are :create or :update:

  ```
  validatates_presence_of :name, :on => :update
  ```

Ensuring values are the proper length

Sometimes, we just want to ensure that a field is the proper length or within an allowed range. For example, perhaps we want to ensure that a person's ZIP code is five digits long. In this cases, we could use another validation rule named validates_length_of like so:

```
class Member < ActiveRecord::Base
  validates_presence_of :login, :name
  validates_length_of :zip, :is => 5

  validates_acceptance_of :accepted
  validates_confirmation_of :password
end
```

You can see the results of this validation in Figure 4-9.

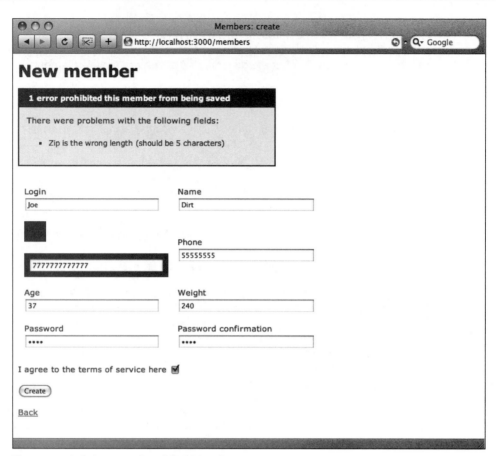

Figure 4-9. Displaying errors for a failed ZIP code

Just like with our validates_presence_of validation rule, we can customize our validates_length_ of validation rules with optional parameters including :message to customize the error message and :on for when a validation should be executed:

```
validatates_numericality_of :age, :on => :create,  ➧
    :message => "must be provided"
```

> *In fact, all validation rules that we'll be discussing support the common options of :message and :on, so to keep things DRY, we'll avoid the repetition by just letting their inclusion be implied for the remainder of this section.*

Other common options for validates_length_of are:

- minimum, :maximum, :is, and :within: These option are used to specify the allowed values for this validation. Minimum and maximum values should be self-explanatory, but :within is a bit more fun in that it allows you to pass a range of values to specify what values the input must fall within:

```
validates_length_of :login, :within => 1..25
```

- :allow_nil and :allow_blank: If set to true allow this field to accept nil or blank values. In other words, Rails won't trigger an error if the value was not set:

```
validates_length_of  :phone, :maximum => 32, :allow_nil => true
```

- :too_long, :too_short, and :wrong_length: These allow you to further customize the message that is returned if the validation fails beyond what it possible with just the :message option. With these options, you can set specific messages for the specific conditions of the value being too_long, too_short, or wrong_length:

```
validates_length_of :name, :within => 6..30,
                          :too_long => "pick a shorter name",
                          :too_short => "pick a longer name"
```

Ensuring values are numbers

We also have the ability to ensure that certain values are numbers and not letters. For example, back in our Member model, accepting anything but numbers for the age or the weight of a new member wouldn't make sense, would it? Using the validation rule validates_numericality_of, we can ensure that a submitted attribute is a number:

```
class Member < ActiveRecord::Base
  validates_presence_of :login, :name
  validates_length_of :zip, :is => 5
  validates_numericality_of :age, :weight

  validates_acceptance_of :accepted
  validates_confirmation_of :password
end
```

You can see the results of adding this validation in Figure 4-10, where our age and weight are restricted to only accepting numbers.

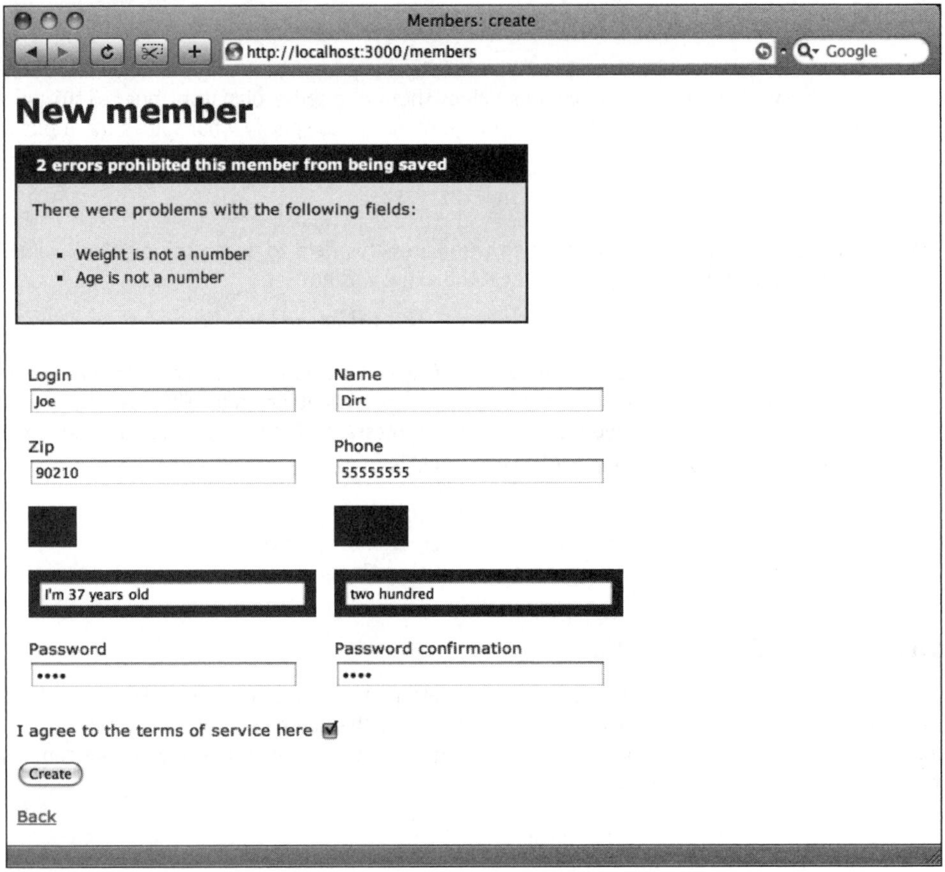

Figure 4-10. Displaying errors for nonnumeric input

And, of course, we also have a number of optional parameters we can use to fine-tune this validation rule as well, such as these:

- :only_integer: This parameter allows you to specify that only whole numbers (i.e., no decimal points) are allowed:

```
validatates_numericality_of :weight, :only_integer => true,
         :message => "must be provided as a whole number"
```

- :allow_nil: If set to true, it allows this field to accept nil values. In other words, it won't trigger an error if the value was not set:

```
validates_numericality_of  :age, :maximum => 120, :allow_nil => true
```

- :greater_than, :greater_than_or_equal_to, :equal_to, :less_than, and :less_than_or_equal_to: These parameters allow you to specify not only that the attribute is a number but that it fits within a specified range:

```
validates_numericality_of :age, :greater_than => 18,
          :message => "You must be a legal adult to use this site"
```

- :odd and :even: These allow you to easily require that the supplied value must be either odd or even (admittedly, I can't imagine why you would ever need this):

```
validates_numericality_of :age, :even => true
```

Ensuring that there can be only one

Hopefully, you caught the reference to the movie *Highlander* in that title, where they yell, "There can be only one!" Just like in *Highlander*, we can use the validates_uniqueness_of validation to ensure that we never allow two records with the same attribute, such as not allowing two people to have the same social security number in an application.

> *It's important to note that this rule isn't 100-percent fail-safe, as two identical records submitted at exactly the same time could both pass this validation test and thus allow for the creation of duplicate records. While the odds of that occurring aren't very high, it is something to be aware of.*

In our application, we surely would never want to allow two users to have the same login name, would we? Let's prevent that by adding a validates_uniqueness_of validation to login:

```
class Member < ActiveRecord::Base
  validates_presence_of :login, :name
  validates_length_of :zip, :is => 5
  validates_numericality_of :age, :weight
  validates_uniqueness_of :login

  validates_acceptance_of :accepted
  validates_confirmation_of :password
end
```

Now Rails will check for the existence of a login before creating a new record. You can see the results of a failed validation in Figure 4-11.

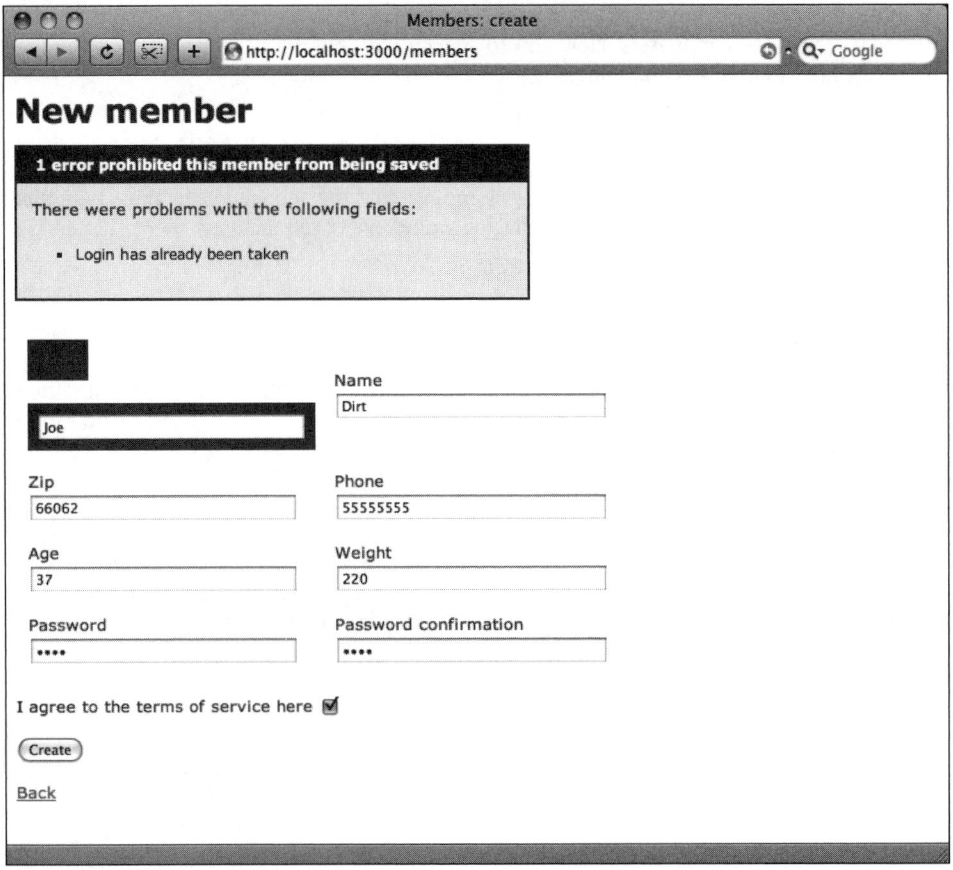

Figure 4-11. Displaying errors for a nonunique login

As with all validation rules, we can customize the validates_uniqueness_of validation:

- :scope: This parameter allows you to specify additional columns to validate the uniqueness of the value within. For example, say that we were creating an application that was tracking members of a family. Within a single family, we don't want to allow more than one person to have the name Joe. But we would want to allow another family to name a child Joe, so we wouldn't want that validation to restrict them.

  ```
  validates_uniqueness_of :name, :scope => 'family_id',
          :message => 'Cannot name two children the same'
  ```

  In this way, the validation will only be relevant within the scope of both the name and the family_id matching.

- :case_sensitive: This parameter is set to true by default; setting its value to false makes the uniqueness requirement non-case-sensitive

  ```
  validates_uniqueness_of :login, :case_sensitive => false
  ```

- :allow_nil and :allow_blank: If set to true, these allow the field to accept nil or blank values. In other words, an error won't be triggered if the value is not set.

  ```
  validates_uniqueness_of :login, :allow_nil => true
  ```

Ensuring that inputs are in the proper format

Another common need is to ensure that any value we accept is in the proper format for what we expect. We would want to use this for things such as phone numbers, social security numbers, or e-mail addresses.

Using the validates_format_of validation rule, we can compare the submitted value against a regular expression. For instance, if we wanted to validate that a social security number was in the proper format, we might use a rule like this:

```
validates_format_of :ssn,
            :with => /(^(\d{3})[-\s.]?(\d{2})[-\s.]?(\d{4})$)|^$/,
            :message => 'Not Recognized as a Valid SSN'
```

> *Regular expressions are an exceptionally powerful string-matching system supported by most programming languages and many text editors and system utilities. Using regular expressions, absolutely amazing feats of string matching, manipulation, and extraction are possible. Unfortunately, regular expressions also tend to come across as a fairly complex and cryptic solution (as you can see in our SSN example). I could recommend a number of wonderful books that explore how to use regular expressions, but for a good free resource, you might check out the screencast and tutorial at http://e-texteditor.com/blog/2007/regular_expressions_tutorial.*

In our own application, earlier we built a validates_length_of validation rule on the zip field to ensure that it was exactly five characters long. However, that validation has a problem. We never ensured that those five characters were digits, therefore we could pass in a ZIP code of aaaaa and that input would have passed the validation. Now, we could solve this problem by simply adding ZIP to the validates_numericality_of rules or we could solve it using our validates_format_of validation rule like so:

```
class Member < ActiveRecord::Base
  validates_presence_of :login, :name
  # validates_length_of :zip, :is => 5
  validates_format_of :zip, :with => /^\d{5}$/
  validates_numericality_of :age, :weight
  validates_uniqueness_of :login, :allow_nil => true
```

```
    validates_acceptance_of :accepted
    validates_confirmation_of :password
end
```

This validation rule is using a regular expression to ensure that the input must consist of only digits (the \d) and that there must be exactly five digits (the {5}). To ensure that our previous validates_length_of rule isn't conflicting, I commented it out of the model. Using this new validation rule, we can move past that previous limitation, as you can see in Figure 4-12.

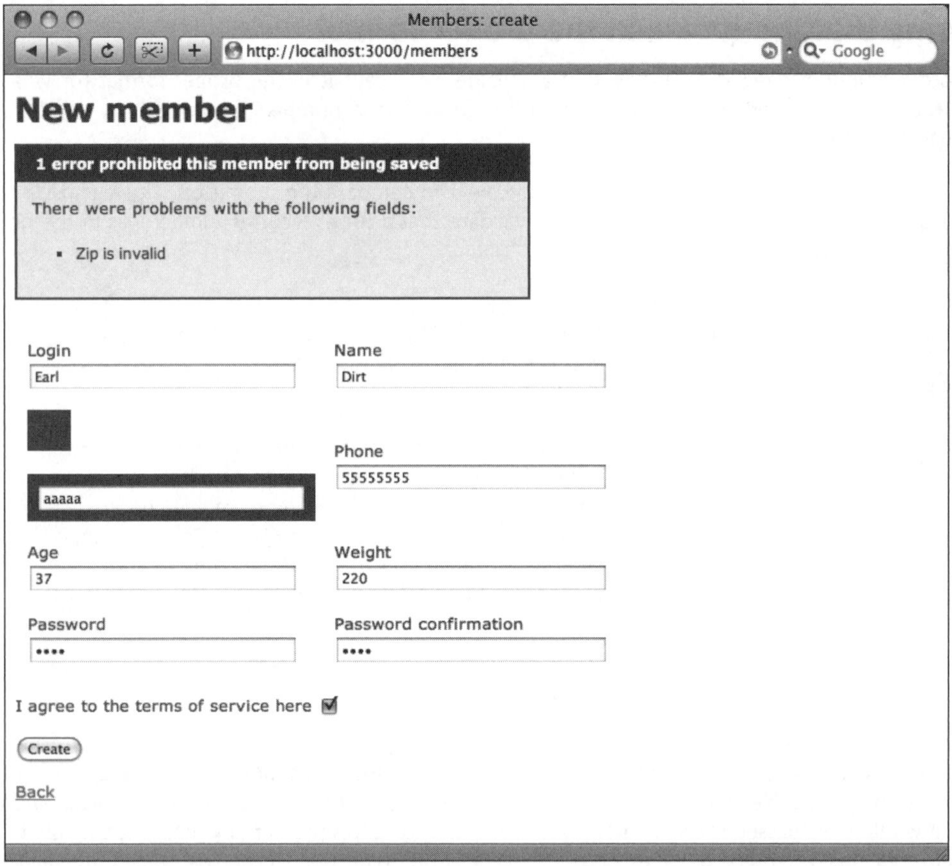

Figure 4-12. Displaying errors for an invalid ZIP format

> *That works fine for our small sample, but of course, we would most likely want something a bit more flexible in production use: we'd want to allow both valid five-digit ZIP codes (e.g., 90210) as well as the five digits plus the optional four digits (e.g., 90210-1234) by using something like /^\d{5}(-\d{4})?$/.*

Ensuring that inputs are the same (confirmation)

Finally, we can address those validation rules that I asked you to add at the very beginning of this section, and we'll start our discussion by explaining why we added that validates_confirmation_of :password line and how it works.

As you would probably guess from our form, this validation makes it easy to validate a confirmation field. For example, many web sign-up forms will ask you to enter your e-mail address twice to confirm that you entered it correctly. Setting this validation allows you to submit a confirmation field from your web form that doesn't have to exist in your database, for example, if we wanted to have users confirm their e-mail addresses. We might have a field named email in the database and add this validation to our model:

```
validates_confirmation_of :email
```

After that, the text fields named :email and :email_confirmation in our form would be compared by our validation when submitted.

You can see this in our form. In our database, we have a single field named password, yet in our form, we had both a password field and password_confirmation field. That's why it was required that we have this validation added to the model; otherwise, our attempt to submit the form would have generated an undefined method error, as shown in Figure 4-13.

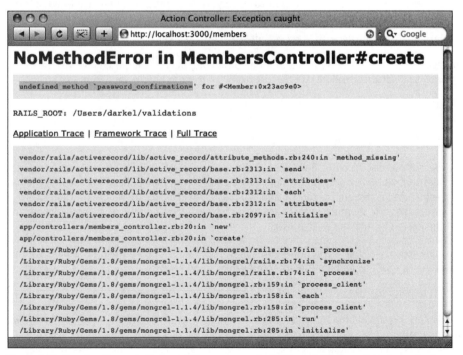

Figure 4-13. Showing the error that would have occurred with the validates_confirmation_of rule

It's a fairly simply rule, but it's certainly useful anytime that we need to have the user confirm their input was correct.

Ensuring that the user accepted something

Another common task is ensuring that users accept some form of agreement, such as terms of service or a privacy policy, through the use of a check box. This validation makes it easy to ensure that this check box has been set; otherwise, the record will not be created:

```
validates_acceptance_of :terms_of_service
```

You can see this validation in effect in the form where we asked the user to agree to our terms of service and in the model where we added a validates_acceptance_of :accepted rule. In our example, there is no accepted field in the database, so this check is done entirely in memory, and in this instance, we simply ensure that no record can be created unless that check box has been set. However, we could also have created a matching field in the database so that the confirmation would be recorded with the record as well. Which way you choose is really a matter of personal preference and business requirements, but I tend to favor not creating the database field in my own development.

This validation rule has one parameter of note:

- :accept: This parameter allows you to specify the value that will be considered accepted. The default is the string "1".

```
validates_acceptance_of :accepted, :accept => "yes"
```

If you're going to save this acceptance to a database column, you should change the :accept option to be set to true, as the attribute will be cast from "1" to true before validation like so:

```
validates_acceptance_of :accepted, :accept => true
```

Other validation rules

We'll close out our discussion of the built-in validation rules with a brief overview of a few other validation rules that we were not able to use in this section's example application. The first that we'll talk about are the validates_inclusion_of and validates_exclusion_of validation rules, which we can use to ensure that any submitted values are either within a specified list of accepted values (or in the case of the exclusion rule, not in that list).

For example to ensure that the gender field can accept values of only male or female, we might use the following rule where we pass the accepted values in an array:

```
validates_inclusion_of :gender, :in =>["male", "female"]
```

Or if we wanted to follow the old rule of never trusting anyone over 40, we could deny them access to our application using an exclusion validation and passing in a range of numbers like so:

```
validates_exclusion_of :age, :in => 40..120
```

Another validation rule that we're not using in this project is the validates_associated rule, which is used to ensure that any associated objects are themselves valid by running their validation rules as well. However, we won't be discussing associations between ActiveRecord models until the next chapter, so this validation will make more sense after you've read that chapter.

Defining your own validations

As powerful and flexible as the built-in rails validation methods are, occasionally, we just need to have that extra bit of flexibility to define our own validations.

For example, looking at our existing form, outside of the standard user sign-up elements that you would normally expect to see, we're also asking for two rather personal pieces of information: a user's age and weight. In our current configuration, a user could simply choose to not provide either piece of information, but what if we wanted to enforce a rule that they complete at least one of those fields? Obviously, we could use the validates_presence_of rule if we wanted to enforce both fields, but adding the conditional logic of requiring that at least one of them is set is a bit more complex.

In this case, we can define a custom validation method named validate that will automatically be called when validations are run. The first thing that we'll want to do is to define that new method in our model; since this isn't something that we would want to allow to be called outside of this model, we should also declare that this method is private by placing the private keyword above the method declaration.

In addition, because we're going to want to allow the possibility for one of these fields to no longer be provided, we need to modify our validates_numericality_of rule to set the allow_nil option to true:

```
class Member < ActiveRecord::Base
  validates_presence_of :login, :name
  # validates_length_of :zip, :is => 5
  validates_format_of :zip, :with => /^\d{5}/
  validates_numericality_of :age, :weight, :allow_nil => true
  validates_uniqueness_of :login, :allow_nil => true

  validates_acceptance_of :accepted, :accept => true
  validates_confirmation_of :password

  private

  def validate

  end

end
```

Here, we have our new validate method added to our model; now we just need to populate it with some code to perform our validation for us. Since we want to ensure that at least one field has been populated, the easiest approach would be to use a conditional statement to test if both of these fields are empty and to raise an error if that occurs. This way, if one or both fields are populated, we will safely pass this validation test but we won't allow both to be empty. The test would look like this:

```
def validate
  if weight.nil? && age.nil?
    # raise errors here
  end
end
```

All that's left to do is to raise our errors, and there are two ways we can do this. In most situations when we hit a point where we want to raise an ActiveRecord error, we can simply do so like this:

```
errors.add :weight, 'Must be provided'
```

We simply add a new error specifying the field that the error should be set on and the message that should be displayed on the page. I don't think it can get more straightforward than that.

However, in our special case, we're actually trying to set a generic message for two fields. So while we could add two errors (one for weight and one for age), it might make more sense to add a single generic error message that wasn't tied to a specific field in the form. In that situation, we can use the add_to_base method to add a general error message like so:

```
errors.add_to_base 'Must provide either your weight or your age'
```

Putting all of that together, our custom validation method would look like this in the model:

```
class Member < ActiveRecord::Base
  validates_presence_of :login, :name
  # validates_length_of :zip, :is => 5
  validates_format_of :zip, :with => /^\d{5}/
  validates_numericality_of :age, :weight, :allow_nil => true
  validates_uniqueness_of :login, :allow_nil => true

  validates_acceptance_of :accepted, :accept => true
  validates_confirmation_of :password

  private

  def validate
    if weight.nil? && age.nil?
      errors.add_to_base 'Must provide either your weight or your age'
    end
  end
end
```

As you can see, we have a tremendous amount of flexibility available to us using both the built-in and the custom validation methods. There's no excuse for us to allow bad and invalid data to make its way into our database with such easy-to-use tools at our disposal.

Migrations

One task that has long been a thorn in the side of most web developers is coordinating changes in database schemas among fellow developers. This is especially true in situations where you have multiple people making changes to an application simultaneously. In these cases, you'll often encounter issues where one developer has added a field to a local development database and forgotten to tell everyone else, which then causes everyone else's version of the code to fail once they synchronize the application code.

Even in cases where I was the sole developer, I have come across challenges with ensuring that changes I made to the database in development were made in the identical fashion to the production database when the new version was deployed. In the old days, we tried solving this problem through sharing flat files that contained the necessary SQL commands or through the use of complex scripts. Fortunately, Rails developers thought there might be an easier way, and thus Rails migrations were created as a solution.

Migrations are a database-independent way of evolving your application's database schema over time without requiring the database to be dropped (erased) and re-created with every change (thus losing your existing data).

With migrations, we simply define our database tables and columns using Ruby in a sequential order and apply each migration one by one through a rake task.

Of course, Rails provides us with a convenient generator for creating our migration files:

```
ruby script/generate migration MigrationName
```

This generator command will create a new migration file for us in /db/migrate that we can then use to specify our changes to the database. Once we have edited the file to our requirements, we can apply those changes to the current database using another rake task named rake:db:migrate.

For some hands-on experience, let's add a migration to the validations project that we were just playing with. For this first migration, we'll use the command line generator to create our migration file like this:

```
ruby script/generate migration MyTest
      exists  db/migrate
      create  db/migrate/20080504181057_my_test.rb
```

You'll notice that the migration is prefixed with the current timestamp so that the file will look something like 20080504181057_my_test.rb.

Before this migration will be useful to us, though, we need to add some commands to it. You can find our newly created migration file in /db/migrate. If you go ahead and open this new migration, which currently looks like this:

```
class MyTest < ActiveRecord::Migration
  def self.up
  end
```

```
      def self.down
      end
end
```

you'll notice that this generator command created a new class with the name that we specified and that it inherits from `ActiveRecord::Migration`. Within this new class we have two pre-defined methods: up and down. These methods are called when we run this migration. If we're executing this migration to move the schema forward, the up method will be called, and if we're backing out this migration, the down method will be called. So it should make sense that whatever we define in the up method, we'll want to define the opposite in the down method.

For example, if we were to create a table in the up method, we would drop that same table in the down method. In this way, we can use our migrations as a form of version control, and we are able to set our database schema to a specific point in time in the development history.

Within these up and down methods, we use a specialized set of methods designed for the easy creation and maintenance of database tables. The methods that we'll be using follow:

- Table modification methods
  - `create_table(name, options)`: Create a new table.
  - `drop_table(name)`: Drop the specified table.
  - `rename_table(old_name, new_name)`: Rename the table from old_name to new_name.
- Column modification methods
  - `add_column(table, column, type, options)`: Add a new column to table.
  - `rename_column(table, old_column_name, new_column_name)`: Rename the specified column from old_column_name to new_column_name.
  - `change_column(table, column, type, options)`: Modify a column by changing it to a different type.
  - `remove_column(table, column)`: Remove the column from the specified table.
- Index modification methods
  - `add_index(table, columns, options)`: Add a new index on the specified columns.
  - `remove_index(table, index)`: Drop the specified index.

The first thing we'll need to do in our first migration is to create a new table, and while we could certainly go ahead and add the necessary methods to create and drop our table here in this sample migration, there is an easier way. Let's first get rid of this empty migration that we created. If you still have it open, close it, and run the following command:

```
ruby script/destroy migration MyTest
notempty   db/migrate
    notempty   db
    rm   db/migrate/20080504181057_my_test.rb
```

Now that we have removed that migration, we'll create it the easier way. If you paid close attention earlier in the chapter when we created our first model, you might have noticed that one of the files that was created by the model generator was a migration file. This file is created because Rails expects that any models we create are naturally going to have a one-to-one relationship to a table. Since we're creating a new model, by default, it makes sense that we'll also have to create an associated table. So let's create a new model in our application named Comment:

```
ruby script/generate model Comment
      exists  app/models/
      exists  test/unit/
      exists  test/fixtures/
      create  app/models/comment.rb
      create  test/unit/comment_test.rb
      create  test/fixtures/comments.yml
      exists  db/migrate
      create  db/migrate/20080427074701_create_comments.rb
```

Sure enough, there at the bottom we can see that a new migration file was also created. Let's open it and see what's inside:

```
class CreateComments < ActiveRecord::Migration
  def self.up
    create_table :comments do |t|

      t.timestamps
    end
  end

  def self.down
    drop_table :comments
  end
end
```

So the migration file that our model generator created for us has populated the up method with a create_table method that creates a comments table, passes that table to a block (you should remember blocks from our discussion in Chapter 2), and places a drop_table method into the down method of our new migration. In the up method, we're creating the table and doing the opposite action (removing that same table) in the down method.

Don't worry about the timestamps method that's also within our create_table block, we'll talk about that shortly. In the meantime, just trust me that it is incredibly useful.

For now, though, let's talk about adding some columns to our new comments table. As we discussed previously, we'll be using the add_column method to add columns to our table. Of course, when we add a column, we also need to specify the type of column that we want to create. When you consider that the possible database solutions have quite a bit of variance in how they name different column types, you might think that would be a difficult task. However, just as Rails strives to make your application independent of the underlying database, it maintains database independence in this area as well by providing us with a common set of field types that will be translated to the correct database-specific implementation when executed. In this way, we don't have to worry that MySQL wants us to use tinyint's for Boolean fields while Postgres and SQLite both offer a custom Boolean column type that we can use. We simply specify that we want to create a :boolean field in the migration, and Rails automatically creates the appropriate field type for the specified database solution.

In Table 4-1, we examine each of the Rails migrations field types and what type column they will create in the most common databases.

Table 4-1. Mapping of Migration Types to Database Types Across Common Database Engines

Type	MySQL	Postgres	SQLite	Oracle	SQL Server
:binary	blob	bytea	blob	blob	image
:boolean	tinyint(1)	boolean	boolean	number(1)	bit
:date	date	date	date	date	datetime
:datetime	datetime	timestamp	datetime	date	datetime
:decimal	decimal	decimal	decimal	decimal	decimal
:float	float	float	float	number	float(8)
:integer	int(11)	integer	integer	number(38)	int
:string	varchar(255)	character varying (255)	varchar(255)	varchar(255)	varchar(255)
:text	text	text	text	clob	text
:time	time	time	datetime	date	datetime
:timestamp	datetime	timestamp	datetime	date	datetime

Let's assume that we want to add two fields to our comments table: a title field and a body field. Within a create_table block, we can use an abbreviated version of the add_column method that looks like this:

```
t.column :title, :string
```

Because we're in the block, we were able to simply call column on the table creation that was passed into the block as t and avoided having to explicitly call add_column :comments, :title, :string.

With that knowledge, we can finish out our migration file with the necessary calls to create the title field as a string and the body field as text like this:

```
class CreateComments < ActiveRecord::Migration
  def self.up
    create_table :comments do |t|
      t.column :title, :string
      t.column :body, :text
      t.timestamps
    end
  end
end
```

```
        def self.down
            drop_table :comments
        end
    end
```

There's no need to explicitly remove each column by hand, as dropping the whole table will also remove all columns that were added.

Now that our migration file is created, go ahead and save it, and let's go back to a command line prompt. From here, we're going to use a rake task to apply our migrations to our existing database. Actually, Rails provides a whole series of rake tasks for performing a variety of tasks on the database; these are shown in Table 4-2.

Table 4-2. Common Database rake Tasks

Task	Description
db:migrate	Applies any pending migrations to the database
db:migrate:redo	Rolls back one database migration and then reapplies it
db:migrate:reset	Drops the database and reapplies all migrations
db:up	Applies the next pending migration
db:down	Rolls back the last applied migration
db:create	Creates the database from the environment specified
db:create:all	Creates all databases defined in database.yml
db:drop	Removes the database from the environment specified
db:reset	Drops and re-creates the database

> All of the tasks in Table 4-2 will use the database defined for the development environment by default. However, they also accept an optional environment parameter that allows you to specify which environment to use. To run our migrations against the production database, for example, we would run it as rake db:migrate RAILS_ENV=production.

To apply our migration to our database, we'll use the rake db:migrate task:

```
rake db:migrate
== 20080504182214 CreateComments: migrating ==========================
-- create_table(:comments)
   -> 0.0031s
== 20080504182214 CreateComments: migrated (0.0033s) =================
```

And our table is now created. If you don't believe me and want to verify it yourself, you could always open the database in the command line SQLite 3 client and check it with the following commands:

```
sqlite3 db/development.sqlite3
SQLite version 3.3.13
Enter ".help" for instructions

sqlite> .tables
comments                members                 schema_migrations

sqlite> .schema comments
CREATE TABLE "comments" ("id" INTEGER PRIMARY KEY AUTOINCREMENT NOT ➥
NULL, "title" varchar(255) DEFAULT NULL, "body" text DEFAULT NULL,➥
"created_at" datetime DEFAULT NULL, "updated_at" datetime➥
DEFAULT NULL);

sqlite> .exit
```

OK, let's imagine that it's now two weeks later, and while continuing to develop our application, we realize that we forgot something important in our comments. It's not enough simply to let users post a comment, we should also allow them to identify themselves as the owner of that comment. In the next chapter, we'll explore how we can associate two tables together so that we could simply include a reference to the member who created the comment, but for the time being, we'll just add a few simple text fields to our comments table to store the name, e-mail address, and home page URL of the person creating the comment.

Once again, I'm going to show you the traditional way, and then we'll back that out, and I'll show the extra-fast way.

Traditionally, we would add a new migration like this:

```
ruby script/generate migration add_missing_comment_fields
      exists  db/migrate
      create  db/migrate/20080504202117_add_missing_comment_fields.rb
```

Then we would open our new migration and modify it with the necessary column modification methods:

```
class AddMissingCommentFields < ActiveRecord::Migration
  def self.up
    add_column :comments, :name, :string
    add_column :comments, :email, :string
    add_column :comments, :website, :string
  end

  def self.down
    remove_column :comments, :website
    remove_column :comments, :email
    remove_column :comments, :name
  end
end
```

The most recent version of Rails has added yet another shortcut for us in this process as well with the addition of a change_table *method. We can use this method in a block in the same way that we did with the* create_table *method. It supports a number of new convenience methods within the block as well, such as* add_XXX *(which allows you to easily add a new column, for example, calling* add_string *to add a new string field),* add_timestamps *(which adds the magic* created_at *and* updated_at *datetime fields),* remove_column *(which allows you to remove a column and can accept multiple fields), and* rename *(which allows you to rename the table).*

So we could have rewritten our last migration like this:

```ruby
def self.up
  change_table :comments do |t|
    t.add_string :name, :email, :website
  end
end

def self.down
  change_table :comments do |t|
    t.remove_column :name, :email, :website
  end
end
```

Very nice and very DRY.

OK, adding all those lines manually is the way that we used to have to do things. But Rails adds a little extra magic to our migrations in that we can build all of this in a single step from the command line. You can name your migrations with descriptive names like add_{something}_to_database and pass in your field names and datatypes to the generator to have it all created for you like this:

```
ruby script/generate migration add_fields_to_comments name:string ➡
email:string website:string
      exists  db/migrate
      create  db/migrate/20080504204133_add_fields_to_comments.rb
```

And that one command creates a migration that looks like this:

```ruby
class AddFieldsToComments < ActiveRecord::Migration
  def self.up
    add_column :comments, :name, :string
    add_column :comments, :email, :string
    add_column :comments, :website, :string
  end

  def self.down
    remove_column :comments, :website
    remove_column :comments, :email
    remove_column :comments, :name
  end
end
```

Pretty cool stuff, huh? Little tricks like this can really speed up your development immensely. In fact, you can also pass the field names and datatypes into a standard migration or even the model generator as well. So there's a lot less reason to ever manually edit you migration files.

Sexy migrations

There's one final migration feature that I wanted to give a quick nod to: a feature named sexy migrations was added in Rails, and it simplifies our work in migrations for table creations.

As you saw earlier, we created a new table by hand like this:

```
class CreateComments < ActiveRecord::Migration
  def self.up
    create_table :comments do |t|
      t.column :title, :string
      t.column :body, :text
      t.timestamps
    end
  end

  def self.down
    drop_table :comments
  end
end
```

With the sexy migrations syntax, we can avoid the need to call the column method in our block, and instead, we can now simply declare the type of column we want to create and pass one or many field names to that column definition. This makes more sense when you can see it in action, so rewriting our migration into the sexy migration format would look like this:

```
class CreateComments < ActiveRecord::Migration
  def self.up
    create_table :comments do |t|
      t.string :title
      t.text :body
      t.timestamps
    end
  end

  def self.down
    drop_table :comments
  end
end
```

Sexy migrations are definitely an improvement of the old form of creating these migrations by hand, but they don't work as parameters to the command line generator. Personally, I recommend that you invest your time in learning to define your migration using the command line shortcuts that we discussed in this section rather than using sexy migrations, as I feel that they offer better time savings.

Magic columns

Remember back when we created our model and I said to just disregard the call to `timestamps` at the moment? Well, it's time to look at that method again.

Have you ever had the need to keep track of when a record was created or when it was last updated in other applications? If not, you've been lucky, as it's a pretty common need in a lot of web applications. So common, in fact, that Rails developers created a solution called magic columns to solve it.

The basic idea is that, since Rails is aware of the schema for each of your tables, it will look for specially named fields within the schema and populate them with data automatically if they exist. This `timestamps` method creates two fields in your schema named `created_at` and `updated_at`. When you create a new record, the current timestamp will automatically (or is it automagically?) be placed within the `created_at` field. On the flipside, whenever you edit and update that record, the current timestamp will then be placed into the `updated_at` field. It's all handled for you like magic.

In addition to those `created_at` and `updated_at` fields, ActiveRecord also has a number of other reserved field names for databases that you're not allowed to use; you can see the majority of these in Table 4-3.

Table 4-3. Reserved Field Names

Field Name	Used For
id	Primary key
{tablename}_id	Foreign key
created_at	Used for automatic timestamping, automatically populated
created_on	Used for automatic timestamping, automatically populated
updated_at	Used for automatic timestamping, automatically populated
updated_on	Used for automatic timestamping, automatically populated
{tablename}_count	Used for the counter cache, automatically populated when configured
type	Used for single-table inheritance, automatically populated when configured
lock_version	Used for optimistic locking, automatically populated when configured

Legacy or difficult databases

We'll close out this chapter with a final bit of advice for how to deal with oddly named or legacy database schemas that don't follow the Rails conventions. Fortunately, Rails provides plenty of tools to make connecting to these easy as well.

We'll start out by looking at issues that can come up with pluralization. As we discussed earlier (and as you saw in Figure 4-1), Rails expects certain naming conventions for the naming of database tables (plural) and model names (singular)

A good way to see some potential issues with pluralization is to open the console and take a look at how Rails is able to map table names to model names, especially since one is plural and the other is single.

Ruby on Rails provides a number of methods that make it easy to do all sorts of string conversions. For example, there are methods that allow you to convert strings from lowercase to uppercase, from plural to singular, and to and from camel case. For determining database table names from model names and vice versa, Rails uses a pair of methods named singularize and pluralize:

```
"Company".pluralize      # "Companies"
"Companies".singularize  # "Company"
```

Pretty nifty, right? But what's going to happen with words that don't have singular or plural forms such as the word "information."

```
"information".pluralize    # "information"
"information".singularize  # "information"
```

Bravo—it seems that Rails is smart enough to handle those correctly as well.

But what if we throw something a little tougher at it, like the word "cactus" whose plural form could be "cacti" or "cactuses":

```
"Cactus".pluralize     # "Cactus"
"Cacti".singularize    # "Cacti"
"Cactuses".singularize # "Cactuse"
```

Well, none of those are correct. So that means that if we had a table named cacti and a model named Cactus, Rails would have some trouble connecting them together because it would be looking for a table named cactus instead.

We can override this easily with a single line addition to our model to explicitly set the name of the table associated to this model:

```
class Cactus < ActiveRecord::Base
  set_table_name 'cacti'
end
```

Of course, legacy databases being what they are, sometimes we also have issues where the primary key was created with a different name than Rails expects. Let's assume that in our cacti table, that instead of id, the primary key was named cactus_id. We can fix this in our model as well using the set_primary_key method:

```
class Cactus < ActiveRecord::Base
  set_table_name 'cacti'
  set_primary_key 'cactus_id'
end
```

Summary

In this chapter, we've taken a whirlwind tour of the basics of ActiveRecord—Rails's solution for the "M" in "MVC." We looked at how to connect ActiveRecord to our database and how to do our basic CRUD (create, read, update, and delete) operations in our database using ActiveRecord. We also looked at how to advance our models by adding validation rules that will help prevent bad data from making its way into our database, and we closed out the chapter by examining how we could use ActiveRecord migrations to create and manage our databases as well.

In the next chapter, we'll be taking a look at some more advanced ActiveRecord features including how we can model complex relationships between tables using ActiveRecord associations. Associations are among my favorite ActiveRecord features, and one of the most powerful, and I'm constantly amazed at how expressive they allow us to be in our code.

Chapter 5

ADVANCED ACTIVERECORD

In the previous chapter, we took the time to explore how incredibly easy the ActiveRecord library makes not only connecting to our database but also defining our database schema, doing the full suite of CRUD operations against any of our tables, and validating any data that will be inserted into our database. That was all pretty exciting and innovative stuff and if that was all there was to ActiveRecord, it would still be a monumental improvement to our web development processes. But of course, ActiveRecord has quite a lot more to it than just those features, and in this chapter, we're going to take our exploration of ActiveRecord quite a bit deeper.

We'll explore how to do things such as performing custom manipulations of our model data before and/or after our validation logic using callbacks and accurately modeling the deep relationships that exist between models (and their underlying tables) using associations. Next, we'll explore how ActiveRecord supports object inheritance through a discussion of single table inheritance. Finally, we'll wrap up with a discussion of two of the newest exciting features added to Rails—named scopes, which allow us to further simplify building advanced queries, and dirty object tracking, which allows ActiveRecord models to keep tabs internally of what attributes have changed.

Let's begin by looking at how we can use callbacks to attach to our models custom code that will be executed before or after key events such as creating, updating, or destroying a record.

Callbacks

In the previous chapter, you saw first-hand the power of ActiveRecord's validations to build sets of rules that any data must meet in order to be saved to our database. And for the majority of our applications, validations are going to be more than enough for our needs, but occasionally, we need just a bit more control over what's happening when ActiveRecord needs to manipulate data in our database.

Whenever we save a record using ActiveRecord, it goes through a series of steps, as you saw in the last chapter where our data is first run through validations before it can be saved to the database. Callbacks are Rails's solution for providing hooks at key points in these steps that enable us to define custom code that will be executed at these hook points. For example, perhaps we have a commonly used yet just as commonly misspelled word that is accepted in one of our data fields. Using callbacks, we could define a method that would automatically correct this misspelling before it is saved to our database.

In fact, callbacks provide us with hooks that we can use to execute any sort of custom code at the following key points:

- Before or after executing the validation rules
- Before or after saving data to the database
- Before or after removing a record from the database

Fortunately, the names of the callback methods were created to be extremely descriptive with method names such as before_validation, after_validation, before_save, after_save, before_destroy, and after_destroy. So it shouldn't be too hard to remember these methods.

To actually use one of these callbacks, we simply need to add a callback method near the top of our Rails model in a declarative manner, such as in this example:

```
class Member < ActiveRecord::Base
  validates_presence_of :login, :name
  before_save :wyn_check

  private

  def wyn_check
    if (state == "KS") && (county[0..1].upcase == "WY")
        self.county = "WYANDOTTE"
    end
  end
end
```

Here, we define a callback that will be called before we attempt to save a new record (using before_save). This callback is set to call a method named wyn_check (referenced as a symbol), and you can see down lower that we defined this method to see if the state is set to Kansas and if the county starts with the letters "WY"—if so, we can safely assume that this is a request for a commonly misspelled county in Kansas named Wyandotte and thus we go ahead and set it to the correct spelling.

> *We should always define any callback methods as protected or private, as we want to ensure that our callback methods can only be called from code within the model, never from any other code in our application.*

Callbacks are a powerful tool that I've often used in my own code to help clean up data before it is inserted into my application's database. For example, I often write callbacks to do things such as removing dollar signs and commas from any fields that would be used to store dollar amounts before they are passed through validations. Or I've used callbacks to convert things like phone numbers and social security numbers into the format that my application expected before saving them to the database. We'll explore using at least one callback method in the final project in this book (see Chapters 11 and 12).

Building associations

For our next tour of advanced ActiveRecord functionality, I'm excited to introduce you to one of my absolute favorite features in Rails—associations. While building simple CRUD-style databases is certainly powerful, it doesn't allow us to take advantage of one of the key features of databases, that is, that they are relational.

Rather than just maintaining simple lists of data, databases are most powerful (and useful) when they are built to have multiple tables that are related to each other via a series of primary and foreign keys.

> *Primary keys are attributes in the table that uniquely identify each record in the table. Foreign keys are an additional field in the table that matches the primary key column of another table. Having a baseline understanding of basic database design principles does help in understanding associations. So just in case you don't know about primary keys or what the database normal forms are and why they're important, I've provided a quick database design primer in Appendix C of this book as a reference for you.*

The importance of primary and foreign keys

To maintain a good database design, it's important that we keep our table designs clean with the data in each table representing only the data that is relevant to its domain. If we wanted to create models in ActiveRecord that represented movies and reviews of that movie, we wouldn't design a table like the one shown in Figure 5-1.

movies
id
name
description
rating
release_date
review_1
review_1_score
review_2
review_2_score
review_3
review_3_score
review_4
review_4_score

Figure 5-1. Storing movie reviews in the movies table

Instead, we'd separate these concerns out into two separate tables and express the relationship between those tables by linking them based on the primary key, so our tables would look like the ones shown in Figure 5-2.

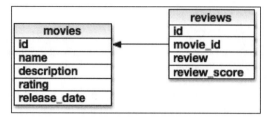

Figure 5-2. Extracting reviews into a separate table

Within the reviews table, each record would need to maintain a reference to the primary key of the record in the movies table that the review is for. This is called building a foreign key reference.

But how would we link these tables to each other from ActiveRecord? Well, the answer to that, once again, comes back to an issue of following the Rails conventions, and as you would expect, Rails has set specific conventions that it expects for foreign keys.

Rails conventions are that our foreign keys are going to be integers (just like our primary keys) and that they will follow the convention of {singular table name}_id. For our movies and reviews tables, we would name the foreign key reference to movies as movie_id.

When that simple convention is followed, we can then easily specify the type of relationship that exists between our tables within our ActiveRecord models. Let's take a look at both the relationships we can build.

Types of associations

We're going to be making extensive use of the script/console again as we explore our associations. However, in order to do that, it would be a good idea to start with a new project. Go ahead and create a new project named associations:

    rails associations

With the project built, change into the associations directory, and let's start our exploration by building our first basic models.

Singular associations (one-to-one)

The most basic association we can define is the one from a child table to its parent table. Let's create a couple of new models that we can then associate. For this example, we'll create a one-to-one relationship, where each record in a parent table has one matching record in a child table. To see that in action, we'll use the example of modeling a list of employees, and to keep things normalized, we'll store their addresses in a separate table as shown in Figure 5-3.

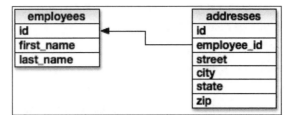

Figure 5-3. The design of a singular association

Let's go ahead and create our Employee and Address models and tables now:

```
ruby script/generate model Employee first_name:string last_name:string
ruby script/generate model Address employee_id:integer street:string➡
 city:string state:string zip:string
```

With the models created, we need to apply the migrations to our database to create the tables:

```
rake db:migrate
```

Running those generators created two models for us in /app/models:

- Employee (employee.rb):

  ```
  class Employee < ActiveRecord::Base
  end
  ```

- Address (address.rb):

  ```
  class Address < ActiveRecord::Base
  end
  ```

Let's fire up a script/console session, so we can explore how we can add associations between these two models:

```
ruby script/console
e = Employee.create(:first_name => "John", :last_name => "Smith")
```

You can see from the response of this create method call that our new employee was created with an id of 1, so we'll use that information to hard-code the employee_id field in a new address record.

```
a = Address.create(:employee_id => 1, :street => "123 Test Lane",
          :city => "Testville", :state => "CA", :zip => "55555")
```

belongs_to

The simplest of our singular association methods is the one that is used to signify that a child table maintains a reference to a parent table. In our example, that's a matter of signifying that in the Address model that there is a relationship to the Employee model. Adding that relationship will also add a number of new methods to our instance of Address to make it easy to traverse that relationship. To see that, let's first grab a copy of the list of methods in our instance of address:

```
original_methods = a.methods
```

Now to add the association, we simply add a belongs_to method call to our Address model, passing it the name of the model that we're associating to:

```
class Address < ActiveRecord::Base
  belongs_to :employee
end
```

Now back in script/console, we need to tell the console that we've changed our application; otherwise, it will still be using our previous version of the model. We do that with the reload! method:

```
reload!
Reloading...
=> true
```

Once we've reloaded our application code, let's reload our address instance and capture its method list:

```
a = Address.find :first
new_methods = a.methods
```

Now, we can simply subtract our collection of the original methods from the new methods collection to see what's different between them:

```
added_methods = new_methods - original_methods
=> ["employee", "employee=", "set_employee_target", "build_employee",
           "create_employee", "belongs_to_before_save_for_employee"]
```

You can see that by simply adding that belongs_to association to our Address model, we've added six new methods. Now two of those methods (set_employee_target and belongs_to_before_save_for_employee) are actually for internal plumbing of ActiveRecord and not meant for our use, so I won't address them. The other four, though, are the bread and butter of our association, so let's examine them.

employee This method allows us to traverse the association to access the parent model:

```
a.employee
```

As you can see, calling this method returns our associated Employee object, and we can even chain the calls to access specific attributes from the employee object.

```
a.employee.first_name      # "John"
```

employee= As you might expect by the equal sign at the end of this method, this is a setter method that allows us to set an association between the address and an employee. We can use it like this:

```
e1 = Employee.create(:first_name => 'Ash', :last_name => 'Williams')

a1 = Address.create(:street => 'none known', :city => ➡
'Deadite Land', :state => 'MI', :zip => '55555')

a1.employee = e1

a1.employee_id    # 2
```

This method allows us to easily assign an employee to an address. When the address is assigned, it sets the employee_id foreign key to the proper value as well.

build_employee This method allows us to simplify the previous setter, by allowing us to build the employee object directly from the address like this:

```
a1.build_employee(:first_name => 'Jean Luc', :last_name => 'Picard')
```

With the new employee built, we can access its attributes through the association as before:

```
a1.employee.first_name      #   "Jean Luc"
```

The one caveat is that, just like our normal build method, this new object isn't actually saved to the database; it's merely created in memory:

```
a1.employee_id     #  2
```

As you can see, employee_id is still set to the previous employee object's ID. However, it updates once we call save:

```
a1.save
a1.employee_id     #  3
```

create_employee This method is exactly the same as build_employee, except that it automatically saves the new employee object immediately.

has_one

The belong_to method is all well and good to get from the Address model to the Employee model, but how do we reciprocate that relationship, so we can call employee.address? Since we're dealing with a one-to-one association, we can do so using the has_one method:

```
class Employee < ActiveRecord::Base
  has_one :address
end
```

If we use the same trick as before to determine the methods that were added by this association, we discover that the employee object has been enhanced with a similar set of methods (that we care about), including address, address=, build_address, and create_address.

```
e = Employee.find :first
e.address.street    #  "123 Test Lane"
```

Collection associations (one-to-many and many-to-many)

Of course, one-to-one associations do tend to be the minority. Much more often, we need to allow a parent record to be associated to many children records in a one-to-many association, as illustrated in Figure 5-4.

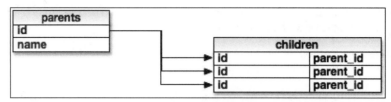

Figure 5-4. In a one-to-many relationship, one parent has many chilldren.

After all, we wouldn't expect a blog post to only accept one comment, or a parent to be limited to only have one child, or for a social network user to have only one friend. In those situations, it makes more sense to build a one-to-many or a many-to-many association.

has_many

We can easily change our existing association between employees and addresses by simply changing the association method in the class as follows:

```
class Employee < ActiveRecord::Base
  has_many :addresses
end
```

Note that we changed not only the method name from has_one to has_many but also the pluralization of our associated model. Rails does this to maintain the natural language flow of the code. Previously, our code read that an employee has one address; now, it reads that an employee can have many addresses.

Using our method comparison trick, we can see that the methods we'd expect to see (such as addresses, addresses=, and addresses.build) are present. Let's walk through a quick example of how we could use them.

Fire up script/console (assuming you weren't still in there), and let's create a new employee and address object:

```
e = Employee.new(:first_name => "neo", :last_name => 'The One')
a = Address.new(:street => 'Source Lane', :city => 'Machine City', ➥
  :state => 'Future', :zip => '101010')
```

Now, to assign the address to the employee, we can use the addresses= method. However, because the addresses method is now holding a collection instead a single record, we have to assign it as a collection, so we wrap the address object in brackets to make it an array of one element:

```
e.addresses = [a]
```

Obviously, this wouldn't be the most natural way to assign addresses to an employee, and thus most developers use the << operator instead to simply append the new address onto the addresses collection like so:

```
a2 = Address.new(:street => 'Level 215', :city => 'Zion', ➥
  :state => 'Underground', :zip => '00001')
```

```
e.addresses << a2
e.addresses.size   #  2
```

Of course, we can also bypass the issues with creating the address separately and then adding it to the addresses collection by simply using the build or create method to build it on top of the association to begin with:

```
e.addresses.build(:street => '11 Imaginary', :city => 'The City', ➥
 :state => "The Matrix", :zip => '199901')
```

Finally, because we're dealing with a collection of objects, we can also perform a find on that collection:

```
e.addresses.find(:all, :conditions => "city ='Zion'")
```

If you know how to read SQL, you'll be interested to know that the preceding method calls created a SQL query like this:

```
SELECT * FROM "addresses" WHERE ("addresses".employee_id = 1 ➥
 AND (city ='Zion'))
```

In other words, ActiveRecord was smart enough to know to scope our queries and search for only addresses in Zion that were associated to this employee. That's a powerful feature of associations that allows us to easily scope our finds through the associations. Remember this, as it will make your life so much better as you build your own applications.

has_and_belongs_to_many

Another common database relationship model is the many-to-many relationship, where rows on both sides of the relationship can be related to multiple records. How is a many-to-many relationship implemented? The trick is to use another table commonly referred to as a join table; Figure 5-5 illustrates a many-to-many relationship.

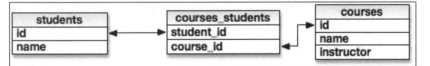

Figure 5-5. A many-to-many relationship between students and courses

To demonstrate the use of join tables, we'll create a new set of tables with a many-to-many relationship that we'll model using the has_and_belongs_to_many method. For our example, we'll imagine that we want to build a course registration system for a school. We'll need to have a model to represent each student and another one to represent each available course. Each course will have more than one student in it, and each student can attend more than one course, therefore this will serve as a good example of how we use has_and_belongs_to_many to represent a many-to-many database relationship.

We'll build a simplified Student model like this:

```
ruby script/generate model Student first_name:string ➥
last_name:string gender:string
```

And a simplified Course model like this:

```
ruby script/generate model Course title:string location:string ➡
  credits:integer
```

Now that we have our Student and Course models, we simply need to add our join table. Because this is simply a join table, we don't need to model this within our application, so to build it, we'll simply build a new migration:

```
ruby script/generate migration create_courses_students
```

This created a new blank migration that we'll populate as follows:

```
class CreateCoursesStudents < ActiveRecord::Migration
  def self.up
    create_table :courses_students, :id => false do |t|
      t.integer :course_id
      t.integer :student_id
    end
  end

  def self.down
    drop_table :courses_students
  end
end
```

You'll notice that we did a few things slightly differently in this migration. First, we named our table a bit differently, and yep, you guessed it, that's because there's a specific convention for doing so. Rails conventions for naming a join table are the names of the two tables that it joins in the manner of {table1_name}_{table2_name}. And the names must be in alphabetic order.

Second, since this is simply a join table and not a first-class model, we don't want a primary key added to our table automatically, so when we create the migration we pass :id => false to the create_table method to let Rails know that we don't want it to create a primary key for us.

With our join table defined in the migration, let's go ahead and run our migrations to build these tables in our database:

```
rake db:migrate
== 20080616024245 CreateStudents: migrating =====================
-- create_table(:students)
   -> 0.0191s
== 20080616024245 CreateStudents: migrated (0.0194s) ==============

== 20080616024532 CreateCourses: migrating =====================
-- create_table(:courses)
   -> 0.0056s
== 20080616024532 CreateCourses: migrated (0.0063s) ==============
```

```
== 20080616025204 CreateCoursesStudents: migrating =================
-- create_table(:courses_students, {:id=>false})
   -> 0.0024s
== 20080616025204 CreateCoursesStudents: migrated (0.0032s) =======
```

With our tables created, we need to configure our models to use the has_and_belongs_to_many association. You'll edit the Student model to look like this:

```
class Student < ActiveRecord::Base
  has_and_belongs_to_many :courses
end
```

And edit the Course model to look like this:

```
class Course < ActiveRecord::Base
  has_and_belongs_to_many :students
end
```

With our model associations built, we can fire up a script/console session and play around with our new has_and_belongs_to_many association.

We'll start by creating a new student and a new course:

```
joedirt = Student.create(:first_name => 'Joe', :last_name => 'Dirt',➡
 :gender => 'Male')

auto_repair = Course.create(:title => 'Auto Repair', ➡
:location => 'Room 123', :credits => 4)
```

Here, we've created a student named Joe Dirt (after the lead character in one of my favorite guilty pleasure movies) and a new course on auto repair. We can test that Joe is currently not associated with any courses and that the auto repair course is currently not associated with any students like so:

```
joedirt.courses       # []
auto_repair.students  # []
```

The easiest way to add the auto repair course to Joe's courses is to simply append it onto the collection, just like we did before with the has_many association:

```
joedirt.courses <<  auto_repair
```

Afterward, we can call joedirt.courses again and see that the auto repair course is now returned. However, look at what happens when we call auto_repair.students:

```
auto_repair.students  #   []
```

It's empty! How can that be? No worries, though, it's not a problem with our association. Actually, it's indicative of the fact that, in an attempt to keep from running unnecessary queries against our database, ActiveRecord recognized that it recently ran that query in this session and thus served us a cached result. We can fix that by calling reload on the auto_repair object to refresh the object and then running our query again:

```
auto_repair.reload

auto_repair.students
[#<Student id: 1, first_name: "Joe", last_name: "Dirt", gender: "Male",
created_at: "2008-06-17 02:24:03", updated_at: "2008-06-17 02:24:03">]
```

Sure enough, we're now able to see our associated objects now.

has_many :through

While has_and_belongs_to_many is a valid and powerful association method, the truth is that fewer and fewer Rails developers use it today thanks to the addition of the has_many :through association. You see, the problem with the has_and_belongs_to_many association is that the join model often hides a real model that you're missing from your application. In other words, we probably have more information that we'd like to store in that join table. Taking our example of students and courses, wouldn't it be useful to also capture information such as the date that students enrolled in the course, how they enrolled (online, in person, etc.), and the semester that enrollment was for? There's really not a good way to capture that additional data with a has_and_belongs_to_many association, and thus the has_many :through association was born out of that need.

With a has_many :through association, we recognize that what we thought was just a join table is actually a missing model in our application and thus needs to be represented as a model. These join models are typically not modeling tangible things, as we're used to with regular models; instead, they typically model things like relationships (such as subscription or membership) between two other models. For our previous example, the missing model would probably be for modeling enrollment and thus we would name it Enrollment. In fact, let's add that Enrollment model to our application and rework our previous has_and_belongs_to_many association into a has_many :through association, so you can see how it works first-hand.

Our first step is to create the new Enrollment model using our script/generate model command:

```
ruby script/generate model Enrollment student_id:integer ➥
course_id:integer enrolled:date how_enrolled:string

       exists  app/models/
       exists  test/unit/
       exists  test/fixtures/
       create  app/models/enrollment.rb
       create  test/unit/enrollment_test.rb
       create  test/fixtures/enrollments.yml
       exists  db/migrate
       create  db/migrate/20080705131256_create_enrollments.rb
```

With our new Enrollment model defined, we next need to run the migration to apply it to the database.

```
rake db:migrate
== 20080705131256 CreateEnrollments: migrating ========================
-- create_table(:enrollments)
   -> 0.0278s
== 20080705131256 CreateEnrollments: migrated (0.0288s) ==============
```

Next, we modify our models to reflect the fact that we're now joining students to courses through the Enrollment model.

We start by first editing the Enrollment model (/app/models/enrollment.rb) to indicate that it has foreign keys that point to the Student and Course models and thus it needs belongs_to associations added:

```
class Enrollment < ActiveRecord::Base
  belongs_to :student
  belongs_to :course
end
```

Pretty standard stuff so far. Next, we'll edit the Student model (found in /app/models/student.rb) to remove the has_and_belongs_to_many association and add in the has_many :through association:

```
class Student < ActiveRecord::Base
  has_many :enrollments
  has_many :courses, :though => :enrollments
end
```

Here's where things change a bit. First, you'll notice that we establish a standard has_many association to the Enrollment model just as before. Next, we defined a relationship to the Course model, but we added the configuration that, in order to access this association, we have to go through the Enrollment model.

We need to also make similar changes to the Course model (/app/models/course.rb):

```
class Course < ActiveRecord::Base
  has_many :enrollments
  has_many :students, :through => :enrollments
end
```

With that, our new has_many :through association is configured. Fire up a script/console session, and let's see how we can use it with our previous example data.

We'll start by loading our previous data into variables and by creating a new course offering:

```
joedirt = Student.find 1
autos = Course.find 1
baking = Course.new(:title => 'Baking', :location => 'Room 227', ➥
 :credits => 2)
baking.save
```

Now since the underlying table that is holding the associations between students and courses has been changed, we currently don't have any associations recorded in the new table:

```
joedirt.courses  # []
joedirt.enrollments  # []
```

Now, we could just add courses to students as we did before:

```
joedirt.courses << autos
```

But if we take a look at Joe's enrollment data, we see that although this solution works, it doesn't allow us to set any of the additional data that we wanted to capture with the enrollment:

```
joedirt.enrollments
  [#<Enrollment id: 1, student_id: 1, course_id: 1, enrolled: nil,
how_enrolled: nil, created_at: "2008-07-05 13:21:40",
  updated_at: "2008-07-05 13:21:40">]
```

Instead, we want to create the enrollment object onto one of the of the models using the create method:

```
baking.enrollments.create(:student_id => joedirt.id, ➥
:enrolled => Date.today, :how_enrolled => "Ruby")
```

From there, we can reload Joe's enrollment and see that he is now enrolled in our new baking course and that the enrollment object contains our additional data:

```
joedirt.enrollments.reload
  [#<Enrollment id: 1, student_id: 1, course_id: 1, enrolled: nil, ➥
  how_enrolled: nil, created_at: "2008-07-05 13:21:40", updated_at: ➥
  "2008-07-05 13:21:40">, #<Enrollment id: 3, student_id: 1, ➥
  course_id: 2, enrolled: "2008-07-05", how_enrolled: "Ruby", ➥
  created_at: "2008-07-05 13:34:55", updated_at: "2008-07-05 13:34:55">]
```

Custom associations

One thing that you may have noticed about that has_many :through association is that it also revealed a fact that I was holding back from you at first. We can customize each of our associations with all sorts of extra parameters. You can read about all of the various parameters that are available in the official API docs for Rails at http://api.rubyonrails.org or at one of the alternative documentation sites I list in Appendix A. However, let me give you a quick tour of some of the most common options and some of my favorites that you should be aware of.

Each of the associations supports some configuration-setting parameters that allow you to override the defaults for the association and set things such as the name of the class that you're associating to:

```
belongs_to :manager, :class_name => "User"
```

Or you can set the name of the foreign key that is being used to join the tables together:

```
belongs_to :manager, :foreign_key => "senior_manager_id"
```

Even cooler than those, though, is the ability to define conditions for the associations:

```
class Privilege < ActiveRecord::Base
  belongs_to :role
  belongs_to :admin, :class_name => "Role", :conditions => ➥
    ["admin = ?", true]
end
```

Being able to define conditions on our associations is a powerful trick for being able to easily scope our data for queries, as you can see previously, where certain privileges are only available to general users and certain privileges are only available to administrators even though a single Role model manages both types.

We're not limited to just specifying search conditions on the association either; we can also set other SQL-like conditions on the association such as

- Specifying the sort order for the returned records:

  ```
  has_many :comments, :order => "created_at DESC"
  ```

- Specifying that only unique records are returned (to eliminate any duplicates from our results):

  ```
  has_many :reviews, :uniq => true
  ```

Finally, one of the most important conditions that we didn't cover before is the option for setting the way to handle the dependencies of associated records after a record is deleted. Imagine if we had a Post model that we used to store blog posts, which was associated with a has_many association to a Comment model so that each one of our blog posts could have many comments associated to it. Now what would happen if we deleted one of those blog posts? Well, if we don't set our dependency level, we would delete the blog post but leave any comments that were associated with it in the database—yet their association would now be invalid. In database terms, these are called orphaned records.

We get around creating orphans by setting a :dependent parameter on the association, which will clean up the associated records if the parent is destroyed. This parameter will act differently depending on the option that we pass to it.

```
has_many :comments, :dependent => :destroy
```

By passing :destroy to the dependent option, we instruct Rails to remove any comments associated with this post if the post is deleted. This option will effectively loop over every comment associated to the post and use ActiveRecord to delete the comment. It ensures that any before or after callbacks that we have defined in the model will also be executed for each comment that's deleted.

```
has_many :comments, :dependent => :delete
```

Using :delete is similar to using :destroy, except that rather than calling the ActiveRecord delete method on each comment, all associated comments are deleted in one fell swoop with a SQL query like delete * from comments where post_id = 12. This option is much faster, but we lose the flexibility of having any before or after callbacks executed on the comments as they are removed.

```
has_many :comments, :dependent => :nullify
```

The final parameter option that we'll look at is the :nullify option. In this option, we choose not to delete the comments, opting instead to set their post_id field back to null so that they no longer point to an invalid record. This option probably doesn't make a lot of sense in this example, because a comment would very rarely be applicable outside of its parent post. However, a more practical example might be something like this:

```
class Author < ActiveRecord::Base
  has_many :posts, :dependent => :nullify
end
```

In this case, we would want to ensure that we didn't lose post content after the removal of a user account.

Recursive relationships (self-referential joins)

A more advanced example of using ActiveRecord associations for modeling our data is in the challenge that arises when one record in a table needs to be able to reference back to another record in the same table. This is often referred to as a self-referential join or a recursive relationship and is a common database problem to encounter.

The most common example for explaining this problem is the situation of having a company database that stores employee information in a single employees table. The challenge comes in that not only is every person in that database an employee, but some of them are managers who have employees reporting to them.

However, I'm far too much of a movie nerd to use such a stock example. Instead, we'll build a self-referential relationship using Rails ActiveRecord associations to model the pattern of Jedi Knights and their Padawan learners.

According to my extensive research on the matter (thank you Wikipedia), I've discovered that there are actually many levels of Jedi, ranging from Jedi candidate to Jedi Master. Jedi candidates who progress to become Padawans (apprentices) are paired with a master who will provide them one-on-one training (it's important to note that a Jedi Knight may train only one Padawan at a time). After this training period, the Padawan may test to ascend to the rank of Jedi Knight. Finally, a Jedi Knight may eventually ascend to the rank of Jedi Master.

For the Jedi Order, we can see that we would need to have a table to store all Jedi. Each Jedi, at some point in her development, learned from a single Jedi Knight. Meanwhile, most senior Jedi will have trained one or more other Jedi during their lifetime. For our example, we'd like to be able to see who each Jedi learned from and trained in her lifetime. Sound simple enough?

Our first order of business will be to define a new model named Jedi that will hold information about each Jedi. For this model, we'll store the Jedi's name, his current rank and a foreign key reference to the Jedi who trained him as a master_id:

```
ruby script/generate model Jedi name:string rank:string ➡
master_id:integer
     exists  app/models/
     exists  test/unit/
     exists  test/fixtures/
     create  app/models/jedi.rb
     create  test/unit/jedi_test.rb
     create  test/fixtures/jedis.yml
     exists  db/migrate
     create  db/migrate/20080619043908_create_jedis.rb
```

With our database defined, go ahead and run the rake db:migrate task to build the jedis tables in our database. Once that's completed, we can build our self-referential associations in our Jedi model like so:

```
class Jedi < ActiveRecord::Base
  belongs_to :master, :class_name => "Jedi",
                      :foreign_key => "master_id"
  has_many :padawans, :class_name => "Jedi",
                      :foreign_key => "master_id"
end
```

In this example, we specified that every Jedi in our database would have had one master using a belongs_to association by overriding the class name and foreign key.

We've also established that each Jedi may have zero, one, or many Padawan learners over time through a has_many relationship that also overrides the class name and foreign key parameters.

With those simple changes, we should be well on our way for being able to represent the relationships among Jedi. Go ahead and fire up a new instance of the script/console to test out our Jedi model and it's self-referential relationships.

We'll start by first creating a number of sample Jedi:

```
yoda = Jedi.create(:name => "Yoda", :rank => "Jedi Master")
qui_gon = Jedi.create(:name => "Qui-Gon Jinn", :rank => "Jedi Master")
obi_wan = Jedi.create(:name => "Obi-Wan Kenobi", ➥
:rank => "Jedi Knight")
anakin = Jedi.create(:name => "Anakin Skywalker", ➥
:rank => "Jedi Knight")
```

Next, we'll assign a relationship stating that the lowest ranking Jedi (Anakin) was trained by Obi Wan:

```
anakin.master = obi_wan
anakin.save
```

Next, let's establish a few more relationships through the Padawan association:

```
yoda.padawans << qui_gon
qui_gon.padawans << obi_wan
```

And with that simple setup, we can test that our relationships are working correctly by querying each Jedi's relationship to a master and Padawans:

```
yoda.padawans     # [Qui-Gon Jinn]
qui_gon.padawans  # [Obi-Wan Kenobi]
obi_wan.padawans  # []
```

D'oh! The caching bug has bitten us again: because we added the association from the opposite side, Rails thinks that its initial load of Obi Wan's record is correct. Let's fix that by reloading Obi Wan:

```
obi_wan.reload
obi_wan.padawans  # [Anakin Skywalker]
```

That's much better. Let's also test those relationships from the reverse side and see that we can see the master for each Jedi in our database as well:

```
anakin.master     # Obi-Wan Kenobi
obi_wan.master  # Qui-Gon Jinn
qui_gon.master  #  Yoda
```

With that, we're able to meet our goal of using a single table to store all Jedi, yet use its data so that when looking at any Jedi we can determine both the master who had trained that Jedi and a list of any Padawans our Jedi has trained. I don't know about you, but I'm always impressed with how easy ActiveRecord makes modeling even more complex relationships like this.

Single-table inheritance

When we come from the Ruby world of object-oriented programming, the idea of using inheritance to solve some of our problems is a natural one. Take, for example, the idea of modeling the different types of people we might use in a wedding-planning application. In this application, we might need to have one model for the groom and one for the bride, as well as models for bridesmaids, groomsmen, guests, and so on.

The problem with these is that, while a few of these models will need to store some unique attributes (dress size, number of guests, etc.), for the most part, all of these are going to be capturing many of the same attributes (name, address, RSVP status, etc.).

While we could simply define a boatload of tables to store all of these different wedding party members' information, but that wouldn't be very efficient. Even worse, it would mean that we would have to define many of the same validations and custom methods again and again and again, which would certainly be a violation of our DRY principles. Finally, imagine the nightmare that it would be to build a simple count of all of the people who have responded to invitations when we would have to query multiple tables to get this one piece of information.

Thinking in terms of object-oriented inheritance, this problem is easy to solve. We would simply define a base class named something like Person that would house all of the attributes and methods that are common and shared among all the individual users. Then, each specific class (bride, groom, guest, etc.) would simply inherit from that base Person class and add in any functionality or attributes that are specific to it. The challenge, of course, is in how would we map that inheritance to our applications database. Fortunately, Rails provides a simple solution for this problem named single-table inheritance.

Using single-table inheritance, we would define a single table in the database that will be used by all classes in the inheritance hierarchy. However, this table would need to have one specially named column called type that would hold string values.

Let's see what this would look like in action. First, we'll create a new Person model in our application storing a variety of attributes that we would need to track:

```
ruby script/generate model Person name:string address:string ➡
dress_size:string tux_size:string wedding_rsvp:boolean ➡
rehearsal_rsvp:boolean type:string
      exists   app/models/
      exists   test/unit/
      exists   test/fixtures/
```

```
create  app/models/person.rb
create  test/unit/person_test.rb
create  test/fixtures/people.yml
create  db/migrate
create  db/migrate/20080831074313_create_people.rb
```

In the preceding code, we created our generic Person model, and in it, we defined a variety of attributes—some that will be used for all classes that inherit from Person (name, address, and wedding_rsvp) and some that will be specific to only people who are in the wedding party (dress_size, tux_size, and rehearsal_rsvp). With our base model created, we can go ahead and apply this migration to our database:

```
rake db:migrate
== 20080831074313 CreatePeople: migrating ===========================
-- create_table(:people)
   -> 0.0047s
== 20080831074313 CreatePeople: migrated (0.0051s) ==================
```

Our generator created a model in /app/models named person.rb; let's edit that file to add some basic validations that will be shared by all classes:

```
class Person < ActiveRecord::Base
  validates_presence_of :name, :address
end
```

From here, we could simply add any number of additional models to our application (in /app/models) for each of the different types of wedding party members and inherit from this Person class, as in the following examples:

- We could create a model for the groom that validates that we've set his tuxedo size in /app/models/groom.rb:

```
class Groom < Person
  validates_presence_of :tux_size
end
```

- We could create a model for the bride that validates that we've set her dress size in /app/models/bride.rb:

```
class Bride < Person
  validates_presence_of :dress_size
end
```

- We could create a model for any guests in /app/models/guest.rb:

```
class Guest < Person
end
```

And now that we have a few models built, we can fire up the console to see how single table inheritance works:

```
ruby script/console
```

Now within the console, we could create a new bride:

```
bride = Bride.new
bride.save        # false
```

Right off the bat, we can see that we can't save an empty bride object. Let's take a look at the ActiveRecord errors that were generated:

bride.errors
```
#<ActiveRecord::Errors:0x182fb0 @errors={"name"=>["can't be blank"],➡
  "dress_size"=>["can't be blank"], "address"=>["can't be blank"]}, ➡
@base=#<Bride id: nil, name: nil, address: nil, dress_size: nil, ➡
tux_size: nil, wedding_rsvp: nil, rehearsal_rsvp: nil, ➡
type: "Bride", created_at: nil, updated_at: nil>>
```

In addition to failing the dress_size validation that we defined in the Bride model, we also failed on the validations that were defined in the Person model, so it seems that our inheritance is working correctly.

Let's fix those errors and save a bride to the database:

```
bride.name = "Cinderalla"
bride.address = "Evil Stepmothers House"
bride.dress_size = "3"
bride.save        #   true
```

Next, let's define a groom for our bride:

```
groom = Groom.create(:name => "Prince Charming", :address => ➡
"Royal Castle", :tux_size => "40 Regular")
```

We've now saved two records in our database, and although both use different model names, they were saved in the same *persons* table.

The magic of single-table inheritance, though, is apparent when we look at what was stored in each of those records in the type column that we added specifically for our single-table inheritance:

```
groom.type    #  "Groom"
bride.type    #   "Bride"
```

That's right; Rails populated the type column with the name of the class that the record belongs to. So when we do a find on one of these inherited models such as this

```
Bride.find :first
```

Rails recognizes that this is a single-table inheritance model and sends the following query to the database:

```
SELECT * FROM "people" WHERE ( ("people"."type" = 'Bride' ) ) LIMIT 1
```

Because Rails keeps track of that type column for you, the task of building single-table inheritance is incredibly easy.

Named scopes

I don't want to over-hype this feature, but I honestly believe it is the most profound and impacting change to Rails in the last few years, and it will revolutionize and simplify the way that many Rails applications are built for the next several years.

Have I piqued your interest yet?

This new feature is called named scopes, and it is absolutely amazing. However the basic idea behind it is actually pretty simple. You saw in the previous chapter that we could build custom methods in our ActiveRecord models. Now, Rails has added a new method for our ActiveRecord models called named_scope, which let's us define a set of find criteria to a name that can then be called on any instance of this model.

To define a series of named scopes on an author model, it might look something like this:

```
class Author < ActiveRecord::Base
  belongs_to :publisher
  has_many :books
  named_scope :active, :conditions => {:active => true}
  named_scope :inactive, :conditions => {:active => false}
  named_scope :male, :conditions => { :gender => 'm' }
  named_scope :female, :conditions => { :gender => 'f' }
end
```

In the preceding example, we've defined four different named scopes (active, inactive, male, and female), each referencing a specific set of conditions that would be used in an ActiveRecord find.

With those few simple named scopes added to that Author model, we've gained an incredible amount of expressiveness for this model.

We can now make calls such as Author.active, which will return the list of active authors from our database (the same as if we had called: Author.find(:all, :conditions => {:active => true})).

Or we could call Author.female and have it return the same result set as if we had called Author.find(:all, :conditions => {:gender => 'f'}).

That's well and good, but things really start to get interesting when we chain multiple named scopes. For example, to find the list of all active female authors, our method call only needs to look like this:

```
Author.female.active
```

> *Alternatively, we could have written that as* Author.active.female. *Order is not important when chaining named scope calls.*

Even better, these named scopes are usable across all of our associations as well. In the author example, we have associations to a publisher and books and thus could write named scope calls like this:

```
pub = Publisher.find_by_name("Friends of Ed")
pub.authors.inactive.books
```

The preceding code will return a list of all the friends of ED books that were written by authors currently marked as inactive. As you can see, using named scopes can be incredibly powerful, and you've only seen the tip of the iceberg. A good resource for digging a bit deeper into named scopes is the free screencast put out by Ryan Bates at http://railscasts.com/episodes/108-named-scope.

Dirty objects

We'll close our discussion of advanced ActiveRecord features with a short introduction to a new and interesting addition to ActiveRecord—Rails support for tracking dirty objects and performing partial updates.

You see, in previous versions of Rails, ActiveRecord didn't keep track of any changes in our objects. If we called update on a record, ActiveRecord would build a SQL update statement that resubmitted every attribute to the database, regardless if that attribute actually needed to be updated. Making matters worse is the fact that it would send that full update statement even if nothing had been changed in the object. However, recently Rails has implemented dirty object tracking, so each ActiveRecord object is now fully aware of what (if any) attributes have been changed.

Let's fire up a console session to see this in action:

```
ruby script/console
```

With a new session started, let's load the groom record for Prince Charming that we created earlier:

```
groom = Grrom.find :first
```

To track changes to an object, Rails provides a number of convenience methods. Let's start by verifying that our object hasn't been changed:

```
groom.changed?    # false
```

Here, you can see that with a pristine copy of our record, calling the new changed? method to query the record comes back false, indicating that the record is the same.

Now, let's take a look at Prince Charming's tuxedo size:

```
groom.tux_size  #  "40 Regular"
```

Not bad—unfortunately, though, Prince Charming has been hitting a few too many buffets (and those bachelor parties haven't helped either), and he's had an aggressively expanding waist size. Thus we need to adjust his tuxedo size to make room and accommodate the new Prince Charming (and hide that belly).

```
groom.tux_size = "42 Long"
groom.changed?    # true
```

You can see here that once we changed an attribute, the changed? method indicates that the record has indeed been updated.

We can also ask the record to give us an array of all attributes that have been modified by calling the changed method:

```
groom.changed   # ["tux_size"]
```

That method lets us know which field changed. Using Ruby's ability to generate dynamic methods on the fly, we can go a few steps further by appending a _was onto the end of the attribute to determine what the value was before the change like so:

```
groom.tux_size_was    # "40 Regular"
```

We can even go a step further by changing to a _change appended at the end to return an array that provides us both the initial and new values for this attribute:

```
groom.tux_size_change    #  ["40 Regular", "42 Long"]
```

After all of that, we can now simply issue our save method to update the database:

```
groom.save    # true
```

Afterward, our changed attributes are all reset to indicate that we are now current with what's in the database again.

```
groom.changed   # []
groom.changed?  #  false
```

This dirty object tracking will be used for partial object updates in future versions of Rails so that when we update an object like we did in this example, Rails will no longer attempt to update every attribute in the record to the database. Instead, it will only update those fields that have changed, like this:

```
UPDATE "people" SET "tux_size" = '42 Long', "updated_at" = ➡
'2008-08-31 09:38:25' WHERE "id" = 3
```

Summary

We covered a lot of ground in this chapter and greatly expanded your knowledge in understanding how you can support the full spectrum of CRUD operations in a database using ActiveRecord. In this chapter, we talked about how we can add callbacks to our models to inject our own code into key points of the creation, updating or deleting of records. We then went into how to model relationships between tables using ActiveRecord's associations, and you discovered that the amount of expressiveness that we can build into our applications using associations is simply amazing. I hope you had as much fun learning about associations in this chapter as I had building the examples. Associations are by far one of my favorite powerful features within the Rails framework.

After associations, we looked at how ActiveRecord supports a simple type of object inheritance with its single-table inheritance feature, before moving into two exciting new developments in ActiveRecord: named scopes and dirty object tracking.

At this point, we've covered the most important points of using ActiveRecord within our Rails applications to serve as the "M" in our MVC architecture. Now, it's time to tour the views and the controllers. After that, we'll move on to the fun business of building our own Rails application.

Chapter 6

PRESENTING THE VIEWS

In the last few chapters, we took a nice tour of the ins and outs of using Rails's ActiveRecord library to connect and interface to our applications database. By doing so, we gained a nice understanding of the "model" in our MVC pattern. Now, it's time to move on to the next portion of the pattern as we take a look at the support in Ruby on Rails for the "view" component of MVC. When we talk about the view, we're typically talking about the scripts that build the user interfaces that we present to allow users to interact with our application.

Action View is the name of the library that Rails provides to give us the necessary features and methods that we need to easily, and with relatively little pain, build our user interfaces pages. Typically, these pages, which you'll commonly hear referred to as templates, will simply be a combination of HTML and embedded Ruby.

For our purposes in this chapter, I'm going to assume that you already have a basic grasp on how to build HTML web pages, so we'll be focusing our attention on the ways that Rails makes it easier for us to build our user interface templates.

We'll start out by looking at how we can embed Ruby into our HTML templates to add dynamic content to the pages in our application. We'll also look at the multiple ways that Rails solves the problem of duplication in our templates: first by providing an easy way for us to define common header and footer elements that can be applied to our templates and second by looking at how Rails provides the ability for us to move duplicated elements out of our views and into subtemplates. Even cooler, we'll look at how Rails provides a large library of methods, called helpers, that help us build the HTML elements and tags that we'll use in our application's user interface.

Naming templates

But before we jump into the mix of exploring what we can do with templates, let's pause for a moment to first give you an understanding of how our templates need to be named and where they are stored in our application.

As you should expect by now, Rails has a set of standard naming conventions for our templates that we need to follow to make things go smoothly. Rails uses a three-level naming mechanism that looks like index.html.erb.

In this example, index refers to the actual name of our template. Next the html level of the filename refers to the content type that this template will render as, and this example shows that our template will return an HTML web page. The final level of our naming convention is used to determine the template rendering engine that will be used to build the final output. The most common one that we'll use in Rails is erb, which represents Embedded Ruby (ERb).

While we won't be covering them here, other common extensions are:

- .xml.builder: Used for creating XML-based templates using the Ruby Builder library
- .js.rjs: Used to return dynamic JavaScript using RJS (most people believe this stands for Ruby JavaScript, but I've seen some definitions list it as Remote JavaScript)

As for the location of our templates, you might have noticed when we built some simple templates back in Chapter 3 that view templates are very tightly bound to controller actions and will typically have a one-to-one relationship with them. So if we have a posts_controller with an index action, then all templates for this controller will be found in /app/views/posts (to match the controller name), and within this folder is a template named index.html.erb (to match our action).

Meet the ERb tags

To embed dynamic content into our templates using Ruby, Rails utilizes a library named ERb, which will seem pretty familiar if you've ever built web applications using solutions such as PHP or JSP.

Using ERb, we simply create our HTML pages as normal and mix in dynamic content throughout the HTML using tags that that look like <%= %>.

Let's take a look at how they work in practice. To do that, let's reopen our previous application from Chapter 3 (where we built a simple Rails application to say "Hello World!"). We'll use that application as our baseline to which we can add some ERb tags to those templates to add dynamic content.

If you recall, in that application, we built an index template in the hello controller that outputs a single quote from the pilot episode of *Futurama* every time you visit http://localhost:3000/hello. You can see that template's output in Figure 6-1.

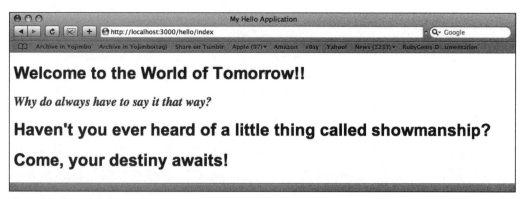

Figure 6-1. Our existing page

Well, that's fine and good, but it's not exactly very dynamic is it? Every user who views this page will always see the exact same content in the page. Let's explore how we can use ERb tags to make the page more dynamic.

Within ERb, there are four different tag combinations that we can use to embed Ruby code into our pages. The first pair that we'll look at are the <%= %> tags.

The <%= %> Tags

When we embed Ruby code within <%= %> tags in a template, that Ruby code will be evaluated when the server renders the template, and the result of that Ruby code will then be injected into the HTML source in its place.

Let's see how that looks by adding some Ruby code into the index template found in /app/views/ hello/index.html.erb. We'll start by outputting the current date when the template is rendered by adding a call to Date.today to the template like so:

```
<!DOCTYPE HTML PUBLIC "-//W3C//DTD HTML 4.01 Transitional//EN"
  "http://www.w3.org/TR/html4/loose.dtd">
<html>
  <head>
    <meta http-equiv="Content-type" content="text/html; charset=utf-8">
    <title>My Hello Application</title>
    <style type="text/css" media="screen">
      h1 {font-family: Arial, "MS Trebuchet", sans-serif;}
      h2 {color: red; font-style: italic;}
    </style>
  </head>
  <body>
    <h1>Welcome to the World of Tomorrow!!</h1>
    <h1>The Current Date is <%= Date.today.to_s(:long) %></h1>
    <h2>Why do always have to say it that way?</h2>
    <h1>Haven't you ever heard of a little thing ➡
            called showmanship? </h1>
```

141

```
            <h1>Come, your destiny awaits!</h1>
        </body>
    </html>
```

Fire up your web application using `ruby script/server`; open a web browser to `http://localhost:3000/hello`; and you'll be rewarded with a page that looks similar to the one shown in Figure 6-2 (of course, your date should be different, and if the date shows the same in your version, you really should fix the date/time settings on your computer!).

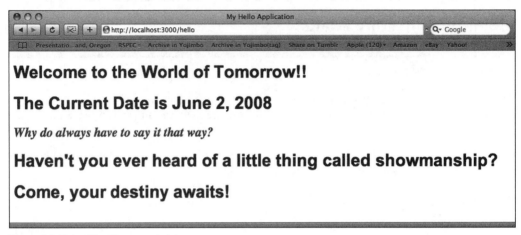

Figure 6-2. Outputting the current date

And that's it—our page is now dynamic and will always return the current date every time it's loaded.

But that's not quite what we wanted though was it? Wouldn't it be better if, instead of displaying the current date, we could display tomorrow's date? This is supposed to be the world of tomorrow after all. As with all good languages, there's more than one way we could accomplish that:

First, we could simply add an additional day to the current date like so:

```
    <h1>The Current Date is <%= (Date.today + 1.day).to_s(:long) %></h1>
```

That works, but it's not very pretty and isn't quite as succinct as it could be. Instead, we could use one of Rails's additions to `Date` and `Time` objects by the name of the `tomorrow` method:

```
    <h1>The Current Date is <%= Date.tomorrow.to_s(:long) %></h1>
```

> It might be worth noting that since the `Date.today` method is executed on the server it's being run from, it will return the current Date as it's set on the server. So if the date's wrong on the server, it'll be wrong to everyone who views this page. This also means that the output will also be set to whatever time zone the server uses.

The <% %> Tags

There are times that we want to execute Ruby code but not actually insert anything into the HTML output of our template. In these cases, we can use the <% %> tags, which work identically to the <%= %> tags except that the return value of the Ruby code between them is not inserted into the HTML.

We would want to use this type of tag mainly for things like variable assignments or the beginnings and endings of things like loops or conditionals. This tag's usefulness should be a bit clearer when we can see them in action by adding a simple loop to our existing page. So let's do just that by adding some <% %> tags to our index template:

```
<!-- Excerpted -->
<h1>The Current Date is <%= Date.tomorrow.to_s(:long) %></h1>
<h2>Why do always have to say it that way?</h2>
<h1>Haven't you ever heard of a little thing called showmanship? </h1>
<h1>Come, your destiny awaits!</h1>
<hr />
<% message = "BLAST OFF!" %>

<% for x in %w(Ten Nine Eight Seven Six Five Four Three Two One) %>
  <%= x %><br />
<% end %>
<h1><%= message %></h1>
<!-- Excerpted -->
```

Assuming your script/server is still running, you can refresh the page in your web browser and see the result of our change to this template, which will look like the page shown Figure 6-3.

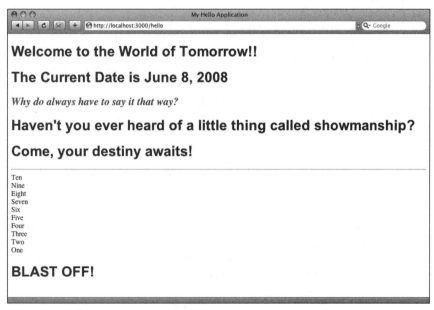

Figure 6-3. Added a simple loop to our template

In this example, we used our new <% %> tags to define a variable named message and to start and end a loop that outputs a countdown timer.

Another cool thing that we can do with ERb tags is to conditionally determine exactly which parts of our template will be output when it's rendered. Hang on; it gets better—we can also use those conditionals to determine which parts of the HTML within the template to render. To see that in action, let's modify our index template to remove our loop code from the previous example and change the template to look like this:

```
<!-- Excerpted -->
<h1>The Current Date is <%= Date.tomorrow.to_s(:long) %></h1>
<h2>Why do always have to say it that way?</h2>
<h1>Haven't you ever heard of a little thing called showmanship? </h1>
<h1>Come, your destiny awaits!</h1>
<% output = false %>
<hr />
<% if output %>
  <h2>I'm only rendered if output is set to true</h2>
<% else %>
  <h2>I'm only rendered if output is set to false</h2>
<% end %>
<!-- Excerpted -->
```

In this example, we wrapped a pair of standard H2 tags within a conditional block (using those <% %> tags), but only one of those tags will make it to the final page that's delivered to the browser. So you can see that using these Ruby tags, we can have a great amount of control over our pages.

The <%- -%> Tags

There's only one small problem with the code in our previous example, and it's not immediately obvious unless you look at the HTML source of the rendered page.

If you were to view the source of the web page in your browser from the previous examples, you'll see that there's a small trouble spot here:

```
<h1>Haven't you ever heard of a little thing called showmanship? </h1>
<h1>Come, your destiny awaits!</h1>

<hr />

  <h2>I'm only rendered if output is set to false</h2>

</body>
```

Do you notice all those extra blank lines that have been added to our HTML source? The issue is that while those <% %> tags don't output the return value of their Ruby code into the template, they do still show up as blank lines within the source. Most of the time, this really isn't a problem, but on rare occasions, it can be the cause of some odd CSS (Cascading Style Sheet) rendering issues when your CSS is expecting a tighter output.

Fortunately, there's an easy fix for this, because we can simply change our <% %> tags to <%- -%> tags, which work the same except that they suppress any additional leading white space and extra new lines that would normally be added. Let's modify our previous code to use these new tags:

```
<!-- Excerpted -->
<h1>Come, your destiny awaits!</h1>
<%- output = false -%>
<hr />
<%- if output -%>
  <h2>I'm only rendered if output is set to true</h2>
<%- else -%>
  <h2>I'm only rendered if output is set to false</h2>
<%- end -%>
<!-- Excerpted -->
```

Save the changes to this file, and refresh the page in your browser. You'll notice that while it looks the same in the browser, viewing the HTML source reveals that our output has been tightened up quite a bit now:

```
<h1>Haven't you ever heard of a little thing called showmanship? </h1>
<h1>Come, your destiny awaits!</h1>
<hr />
  <h2>I'm only rendered if output is set to false</h2>
  </body>
</html>
```

Why wouldn't you always use the <%- -%> tags then? Well, the simplest answer is that it rarely matters as users are going to see the rendered version of your HTML and not the pure source, and the extra output doesn't normally cause issues with CSS rendering. However, in the cases where it does matter, it's nice to have such an easy way to fix it.

The <%# %> Tags

Sometimes, while we're developing our templates, we want to be able to block some code in a template from being executed but don't really want to have to go through the hassle of deleting it and potentially re-adding it later.

An easy way to do that is to change the ERb tags to their comment variants <%# %>. Using these, any code within these tags is simply ignored. Of course, it should go without saying that it would be bad form to leave these comment tags in our templates once they're released.

Layouts

In addition to adding dynamic content to our pages using ERb tags, another cool thing that Rails provides us with is the ability to define a common header and footer for all of our pages. Of course, like most things in Rails, it does so in the most pain-free way imaginable. If you look within your app/views folders, you should see a folder named layouts (see Figure 6-4).

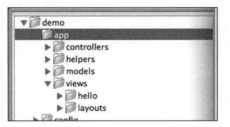

Figure 6-4. The layouts folder

This is a special folder because our controllers will look within this folder for a matching template to use for the current request. The layout files we'll create in this folder are actually pretty simple things, as they're really just another example of HTML with ERb templates that we use to build our common header and footer options.

Determining which layout to use with a view template is actually done by the controller based on the following rules:

- A specific layout can be explicitly specified in the controller in the code.
- A layout file in /app/views/layouts exists with the same name as our controller (e.g., hello.html.erb for the hello controller).
- Barring either of those, Rails will look to see if a generic application.html.erb layout file exists in /app/views/layouts in order to match the application controller (which all of our controllers inherit from).

Of course, for that to become a bit clearer, it would help to see it in action, so let's build some layouts.

Create a new file named application.html.erb within /app/views/layouts, and let's move the standard header and footer elements out of our existing template and into this new file. So place the following content in it:

```
<!DOCTYPE HTML PUBLIC "-//W3C//DTD HTML 4.01 Transitional//EN"
  "http://www.w3.org/TR/html4/loose.dtd">
<html>
  <head>
    <meta http-equiv="Content-type" content="text/html; charset=utf-8">
    <title>My Hello Application</title>
    <style type="text/css" media="screen">
      h1 {font-family: Arial, "MS Trebuchet", sans-serif;}
      h2 {color: red; font-style: italic;}
    </style>
  </head>
  <body>
    <h1>Hello from the Application Layout!! </h1>

    <!-- Here's where our normal template content was -->

  </body>
</html>
```

You can see here that we've moved the elements that we expect to remain the same across all our HTML pages (in this case our HTML header information, CSS styles, and H1 tag, as well as the closing HTML tags) into our new layout file. Meanwhile we'll also need to remove that same header and footer code out of our view template (/app/views/hello/index.html.erb)—leaving it to look like this:

```erb
<h1>The Current Date is <%= Date.tomorrow.to_s(:long) %></h1>
<h2>Why do always have to say it that way?</h2>
<h1>Haven't you ever heard of a little thing called showmanship? </h1>
<h1>Come, your destiny awaits!</h1>
<%- output = false -%>
<hr />
<%- if output -%>
  <h2>I'm only rendered if output is set to true</h2>
<%- else -%>
  <h2>I'm only rendered if output is set to false</h2>
<%- end -%>
```

Saving our new application layout and refreshing our page, we'll see the result shown in Figure 6-5.

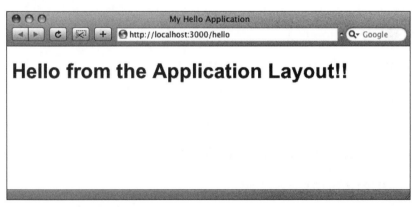

Figure 6-5. The application layout

Well, the good news is that Rails found our new layout, but where is the output from our index view template?

It's missing because we didn't tell Rails where to insert it within our layout. You see, Rails recognized that we had a layout and began rendering it, but we also need to specify a place within that layout to tell the rendering engine to also render the view template. This is easily remedied with the simple addition of a yield method.

yield is a special method that we use in our layout templates to tell the rendering engine to stop rendering the layout at this point and instead begin rendering the view template. Once the view template completes rendering, control of the output returns to the layout.

So let's fix our current layout issue by adding the yield method to our layout so that our layout template looks like this:

```
<!DOCTYPE HTML PUBLIC "-//W3C//DTD HTML 4.01 Transitional//EN"
  "http://www.w3.org/TR/html4/loose.dtd">
<html>
  <head>
    <meta http-equiv="Content-type" content="text/html; charset=utf-8">
    <title>My Hello Application</title>
    <style type="text/css" media="screen">
      h1 {font-family: Arial, "MS Trebuchet", sans-serif;}
      h2 {color: red; font-style: italic;}
    </style>
  </head>
  <body>
    <h1>Hello from the Application Layout!!</h1>
    <%= yield %>
  </body>
</html>
```

Save the layout file, and when we refresh the page in our web browser, we'll see the page that we expected to see last time (see Figure 6-6).

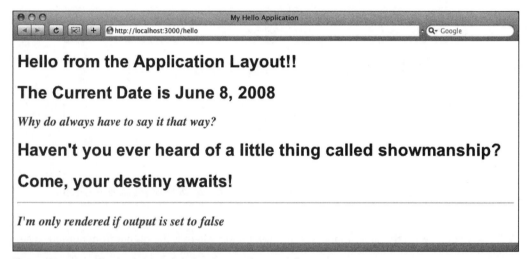

Figure 6-6. Our application layout rendering the template as well

Creating an application layout is a useful tool for when we want to have a standard, applicationwide layout that wraps around all of our view templates. However, we can also create a layout that will be specific to a single controller by creating a layout file with the same name as the controller.

Let's see what happens when we create a new layout file in our layouts folder named hello.html.erb (to match the controller name) that contains the following:

```
<!DOCTYPE HTML PUBLIC "-//W3C//DTD HTML 4.01 Transitional//EN"
  "http://www.w3.org/TR/html4/loose.dtd">
<html>
```

```
    <head>
      <meta http-equiv="Content-type" content="text/html; charset=utf-8">
      <title>My Hello Application</title>
      <style type="text/css" media="screen">
        h1 {font-family: Arial, "MS Trebuchet", sans-serif;}
        h2 {color: red; font-style: italic;}
      </style>
    </head>
    <body>
      <h1>Greetings from the Hello Layout!!</h1>
      <%= yield %>
    </body>
  </html>
```

After saving this new layout file and refreshing our web page, we can see result in Figure 6-7—our new layout was used in the rendering rather than the application layout we defined earlier.

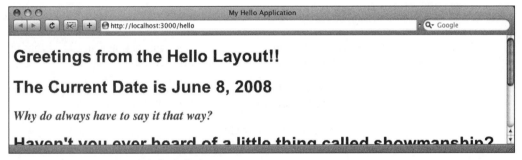

Figure 6-7. Our view wrapped by the hello layout

So we can see that even though we still have an applicationwide layout, our new layout with the same name as the controller took precedence. This is an important thing to remember when you're building your own Rails applications, as some Rails generator commands will also automatically generate a default layout that will need to be deleted if you're trying to create a single application-wide layout.

Our final exploration of layouts will require us to dip into the controller as well, because we'll explicitly specify which layout to use from within the controller. To do that, we'll start by first creating a new layout file named something unique, such as mylayout.html.erb.

Within this new layout file, let's place the following content:

```
<!DOCTYPE HTML PUBLIC "-//W3C//DTD HTML 4.01 Transitional//EN"
  "http://www.w3.org/TR/html4/loose.dtd">
<html>
  <head>
    <meta http-equiv="Content-type" content="text/html; charset=utf-8">
    <title>My Hello Application</title>
  </head>
  <body>
    <h1>Ruh Roh! This layout doesn't match any Controllers</h1>
```

```
    <%= yield %>
  </body>
</html>
```

Currently, our views in the hello controller will utilize the named hello.html.erb layout, because it's named the same as the controller, so in order to use our newest layout, we need to override that. As we said earlier, layouts are determined at the controller level, so to change it, we'll need to open our hello controller, which can be found in /app/controllers as hello_controller.rb. This hello controller currently looks like this:

```
class HelloController < ApplicationController

  def index
  end

  def world
    render :text => "Hello World!"
  end
end
```

To override the layouts that are being discovered by naming convention, we simply need to explicitly define the layout we want to use in the controller using the layout method.

For example, if we wanted to override the default behavior and ensure that no layout would be used for this controller, we could do so by adding layout nil to the controller like so:

```
class HelloController < ApplicationController
  layout nil

  def index
  end

  def world
    render :text => "Hello World!"
  end
end
```

Make that change and refresh our page, and you'll see that our view template is now rendered sans layout. However, what we really wanted was the ability to specify a different layout, which we do by changing our call to the layout method to now pass the name of the layout we want like so:

```
layout 'mylayout'
```

Refresh the page, and you'll see that it is now using our custom layout. Bang-a-rang!

As a side note, we can also limit the use of our layout by passing :only or :except parameters to the layout method. Imagine that in our controller, we only wanted to use that layout for the index method but not for the world method. We could do that by explicitly listing the methods that we want this layout applied to like this:

```
layout 'mylayout', :only => :index
```

Or we could list the methods that we don't want the layout to apply to like this:

```
layout 'mylayout', :except => :world
```

Choosing whether to use :only or :except is typically just a matter of deciding which requires less typing for you. A good programmer is a lazy programmer!

Custom layout content from the view

One final cool thing about layouts that we'll cover in this section is that we can also specify multiple sections in our layout in which to insert content from our view. Some examples of places we might want to specify are buttons in a subnavigation menu with links specific to the current content or perhaps just to specify some custom style sheet or JavaScript files to include in our header for this view. To illustrate what this might look like, let's modify the mylayout layout file we created to yield some other areas like so:

```html
<!DOCTYPE HTML PUBLIC "-//W3C//DTD HTML 4.01 Transitional//EN"
  "http://www.w3.org/TR/html4/loose.dtd">
<html>
  <head>
    <meta http-equiv="Content-type" content="text/html; charset=utf-8">
    <title>My Hello Application</title>
    <%= yield :custom_styles %>
  </head>
  <body>
    <ul id="navigation">
      <%= yield :subnav %>
    </ul>
    <h1>Ruh Roh! This layout doesn't match any Controllers</h1>
    <%= yield %>
  </body>
</html>
```

So, what did we just do? We created two additional yield blocks in our layout file. However, you'll notice that, for these additional blocks, we also specified a unique symbol name for the content that should go there. We'll create special content blocks in our view templates with names that match these new yield blocks to place their content in the layout at these points.

If you were to save the new layout and view the page in a web browser now, you'll see that things are still working just fine; it's good to know that merely adding those blocks didn't break anything. So all we need to do now is specify some content for those additional yield blocks within our view. Open /app/views/hello/index.html.erb, and modify it with these special content blocks like this:

```erb
<h1>The Current Date is <%= Date.tomorrow.to_s(:long) %></h1>
<h2>Why do always have to say it that way?</h2>
<h1>Haven't you ever heard of a little thing called showmanship? </h1>
<h1>Come, your destiny awaits!</h1>
<%- output = false -%>
<hr />
<%- if output -%>
```

151

```
    <h2>I'm only rendered if output is set to true</h2>
<%- else -%>
    <h2>I'm only rendered if output is set to false</h2>
<%- end -%>

<% content_for(:custom_styles) do %>
  <style type="text/css" media="screen">
    #navigation {margin: 0; padding: 0; background-color: #69C;
      list-style-type: none; float: left; width: 100%;}
    #navigation li {margin: 0; padding: 0; float: left;}
    #navigation a {float:left; width: 127px; color: #000;
      text-decoration: none; line-height: 2.5; text-align:
      center; border-right: 1px solid #000;}
  </style>
<% end %>

<% content_for(:subnav) do %>
  <li><a href="/">Home</a></li>
  <li><a href="/">Logout</a></li>
<% end %>
```

Now, we didn't have to put those content_for blocks at the bottom of our view—technically, they could have gone anywhere in the view, but their use should seem pretty self-explanatory. When the layout is being rendered and it hits the command to yield :customer_styles, the rendering engine looks in the view template for the existence of a content_for(:custom_styles) block and, if the block is found, places that content in the layout at this point.

Save the view template, and refresh the page in your web browser. You can see the result of all this in Figure 6-8.

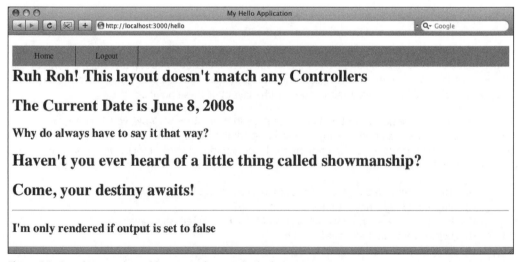

Figure 6-8. Our view template with custom elements in the layout

You can see that our final HTML template is now being rendered with all of our custom content blocks placed into the proper places in the layout. You've not only seen that layouts are a powerful tool in our Rails arsenal that we can use to reduce duplication and simplify our view templates, but you've also seen that they can be incredibly flexible tools that we can use for even more complex layouts.

Helper methods

In addition to layouts, Rails provides an impressive number of helper methods within our views to simplify many of our common tasks in building our view templates. So what are helper methods? Well, I could be obnoxious and simply say that they are methods meant to help us—but in reality, they're special methods intended to extract complicated (or repetitive) logic out of our views. Not only does Rails provide us with a large collection of helper methods for our use but the framework also provides us with an easy ability to create our own helper methods.

You should experiment with each of these helpers by adding them to your template so that you can see them in action yourself, or you could view their output in the console by preceding each method name with the `helper` keyword. So to view the output of the `stylesheet_link_tag` helper method we'll discuss next, you would just type this into a script/console session:

```
helper.stylesheet_link_tag 'scaffold'
```

With those basic instructions, let's a take a quick tour of some of the more useful helper methods that you'll want to use.

Rails-provided helpers

Let's start our tour of helper methods by looking at some of the more useful Rails-provided helper methods for dealing with static assets in our /public directory. As you recall, we have three subdirectories within /public for holding the various static assets that our web application will typically need (style sheets, JavaScript files, and images)

stylesheet_link_tag

We can use this helper method to link to style sheets within our /public/stylesheets directory. Say that we wanted to use a style sheet named `scaffold` in our application. We could easily add it using this helper method like so:

```
stylesheet_link_tag "scaffold"
```

This would output something like this into your HTML:

```
<link href="/stylesheets/scaffold.css?1213337145" media="screen" rel="stylesheet"
type="text/css" />
```

There are a couple of important things that I want to draw your attention to about the output of the `stylesheet_link_tag` helper method. First, you'll notice that using the helper method was a lot less typing for us to build that link, and that's certainly a good reason to use the helper. However, the helper method is also doing something extra sweet for us. It appended a timestamp noting when the style sheet was last modified to the end of the style sheet name (i.e., `scaffold.css?1213337145`).

This is a great trick for ensuring that users are always downloading the latest style sheet. If we add or change styles in this file, the timestamp that's appended to the end will update, so browsers would interpret it as a style sheet they don't have and thus download it, rather than continuing to use their locally cached version.

javascript_include_tag

Much like the stylesheet_link_tag, this helper is used to include JavaScript files from the /public/javascripts directory:

```
javascript_include_tag "jquery"
```

The preceding line would output an HTML tag like this:

```
<script src="/javascripts/jquery.js?1213337144" type="text/javascript">
</script>
```

You can see that this helper method appends a timestamp to the JavaScript file as well, so we're sure that our users are always using the latest version of our JavaScript file. In addition to that, this helper also has a couple of extra helpful presets: you can include all the default (prototype and script.aculo.us) JavaScript libraries by calling this:

```
javascript_include_tag :defaults
```

which will create the following HTML output:

```
<script src="/javascripts/prototype.js?1213337144" ➡
                              type="text/javascript"></script>
<script src="/javascripts/effects.js?1213337144" ➡
                              type="text/javascript"></script>
<script src="/javascripts/dragdrop.js?1213337144" ➡
                              type="text/javascript"></script>
<script src="/javascripts/controls.js?1213337144" ➡
                              type="text/javascript"></script>
<script src="/javascripts/application.js?1213337144" ➡
                              type="text/javascript"></script>
```

And you could simply have the template load every JavaScript file it finds in /public/javascripts with this preset:

```
javascript_include_tag :all
```

image_tag

As the name implies, this helper is for displaying images from our /public/images directory:

```
image_tag 'bg.jpg'
```

Its output would look like this:

```
<img alt="Bg" src="/images/bg.jpg?1213337144" />
```

Formatting helpers

We also have a number of helpers that are useful for helping us format our data.

time_ago_in_words This helper is useful for measuring the amount of time between now and the specified time. It returns a natural-language–formatted result:

```
time_ago_in_words(Time.local(2008, 12,25))   #  6 months
time_ago_in_words(Time.now - 28.hours)        #  1 day
time_ago_in_words(Time.now - 10.minutes)      #  10 minutes
```

Number helpers We also have a group of helpers designed to help us easily reformat numbers:

```
number_to_currency 25          #  $25.00
number_to_human_size 1024      #  1 KB
number_to_percentage 25        #  25.000%
number_to_phone 5555555555     #  555-555-5555
number_with_delimiter  25000   #  25,000
```

Of course, any international readers may notice that many of these helpers are outputting U.S.–style formatting. Fortunately, those are merely the defaults, and all of these helpers support a number of optional parameters that you can pass to them to customize them for your specific uses.

For example, let's say that we wanted to output our currency in pounds instead of dollars; we could do that like this:

```
number_to_currency(25.50, :unit => "&pound;",
                          :separator => ",",
                          :delimiter => "",
                          :format => "%n %u")
```

The preceding lines would output this:

```
25,50 &pound;
```

You can read about all the possible options each helper has in the Rails documentation (I've provided references to the documentation's location and some tips on how to use it in this book's appendix).

Text helpers In addition to helpers that help us format numbers, we also have a group of helpers designed to make working with text easier:

- auto_link: This transforms all URLs or e-mail addresses within the string into clickable HTML links.
- highlight: This helper makes it easy to highlight strings within text by wrapping the searched-for words or phrases in a CSS class named highlight:

  ```
  highlight(' Lorem ipsum dolor sit amet', 'dolor')
    #  Lorem ipsum <strong class="highlight">dolor</strong> sit amet
  ```

- pluralize: This helper is one of my favorites. It uses Rails pluralization rules to add pluralization to a word based on a count that you provide, so that you can do things like this:

```
<%= pluralize(1, 'Person') %>     #  1 Person
<%= pluralize(15, 'Person') %>    #  15 People
<%= pluralize(0, 'Person') %>     #  0 People
```

- truncate: Another incredibly useful helper, this one is designed to truncate our text string to only a specific number of characters (along with a trailing ellipsis for good measure):

```
truncate("Lorem ipsum dolor sit amet, consectetur adipisicing", 25)
   # Lorem ipsum dolor sit ...
```

URL helpers The final group of helper methods we'll look at includes a group of helpers to make working with and creating URLs extra easy.

- link_to: This is one of the most important helpers to remember, as you'll be using it constantly. This helper automates the process of creating links to our various controller actions or even to external sites:

```
link_to "Visit Rails API", "http://api.rubyonrails.org/"
link_to "Home", "/"
link_to "Edit Page", :action => :edit
link_to "Edit Comment", :controller => :comments,  :action => :edit
```

- mail_to: Use this helper to create mail-to link tags:

```
mail_to "eldon@railsprojects.com"
mail_to "support@railsprojects.com", "E-mail Support"
```

The preceding lines would output a set of links like these:

```
<a href="mailto:eldon@railsprojects.com">eldon@railsprojects.com</a>
<a href="mailto:support@railsprojects.com">E-mail Support</a>"
```

- button_to: This helper method creates a form within the template that contains a single button. When that button is clicked, the form will submit to the specified URL:

```
<%= button_to "Edit", :action => :new %>
```

The preceding line would create an HTML element like this within the page:

```
<form method="post" action="/hello/new" class="button-to">
  <div>
    <input type="submit" value="Edit" />
    <input name="authenticity_token" type="hidden"
       value="40c07ffd357318be96533bc27d8ecac39485601d" />
  </div>
</form>
```

Form helpers

Without a doubt, one of the most commonly created elements in web applications is the form. We use forms anytime that we want to allow a user to submit or edit data within our application, so it only makes sense that Rails would provide helper methods to simplify the creation of forms as well.

There are two main variants of helper methods for the creation of forms: one for when we're creating a form that will be used to edit/update an ActiveRecord object and another for when we need to create a form that doesn't map to an ActiveRecord object.

To help you learn how to create forms, we'll use a new simple Rails application that I put together in the source archive for you named posts. This is an incredibly simple application that just handles the basics of managing an ActiveRecord model named Posts. In essence, it's the most simplistic version of a blog engine. Unfortunately, even in the simplest sense, it's not a complete application. Once you open the application in your text editor and take a look at the edit.html.erb and new.html.erb templates in /app/views/posts, you'll find that they are both currently empty. That's right; you're going to create the necessary code to build the forms in these templates. Before we do, let's take a quick tour of what's already built for you in the application.

We'll talk about how routing works in Chapter 8, but if you look in /config/routes.rb, you'll see that our sample application provides a couple of simple routes:

```
ActionController::Routing::Routes.draw do |map|
  map.resources :posts
  map.root :posts
end
```

This just says that we've set up the necessary routing for all of the basic CRUD operations to the posts controller, and that we want the default page of the application to go to the posts controller as well.

We also have a very basic Post model in /app/models/post.rb that simply has a few validations on it:

```
class Post < ActiveRecord::Base
  validates_presence_of :title, :body, :category, :active
end
```

To understand what the underlying posts table in the database looks like, you can view its definition in the migration that created it in /db/migrate/20080608093637_create_posts.rb, which looks like this:

```
class CreatePosts < ActiveRecord::Migration
  def self.up
    create_table :posts do |t|
      t.string :title
      t.text :body
      t.string :category
      t.boolean :active

      t.timestamps
    end
  end

  def self.down
    drop_table :posts
  end
end
```

> *Alternatively, you could also look in /db/schema.rb, which is an automatically generated file that shows the current database structure for all tables.*

We won't be taking a full tour of how controllers work until the next chapter, so you might not fully understand what's going on in our posts controller at /app/controllers/posts_controller.rb until then, but there's no harm in looking at it now. You'll see that it currently looks like this:

```ruby
class PostsController < ApplicationController
  before_filter :find_post, :only => [:show, :edit, :update, :destroy]

  def index
    @posts = Post.find :all
  end

  def show
  end

  def new
    @post = Post.new
  end

  def create
    @post = Post.create(params[:post])
    if @post.save
      redirect_to @post
    else
      render :action => :new
    end
  end

  def edit
  end

  def update
    if @post.update_attributes(params[:post])
      redirect_to @post
    else
      render :action => :edit
    end
  end

  def destroy
    @post.destroy
    redirect_to :index
  end
```

```
    protected
    def find_post
      @post = Post.find(params[:id])
    end
  end
```

Notice how pretty much every method in this controller sets an instance variable? Well, that's important because it's the primary way that the controller makes data available for the view (instance variables created in the controller are accessible in the views; local variables are not).

Now look at the index action in the controller that looks like this:

```
def index
  @posts = Post.find :all
end
```

You can see that in the controller, we're simply creating a new instance variable named @posts and that we're using one of the ActiveRecord queries from our last few chapters to populate this instance variable with a collection of all the posts in our database.

If we also open the matching view for this action (/app/views/posts/index.html.erb), you can see that we're using this @posts instance variable in the view as we iterate over all the posts in the collection and output a link to the specific post each time.

```
<h1>Listing of All Posts</h1>

<% for post in @posts %>
  <%= link_to post.title, post %><br />
<% end %>
<hr />
<%= link_to 'Create New Post', :action => 'new' %>
```

Feel free to explore the other controller actions and their views to get a better feel for how the two work together, but it's time for us to get back to solving the problem of the missing edit and new forms in this application.

Using form_for To create a new form when we have an ActiveRecord object (both of these actions have set the @post instance variable with an ActiveRecord object in the controller), we would use a method named form_for that will create a form element in our HTML output and a block where we will define our individual form elements in this pattern:

```
<% form_for @post do |f| %>
    …….
<% end %>
```

In the top line, we're calling the form_for method and passing it our @post instance variable and a block. As I said, this method will create an empty form tag. We're then passing that newly created form into a block as the variable f. Within this block, we'll call other helper methods to build our individual form elements; some examples of our element helper methods include label, text_field, text_area, select, and check_box.

Let's build our forms for the application by adding the following into both the new and edit templates:

```
<% form_for @post do |f| %>
  <p>
    <%= f.label :title, "Post Headline" %><br>
    <%= f.text_field :title %>
  </p>

  <p>
    <%= f.label :body, "Post Content" %><br>
    <%= f.text_area :body %>
  </p>

  <p>
    <%= f.label :category %><br>
    <%= f.select :category, %w(Personal Technical) %>
  </p>

  <p>
    <%= f.label :active %><br>
    <%= f.radio_button :active, :true %> Yes
    <%= f.radio_button :active, :false %> No
  </p>

  <p>
    <%= f.submit "Submit" %>
  </p>
<% end %>
```

If you have some basic HTML experience with building forms, this should be pretty easy to understand. Within the form_for block, we've added paragraph tags that surround each of our form elements. Within those paragraph tags, we've added helper methods to define a label and a form element, which, when rendered, would be converted into HTML that looks like this:

```
<form action="/posts" class="new_post" id="new_post" method="post">
  <div style="margin:0;padding:0">
    <input name="authenticity_token" type="hidden"
      value="0c18ebb1f8185728f859166b8cc6b7c0e6ac77ac" />
  </div>
  <p>
    <label for="post_title">Post Headline</label><br>
    <input id="post_title" name="post[title]" size="30"
                                              type="text" />
  </p>

  <p>
    <label for="post_body">Post Content</label><br>
    <textarea cols="40" id="post_body" name="post[body]" rows="20">
    </textarea>
  </p>
```

```
<p>
  <label for="post_category">Category</label><br>
  <select id="post_category" name="post[category]">
    <option value="Personal">Personal</option>
    <option value="Technical">Technical</option>
  </select>
</p>

<p>
  <label for="post_active">Active</label><br>
  <input id="post_active_true" name="post[active]"
                               type="radio" value="true" /> Yes
  <input id="post_active_false" name="post[active]"
                               type="radio" value="false" /> No
</p>

<p>
  <input id="post_submit" name="commit" type="submit" ➥
                                        value="Submit" />
</p>
</form>
```

The output looks like the form shown in Figure 6-9.

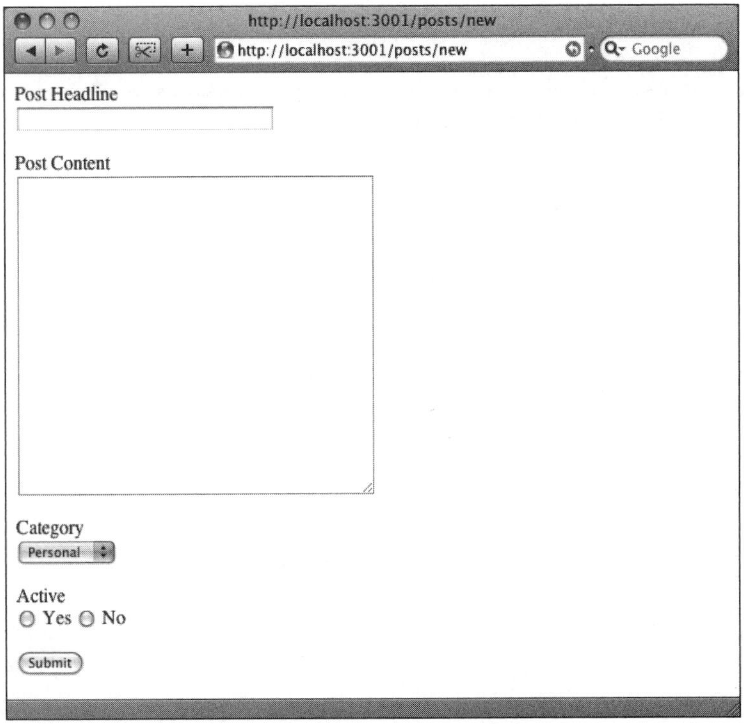

Figure 6-9. Building a form using Rails helpers

And now you can go ahead and play around with creating and editing posts using our new forms. Admit it; you think that's pretty cool, don't you?

Well, it's about to get a little cooler still. Remember all our talk back in Chapter 5 about adding validations to our ActiveRecord models? This post model currently has a couple validations enabled on it as well:

```
class Post < ActiveRecord::Base
  validates_presence_of :title, :body, :category, :active
end
```

Wouldn't it be cool if there were an easy way to display any validation errors back to a user who attempted to create or save an invalid post? Do you really think I would bring it up if there weren't?

All we have to do is add another helper method by the name of error_messages_for to the top of each of our edit and new templates so that they look like this:

```
<%= error_messages_for :post %>
<% form_for @post do |f| %>
   <p>
      <%= f.label :title, "Post Headline" %><br>
   <! --- Except  -->
```

Afterward, if we attempt to save an invalid post, we'll be treated to a detailed explanation of our errors, which you can see in Figure 6-10.

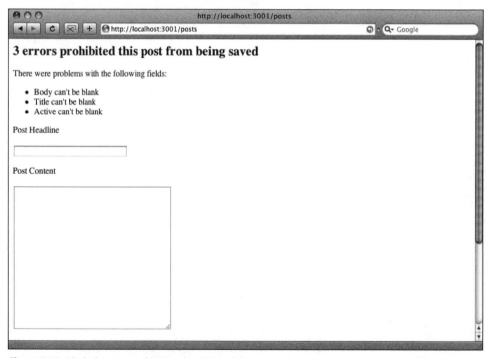

Figure 6-10. Displaying errors about an invalid model

One final thing to point out about the form_for method, which you might have noticed, is that the forms we're using here are also displaying our post data. Even though it's the exact same code in both templates, if we were looking at an existing post in the edit form, we can see that all of the form elements are populated. In addition, when we submit a post that fails validations, our new form is populated with the data that was originally submitted. How does it do that?

It's actually pretty simple. Recall that when we created this form we did so by passing in the @post instance variable:

```
<% form_for @post do |f| %>
```

This essentially meant that our form was going to be built using whatever data existed in @post. In the case of the new action, that was an empty post record (i.e., @post = Post.new), whereas in the edit action, we had populated the @post variable using a find_post method called in a before_filter to load @post with a preexisting record (@post = Post.find(params[:id])).

In our form, this @post data is available as part of the form that we passed in as the local variable f. We then called the helper methods on that f variable (i.e., f.text_field :title), so that those helper methods are essentially always displaying whatever data is set in the ActiveRecord object in @post. Easy peasy and darn cool.

Using form_tag Lots of times, we want to create a form that wasn't meant to work with an ActiveRecord object, so we'd want to provide a form that's meant to neither add data to our database nor be used to display data from the database. A good example might be a login form where we'd be using the data from the form to query the database, but we don't want a login form to create a new user and would never want it to display a user's login name and password. In those cases, we would use a different helper method for building forms named form_tag that looks like this.

```
<% form_tag :controller => "sessions" do %>
……..
<% end %>
```

You'll notice that it's fairly similar to our previous form_for method except that with this variant we're passing it a path instead of an ActiveRecord object.

Once we have a new form started, we simply pass it a smattering of helper method calls to create the individual form elements.

However, since we don't have an ActiveRecord object that those methods could be called on, we need to use stand-alone versions of these form element helper methods that end with _tag. So to add a text field to this form, we call the text_field_tag helper method. Here's what a simple login form using these helpers would look like:

```
<h1 class="section_header">Login Form</h1>
<% form_tag :controller => "sessions" do -%>
  <p>
    <%= label_tag 'login' %><br/>
    <%= text_field_tag 'login' %>
  </p>
```

```
<p>
  <%= label_tag 'password' %><br/>
  <%= password_field_tag 'password' %>
</p>

<p><%= submit_tag 'Log in' %></p>
<% end -%>
```

In this code, you can see that we've created a new form block, but this isn't built around an ActiveRecord object. Instead, it's built simply to post to a specific path. Within the form block, we've created paragraph tags surrounding our form elements again. This time, however, we're using the stand-alone variants that aren't meant to display ActiveRecord data. You can see the output of this form in Figure 6-11.

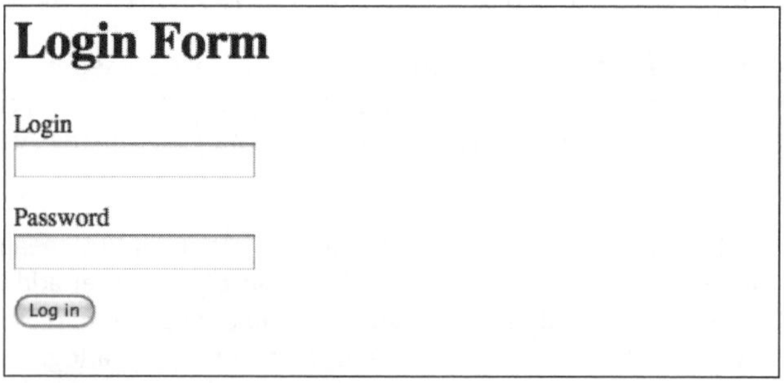

Figure 6-11. A simple stand-alone login form

Building your own helpers

Obviously, Rails has provided us with a pretty impressive collection of helper methods (and there are a lot of additional ones that we didn't look at), but to make the deal even sweeter, it also allows you to create your own. In fact, if you look within the /app directory, you'll notice that it already contains a helpers subdirectory, which contains default helper files for the application and hello controllers. Looking at the posts_helper.rb file within that directory, you'll see that it currently looks like this:

```
module PostsHelper
end
```

That's right; it's a module! Just as we discussed back in Chapter 2, modules can be used to mix in new methods and functionality to an existing class, so that must be what's happening here. When Rails goes to render our template, it mixes in the appropriate helper modules to add their methods to our available repertoire.

We can add a new helper method easily by simply adding the appropriate method to this module.

Let's imagine that we have a User model to keep track of members of our web application. Within this User model, we allow users to also upload simple avatar images of their own. Within our view templates, we want to display each user's uploaded avatar, or we want to display a generic default avatar if the user hasn't added one yet.

Adding that kind of logic in multiple places in a view would obviously cause our templates to get ugly pretty fast, so instead, that logic would make a good choice for a custom helper method. Since it also makes sense that this helper would be needed across many controllers, we would add it to the application_helper.rb to make it available to all controllers.

With all that background, our new helper might look something like this:

```
module ApplicationHelper
  def show_avatar
    if @user.avatar
      @user.avatar.public_filename
    else
      "no_avatar.gif"
    end
  end
end
```

Within our view templates, anytime we wanted to display a user's avatar, we could do so with a simple call to this:

```
<%= image_tag show_avatar %>
```

And our helper would handle the logic of checking for the existence of a user avatar and return the filename of that avatar or of a generic avatar image if the user has none.

Of course, it's worth mentioning that we could simplify our helper method by rewriting it to use a ternary operator instead of the if-else-then clause like so:

```
def show_avatar
  @user.avatar ? @user.avatar.public_filename : "no_avatar.gif"
end
```

Partials

The final component of Action View that we'll look at in this chapter—partials—is also designed to help us remove duplicate code from our templates. Partials are one of those extremely powerful tools for maintaining your templates that, unfortunately, are often underutilized by people who are first learning Rails development.

However, understanding partials is fairly simple. In essence, they are a tool for removing commonly repeated elements from view templates and placing them into separate mini-templates (that can then be included into any view).

To understand what that means, though, you really need to see it in action. Fortunately, we already have an excellent example in front of us with the two forms that we just created in this chapter. Those two forms were identical in every way and allowing duplication like that in our views can become a royal pain when maintaining this application. You see, if we ever decided to add another field to those forms or modify the way they look in some way (such as removing the paragraph tags), we'd have to make the same changes in multiple places to modify those forms.

However, if we move these forms out into a single partial, we could simply edit that one partial file and see the changes replicated in both locations. To create the partial, we can simply create a new template in /app/views/posts and precede its name with an underscore. Create a new file named _form.html.erb, and let's move our form code into this partial template:

```
<%= error_messages_for :post %>
<% form_for @post do |f| %>
  <p>
    <%= f.label :title, "Post Headline" %><br>
    <%= f.text_field :title %>
  </p>

  <p>
    <%= f.label :body, "Post Content" %><br>
    <%= f.text_area :body %>
  </p>

  <p>
    <%= f.label :category %><br>
    <%= f.select :category, %w(Personal Technical) %>
  </p>

  <p>
    <%= f.label :active %><br>
    <%= f.radio_button :active, :true %> Yes
    <%= f.radio_button :active, :false %> No
  </p>

  <p>
    <%= f.submit "Submit" %>
  </p>
<% end %>
```

With a new partial at the ready, we can remove that code from our new and edit templates, replacing them with a simple callout to render our new partial. So we can change our new template to look like this:

```
<h1>Create a new Post</h1>
<%= render :partial => 'form' %>
```

and our edit template to look like this:

```
<h1>Edit this post</h1>
<%= render :partial => 'form %>
```

And that's all there is to creating a basic partial. We've removed duplication from these two templates so that now, if we want to make changes to both, we have to make our changes in only a single place. Pretty easy stuff, huh? But as they say on every late-night infomercial, "But wait! There's more!" So before we close out this chapter, let's take a slightly deeper look at some other interesting things we can do with partials.

Calling a partial from another template

You might have deduced that our previous call to render the form partial worked because we created the partial in the same directory as the templates that were calling it. But what would happen if we wanted to reuse that same partial from another controller's templates (a common example being a comment form)? Well, we can do that with just a minor tweak to our render method:

```
<%= render :partial => 'posts/form' %>
```

Rails will interpret that to mean, "Look in the /posts view templates folder for a partial named form."

Passing variables into a partial

In our previous examples, Rails did a little bit of magic for us in the call to render the partial in that, even though the partial technically lives in its own scope, our instance variables are shared with the partial. So we didn't have to jump through any hoops to get our @post variable into the partial like this:

```
render :partial => 'form' , :object => @post
```

In that example, we're explicitly passing the @post instance variable into the partial as an object that it can access. Doing so is perfectly valid but unnecessary, since instance variables are already shared.

However, the same can't be said for local variables that we might have created in the view. In order to make those available to the partial, we would need to explicitly pass them into the render partial method call.

For example, let's say that we wanted to be able to customize the text on the submit button to reflect if it's being rendered from the new or the edit template. Our first step in doing that would be to modify the partial to render a new variable name instead of a static string; we'll call this new variable button_text:

```
<%= f.submit button_text %>
```

Now, we just need to modify our new and edit templates to pass in some local data to populate that variable. So our new template could be changed to this:

```
<h1>Create a new Post</h1>
<%= render :partial => 'post', ➥
                    :locals => {:button_text => "Create New Post"} %>
```

And our edit template could be changed to this:

```
<h1>Create a new Post</h1>
<%= render :partial => 'post', ➥
                    :locals => {:button_text => "Edit This Post"} %>
```

And with that, our button text in the partial has been set from the view that renders it.

Render a collection

The final use of a partial that we'll look at here is the ability to use a partial to render a collection. If you look at our index.html.erb in /app/views/posts, you'll see that currently we're still just looping over the collection of all @posts:

```
<h1>Listing of All Posts</h1>

<% for post in @posts %>
  <%= link_to post.title, post %><br />
<% end %>
<hr />
<%= link_to 'Create New Post', :action => 'new' %>
```

That's not so bad in this example, since with each iteration over the collection, we're simply creating a single link. But what if we were doing more complex logic within that loop? For example, take this code I pulled out of my own archives; it loops over comments on a photo but with quite a bit more display logic with each comment than our previous example (including displaying things such as the user's name and avatar):

```
<% for comment in @photo.comments %>
  <li>
    <div class="comment-head">
      <div class="comment-author-details">
        <h3>
          <div class="user-img">
            <%= link_to(image_tag(@user.small_avatar),
                                        showuser_path(@user)) %>
          </div>
                  <%= link_to @user.name, showuser_path(@user) %> posted
        </h3>
      </div>
    </div>

    <div class="comment-body">
      <div class="comment-body-paragraph">
        <p><%= comment.comment %></p>
      </div>
    </div>
    <p class="comment-link small"><em> </em></p>
  </li>
<% end %>
```

It's not hard to see that a bunch of code like this in your template could quickly make the whole page look a lot more cluttered, make it harder to follow, and cause us some heartburn anytime we needed to edit it. Let's go back to our simple loop in the index template, so we can see how easy it is to convert that to a collection partial so that we'll be prepared to prevent logic like the above from ever making its way into our templates.

First, let's create a new partial template named _post.html.erb and place the code from within our existing loop into this partial. However, an interesting thing about collection partials is that when we call them, each element of the collection will be passed into the partial with the same name as the partial itself.

```
<%= link_to post.title, post %><br />
```

Then in our index template, we call the partial, passing it our @posts variable as a collection like so:

```
<h1>Listing of All Posts</h1>

<%= render :partial => @posts %>
<hr />
<%= link_to 'Create New Post', :action => 'new' %>
```

Even in the simplest example, we've removed several lines of code from our view template. Imagine how much easier reading and maintaining partials can make a more complex template.

Summary

In this chapter, we took a quick tour of the ActionView library and how we can use it to build our view templates. Along the way, we touched on the various ways that we can embed Ruby code into our templates and the uses for each of the available ERb tags. Afterward, you saw how you could use layouts to build standard header and footer content that can be reused across multiple templates and controllers.

Next, we took some time to explore the various helper methods that Rails provides to further simplify the building of our view templates, and you learned how to build your own helpers.

Finally, we closed out the chapter by looking at how we can further remove redundancy from our view templates through the use of partials.

Chapter 7

EXPLORING ACTION PACK: UNDERSTANDING THE CONTROLLER

Can you believe it? We're finally near the end of our whirlwind tour of MVC land! Our final stop on this trip is a quick tour of ActionController, which is responsible for providing the "C" of MVC.

We've touched on this in the last few chapters, but as a reminder, controllers serve as the traffic cops in our applications. When a user requests a page from our application, the controller is the first stop in the application logic. Controllers interact with our models to gather any data and finally determine what response (which could be a view template or an HTTP status code) will be sent back to the user.

At the end of the day, the controller really only has one job—to respond to requests.

Application.rb and controller inheritance

For the purposes of this chapter, I've provided you with another sample application within the source directory that we'll be using to explore controllers together. The project is aptly named "controllers," and you'll want to have it ready to test out a few things as we go through this chapter.

As I'm sure you've probably noticed by now, our controllers all reside within the /app/controllers directory within our Rails project. What you might not have noticed, though, is that every new Rails project automatically creates one controller in that directory named application.rb. If you go ahead and open that file now, you'll see that it currently looks like this:

```
# Filters added to this controller apply to all controllers in the ➥
application.
# Likewise, all the methods added will be available for all controllers.

class ApplicationController < ActionController::Base
  helper :all # include all helpers, all the time

  # See ActionController::RequestForgeryProtection for details
  # Uncomment the :secret if you're not using the cookie session store
  protect_from_forgery # :secret => 'd8e9f8cd03b09d935a3004d7d1873c4d'
end
```

In the preceding example, I styled the actual code in this controller in bold to help it stand out from all the comments. Let's compare this controller with a new empty controller that we'll create in our application. Go ahead and open a command prompt. Let's create a new empty controller using another one of our generators. We'll name our new controller "dragons."

```
ruby script/generate controller dragons
        exists   app/controllers/
        exists   app/helpers/
        create   app/views/dragons
        exists   test/functional/
        create   app/controllers/dragons_controller.rb
        create   test/functional/dragons_controller_test.rb
        create   app/helpers/dragons_helper.rb
```

If you look at the output of our generator, you'll see that it created three files for us. In addition to the dragons_controller.rb file that we asked it to make in /app/controllers, it also created a test file in /test/functional and a helper file (where we could store the helper methods that we discussed in Chapter 6).

Now that we have a controller of our own, let's compare and contrast it with the application controller we looked at earlier. If you look in /app/controllers, you'll notice that these two controllers are named differently: while the application controller is simply named application.rb, the controller that we created is named dragons_controller.rb. The reason for this is that all user-created controllers need to follow the {name}_controller naming convention.

I read a response from the Rails core team to a question asking why the naming conventions differ: they stated that the variation is simply to help highlight the fact that the application controller is special. However, this difference has been the source of some debate within the Rails community, as some developers would prefer to see the application controller follow the standard naming convention and thus be named application_controller.rb. Personally, I'd prefer to see the name changed to match the convention, but I wouldn't expect to see this changed anytime soon. For now, it's just important to remember that the application controller has a special filename.

Next, let's compare the code that is in our dragons controller and the code that is in the application controller. Open dragons_controller.rb, and you should see the following:

```
class DragonsController < ApplicationController
end
```

The most important thing to notice is that both of these controllers are simply Ruby classes; however, they each inherit from different sources. The application controller class inherited from ActionController::Base, so in the same way that the models that we created in Chapters 4 and 5 gained all of their advanced functionality by inheriting from ActiveRecord::Base, a controller gains its advanced functionality from the ActionController library.

But our dragons controller doesn't inherit from ActionController::Base; it actually inherits from our application controller. This means that it inherits all of the advanced functionality that was in ActionController::Base *plus* any functionality that we add into the application controller. This powerful abstraction makes it easy for us to define functionality or data that can then be shared across all controllers without having to repeat ourselves. A common use for this is to define a custom method in our application controller for verifying that the user is logged in, which then makes that method available for use in all of our controllers. We'll talk more about this when we discuss applying filters to our controllers later in this chapter.

Defining actions

In order for our controller to be of any use, we need to define some methods (which are called "actions" within the context of a controller) that will be used to respond to requests. Creating a new action is as simple as defining a new method within the controller like so:

```
class DragonsController < ApplicationController
  def index
  end
end
```

That's all it takes. Now it's possible to send requests to the /dragons/index URL. We could now add code within this index action to use our models to pull data out of the database, select a view template to display to the user, or even render data directly back to the user (as we did back in Chapter 3).

But what would happen if we were to fire up the script/server and run this application as it sits right now by requesting this action? You can see the result in Figure 7-1.

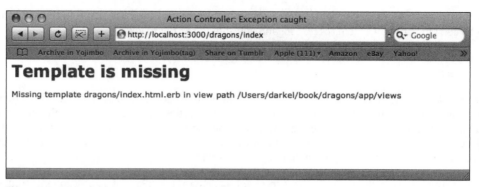

Figure 7-1. Rails provides us with an error for a missing template.

Even though our controller action was empty, it still attempted to render a template. This is because Rails is smart enough to understand that the default end of any action should be to render a template, so if the developer hasn't coded any explicit code to redirect or render something else, then Rails will look within the /app/views/{controller_name}/ directory for a template that has a name that matches the action's name.

Hence for our index action, Rails looked in /app/views/dragons for an index.html.erb template. It was only when it couldn't find this template that it rendered an error back to the user to say that it had nothing to respond with. So you can see that controller actions and view templates are very tightly bound together.

To move past that error, let's add a simple template that can be rendered instead. Go ahead and create our missing file (/app/views/dragons/index.html.erb), and place the following code in it:

```
<!DOCTYPE HTML PUBLIC "-//W3C//DTD HTML 4.01 Transitional//EN"
  "http://www.w3.org/TR/html4/loose.dtd">
<html>
  <head>
    <meta http-equiv="Content-type" content="text/html; charset=utf-8">
    <title>Dragons Be Here</title>
  </head>
  <body>
  <h1>Welcome to all Dragons</h1>
  </body>
</html>
```

With the template added, now if we were to reload our page in a web browser we can say buh-bye to that error message, as you can see in Figure 7-2.

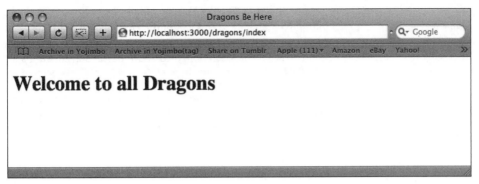

Figure 7-2. Rails found our template

As a side note, let's see what happens if we add a template without a matching controller action. Within /app/views/dragons/, add a new file named boo.html.erb, and place the following code within it:

```
<!DOCTYPE HTML PUBLIC "-//W3C//DTD HTML 4.01 Transitional//EN"
  "http://www.w3.org/TR/html4/loose.dtd">
<html>
  <head>
    <meta http-equiv="Content-type" content="text/html; charset=utf-8">
    <title>Ghost Action</title>
  </head>
  <body>
  <h1>Boo!!!!</h1>
  </body>
</html>
```

Now if you view http://locahost:3000/dragons/boo within a web browser, you'll get the result shown in Figure 7-3.

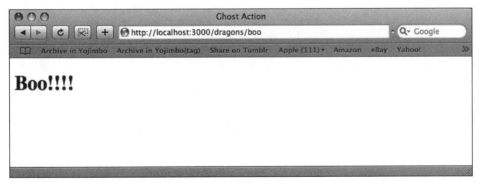

Figure 7-3. Rendering a template without a controller action

175

That's right. Rails was smart enough to know that since rendering something back to the end user is the preferred response, if it couldn't find a matching action within the controller, it then knew to look for a template with the correct name in the views directory. So even though our action was undefined, simply placing the template with the correct name was enough to cause our action to work successfully.

Enough theory, let's see what happens with some real code. To do that we'll create a new controller named "pirates." As a quick tip to save time, we can also pass in the name of the actions that we want, and our generator will not only create them in our controller but also create sample template files for each:

```
ruby script/generate controller Pirates index show

        exists  app/controllers/
        exists  app/helpers/
        create  app/views/pirates
        exists  test/functional/
        create  app/controllers/pirates_controller.rb
        create  test/functional/pirates_controller_test.rb
        create  app/helpers/pirates_helper.rb
        create  app/views/pirates/index.html.erb
        create  app/views/pirates/show.html.erb
```

This generator command created our pirates controller, which currently looks like this:

```
class PiratesController < ApplicationController

  def index
  end

  def show
  end
end
```

It also created a pair of view templates with some basic helpful information to point us to where they exist in case we attempt to render these templates without changing them. For example, index. html.erb in /app/views/pirates currently looks like this:

```
<h1>Pirates#index</h1>
<p>Find me in app/views/pirates/index.html.erb</p>
```

In our sample project, I've already preloaded the SQLite database with a pirates table, some sample pirate data, and a basic Pirate model. Our pirates table simply captures the name of a pirate and the name of the ship that person captains. Our Pirate model has only a simple set of validations defined on those fields as follows:

```
class Pirate < ActiveRecord::Base
  validates_presence_of :name, :ship
end
```

Let's use that data to finish building the index and show actions that we've started. For our initial purposes, we'll use the index action to display the full collection of pirates from our database, while the show action will be used to display a single pirate.

Our first task will be to add some code to the index action to get a list of all pirates. To gather that list of all pirates, we'll use the ActiveRecord find :all method and place its results into an instance variable named @pirates.

```
class PiratesController < ApplicationController
  def index
    @pirates = Pirate.find :all
  end

  def show
  end
end
```

> You should recall from our discussion of instance variables back in Chapter 2 that they are identified by the preceding @ sign and that they have an expanded scope, in that they are visible (and shared) between all methods within the object. Any instance variables that we create in the controller are accessible from within the view.

With our @pirates instance variable set, we can populate the index view template with some ERb code to display our collection of pirates like so:

```
<!DOCTYPE HTML PUBLIC "-//W3C//DTD HTML 4.01 Transitional//EN"
  "http://www.w3.org/TR/html4/loose.dtd">
<html>
  <head>
    <meta http-equiv="Content-type" content="text/html; charset=utf-8">
    <title>Pirates</title>
  </head>
  <body>
    <h1>Listing of all Pirates</h1>
    <ul>
      <% for pirate in @pirates %>
        <li><%= pirate.name %> is Captain of the <%= pirate.ship %></li>
      <% end %>
    </ul>
  </body>
</html>
```

This code, when viewed in a web browser, will give us the result shown in Figure 7-4.

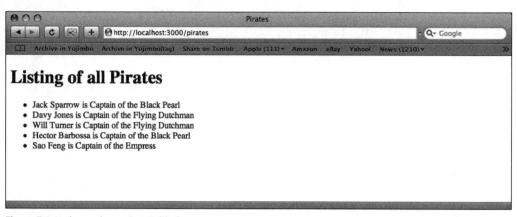

Figure 7-4. Yo ho, yo ho, a pirate's life for me

Pretty simple stuff, huh? Let's take it a step further by populating the show action and associated view template.

The purpose of the show action is to display the information relating to a single pirate, so we simply need to code this action to perform a find for the pirate specified by the URL and place that pirate's information into an instance variable for our view to display.

> *You should recall from our tour of Rails back in Chapter 3 that our default route comes in as* controller/action/id, *so our URLs will look like* http://localhost: 3000/pirates/show/1 *if we wanted to view the pirate with the id of 1. We'll be taking a much more detailed view of routing in the next chapter.*

But you might be wondering how we reference that id variable within our controller. Rails provides a method named params for that purpose. The params method is actually a fairly useful abstraction, because it provides you simple access to any arguments that were sent along with the request (in the URL or in a form POST), such as the ID of the pirate that we want to look up. To access any parameter, we simply access it as if it were an element of a hash, so to obtain the id that was passed along via the URL, we would simply use params[:id].

Let's use that now to build our show action:

```
class PiratesController < ApplicationController

  def index
    @pirates = Pirate.find :all
  end

  def show
    @pirate = Pirate.find(params[:id])
  end
end
```

Here, we've simply done an ActiveRecord find on the Pirates model, using the id that was passed in via the URL as the parameter in that find and saving the result into an instance variable named @pirate.

With an @pirate instance variable is created that contains the specified pirate, we can build our show template (/app/views/pirates/show.html.erb) with the following code to display that pirate's attributes:

```
<!DOCTYPE HTML PUBLIC "-//W3C//DTD HTML 4.01 Transitional//EN"
  "http://www.w3.org/TR/html4/loose.dtd">
<html>
  <head>
    <meta http-equiv="Content-type" content="text/html; charset=utf-8">
    <title><%= @pirate.name %></title>
  </head>
  <body>
    <h1>Pirate:  <%= @pirate.name %></h1>
    <h2>Ship:   <%= @pirate.ship %></h2>
  </body>
</html>
```

After creating this template, viewing it at http://localhost:3000/pirates/show/1 gives us the result shown in Figure 7-5.

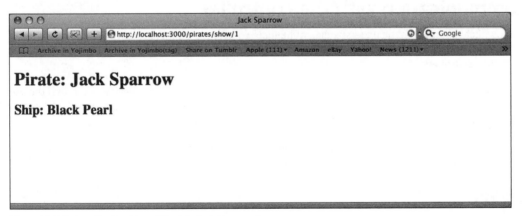

Figure 7-5. That really should say "*Captain* Jack Sparrow."

All that we have left to do to make this a little more functional is to simply modify our index template to provide a link to the show action on each pirate's name using the link_to method that we discussed in the last chapter. Open up /app/views/pirates/index.html.erb, and modify it like this:

```
<h1>Listing of all Pirates</h1>
  <ul>
    <% for pirate in @pirates %>
      <li><%= link_to pirate.name, :action => 'show', :id => pirate %>
              is Captain of the <%= pirate.ship %></li>
    <% end %>
  </ul>
```

This, of course, changes our index template to look like the one shown in Figure 7-6, where the name of each pirate is now a link to the show action with URLs that look like http://localhost:3000/pirates/show/2.

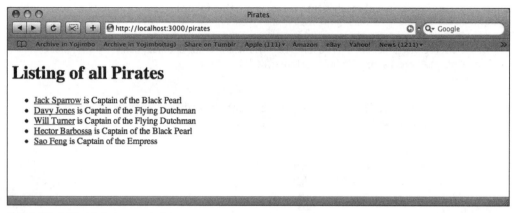

Figure 7-6. Adding links to our pirates

Communication with the controller

Now that you have a basic understanding of building controllers, defining actions, and the relationship of controllers to view templates, let's take a deeper look at the ways that we can get data into and out of our controllers.

You've already seen that the main way we pass data from the controller to the view is through the use of instance variables, and in the last section, I introduced how we use the params method to access any data passed to the action via the URL or within a form POST.

While those are certainly the most commonly used forms of communication with the controllers, they aren't our only options. Let's take a look at the others.

Sessions

Perhaps the method that most developers are used to using for making data available from request to request or from controller to view is the session. So it only makes sense that, of course, Rails would provide support for making interacting with a session easy as well.

> *In case you're not aware, sessions are a server-side solution for storing small bits of user data that can be then used from page to page. Sessions are like a container for variables that are accessible regardless of which page the user is currently on (so that we don't have to keep passing them in the URL). Perhaps one of the most common uses for sessions is for storing items within a shopping cart on an e-commerce site.*

Writing to and reading from the session store is incredibly simple. As proof of that, let's modify our Pirates controller to store a string in the session in one request and then see how that data can then be retrieved from the session in a separate request. We populate data into our session using a session[:key] = value method call, let's use that method to populate a message in the index action of the pirates controller now:

```
class PiratesController < ApplicationController

  def index
    @pirates = Pirate.find :all
    session[:message] = "Hello from the Index Action"
  end

  def show
    @pirate = Pirate.find(params[:id])
  end
end
```

All we did was assign a simple hello message into the session and store it so it can be referenced with the key message—pretty simple stuff, huh? Now, let's modify the show template to see if that value is populated and, if so, to display it. An easy way to do that is to use the || (OR) operator in a way that will display the session data if it's populated or another piece of data in case it's not. Within our show template, let's modify the code to display our session message as the page title or the pirate's name if the session message data is empty:

```
<!DOCTYPE HTML PUBLIC "-//W3C//DTD HTML 4.01 Transitional//EN"
  "http://www.w3.org/TR/html4/loose.dtd">
<html>
  <head>
    <meta http-equiv="Content-type" content="text/html; charset=utf-8">
    <title><%= session[:message] || @pirate.name %></title>
  </head>
  <body>
    <h1>Pirate:  <%= @pirate.name %></h1>
    <h2>Ship:   <%= @pirate.ship %></h2>
  </body>
</html>
```

If in our web browser, we navigated directly to this show action, we would display the current pirate's name as the page title. However if we went to the index action and clicked a pirate's name, we would get the result shown in Figure 7-7.

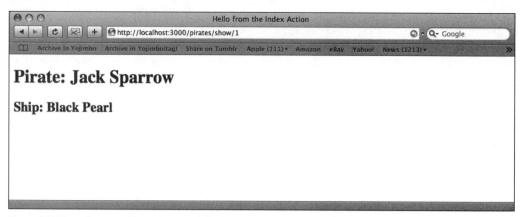

Figure 7-7. Note the page title at the top of the bar.

While this example may seem a little contrived, it shouldn't take much to see the useful implications of using the session. If we were building a shopping cart for an e-commerce application, we could simply store each item that a user added to the cart into a session variable and then use this same || (OR) operator to display the current contents of the shopping cart or a message displaying that the cart was currently empty.

Disabling the session

Obviously the session store was already available to us by default; we didn't have to do any additional configuration or make any method calls to initialize it. This is extremely convenient, because the majority of web applications are going to need to use the session store for some form of data passing, whether it be allowing users to log in or providing some form of shopping cart. But in some applications, we know that we have absolutely no need for sessions. In those cases, we can disable the session store and gain a significant performance boost. You see, when sessions are enabled, every request to your Rails application must assign a session to the user and create a cookie with the session ID in the user's browser for future requests, even if you never use the session. Therefore removing this extraneous processing from each request helps the overall performance and scalability of your Rails application.

At the top of your controller, you can disable the session simply by adding a simple call to session :off, like so:

```
class DragonsController < ApplicationController
  session :off

  def index
  end
end
```

You can disable the session in each of the relevant controllers, or if you want to disable sessions for the entire application, simply add this method call into your application controller.

Session options

Rails also provides us with a variety of options for where our session data is stored. Traditionally, Rails sessions were stored on the server using a file-based storage system, but with Rails 2 came a radical change—the default is now to use cookies as the storage system for session data.

The primary motivation for this change was to enhance Rails's performance, as cookie-based sessions are dramatically faster than any of the alternatives. Many Rails developers were less than thrilled with this change to the default, because cookie-based sessions also impose more restrictions, which we'll discuss in a moment, and thus many developers often change their session storage to one of the other options. Let's take a quick tour of the available options and discuss how to change each one.

Session storage is actually defined in one of our main configuration files for our Rails application—environment.rb in /config. Within this file, about three-quarters of the way down the page, you'll find a commented out section that allows you to redefine the session storage; it looks like this:

```
# Use the database for sessions instead of the cookie-based default,
# which shouldn't be used to store highly confidential information
# (create the session table with 'rake db:sessions:create')
# config.action_controller.session_store = :active_record_store
```

To change our session store, we simply uncomment that last line and set the session store to the proper value.

Cookie-based sessions As we discussed, this is the new default for Rails applications, so any data that we populate into the session will be stored on the user's browser within a cookie. This might sound a bit scary because users might be able to modify their cookie values. However, the cookies are also stored with a secure hash that ensures that the data integrity of the cookie is still valid when it is returned by the browser. If you want to configure the secret key used to generate that secure hash (and you should!), you can simply replace the string that is set as the :secret in this section of the environment.rb with one of your own choosing:

```
config.action_controller.session = {
    :session_key => '_dragons_session',
    :secret      => '656e4744a4acf68e2ce860eb73689f81ff177a87ec43e03➡
b21b83c5cc2ea1f67a992d9426d9dacc5565d12a0829654ebaf861703ee3fbe6535b➡
b362c81e715de'
    }
```

Another consideration to be aware of when using the cookie-based session store is that cookies have a hard limit of only allowing 4KB of data (about 4,000 characters), so you need to ensure that you don't try to place too much data into the session.

ActiveRecord-based sessions One of the most popular session stores is the ActiveRecord session store, which allows you to store your sessions into the database. Why is this popular? Well, for one thing, querying the database is much faster than querying the file system. Plus, the database is a shared resource so using it makes scaling our sessions across multiple web servers much easier. To enable this session store requires you to first create a table named sessions in your application's database with some specific fields. Fortunately, creating the table is made simple through a rake task that will create the necessary database migration for you:

```
rake db:sessions:create
    exists  db/migrate
    create  db/migrate/001_create_sessions.rb
```

Once we create our new migration, all that's left is to apply it using the rake db:migrate task and modify our environment.rb to set the session store to use ActiveRecord.

```
config.action_controller.session_store = :active_record_store
```

Memcache-based sessions These days, high-traffic web applications and memcache seem to be synonymous, so it's common for many web applications to set up memcache and use it to store their session data for even faster performance than a database. Once you have a memcached server installed, enabling support for it in our Rails application is only slightly more difficult than configuring our other session stores.

> *What is memcache? Memcache is a system that was originally built by Danga Interactive for the web application LiveJournal as a means of alleviating database load. It provides a high-performance, distributed caching system in memory where our applications can store any type of commonly referenced data such as HTML fragments, data from the database, and so on. Because the data is stored in memory, it can be accessed at speeds far faster than any database system can compete with.*

Like in all the other session storage option, first, we change our session store configuration option in environment.rb to use memcache:

```
config.action_controller.session_store = :mem_cache_store
```

In addition to that configuration option, we must also require the Ruby memcache library (so that Rails can interface to memcache) and provide a number of memcache-specific configuration options into our environment.rb like this:

```
require 'memcache'
memcache_options = {
  :c_threshold => 10_000,
  :compression => true,
  :debug => false,
  :namespace => :app-#{RAILS_ENV}",
  :readonly => false,
  :urlencode => false
}

CACHE = MemCache.new memcache_options
CACHE.servers = 'localhost:11211'

ActionController::Base.session_options[:expires] = 1800
ActionController::Base.session_options[:cache] = CACHE
```

Obviously, you would need to modify those parameters to match your installation of memcache, but once you did that and restarted your Rails application, your application would be using memcache to store its session data.

Cookies

In addition to sessions, we also have the ability to manually read and set our own cookies from our Rails controllers. While we might use sessions to track data between page requests for a single visit, we could set our own cookies for storing data that has a much longer lifetime, such as user preferences or some form of tracking ID. However, it's important to note that standard cookies are not a very secure system and thus you should not be storing any private or sensitive data within them.

Setting a cookie is similar to setting sessions:

```
cookies[:message] = 'This is my cookie message'
```

Of course, it's also frequently useful to set a cookie expiration time, which you can do by providing your data in a hash with one of the keys being :expires that sets an expiration time, like so:

```
cookies[:message] = { :value => 'This is my cookie message', ➥
    :expires => Time.now + 2.months}
```

Reading a cookie is equally easy. However, it's important to note that cookies are not accessible from the view templates, so you should be accessing them in your controller and passing their data into your view in an instance variable:

```
@message = cookies[:message]
```

Removing a cookie is as simple as using the delete method:

```
cookies.delete :message
```

Flash

Another problem that occurs often in web applications is the issue of passing messages between requests, especially in situations where we need to redirect a request from one action to another. For example, it's common to redirect users to a listing page when they delete items from the database, but we still provide them some feedback that their delete request was successful.

The problem, however, is that whenever we do a redirect, we're essentially creating a completely new request, so data or variables that we had in memory from the original request are lost.

While we could certainly utilize the session or a cookie to pass these messages around, it can be a bit of a pain to manage the constant writing and erasing of short-lived messages.

Rails's solution for being able to pass one-time use messages between separate requests is called the flash, which is sort of like a hash that only lives for one additional request. We can pass a message into the flash with a simple call to the flash method, specifying the key we want to use and the message that we want to pass into the flash:

```
flash[:notice] = "We threw your worthless comment away"
```

In essence, the flash really isn't that complex. In one request, we store a message into the current session. The next request simply reads any messages out of this session variable and flushes the data out of the flash. In this way, the flash is the perfect solution for messages that only need to last for one additional request such as in this create action:

```ruby
def create
  @company = Company.new(params[:company])
  if @company.save
    flash[:notice] = 'Company was successfully created.'
    redirect_to(@company)
  else
    render :action => "new"
  end
end
```

In this example, the create action is being used to add a new company record to the applications database. Once that record has been successfully saved (if @company.save), the request will be redirected to the index action to display a list of all companies (redirect_to(@company). However, we still want to let the user know that the company was created, so we're setting a notice message in the flash (flash[:notice] = 'Company was successfully created.'). In this way, our index view template simply needs to display any flash messages for us to be able to communicate this message to the user.

A deeper look at the controller's response

After we've evaluated the data available from our incoming parameters or sessions and then used our models to populate or query our database, our controllers need to be used to make a choice about how to respond to the user. In this section, we'll take a tour of the various options available to our controller actions

Rendering templates

As we demonstrated earlier, the default response for any controller action is to render a template with the same name as the action. When we have an action in our controller that looks like this:

```ruby
def index
  @pirates = Pirate.find :all
end
```

it is really the equivalent of making an explicit call to render a template like this:

```ruby
def index
  @pirates = Pirate.find :all
  render :template => "pirates/index"
end
```

Notice that we can explicitly render a template by providing the call with a relative file path to the template that we want to render. Obviously, this isn't very useful in normal situations when we're simply setting it to render the default template, but it can be rather helpful for anytime we want to override the default. In addition to rendering a specific template, we can also explicitly render a specific file using the absolute file system path:

```
render :file => '/apps/pirates/app/views/shared/standard.html.erb'
```

Or we can simply choose to render another action's template, which is the most common choice:

```
render :action => "show"
```

In fact, you recently saw a block of code that would render another action's template. Let's take another look at it:

```
def create
  @company = Company.new(params[:company])
  if @company.save
    flash[:notice] = 'Company was successfully created.'
    redirect_to(@company)
  else
    render :action => "new"
  end
end
```

In this create action, we're attempting to save a new company that was submitted via a form post from the new action. If the record is successfully saved, we populate a flash message and redirect the user to the index action. However, if it could not be saved for some reason (which will typically mean it failed some validation rule), we want to redisplay the @company object (with its error messages for why it was not saved) back in the same form, so the user can correct the issues and resubmit. Thus we're simply rendering the template from the new action here.

It's important to note, however, a call to render :action merely renders that action's template; it does not run the code within the action. In order to avoid any ugly error messages, you must first set any instance variables that the other template requires before rendering another action's template.

Directly rendering

In addition to rendering one of our templates back to the user, we can sometimes choose to bypass the view system entirely and render a response directly to the user from our controller. We can choose to send text back to the user directly like so:

```
render :text => "Hello World!"
```

However, the real power comes into play when we convert our object to a data serialization format such as XML or JSON and render that back to the user.

> *JSON stands for JavaScript Object Notation and is an alternative to using XML for transmitting data in web applications (particularly in AJAX requests). It's far less verbose and thus is able to be transmitted faster.*

We even have powerful methods available to all of our objects that convert them to XML and JSON easily, so that we can render them like so:

```
render :json => @pirate.to_json
render :xml => @ pirate.to_xml
```

Finally, we have the option to choose to send nothing back to the user request like so:

```
render :nothing => true
```

Now you might be scratching your head as to why we might want to send no response back to a user's request, but the answer is simple when you consider that can also send along an HTTP status message for the browser, for example:

```
render :nothing => true, :status => 404
```

In this example, we're not sending any content back to the user, merely an HTTP status message of 404 (which means that the server could not find what was requested).

Redirect

Sometimes, however, we don't want to simply render another template, we want to end the current request and start an entirely new one. A good example of this is when we create a new object. Oftentimes, after we attempt to save the object, we want to test if the save was successful. If it wasn't (most likely due to validations), the action should render the new form again (displaying our previous entries and any error messages). If the save was successful, we would want to redirect to the show action like so:

```
def create
  @order = Order.new(params[:order])
  if @order.save
    flash[:notice] = 'Order was successfully created.'
    redirect_to :action => 'show', :id => @order
  else
    render :action => "new"
  end
end
```

Sending data

Another response capability from our Rails controllers that is used infrequently is the ability to send or stream binary data from the controller to the end user. The two methods that we can use to send binary data back to the end user are send_data and send_file.

send_data

The send_data method allows you send data to the user as a named file. It accepts a number of options such as these:

- :filename: The suggested name for the web browser to use
- :type: The HTTP content type, defaults to application/octet-stream
- :disposition: Whether the data should be shown inline (inline) or downloaded (attachment)
- :status: The HTTP status code, defaults to 200 (OK)

An example of use follows:

```
send_data(@photo.data,
                :filename => @photo.name,
                :type => 'image/jpg',
                :disposition => "inline")
```

send_file

Our other method for sending binary data back to the client is the send_file method, which has options for streaming the data to the client at 4096 bytes at a time (by default).

Unfortunately, the method does read the entire file into memory before attempting to send, so it can cause some performance issues. Valid options for the send_file method include the following:

- :filename: The suggested name for the web browser to use
- :type: The HTTP content type, defaults to application/octet-stream
- :disposition: Whether the data should be shown inline (inline) or downloaded (attachment)
- :buffer_size: Amount of data that will be streamed at a time (defaults to 4096 bytes)
- :stream: Used to determine if the server should send the file as it reads it (true) or to read the whole file into memory and then send (false)
- :status: The HTTP status code, defaults to 200 (OK)

An example of use follows:

```
send_file "files/20080928_12574.mov", :filename => 'trailer.mov',
                :disposition => "attachment"
```

Proper controller design

In the early days of building web applications with Rails, the poor controller suffered much abuse from many Rails developers. Our controllers would become these huge abominations of code that became overly complex and difficult to maintain. Lucky for you, you won't have to go through that pain because there have been two different lessons (or movements, some might say) within the Rails community that brought us all back to the right way.

Skinny controllers

The first movement began with a blog post by Rails core team member Jamis Buck called "Skinny Controller, Fat Model" (http://weblog.jamisbuck.org/2006/10/18/skinny-controller-fat-model). In his post, he explained the temptation to place too much of our application logic into our views and controllers, leaving our models anemic and powerless. As an example, here's a controller action from one of my first Rails applications that I'm particularly ashamed of:

```
def search_orders
  user = User.find(session[:user_id])
  username = user.name.capitalize
  @order = Search.find_by_FirmFile(params[:FirmFile])
  if(@order)
    current_status = @order.status.state
    order_id = Ntes.new(current_status, @order.FirmFile, username)
    @assigned_to = order_id.assigned_to
    message = order_id.get_task
    flash[:notice] = "<strong>Next Task: </strong>" + message
    @attachments = @order.attachment
    @borrower = Party.get_ssn(@order.FirmFile)
    render(:template => "interface/summary")
  else
    render(:nothing => true)
  end
end
```

Seriously, taking a look at that now, I'm not 100-percent sure what it's doing even though I wrote it. It obviously violates all of our goals of writing code that's readable and maintainable.

Here's another example from the same time period:

```
def index
  @appts = Appointment.find(:all,
           :conditions => "status =1 and date = '#{@concatdate}'")
  @prev = Appointment.find(:all,
           :conditions =>[ "status =1 and appointment between ? ➥
and ?",12.days.ago, Time.new])

  @upcoming = Appointment.find(:all,
           :conditions =>[ "status = 1 and appointment > ? ",➥
  Time.new])
end
```

I've got all this noise in my controller action; meanwhile, my model is sitting nearly empty:

```
class Appointment < ActiveRecord::Base
  belongs_to :customer
  belongs_to :fitter
end
```

If I were to have followed the "skinny controller, fat model" guidelines back when I wrote this code, at the very least, I would have moved those finders into my Appointment model like so:

```
class Appointment < ActiveRecord::Base
  belongs_to :customer
  belongs_to :fitter

  def self.find_current(date)
    find :all, :conditions => ["status = 1 and appointment = ?", date]
  end

  def self.previous
    find :all, :conditions =>[ "status = 1 and appointment between ?➥
and ?", 12.days.ago, Time.new]
  end

  def self.upcoming
    find :all, :conditions =>[ "status = 1 and appointment > ? ",➥
Time.new]
  end
end
```

> *Actually, I want to make quite a few other changes to this code right now, just because I know better, and Rails has advanced quite a bit since then, but we'll just focus on the important changes for this lesson.*

With those changes, we can now clean up that controller action to look like this:

```
def index
  @appts = Appointment.find_current(@concatdate)
  @prev = Appointment.previous
  @upcoming = Appointment.upcoming
end
```

It's a small change, but now our code is less noisy and we have standard methods that we can call from any other controller action the next time we need to gather a list of the upcoming or previous appointments. We've moved logic to the correct location, improved readability of our code, and reduced duplication.

CRUD

The second major shift in controller design came from the creator of Rails, David Heinemeier Hansson, during his keynote address during RailsConf 2006. In his presentation, entitled "A World of Resources," Hansson demonstrated how developers who embrace a CRUD-based design methodology in their applications can be rewarded with cleaner and more consistent applications.

> You should recall from our earlier chapters in ActiveRecord that "CRUD" is a traditional database term that stands for the four main operations of create, read, update, and delete.

In the same way that our has_and_belongs_to_many association can often really be hiding a full-fledged model from us that should instead be using the has_many :through association, oftentimes, it's tempting to code additional actions into our controllers that complicate our actions and hide relationships that we should be modeling. Hansson presented the argument that a good design aspiration for our controllers is to provide simply the actions necessary for basic CRUD operations. For a controller, that would mean the following seven actions:

1. index: Responsible for presenting a collection back to the user
2. show: Responsible for showing a single specific object to the user
3. new: Responsible for providing the user with an empty form to create a new object
4. create: Receives the form submission from the new action and creates the new object
5. edit: Responsible for providing the user with a form populated with the details of a specific object for use in editing the object's attributes
6. update: Receives the form submission from the edit action and updates the specific object
7. destroy: Deletes the specified object from the database

Compare that design goal with another bad example from my own coffers:

```
class OrdersController < ApplicationController
  def index…

  def summary…

  def shipments…

  def add_manual_note…

  def view_notes…

  def mark_complete…

  def mark_incomplete…

end
```

In this example, I collapsed the code blocks so you could easily see the action names without being distracted by more embarrassing code. However, just looking at the method names, you should be able to instantly see some bad design going on here. Why would my orders controller need methods for adding and viewing notes? Doesn't it make a lot more sense for me to add a notes controller that would focus on those seven CRUD actions? These two methods could easily be handled better there than in the orders controller, and the actions in the notes controller could easily be scoped to associate each note with a specific order.

How about those last two methods, mark_complete and mark_incomplete? Those don't really fit into our CRUD design aesthetic either, do they? They really could be considered states of an order, so we could create a states or a statuses controller that could be used to manage those states for an associated order. The goal, of course, is to get beyond just modeling things and model items such as relationships (membership, subscription), events (changed, closed), and states (reviewed, accepted) in an effort to fully model the problem domain while keeping our controllers straightforward.

> After embarrassing myself with all my examples of bad code that I've written, I would like to note that all of those examples were from applications that I wrote during my first three months with Rails back in September and October of 2005. Just like the peasant who claimed that a witch had turned him into a newt in Monty Python and the Holy Grail, "I got better."

Building our CRUD controller

It's one thing to simply talk about building the seven CRUD actions for a controller, but doing it is quite another. In our pirates controller, we've already built the index and the show actions, so let's go ahead and finish it by adding the remaining actions of new, create, edit, update, and destroy:

As a reminder (after removing our session testing), our current pirates controller looks like this:

```
class PiratesController < ApplicationController

  def index
    @pirates = Pirate.find :all
  end

  def show
    @pirate = Pirate.find(params[:id])
  end
end
```

Let's use this as our baseline as we build the remainder of our CRUD actions. However, since we'll be creating all the associated views as well with each of these actions, let's save ourselves a little typing by implementing a layout for our common HTML header and footer code.

To do that, create a new file in /app/views/layouts named application.html.erb (if it doesn't already exist), and place the following code in it:

```
<!DOCTYPE HTML PUBLIC "-//W3C//DTD HTML 4.01 Transitional//EN"
  "http://www.w3.org/TR/html4/loose.dtd">
<html>
  <head>
    <meta http-equiv="Content-type" content="text/html; charset=utf-8">
    <title>Pirates</title>
  </head>
```

```
        <body>
          <%= yield %>
        </body>
      </html>
```

Now that we've created an applicationwide layout that will wrap each of our view templates, we'll also need to modify the index and show templates that we've built previously to remove this shared code (these templates reside in /app/views/pirates)

We'll simplify our index template (index.html.erb) to look like this:

```
      <h1>Listing of all Pirates</h1>
      <ul>
        <% for pirate in @pirates %>
          <li><%= link_to pirate.name, :action => 'show', :id => pirate  %>
                 is Captain of the <%= pirate.ship %></li>
        <% end %>
      </ul>
```

Here, the template simply loops over the pirates in our @pirates instance variables and displays each of them along with the name of the ship that he or she captains.

We'll simplify the show template (show.html.erb) to look like this:

```
      <h1>Pirate:  <%= @pirate.name %></h1>
      <h2>Ship:   <%= @pirate.ship %></h2>

      <p><%= link_to "back", :action => 'index' %></p>
```

Now, the template will display the name of a single pirate and ship.

The new action

The new action is fairly straightforward because it only needs to provide the end user with a form to create a new pirate, so our controller action simply needs to create a new empty pirate object in memory (note that the object is not saved to the database at this point):

```
      def new
        @pirate = Pirate.new
      end
```

Meanwhile, our associated view template (/app/views/pirates/new.html.erb) will simply display the new form using the same form helpers that we discussed in the Action View chapter.

```
      <h1>Create a New Pirate</h1>

      <%= error_messages_for :pirate %>

      <% form_for :pirate, :url => {:action => :create} do |f| -%>
        <p>
          <%= f.label :name, "Name" %><br />
```

```
        <%= f.text_field :name %>
      </p>
      <p>
        <%= f.label :ship, "Ship" %><br />
        <%= f.text_field :ship %>
      </p>
      <p><%= f.submit "Submit" %> </p>
    <% end -%>

    <p><%= link_to "back", :action => 'index' %></p>
```

Here, we are defining the necessary form to create a new pirate in our application's database (form_for :pirate, :url => {:action => :create} do |f|), using the form_for method that we talked about in Chapter 6. Next, we create each of the form fields using the standard form helper methods, such as f.text_field :name to create the form field for the pirate's name. When the form is saved and viewed at http://localhost:3000/pirates/new, it gives us the page shown in Figure 7-8.

Figure 7-8. Our create pirate form

The create action

The purpose of the create action is to be the target of the form submission from our new action. This action will attempt to save the submitted pirate and if successful will redirect the user to the show action and display the newly created pirate. If the pirate cannot be saved for any reason, we'll simply render the new template again. However, this time, the @pirate instance variable would be populated with the previous form submission and would display the previous entries and any error messages that were now added to the object. That probably sounds a lot more complex than it really is. Our create action should look like this:

```
def create
  @pirate = Pirate.new(params[:pirate])
  if @pirate.save
    redirect_to :action => 'show', :id => @pirate
  else
    render :action => 'new'
  end
end
```

Of course, we've already reviewed this block of code several times in his chapter, but just as a reminder since this action will always either redirect to or render another action, there's no purpose in building an associated template for the create action.

The edit action

The edit action and template will be nearly identical to our new action and template, except that rather than displaying an empty pirate object, we'll load the URL-specified pirate:

```
def edit
  @pirate = Pirate.find(params[:id])
end
```

And our edit template will be nearly identical to our new template outside of the header text and the destination of the form:

```
<h1>Edit <%= @pirate.name %></h1>

<%= error_messages_for :pirate %>

<% form_for :pirate, :url => {:action => :update} do |f| -%>
  <p>
    <%= f.label :name, "Name" %><br />
    <%= f.text_field :name %>
  </p>
  <p>
    <%= f.label :ship, "Ship" %><br />
    <%= f.text_field :ship %>
  </p>
  <p><%= f.submit "Update" %> </p>
<% end -%>

<p><%= link_to "back", :action => 'index' %></p>
```

The template will create a display like the one shown in Figure 7-9.

Figure 7-9. In the market for a new boat

The Update Action

The update action will also be incredibly similar to the create action and will look like this:

```
def update
  @pirate = Pirate.find(params[:id])
  if @pirate.update_attributes(params[:pirate])
    redirect_to :action => 'show', :id => @pirate
  else
    render :action => 'edit'
  end
end
```

Much like the create action is the destination of the form from the new action, the update action is the destination of the form from the edit action. Here, we first load the pirate's record based on the id (@pirate = Pirate.find(params[:id])). Then, we want to update all of that pirate's attributes based on what was submitted via the form, so we'll use the ActiveRecord method update_attributes to set the data in the @pirate equal to the values that were submitted in the form (@pirate. update_attributes(params[:pirate])). If our update was successful, we'll redirect the request back to the show action. If our update failed for some reason, we want to redisplay the edit action's form again.

The delete action

Our final action will be to provide the link to remove a pirate record from our database. The action will be fairly simple, as it merely looks up the specified record, deletes it, and then redirects the user to the index action:

```
def destroy
  @pirate = Pirate.find(params[:id])
  @pirate.destroy
  redirect_to :action => 'index'
end
```

197

Updating the index template

The final step we should do is to modify our index template to provide links to the new, edit, and destroy actions. This is fairly easy and only requires a few additional snippets of code within /app/views/pirates/index.html.erb:

```erb
<h1>Listing of all Pirates</h1>
<ul>
  <% for pirate in @pirates %>
    <li><%= link_to pirate.name, :action => 'show', :id => pirate  %>
        is Captain of the <%= pirate.ship %>
      <%= link_to "edit", :action => 'edit', :id => pirate %> |
      <%= link_to "remove", :action => 'destroy', :id => pirate %>
    </li>
  <% end %>
</ul>

<%= button_to "Create New Pirate", :action => 'new' %>
```

The preceding code provides us with the template shown in Figure 7-10.

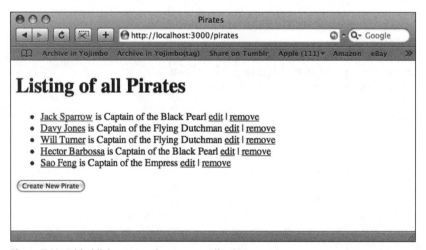

Figure 7-10. Added links to round out our application

Putting it all together, our final pirates controller with full CRUD support looks like this:

```ruby
class PiratesController < ApplicationController

  def index
    @pirates = Pirate.find :all
  end

  def show
    @pirate = Pirate.find(params[:id])
  end
```

```ruby
  def new
    @pirate = Pirate.new
  end

  def create
    @pirate = Pirate.new(params[:pirate])
    if @pirate.save
      redirect_to :action => 'show', :id => @pirate
    else
      render :action => 'new'
    end
  end

  def edit
    @pirate = Pirate.find(params[:id])
  end

  def update
    @pirate = Pirate.find(params[:id])
    if @pirate.update_attributes(params[:pirate])
      redirect_to :action => 'show', :id => @pirate
    else
      render :action => 'edit'
    end
  end

  def destroy
    @pirate = Pirate.find(params[:id])
    @pirate.destroy
    redirect_to :action => 'index'
  end

end
```

As you can see, keeping our controllers skinny and focused on the CRUD actions also keeps them very easy to understand. Whereas other Rails developers have had to learn these lessons painfully, you have a great advantage in the fact that you're going to start out with this understanding. As such, all of your Rails applications should be easier to maintain over time.

Filters

We'll close out our discussion of controllers in Rails with one last powerful feature that you'll want to take advantage of in your own controllers—filters.

Filters are a way to run code before, after, or around our controller actions. In that regard, they are similar to the callbacks that we were able to define in our ActiveRecord models. However, while ActiveRecord callbacks are typically used for data manipulation and processing, filters are typically used for things such as protecting access to certain actions or auditing.

The three main filters that you'll be using are before_filter, after_filter, and around_filter, and they are defined macro-style at the top our controller just like our ActiveRecord associations. They do exactly as their names suggest. The before_filter allows us to execute code before our action executes. The after_filter defines code that we can execute after our action is executed yet before the template is rendered. Lastly, the around_filter defines code that will execute both before and after our action (often used for things such as benchmarking).

The most common use of a filter, though, is for authentication, which might look like this:

```
class FittersController < ApplicationController
before_filter :check_authentication, :except => "signin_form"

  def index…

  def show…

  def signin_form…

protected
  def check_authentication
    unless session[:user]
      session[:intended_action] = action_name
      redirect_to :action => "signin_form"
    end
  end
end
```

In this controller, we defined a before_filter that will call the check_authentication method before it runs any other controller action. We define this method to be either protected or private, so that it will not be directly accessible from the web (i.e., someone couldn't load /fitters/ check_authentication in a web browser). In this regard, any requests to the index or show actions will first execute the check_authentication method to determine if the user is already logged in; if the user is logged in, the controller action will run correctly. If for some reason, the user is not logged in, the request will be redirected to the signin_form. In addition, we excluded the signin_form from the before filter, so people will always be able to reach the sign-in page.

Another common use for filters is to reduce duplication of code in our controllers by providing a single method that will be used to look up our data and populate our instance variable. Let's open the pirates controller one last time (/app/controllers/pirates_controller.rb) and see how we can use a before_filter to eliminate some duplication.

You might have noticed that many of our actions all duplicate exactly the same finder method:

```
@pirate = Pirate.find(params[:id])
```

This one method is duplicated in our show, edit, update, and destroy actions. In cases like this, I sometimes like to build a single before_filter to do that lookup only once per controller. Our first step in doing this will be to add our before_filter to the top of our controller. However, because we want this filter to be used for only specific actions, we'll want to either apply an only or an except condition on our filter to limit its scope. I chose to use an except condition simply because there are fewer actions to have to type.

```
class PiratesController < ApplicationController
  before_filter :lookup_pirate, :except => [:index, :new, :create]
```

Now with our filter defined, we'll create the lookup_pirate method at the bottom of our controller as a protected action.

```
protected
  def lookup_pirate
    @pirate = Pirate.find(params[:id])
  end
```

Finally we'll remove those @pirate = Pirate.find(params[:id]) calls out of the show, edit, update, and destroy action, which leaves our final controller looking like this:

```
class PiratesController < ApplicationController

  before_filter :lookup_pirate, :except => [:index, :new, :create]

  def index
    @pirates = Pirate.find :all
  end

  def show
  end

  def new
    @pirate = Pirate.new
  end

  def create
    @pirate = Pirate.new(params[:pirate])
    if @pirate.save
      redirect_to :action => 'show', :id => @pirate
    else
      render :action => 'new'
    end
  end

  def edit
  end

  def update
    if @pirate.update_attributes(params[:pirate])
      redirect_to :action => 'show', :id => @pirate
    else
      render :action => 'new'
```

```
      end
    end

    def destroy
      @pirate.destroy
      redirect_to :action => 'index'
    end

  protected

    def lookup_pirate
      @pirate = Pirate.find(params[:id])
    end

  end
```

Now we've removed the duplicated code out of our show, edit, update, and delete actions and placed that code into a single method that will be called by the before_filter. Always feels good to simplify our code, doesn't it?

Summary

In this whirlwind of a chapter, we took a look at the controller and its responsibility for responding to requests. We talked about how to build our own actions, and we talked about the options and differences between rendering a response and redirecting to another request. More importantly, we spent time talking about the proper design of controllers as we built a controller using the principles of both CRUD-based design and the lessons learned from the "Skinny Controller, Fat Model" blog post.

In the next chapter, we're going to dig deep into the Rails routing system, which is primarily responsible for mapping our URLs to our controllers and actions. In that chapter, we'll explore how we can break out of the default :controller/:action/:id URL patterns that we have been using and bend our URLs into any fashion that will fit with our application goals. It's going to be a fun ride.

Chapter 8

CONTROLLING OUR ROUTING

At this point in the book, we've completed a nice high-level tour of each leg of the MVC architecture and how Rails supports it using the ActiveRecord and the ActionPack libraries. Along the way, we even touched a little on how those three elements work together as we've built some simple forms and looked at how controllers serve as the bridge between model data and views. But we've merely breezed by one area in those discussions: understanding how Rails determines the way to map web requests to those components. In other words, how does Rails know to map a URL like `http://localhost:3001/posts/edit/23` to the edit action in the posts controller (setting the `id` parameter to 23 for the ActiveRecord find)?

Well that's exactly the question that we'll work at answering in this chapter as we take a tour through the Rails routing system. Along the way, you'll gain not only an understanding of how Rails interprets URLs but also how we can configure it to provide our web applications with the URLs that we want. In some ways, the Rails routing system is similar to the traditional Apache `mod_rewrite` module, except that we use Ruby to define our URLs and control how each URL maps to specific controllers and actions.

Introducing routing

Even though it's taken us a bit of time to get here, that doesn't in any way indicate that the routing system is less important. In fact, if you think about it, the system that determines how requests are directed to controllers and actions is vitally important, and gaining a solid understanding of what is possible within the Rails routing system will pay you immense dividends as you launch into building your own applications.

Fortunately, we won't have to go very far, as all routes in Rails applications are defined in a single location—the routes.rb file that's located in /config.

If you were to open this file from any of our previous demonstration applications, you would see that (outside of the numerous comments) the actual code in this file is incredibly short:

```
ActionController::Routing::Routes.draw do |map|
  map.connect ':controller/:action/:id'
  map.connect ':controller/:action/:id.:format'
end
```

So what's going on in this code? Well, you should immediately notice that once again we have a block defined; this time, it's calling the draw method in the Rails Routing module and passing that method into the block as a local variable named map. Within the block, we're calling the connect method on that map object twice and passing it some route definitions. Those two map.connect calls make up what we typically refer to as the default routes (the routes that are defined automatically in every new Rails application). Back in Chapter 3, we actually had a short discussion about these default routes and how they follow the URL pattern. That first parameter represents the controller; the second parameter in the URL is used to determine which action is called in that controller; and the final parameter is used to populate the id field, as you can see in Figure 8-1.

Figure 8-1. How a URL maps to the default route

You've probably noticed in the past few chapters that when using these default routes, not all the parameters in the URL string are required. For example, if we don't provide a third parameter (id) in the URL string, we still match the route based on the other parameters, and id is just set to nil. However, you might not have noticed that if we leave off the second parameter (action) like in http://localhost:3000/hello, we will still match this default route, and the request will simply be routed to the index action by default. Anytime we reference a controller in Rails without specifying an action, Rails will default to the index action.

The default routes have certainly served us well in our previous examples, and it's absolutely possible to build fully functional Rails applications using nothing more than these defaults. Those applications would certainly be good and have some nice pretty URLs (much nicer than many other languages have by default), but what would we do if we wanted to provide a URL scheme that hid one of our controller names behind a friendlier public name?

For example, what if we were using a posts controller to interface to blog posts, but we wanted our URLs to say "blog" instead of "posts" (e.g., www.mydomain.com/blog instead of www.mydomain.com/posts)?

Or what if, instead of having to pass the id of a record we wanted in the URL, we wanted to select a record based on the date such, as www.mydomain.com/post/2008/12/06?

Or wouldn't it be nice to allow users to specify a book's title in the URL, like www.mydomain.com/book/foundation_rails_2, instead of having to know the book's primary key?

Well, we can do all of that and much, much more merely by creating custom routes using Rails's routing system. In this chapter, we're going to explore what routing is and how it works, and we're going to build some custom routes to support special cases like the ones I just listed.

But to do that, we're going to need another sample application that we can use as our sandbox to play in. Within this book's source archive, you'll find a sample project I put together named demoblog that provides a few basic pages for the creation and management of simple blog posts. The project is shown in Figure 8-2.

Figure 8-2. A quick view of our blog post manager

This is a very simple blog management application that's fairly similar to the one that we were using in Chapter 6, with one exception; in this application, I've added some styles and visual tweaks so it wouldn't look quite as plain. In fact, one thing that you can see in the screenshot in Figure 8-2 is that I'm using images instead of text for the links to the show, edit, and delete actions.

I added the images for the links by simply combining two of the helpers that we discussed back in Chapter 6—the link_to method and the image_tag method—like so:

```
<%= link_to image_tag('show.jpg'), :controller => 'posts',
                                    :action => 'show', :id => post %>
```

As for the data that we use for a blog post, we simply capture three fields: the headline, the body text, and a specially formatted version of the headline called "permalink," as you can see in Figure 8-3.

> What is a permalink? It's a condensed version of the words "permanent link" and is typically used to describe the URL that will point to a specific entry on the site. Over time, the standard has also developed that a permalink should be a human readable phrase or description rather than simply an ID value.

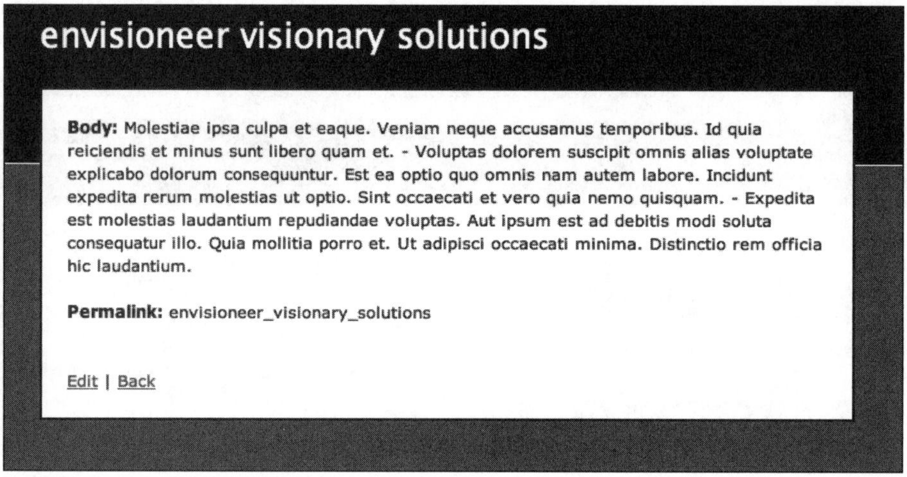

envisioneer visionary solutions

Body: Molestiae ipsa culpa et eaque. Veniam neque accusamus temporibus. Id quia reiciendis et minus sunt libero quam et. - Voluptas dolorem suscipit omnis alias voluptate explicabo dolorum consequuntur. Est ea optio quo omnis nam autem labore. Incidunt expedita rerum molestias ut optio. Sint occaecati et vero quia nemo quisquam. - Expedita est molestias laudantium repudiandae voluptas. Aut ipsum est ad debitis modi soluta consequatur illo. Quia mollitia porro et. Ut adipisci occaecati minima. Distinctio rem officia hic laudantium.

Permalink: envisioneer_visionary_solutions

Edit | Back

Figure 8-3. A view of an individual post

Getting back to the application's routing, currently, this application is simply configured to use the default routes that we discussed at the beginning of this chapter. This means that the application supports URLs like these:

- /posts: Provides an index page of all posts
- /posts/show/4: Provides a view of a single post (in this case, the post with ID of 4)
- /posts/edit/4: Provides a form for editing a single post (in this case, the post with ID of 4)
- /posts/new: Provides a form for creating a new post

While these URLs are certainly functional, it's fairly common that many popular blogs today employ the use of URLs that could be considered a bit more user friendly, such as URLs that reference a specific web post via a permalink instead of an ID (www.mydomain.com/blog/merry_christmas_2008 instead of using something like www.mydomain.com/blog/12). Doing so may seem like just a bit of vanity to some people; however, it is often seen as a nicer way to link to a specific article. After all, if a friend were to e-mail you a link with a URL like www.mydomain.com/blog/merry_christmas_2008, you would probably feel more comfortable clicking through the link to the web site simply because you'd have a better idea of what to expect the content of that web page is going to be. However, you have no idea what to expect if you simply received a link like www.mydomain.com/blog/12.

This same technique is often employed on professional business sites as well so that the name of the product is in the URL rather than just some arbitrary ID field.

What routing does

At its simplest, the routing system in Rails is nothing more than a glorified pattern-matching system that responds to different types of requests.

On one hand, it is used to examine URL strings from any incoming requests and match them to a route to select the controller and action that should respond to this request. So when our application receives a request like http://localhost:3000/posts/update/3, routing determines that this request should go to the posts_controller and execute the update action while passing it the id of 3 in the parameters.

On the other hand, whenever we use link-generating helper methods in our views (e.g., link_to or url_for) like the ones we discussed in Chapter 6, the routing system is also used. In this case, Rails uses the routing system in reverse as it evaluates the parameters that were passed to that method against our routes configuration to generate the correct URL. So when we create a link in our application using the link_to helper like this

```
link_to 'Show Post ', :controller => 'posts',  ➡
                                :action => 'show', :id => post
```

the routing system determines that this helper method should generate a link to the URL http://www.mydomain.com/posts/show/3.

Using the routing system to generate the URLs might sound unnecessarily complicated, especially since up to now we've only been dealing with the default routes and thus standard link generation methods like link_to "Update Post", :controller => 'posts', :action => 'update', and :id => 3 that don't require much complexity to convert into a URL. However, most real-world applications will add more complexity to their routing, and thus once we start building custom routes, it should become quite obvious why we need the routing system to assist with URL generation.

Of course, not all routes are created equal, so we need to have some form of system for ensuring that we select the correct route if more than one line in our routes configuration *could* match. Rails provides this prioritization in a fairly simple manner by evaluating our routes from top to bottom and selecting the *first* route that matches. Thus it's very important when creating your routes that you place the most specific routes at the top, and the more generic catch-all routes (such as our default route) at the bottom of the routes.rb file.

Setting the home directory

The most common route that we'll set in most of our applications is determining what we need to display for the root or home URL for our application. There are actually two approaches to solving this.

First is the legacy approach, where we simply specify which controller an empty request should be routed to:

```
map.connect '', :controller => 'posts'
```

This route says that if we receive no additional parameters in the URL (e.g., www.mydomain.com/), then that request should route to the posts controller, and though not explicitly defined, the default behavior is that it would also go to the index action in that controller.

That approach has worked fine for a number of years. However, recently Rails added a new approach that requires a little less typing to build this same route:

```
map.root :controller => 'posts'
```

In this shorter version, we simply call map.root instead of map.connect to specify that any requests to the root of our application should go to the posts controller and the index action. Besides saving us a few extra keystrokes, this method also provides us with a number of nice new helper methods, which we'll look at shortly when we dig into named routes.

Let's go ahead and add this map.root line to our routes configuration so that our routes file should now look like this:

```
ActionController::Routing::Routes.draw do |map|
  map.root :controller => 'posts'
  map.connect ':controller/:action/:id'
  map.connect ':controller/:action/:id.:format'
end
```

Once you make a change to your routes configuration, though, you'll need to restart your application (assuming it was already running). Once you do, just open a web browser to http://localhost:3000/, and you'll be greeted by the same page that you saw back in Figure 8-2.

> *In fact, it's important to remember that anytime you make a change to the routes configuration, you must restart your Rails application in order for the changes to take effect.*

Regular routes

As you've already seen, we can use the map.connect method to generate our default routes, but there's actually quite a bit more that we can use it for. For one, we can hard-code parameters within our routes rather than merely letting them be specified in the URL.

To see that in action, let's do a quick exercise. Let's say, for example, that our application has a blog post with an id of 101 (with a headline of "Reasons I Rock") that has become exceedingly popular (I guess everyone else wants to know just why you rock so much). To make it even easier for our fans to get to this article or to share with other people, we'd like to create a custom route that links directly to this page.

We can do so rather easily with the addition of a new route that interprets requests to /Reasons_I_Rock and directs them to the show action of the posts controller:

```
ActionController::Routing::Routes.draw do |map|
  map.connect '/Reasons_I_Rock', :controller => 'posts', ➥
                      :action => 'show', :id => 101
  map.root :controller => 'posts'
  map.connect ':controller/:action/:id'
  map.connect ':controller/:action/:id.:format'
end
```

The next time someone goes to visit our site using the URL http://localhost:3000/Reasons_I_Rock, they'll be directed straight to the content (after restarting our web application, of course).

Prefixing our blog posts

That's fine and good, but let's imagine instead that we want to change the name that people use to access our blog posts. While posts is certainly a descriptive word for us as developers, it's probably not the clearest term for an end user. Instead, let's preface all of our posts with the word "blog":

To do this, we would need to change our route entries to look like this:

```
ActionController::Routing::Routes.draw do |map|
  map.connect 'blog/Reasons_I_Rock', :controller => 'posts',
                          :action => 'show', :id => 101
  map.connect 'blog', :controller => 'posts'
  map.connect 'blog/:id', :controller => 'posts', :action => 'show'

  map.root :controller => 'posts'
  map.connect ':controller/:action/:id'
  map.connect ':controller/:action/:id.:format'
end
```

With these changes loaded, the main index page listing all of our blog posts would be available at http://localhost:3000/blog, a specific blog post would be accessible using its ID at http://localhost:3000/blog/23, and our hard-coded "Reasons I Rock" post would be visible at http://localhost:3000/blog/Reasons_I_Rock. Pretty cool, huh?

Routing by date

As another exercise, what if we wanted to route to our blog posts using the date that the blog post was created instead of routing based on each post's primary key? In that situation, we're saying that we would want our URLs to look something like http://localhost:3000/blog/2008/08/18. Once again, Rails makes it easy for us to do this seemingly complex task.

The first step would be to define a new route that captures the year, month, and day in the URL:

```
map.connect "blog/:year/:month/:day",
  :controller => "blog",
  :action => "show_by_date",
```

Well, that was easy, but there's still a small problem with it. Because Rails is simply going to match any URL that fits into the /blog/XX/XX/XX style to the route, someone could type in a URL such as /blog/you/are/lame, and your show_by_date action would then look for a blog post with a year of you, a month of are and a date of lame! Fortunately, we can fix this by adding a few regular expressions within our route to ensure that we only match for URLs with the correctly formatted parameters:

```
map.connect 'blog/:year/:month/:day',
              :controller => 'posts',
              :action     => 'show_by_date',
              :year       => /\d{4}/,
              :month      => /\d{1,2}/,
              :day        => /\d{1,2}/
```

> Regular expressions are an exceptionally powerful string-matching system supported by most programming languages and many text editors and system utilities. Using regular expressions, absolutely amazing feats of string matching, manipulation, and extraction are possible. Unfortunately, regular expressions also tend to come across as a fairly complex and cryptic solution (as you can see in our routing-by-date example). I could recommend a number of wonderful books that explore how to use regular expressions, but for a good free resource, you might check out the screencast and tutorial at http://e-texteditor.com/blog/2007/regular_expressions_tutorial.

In the preceding route, we use regular expressions to specify that the year, month, and day parameters must be digits (using \d). We also require that years be given in the full four-digit manner and allow that months and days can be either one or two digits long.

Our routes are shaping up quite nicely. However, one little thing might be bugging you, and that is that there is currently a small bit of duplication in each of the routes that we just created.

In each of our new routes, you'll notice that we had to include the same :controller => 'blog' command. Obviously, that isn't too painful when we only have three routes, but you can imagine that if we had a larger application that had a large number of these routes, it could get a little tedious to deal with all of those. Well, fortunately, that duplication bugged some of the Rails core developers as well, so they created a method to eliminate that duplication named with_options:

```
map.with_options :controller => 'blog' do |blog|
    blog.connect 'blog/reasons_i_rock', :action => 'show, :id => 101
    blog.connect 'blog'
    blog.connect 'blog/:id', :action  => 'show'
  end
```

Using with_options, we can move the common elements of our routes out of each line and use a block to apply it dynamically to each route we define. In essence, we define a set of common route options that we want to be merged with any routes that we define within the block. It's a small change, but it can save you quite a bit of typing in larger route sets.

Named routes

Traditionally, Rails developers always used map.connect, which was used to build our generic /:controller/:action/:id routes like this:

```
map.connect '', :controller => 'home', :action => 'welcome'
map.connect '/post/:id', :controller => 'post', :action => 'show'
map.connect '/weather/:year/:month/:date, ➡
                        :controller => 'weather', :action => 'archive'
```

While the map.connect method works fine, it can force Rails developers to be rather verbose when they want to refer to a specific route from within their application. For example, if we wanted to create links to the preceding routes, our link_to methods would have looked like this:

```
link_to 'Home', :controller => 'home', :action => 'welcome'
link_to 'Show Post', :controller => 'post', ➡
                                :action => 'show', :id => @post
link_to 'Weather Last Christmas', :controller => 'weather',
                                :action => 'archive',
                                :year => '2006'
                                :month => '12',
                                :date => '25'
```

You can see how quickly it would become bothersome to constantly generate links by manually typing the controller, actions, and ID parameters each time, and you can imagine how quickly this would increase the noise ratio within our view templates.

As a means to simplify the process of building links in our application, named routes were added to our Rails arsenal to ease this pain for Rails developers. Building a named route is almost identical to building a regular route—except that we replace the connect method with a custom name of our own choosing for the route. So to convert the regular routes you saw previously, we could instead write them like this:

```
map.home '', :controller => 'home', :action => 'welcome'
map.post '/post/:id', :controller => 'post', :action => 'show'
map.weather_archive '/weather/:year/:month/:date, ➡
                        :controller => 'weather', :action => 'archive'
```

While this may seem like just a minor change, it makes these named routes and that makes a big difference for us.

When we create a named route, Rails uses its magic to build two new URL methods for each named route that we can use to make our lives much easier. Those methods are based on the name that we provided for the named route and look like {named_route}_path and {named_route}_url.

Our previous map.home route would generate named route methods named home_path and home_url, each of these methods would simply generate the URLs for this specific route. The only difference between these two methods is that home_url will generate a fully qualified link including host and port (e.g., http://localhost:3000/) while home_path will generate only the relative path (i.e., /). So armed with our named routes, we could quickly convert our previous links to those routes like this:

```
link_to 'Home', home_path
link_to 'Show Post', post_path(@post)
link_to 'Weather Last Christmas', ➥
                    weather_archive_path('2006', '12', '25')
```

As you can see, while named routes don't have any effect on our end users (the URLs are still the same), they can make the process of building links in our templates quite a bit easier. In fact, because of this, most Rails developers prefer to use named routes over traditional routes these days.

RESTful routing

The newest type of routing that was added to Rails is commonly referred to as RESTful routing. It's called that because it was added to support easily adding REST-based web services to our Rails applications.

REST, as you may be aware, stands for Representational State Transfer and is an architecture for providing access to resources by interpreting the URL and the HTTP method that was used to access the URL. Or in layman's terms, it's a set of conventions for interfacing with our application where the HTTP method (GET, POST, etc.) that was used to access the URL has great significance.

You see, unlike traditional web-service technologies such as SOAP or XML-RPC that would require us to build a completely separate set of controllers and actions to provide the web service interface to our application, REST is unique in that it's possible to provide our web service from the same controllers and actions that provide the HTML version of our application. Rather than being a solution that's been tacked on top of our traditional web technologies, REST-based services solve the problem by providing services through the native constructs of HTTP.

But what are those constructs? Well, if you've been around web applications for a while, then you're probably already well aware of the two common HTTP methods that are used in web application: GET and POST.

The GET method is used to retrieve information, and this is the method that we typically use for links. Any additional parameters in a GET request must be passed within the URL. An example of an application that uses GET requests is Google, where whatever search parameters that we're searching for are passed along into the URL string like http://www.google.com/search?&q=rails.

We also have the POST method, which is most often used for submitting data to our web application, typically through the use of a form. A good example would be the form in the new template in our example application for this chapter where when you submit the form all of the parameters are sent in the HTTP headers and not in the URL.

But those aren't the only options; there are several others that are defined in the HTTP specifications that we rarely see used in web applications, including the two that are most important for REST services: PUT and DELETE.

The PUT method is similar to the POST method but was designed for updating an already existing resource.

The DELETE method acts like a GET request in that its parameters are passed via the URL, but it differs in that instead of requesting the server to return a resource, it asks the web application to delete the specified resource.

So for RESTful interfaces we have four HTTP verbs that we'll need to use:

- GET for reading data
- POST for creating new data
- PUT for updating existing data
- DELETE for removing data

Does that sound familiar? It should, because those match up perfectly with the common CRUD (create, read, update, destroy) operations of a database, as shown in Table 8-1.

Table 8-1. Correlation of HTTP Methods to Database Operations

Action	Database Operation	HTTP Method
Create	INSERT	POST
Read	SELECT	GET
Update	UPDATE	PUT
Destroy	DELETE	DELETE

It gets even better than that. Recall that we talked about designing our controllers around CRUD operations in the last chapter? Well, that puts us in the perfect position to also support REST interfaces. When we've built our controller actions in line with a CRUD design, they immediately line up, as shown in Table 8-2.

Table 8-2. Comparing Controller Actions, HTTP Methods, and Database Operations

Action	Database Operation	HTTP Method	Controller Action
Create	INSERT	POST	Create
Read	SELECT	GET	Show
Update	UPDATE	PUT	Update
Destroy	DELETE	DELETE	Destroy

Does all this sound a little too good to be true? Wondering why we haven't been building REST interfaces all along? Well, here's the rub—existing web browsers only support the HTTP methods GET and POST. That's right; we don't have a way to do PUT and DELETE requests from a web browser. So how in the heck do we handle RESTful routes in a Rails application?

Rails gets around this limitation through some clever manipulation of parameters: it sends the PUT and DELETE methods as hidden parameters in the header. Yes, it's a hack, but it's a necessary one that makes it possible for us to build powerful REST services.

As I said, in a RESTful service, requests will be routed to our controller actions based on the URL and the HTTP method used to invoke it. I just showed you how we interact with the four basic ones that map directly to the CRUD operations, but when we built our CRUD–based controllers in the last chapter, we had seven methods: index, show, new, edit, create, update, and destroy. What about the index, new, and edit actions? They're actually easy to support, because they're really just variations on the GET request. The index action simply uses GET to obtain a list of all resources instead of a single resource, while the new and edit actions simply use GET to open a form that will be used to submit data back to the server to either the create or the update actions.

Notice that in the examples in Table 8-3 many of the URLs are exactly the same. The only difference between them is the HTTP verb used to access that URL.

Table 8-3. Mapping Controller Actions to HTTP Verbs and URLS

Action	HTTP Method	URL
Index	GET	/posts
Show	GET	/posts/12
New	GET	/posts/new
Edit	GET	/posts/12/edit
Create	POST	/posts
Update	PUT	/posts/12
Destroy	DELETE	/posts/12

So in order to build our routes to support REST, we simply need to build the necessary routes to connect the proper URL and HTTP method to the correct controller and action. Sounds pretty easy, doesn't it? Let's take a look at the routes necessary for these seven actions, and for good measure, we'll build them with named routes to make it easy for us to reference them from within our Rails application:

```
map.posts 'posts', :action => 'index', ➥
                   :conditions => {:method => :get}
map.connect 'posts', :action => 'create', ➥
                   :conditions => {:method => :post}
map.formatted_pst 'posts'.:format', :action => 'index', ➥
                               :conditions => {:method => :get}
map.exercise 'posts/:id', :action => 'edit', ➥
                       :conditions => {:method => :get}
map.connect 'posts/:id', :action => 'update', ➥
                       :conditions => {:method => :put}
map.connect 'posts/:id', :action => 'destroy', ➥
                       :conditions => {:method => :delete}
map.formatted_post 'posts/:id.:format', :action => 'edit', ➥
                                   :conditions => {:method => :get}
map.connect 'posts/:id.:format', :action => 'update', ➥
                               :conditions => {:method => :put}
map.connect 'posts/:id.:format', :action => 'destroy', ➥
                               :conditions => {:method => :delete}
map.new_post 'posts/new', :action => 'new', ➥
                       :conditions => {:method => :get}
map.formatted_new_post 'posts/new.:format', :action => 'new', ➥
                                       :conditions => {:method => :get}
map.edit_post 'post/:id;edit', :action => 'edit', ➥
                           :conditions => {:method => :get}
map.edit_post 'post/:id.:format;edit', :action => 'edit', ➥
                                   :conditions => {:method => :get}
```

Ugh! That wasn't quite as easy as we had hoped, was it? If that's how much typing we have to do to support just one RESTful controller, can you imagine how much typing we'd have to do to support many? That would be almost unbearable. Named routes are an incredible tool, but unfortunately, it seems that they're still a bit underpowered for building RESTful routes, as we'd be forced to build far too many named routes to support our seven CRUD actions.

Of course, by now, you know I wouldn't be making such a point of this if a ready-made solution weren't already present within Rails. Believe it or not, we can bypass all of that typing and get all those same named routes created through the use of a single route that looks like this:

```
map.resources :posts
```

Considerably easier, wouldn't you agree? In fact, to support multiple RESTful controllers, we can even string them together on a single line like so:

```
map.resources :posts, :users, :comments
```

Here, we've defined multiple RESTful routes in a single line to save space. If we wanted to be more explicit we could alternatively have written these routes like this:

```
map.resources :posts
map.resources :users
map.resources :comments
```

Hopefully, you'll agree that it's more desirable to string them together onto a single line to avoid the duplication of effort for defining each route individually.

Now you can see that as long as we're building our controller actions to fit into the CRUD based design, it makes a lot more sense to use the new RESTful routes that Rails provides in order to clean up our routing configuration.

Singular routes

Of course, in very special circumstances, there are times when we have a resource that can only be singular. That is, not only is there only one, but that there can be only one instance of that resource within the current context. In these cases it wouldn't make sense to have methods and views for an index (since there is only one), and there is no need to specify an ID for any of the show, edit, or update methods either.

A good example of this would be a user resource that represents the currently signed in user. Rails provides support for this with a singular version of map.resources named map.resource. We call it like this:

    map.resource :user

This generates a series of routes very similar to map.resources except that URLs are singular, there is no index method, and many of the methods do not require an identifier parameter; see Table 8-4.

Table 8-4. Routes Generated by the Singular map.resource Method

Action	HTTP Method	URL
Show	GET	/user
New	GET	/user/new
Edit	GET	/user/edit
Create	POST	/user
Update	PUT	/user
Destroy	DELETE	/user

Nested routes

There's another variation to our standard routes that we need to be able to address—when one resource is only valid within the context of its relationship to another resource. For example, let's use the analogy of modeling a family unit of parents and children. If I were building a RESTful application and wanted to obtain a list of all parents, I could simply issue a GET request to /parents for the index method of the Parents controller. Also if I wanted to obtain details about a specific parent, I might issue a GET request to /parents/1.

Similarly, if I wanted to obtain a list of all children in my application, I would do a GET request to /children, or I could use a GET request to /children/5 for details on a specific child.

The problem is that, in my application, I'm not really interested in accessing children except within the context of their parents. In other words, I care about only the children associated with the parents that I'm currently looking at. So what we need is a way to make our RESTful routes recognize that children are only valid in relation to their parents, and that's exactly what nested routes provide us with. When we're dealing with a nested route, our routes change so that to access the index method of the child controller, we now have to add the specific parents first; the route changes to /parents/1/children. In other words, the parents prefix their associated children.

Some other examples of possible nested routes would be the relationships of a book to chapters, a forum to posts, a state to cities, and so on.

We can represent nested routes in our Routes configuration in two different ways. The first way is to generate the route as a block:

```
map.resources :parents do |parent|
  parent.resources :children
end
```

The second way is to use the same type of association methods that we used in our ActiveRecord associations to build the nested routes:

```
map.resources :parents, :has_many => :children
```

The second way is certainly a bit more concise, but I tend to prefer the block method simply because it helps make those routes not get lost in the noise of a larger routes configuration. However, both methods produce the exact same named route set that you can see in Table 8-5.

Table 8-5. Mapping Controller Actions to HTTP Verbs and URLS for Nested Resources

Action	HTTP Method	URL
Index	GET	/parents/:parent_id/children
Show	GET	/parents/:parent_id/children/:id
New	GET	/parents/:parent_id/children/new
Edit	GET	/parents/:parent_id/children/:id/edit
Create	POST	/parents/:parent_id/children
Update	PUT	/parents/:parent_id/children/:id
Destroy	DELETE	/parents/:parent_id/children/:id

In addition, it's important to note that, in our views, when we link to a nested resource we need to use a specialized method that takes into account the nested nature of the route, so rather than simply linking to children_url like we might normally do, we need to use the extended version parent_children_url(@parent), making sure to pass a reference to the parent resource as a parameter .

Customizing RESTful routes

So far, we've been enjoying the fact that the map.resources method builds all the routes to our controller as long as they're following the CRUD design pattern. Unfortunately, there are going to be times when we need to add additional methods to our controllers beyond the basic CRUD methods. In those cases, we'll need to modify our RESTful routes to be able to support these additional methods. Rails provides two different modifications that we can apply, which one you implement depends on whether your method is affecting a single element or a collection of elements.

Member routes

If your custom method interacts with a single resource, you'll want to define a custom member route. The best way to learn, though, is through an example. For this example, we have a controller that has the seven basic methods plus one additional method named retract. The retract method works on a single resource, but currently, there is no way to route a request to it. We'll fix that. Open routes.rb in /config, and find the line that looks like this:

```
map.resources :posts
```

Since this single line is what controls the routing to our Posts controller, it's here that we'll need to define our new member route. We do so by modifying the route like so:

```
map.resources :posts, :member => {:retract => :get}
```

This small addition of defining the name of the member and the HTTP method used to access that method has added the following named routes to our routes:

```
retract_post_path
```

> Obviously, this route was defined as a GET request, because it is simply retrieving a result from the server. If, however, we were wishing to push data to or modify data on the server in some way, we would have needed to define the member route as a POST request instead.

Collection routes

Conversely, if our custom method were applicable to a collection or group of resources, we would define a collection route for it. Collection routes tend to be fairly identical to our member routes, and we define them in pretty much the same way:

```
map.resources :posts, :collection => {:showall => :any}
```

However, the generated named route will use a pluralized form:

```
showall_posts_path
```

In the end, the only difference between a collection and a member route is whether you're interacting with one record or many records.

rake routes

As our routes grow, it can sometimes become a little confusing determining all the named and RESTful URLs that our application supports. Back in the old days, Rails developers used custom console scripting to evaluate and print out a list of the generated routes, but with Rails 2.0 came a new rake task that solves this problem.

Now if we want a detailed look at our routes we can simply run this:

```
rake routes
```

It will print out all the generated routes to the screen in four columns that map to this:

```
route_name, HTTP method, path, requirements
```

Currently, the routes configuration for our demoblog application is a bit eclectic (being that it's a sandbox for us to learn routing), but if we were to run the rake routes task on this application, it will output something like you can see in Figure 8-4.

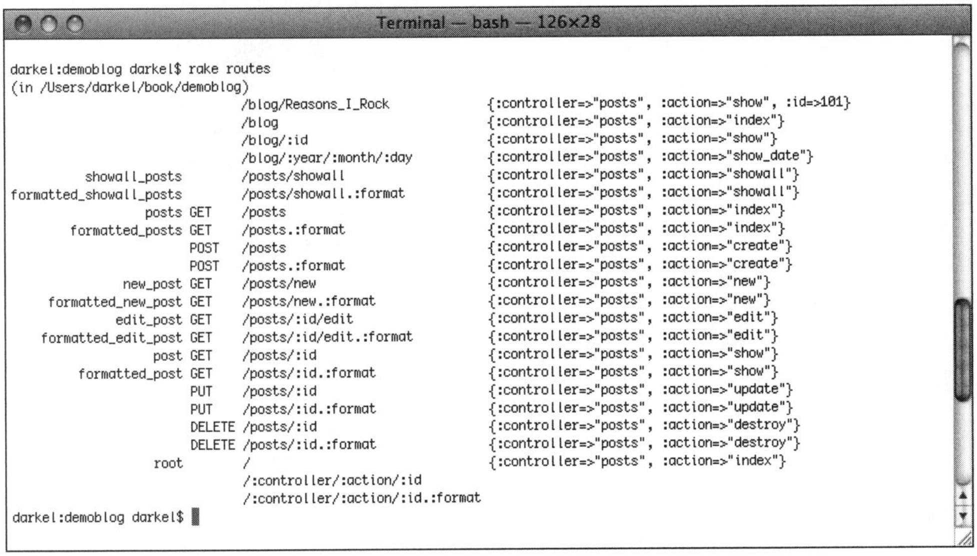

Figure 8-4. The output of the rake routes task

Summary

In this chapter, we were able to expand our routing beyond just the simple /controller/action/id default that every Rails application starts with, and you learned how to build custom routing to bend URLs to the exact format that you want.

Along the way, we also explored some of the newer enhancements to routing, such as named routes; while only being a small change within the context of the routes.rb file, these make a big difference for our views when we need to create links.

Finally, we took a quick tour of the new RESTful routing support that's available within Rails applications, which allows you to use the HTTP verbs GET, POST, PUT, and DELETE to add more meaning to your URLs and provide simplified access to your resources.

Chapter 9

SCAFFOLDING AND PLUG-INS

All your efforts up to this point are about to be rewarded, as we've finally reached the point where you are going to begin seeing the knowledge you've built up in the previous chapters combine to build a simple Rails application together. In the last several chapters, we've examined all of the individual aspects of building Rails applications—you learned how to use Rails to define our database schema and how to build Rails models to interact with those databases. We've discussed not only how to build controllers but also how to properly design them, and we looked at how we can embed Ruby to add dynamic content to our HTML templates (views). Last but not least, we examined the power of the Rails routing system and how it allows us to effectively map URLs to our controllers and pages.

You've already seen how using Rails can speed up your development time. However, in this chapter, I'm going to introduce two new tools that will strap turbo-powered rocket packs onto our development backs.

The first tool we'll explore for speeding up development is the Rails scaffolding generator. The scaffolding generator will build a complete set of Rails code for managing a single resource including a data migration, model, and controller that supports RESTful routing and view templates. This scaffold-generated code forms a complete solution for interacting with your model data and provides a complete CRUD–based solution. While the code that the scaffold generates is good, it's probably not something that you would want to deploy into a real production application. That's not to say it isn't useful, however, as it can be quite a timesaver for quickly getting your application up and running with a generic set of code that you can then modify and mold into something that's more suitable for your project.

The second tool that I'll be introducing in this chapter is the Rails plug-in system, which is a system that allows developers to easily share code solutions between Rails applications. Plug-ins are a powerful way to enhance Rails with exciting new features that are not inherent to the framework, and there is an immense wealth of functionality available in plug-ins. In fact, at the time of this writing, there are over 1,100 plug-ins available for you to use to enhance your Rails applications. Some examples of popular plug-ins available include those for adding pagination to our applications, building complete authentication systems for us, and extending ActiveRecord with enhanced functionality such as tagging, geocoding, or even file upload capabilities.

Overview of what we're going to build

Obviously, with over 1,100 plug-ins available, a simple list of them all would be horribly inefficient; instead what's needed is some form of catalog that can be used to help organize and categorize the available plug-ins, and in fact, there are several available including the most popular one at http://agilewebdevelopment.com/plugins. In this chapter, we're going to explore how easy it would be to build a quick and simple version of a plug-in catalog application similar to the one at the Agile Web Development site or even the Jquery JavaScript plug-in catalog (http://plugins.jquery.com/).

Our application will provide the ability to do a full set of CRUD operations on a catalog of available plug-ins, and we'll even add a touch of advanced functionality to our application by implementing one of those plug-ins. The application that we're going to build here isn't going to be feature-complete (we'll build a full application in just a couple chapters from now); instead, we're going to focus on demonstrating how we can create a fairly useful beta-level application in a very short amount of time using the power of scaffolding and plugins.

Along the way, this application will also serve as a good refresher to help bring together many of the concepts that we've discussed in the last several chapters into a cohesive whole.

Creating our application

Let's get things kicked off by starting our new application using the rails generator and naming our new project "plugins":

```
rails plugins

    create
    create  app/controllers
    create  app/helpers
    create  app/models
    create  app/views/layouts
    -- excerpt --
```

> You'll notice that we're using the default database of SQLite for our application. You can feel free to change this to another RDBMS if you choose. However, you'll need to ensure that you set the /config/database.yml file correctly and create the necessary databases and permissions.

From here, we'll go ahead and open a command line prompt into our new plugins application directory, and for good measure, we'll freeze the Rails gems into our application:

```
rake rails:freeze:gems
```

Once that's done, let's go ahead and get rid of the default index page from our application:

```
rm public/index.html
```

Your first scaffold

We can jumpstart our application by using scaffolding to help us build our first full set of models, controllers, views, and so forth. At this point, we're ready to add our first scaffold to our application. While our first temptation might be to jump right in and create a scaffold to manage plug-ins, that appraoch would probably be inefficient, as I know that we're going to need to link our plug-ins to a category. Therefore, it makes sense to start by building our category model, controller, and such by using the scaffold generator.

To do that, we'll run this generator command from the root of our application:

```
ruby script/generate scaffold category name:string
      exists   app/models/
      exists   app/controllers/
      exists   app/helpers/
      create   app/views/categories
      exists   app/views/layouts/
      exists   test/functional/
      exists   test/unit/
      create   app/views/categories/index.html.erb
      create   app/views/categories/show.html.erb
      create   app/views/categories/new.html.erb
      create   app/views/categories/edit.html.erb
      create   app/views/layouts/categories.html.erb
      create   public/stylesheets/scaffold.css
      create   app/controllers/categories_controller.rb
      create   test/functional/categories_controller_test.rb
      create   app/helpers/categories_helper.rb
       route   map.resources :categories
  dependency   model
      exists     app/models/
      exists     test/unit/
      exists     test/fixtures/
```

```
create    app/models/category.rb
create    test/unit/category_test.rb
create    test/fixtures/categories.yml
create    db/migrate
create    db/migrate/20080525181258_create_categories.rb
```

You can see that this generator command is fairly similar to ones we've called in previous chapters. We pass this generator the name of our new scaffold (which will also be the name of the model that will be created), and just like with our model generator, we can pass any number of data migration parameters to the scaffold that will be used for our migration file. You can see by looking over that output that quite a lot of things were created from that one command—let's take a closer look at everything that the scaffold generator created for us.

Open our routes file (/config/routes.rb), and you'll notice that the scaffold added a new RESTful route for our categories within:

```
ActionController::Routing::Routes.draw do |map|
  map.resources :categories
...
```

So right out of the box, our new category resource has route support for the full spectrum of both CRUD operations and RESTful routing.

The second thing that the scaffold generator did was create a new migration in /db/migrate for our categories table using the parameters that we passed at the end of our scaffold command (i.e., name:string):

```
class CreateCategories < ActiveRecord::Migration
  def self.up
    create_table :categories do |t|
      t.string :name

      t.timestamps
    end
  end

  def self.down
    drop_table :categories
  end
end
```

A category model shouldn't need too much more than that, so that migration seems to be fine for now. Let's go ahead and run our migration now to apply it to our database:

```
rake db:migrate

== 20080525181258 CreateCategories: migrating ==========================
-- create_table(:categories)
   -> 0.0039s
== 20080525181258 CreateCategories: migrated (0.0041s) ================
```

Next, we can look at the model that was created by the scaffold (/app/models/category.rb), and you can see that it's pretty basic thus far:

```ruby
class Category < ActiveRecord::Base
end
```

This model provides connectivity to the table we just created in the migration, but at the very least, we should probably add some basic validations to this model to ensure that we don't allow someone to create a blank category. As an extra good measure, we'll also ensure that our category names remain at a reasonable length by setting that they must be between 2 and 30 characters.

```ruby
class Category < ActiveRecord::Base
  validates_presence_of :name
  validates_length_of :name, :within => 2..30
end
```

Saving our changes to this model, let's move onto taking a look at the RESTful controller actions and views that the scaffold created for us. Our new controller can be found as app/controllers/categories_controller.rb; we'll take a look at the whole thing and then pick out a few key elements of it.

```ruby
class CategoriesController < ApplicationController
  # GET /categories
  # GET /categories.xml
  def index
    @categories = Category.find(:all)

    respond_to do |format|
      format.html # index.html.erb
      format.xml  { render :xml => @categories }
    end
  end

  # GET /categories/1
  # GET /categories/1.xml
  def show
    @category = Category.find(params[:id])

    respond_to do |format|
      format.html # show.html.erb
      format.xml  { render :xml => @category }
    end
  end

  # GET /categories/new
  # GET /categories/new.xml
  def new
    @category = Category.new
```

```ruby
    respond_to do |format|
      format.html # new.html.erb
      format.xml  { render :xml => @category }
    end
  end

  # GET /categories/1/edit
  def edit
    @category = Category.find(params[:id])
  end

  # POST /categories
  # POST /categories.xml
  def create
    @category = Category.new(params[:category])

    respond_to do |format|
      if @category.save
        flash[:notice] = 'Category was successfully created.'
        format.html { redirect_to(@category) }
        format.xml  { render :xml => @category, :status => :created,➥
                                            :location => @category }
      else
        format.html { render :action => "new" }
        format.xml  { render :xml => @category.errors,➥
                                    :status => :unprocessable_entity }
      end
    end
  end

  # PUT /categories/1
  # PUT /categories/1.xml
  def update
    @category = Category.find(params[:id])

    respond_to do |format|
      if @category.update_attributes(params[:category])
        flash[:notice] = 'Category was successfully updated.'
        format.html { redirect_to(@category) }
        format.xml  { head :ok }
      else
        format.html { render :action => "edit" }
        format.xml  { render :xml => @category.errors, ➥
                                    :status => :unprocessable_entity }
      end
    end
  end
```

```
  # DELETE /categories/1
  # DELETE /categories/1.xml
  def destroy
    @category = Category.find(params[:id])
    @category.destroy

    respond_to do |format|
      format.html { redirect_to(categories_url) }
      format.xml  { head :ok }
    end
  end
end
```

One of the first things that you should have noticed is that, within this controller, we have those same seven CRUD actions that we discussed as proper controller design back in Chapter 7 (index, show, new, create, edit, update, destroy). In addition, each of these actions was built using the respond_to method so that they support responding to multiple formats. The scaffold built support for both HTML and XML requests, as you can see in the following index method snippet:

```
def index
  @categories = Category.find(:all)

  respond_to do |format|
    format.html # index.html.erb
    format.xml  { render :xml => @categories }
  end
end
```

While we're looking at the index action, let's take a look at the associated HTML view that was also created for this action; you'll find it in /app/views/categories/index.html.erb:

```
<h1>Listing categories</h1>

<table>
  <tr>
    <th>Name</th>
  </tr>

<% for category in @categories %>
  <tr>
    <td><%=h category.name %></td>
    <td><%= link_to 'Show', category %></td>
    <td><%= link_to 'Edit', edit_category_path(category) %></td>
    <td><%= link_to 'Destroy', category, :confirm => 'Are you sure?',➡
                                      :method => :delete %></td>
  </tr>
<% end %>
</table>
```

```
<br />

<%= link_to 'New category', new_category_path %>
```

Here, you can see that we're looping over the @categories instance variable that was created in the controller using a for loop and outputting each category into a table (ugh!) along with links to view the category, edit the category, or even to delete the category.

You should also notice that the scaffolding is using the named routes (i.e., new_category_path) for all of its links, so if you were a little fuzzy on named routes from the last chapter, studying this scaffold-generated code is a good way to get a better feel for how to use them.

For good measure, let's also take a look at the new template at /app/views/categories/new.html.erb to see how it was built:

```
<h1>New category</h1>

<% form_for(@category) do |f| %>
  <%= f.error_messages %>

  <p>
    <%= f.label :name %><br />
    <%= f.text_field :name %>
  </p>
  <p>
    <%= f.submit "Create" %>
  </p>
<% end %>

<%= link_to 'Back', categories_path %>
```

Again a fairly standard template, but I wanted to highlight this template so we could take a short bunny trail for a moment to look closer at one line:

```
<% form_for(@category) do |f| %>
```

This is a new bit of sweetness that was added to Rails recently. Previously, we had to explicitly specify the action that we wanted a form to route to in the form_for method, so previously, this line would have been written like this if it was in a new template:

```
<% form_for :category, :url => {:action => :create} do |f| -%>
```

or written like this if it was a form in an edit template:

```
<% form_for :category, :url => {:action => :update} do |f| -%>
```

However, in modern Rails applications, both our new and edit form templates can be built using the exact same line of code:

```
<% form_for(@category) do |f| %>
```

How does Rails know whether our form needs to be submitted to either the create or update action when we're giving it the exact same command? That answer resides within the category object itself. Within the object, ActiveRecord keeps track of whether or not the object is a new object or an existing one that was loaded from the database. We can see the object tracking this data using the script console by outputting the data of both a new and an existing category object (obviously, we would have had to create a record in the database before we'd be able to load an existing one though).

```
ruby script/console
Loading development environment

c1 = Category.find :first

puts c1.to_yaml
--- !ruby/object:Category
attributes:
  name: Model Plugins
  updated_at: 2008-05-25 13:28:22
  id: "1"
  created_at: 2008-05-25 13:28:22
attributes_cache: {}

c2 = Category.new
=> #<Category id: nil, name: nil, created_at: nil, updated_at: nil>

puts c2.to_yaml
--- !ruby/object:Category
attributes:
  name:
  updated_at:
  created_at:
attributes_cache: {}

new_record: true
```

So in the preceding output, you can see that when we created a new category the object had an additional attribute named new_record that was set to true. When a form is built, Rails evaluates the @category object and checks to see if it's a new or an existing record. If it has the new_record attribute set to true, the form is routed to the create action; otherwise, it will be routed to the update action. Pretty slick, huh?

Viewing the scaffold

OK, our bunny trail has ended, and we're back to our regularly scheduled application. Now that we've examined the underlying code, let's go ahead and start up our new Rails application to see what it looks like. As you should know, we can start our application using the script/server command:

ruby script/server

```
=> Booting Mongrel (use 'script/server webrick' to force WEBrick)
=> Rails application starting on http://0.0.0.0:3000
=> Call with -d to detach
=> Ctrl-C to shutdown server
** Starting Mongrel listening at 0.0.0.0:3000
** Starting Rails with development environment...
** Rails loaded.
** Loading any Rails specific GemPlugins
** Signals ready.  TERM => stop.  USR2 => restart.  ➥
INT => stop (no restart).
** Rails signals registered.  HUP => reload (without restart).  ➥
   It might not work well.
** Mongrel 1.1.4 available at 0.0.0.0:3000
** Use CTRL-C to stop.
```

Once the server is started, open a web browser to http://localhost:3000/categories, and you should be greeted with a page like the one shown in Figure 9-1.

Figure 9-1. Our index template created by the scaffold

Click the New category link, and you'll be taken to the new template at http://localhost:3000/categories/new, which you can see in Figure 9-2.

Let's go ahead and use this form to create a new category. I created a category named Model Plugins, but you can create anything you want.

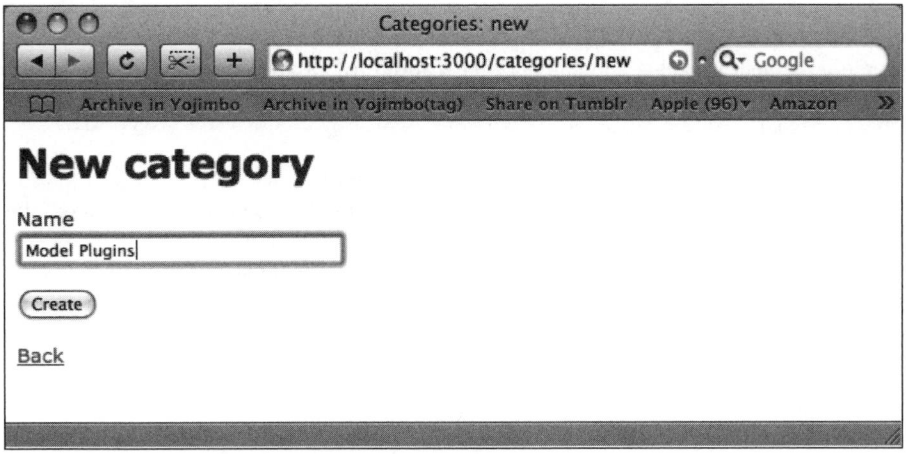

Figure 9-2. Creating a new category

Once our category is created, we'll be taken to the show template, where you can see the results of our form submission. Clicking the Back link will take us back to our index template, which is now populated with our new category, as you can see in Figure 9-3.

Figure 9-3. The index page showing our new category

That's a pretty amazing amount of functionality that was created in a few seconds with just a couple commands, isn't it?

At this point, why don't you go ahead and play around with the scaffold interface by creating some additional categories yourself.

It doesn't really matter what names you add, but just in case you're stumped for some creative categories to add, here are a few ideas to help you get started: View Extensions, AJAX, Testing, Authentication, or File Upload.

Generating the plug-in scaffold

Let's keep the momentum going and add another scaffold to our application. This time, we'll build a scaffold to track plug-ins. If you haven't already, stop your development server, so we can run the scaffold generator again.

Thinking about the attributes of a plug-in that we would want to track, I came up with the following list for our initial scaffold: to track a plug-in, we will need to be able to capture the name of the plug-in, a description of its functionality, a link to the URL where the plug-in can be found, and a foreign key reference to the category that the plug-in is associated to. Using that simple design we can create our new scaffold like so:

```
ruby script/generate scaffold Plugin name:string description:text ➡
url:string category_id:integer
      exists   app/models/
      exists   app/controllers/
      exists   app/helpers/
      create   app/views/plugins
      exists   app/views/layouts/
      exists   test/functional/
      exists   test/unit/
      create   app/views/plugins/index.html.erb
      create   app/views/plugins/show.html.erb
      create   app/views/plugins/new.html.erb
      create   app/views/plugins/edit.html.erb
      create   app/views/layouts/plugins.html.erb
   identical   public/stylesheets/scaffold.css
      create   app/controllers/plugins_controller.rb
      create   test/functional/plugins_controller_test.rb
      create   app/helpers/plugins_helper.rb
       route   map.resources :plugins
  dependency   model
      exists     app/models/
      exists     test/unit/
      exists     test/fixtures/
      create     app/models/plugin.rb
      create     test/unit/plugin_test.rb
      create     test/fixtures/plugins.yml
      exists     db/migrate
      create     db/migrate/20080525191142_create_plugins.rb
```

We don't need to review everything that was created again, but you should feel free to pause in your reading to look around the newly generated code if you wish. When you're ready to continue on, we'll focus on the changes that we're going to make to the generated scaffold.

To start with, let's go ahead and run our migrations with the rake db:migrate task to build the plugins table in our database. After which, open the category and plug-in models (in /app/models) to add associations between the two (as well as some basic validations to our plug-in model).

Associating our models

Since one category will have many plug-ins associated with it, we'll want to build a has_many associa-tion from categories to plug-ins. Add the following to the category model:

```
class Category < ActiveRecord::Base
  validates_presence_of :name
  validates_length_of :name, :within => 1..30
  has_many :plugins
end
```

Meanwhile, in our plug-ins' model, we'll want to add a reciprocal belongs_to association back to our categories, along with adding some basic validation logic.

```
class Plugin < ActiveRecord::Base
  validates_presence_of :name, :description, :url, :category_id
  validates_uniqueness_of :name
  validates_numericality_of :category_id

  belongs_to :category
end
```

So in our model, we've added validations to ensure that all of the fields that describe a plug-in are required (using the validates_presence_of validation). We also want to prevent duplication in our database, so we're using a validates_uniqueness_of validation on the name field to ensure that we don't save two plug-ins with exactly the same name. Finally, for good measure, we're using a validates_numericality_of rule to ensure that our category field will accept only a numeric value.

Once those changes are saved to our models, let's also open the routes configuration (/config/routes.rb) and remove all those extraneous comments and the default routes. In addition, we'll set the root of the application to point to the plugins controller. Afterward, our routes configuration should look like this:

```
ActionController::Routing::Routes.draw do |map|
  map.resources :plugins
  map.resources :categories
  map.root :controller => 'plugins'
end
```

Since we've modified our routes, we'll need to restart our application for the changes to be loaded.

Cleaning up the views

It would also be a good idea to clean up some of the generated view templates. We'll start by first cleaning up the layout files. You see, each scaffold that we ran automatically created a matching con-troller-specific layout file in /app/views/layouts. Unfortunately, we need to get rid of these, as we're going to want to have a standard global template. The easiest way to perform that task is to rename one of those layouts to application.html.erb and then remove the other; see Figure 9-4.

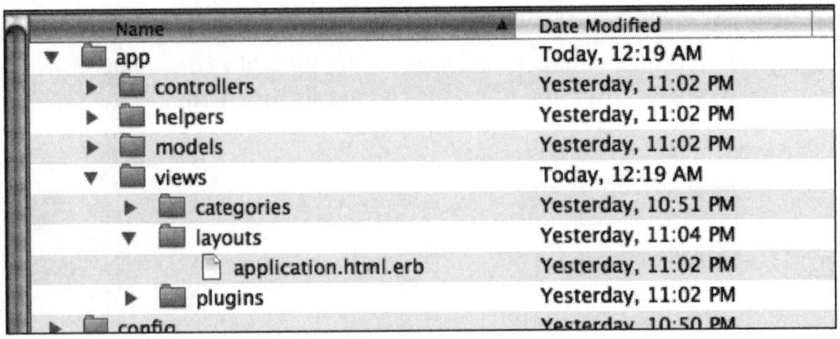

Figure 9-4. Creating a single global layout

With a single layout file now, we can also modify the forms that are used in the edit and new templates for our plug-ins scaffold.

First off, it would be a good idea to move this form to a single partial, so we only have to make changes to it once. Recall that we covered partials in Chapter 6. The first step in doing that is to create a new partial template in /app/views/plugins named _form.html.erb and place the following code into it:

```
<% form_for(@plugin) do |f| %>
<%= f.error_messages %>
<p><%= f.label :name %><br />
      <%= f.text_field :name %></p>
<p><%= f.label :description %><br />
      <%= f.text_area :description %></p>
<p><%= f.label :url %><br />
      <%= f.text_field :url %></p>
  <p><%= f.label :category_id %><br />
    <%= f.select :category_id,
              Category.find(:all).collect {|c| [c.name, c.id] },
                                      {:include_blank => true} %>
  </p>
  <p>
    <%= f.submit "Submit" %>
  </p>
<% end %>
```

This code is pretty close to what the scaffold generated with the exception that we changed the category_id field to be a drop-down box that's populated with our category records instead. Now we just need to change our new and edit templates to render our new partial:

The new template (/app/views/plugins/new.html.erb) looks like this:

```
<h1>New plugin</h1>

<%= render :partial => 'form' %>

<%= link_to 'Back', plugins_path %>
```

And the edit template (/app/views/plugins/edit.html.erb), like this:

```
<h1>Editing plugin</h1>

<%= render :partial => 'form' %>

<%= link_to 'Show', @plugin %> |
<%= link_to 'Back', plugins_path %>
```

If we fire up a web browser and go to http://localhost:3000/plugins/new, we can see that our templates are displaying our new form partial, as shown in Figure 9-5.

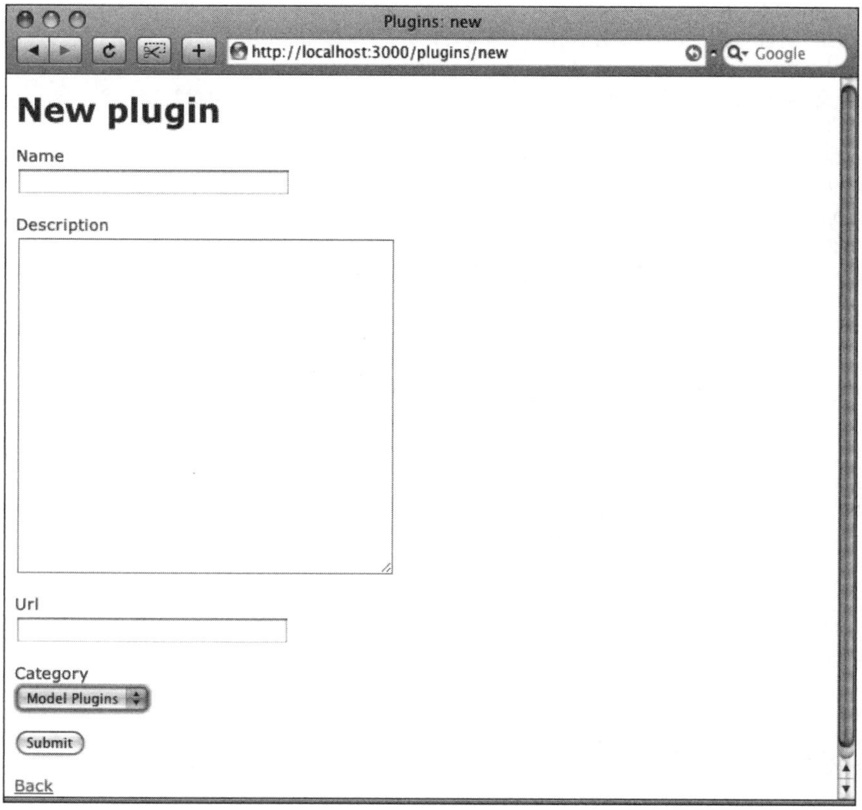

Figure 9-5. Rendering our new partial

Things are coming along pretty nicely thus far: we can manage categories and create plug-ins that we can associate to those categories, thus our application is fairly functional. But it is still fairly plain looking, isn't it? Let's fix that by finishing our layout to give our application a slightly improved look and feel.

In the source archive for this book, I've provided you with some images and style sheets that you should download and store in your /public/images and /public/stylesheets directories. Once those are loaded into your application, open /app/views/layouts/application.html.erb, and let's modify our global layout template to look like this:

```erb
<!DOCTYPE html PUBLIC "-//W3C//DTD XHTML 1.0 Transitional//EN"
        "http://www.w3.org/TR/xhtml1/DTD/xhtml1-transitional.dtd">

<html xmlns="http://www.w3.org/1999/xhtml" xml:lang="en" lang="en">
<head>
  <meta http-equiv="content-type" content="text/html;charset=UTF-8" />
  <title>Plugins: <%= controller.action_name %></title>
  <%= stylesheet_link_tag 'scaffold' %>
</head>
<body>
  <div id="container">
    <div id="header">
      <h1>Plugins 'R Us <span>  Your Source for Plugin Fun</span></h1>
    </div>
    <ul id='nav'>
      <li id='nav_plugins'><%= link_to "Home", plugins_path %></li>
      <li id='nav_categ'><%= link_to "Categories", categories_path %></li>
    </ul>

    <div id="main">
      <p style="color: green"><%= flash[:notice] %></p>
      <%= yield  %>
    </div>
  </div>
</body>
</html>
```

After we make those changes, a quick refresh of our web browser reveals that we've spruced up the application a bit, as you can see in Figure 9-6.

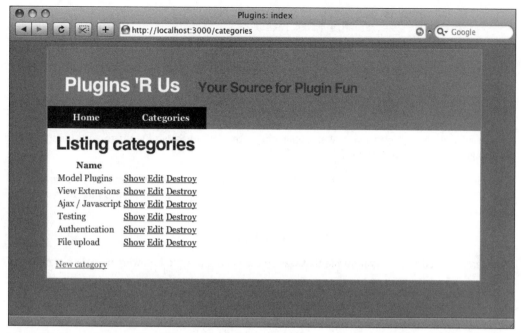

Figure 9-6. Our application with a little style applied

Adding a plug-in to our application

At this point in our application, even though we've only spent a pretty short amount of time, we've put together a fairly large amount of functionality with just a few scaffold commands. Now, we'll further enhance our application by using some shared code via the plug-in system.

A good addition for our application would be the ability for us to allow people to not only view plug-ins but also to rate them to help others separate the wheat from the chaff.

After doing a bit of research on the Agile Web Development plug-ins site that we discussed earlier (http://agilewebdevelopment.com/plugins), I found a number of available plug-ins that we could use to add rating capabilities to our application. However, one of the most popular is acts_as_rateable, which extends our ActiveRecord models with a number of new methods that provide support for ratings.

Rails provides a set of command line tools for the management of plug-ins. To install the acts_as_rateable plug-in into our application, we simply need to run the following command:

```
ruby script/plugin install http://juixe.com/svn/acts_as_rateable/
+ ./MIT-LICENSE
+ ./README
+ ./init.rb
+ ./install.rb
+ ./lib/acts_as_rateable.rb
```

```
+ ./lib/rating.rb
+ ./tasks/acts_as_rateable_tasks.rake
+ ./test/acts_as_rateable_test.rb
```

You might want to take a couple minutes to read through the README file that was installed with this plug-in (/vendor/plugins/acts_as_rateable/README), in order to get a good feel for how this plug-in works. This plug-in will simply enhance an existing ActiveRecord model with a few additional methods to support adding rating functionality to each record.

It's also a good idea to restart your web application after you add any plug-ins to your Rails application, so go ahead and do that now.

According to the README that was bundled with this plug-in, we need to create a new migration to build a ratings table in our database to store all of our ratings. We'll generate this migration with the following command:

```
ruby script/generate migration add_ratings
```

Afterward, we'll edit the migration file that was created and place the following migration statements in it:

```ruby
class AddRatings < ActiveRecord::Migration
  def self.up
    create_table "ratings", :force => true do |t|
      t.column "rating", :integer, :default => 0
      t.column "created_at", :datetime, :null => false
      t.column "rateable_type", :string, :limit => 15, ➥
                                    :default => "", :null => false
      t.column "rateable_id", :integer, :default => 0, :null => false
    end
  end

  def self.down
    drop_table :ratings
  end
end
```

Once you've saved this new migration, let's run our new migration using the rake db:migrate command. Afterward, we'll want to enable ratings on our plug-in model by adding the acts_as_rateable method to our plugin.rb in /app/models:

```ruby
class Plugin < ActiveRecord::Base
  validates_presence_of :name, :description, :url, :category_id
  validates_uniqueness_of :name
  validates_numericality_of :category_id

  belongs_to :category
  acts_as_rateable
end
```

With the acts_as_rateable plug-in now added to our application, we can fire up a script/console session to get a quick feel for how we will work with it:

```
ruby script/console
Loading development environment (Rails 2.1.0)
```

Now, assuming that you've added at least one plug-in record to the application so far, we can load that record with a quick ActiveRecord find:

```
p = Plugin.find :first
```

We can then build a new rating and assign to our model:

```
rating = Rating.new(:rating => 4)
p.ratings << rating
```

At this point, we now have at least one rating assigned to our model, and we can use some of the additional methods added by the acts_as_rateable plug-in to gather our rating information. To get the current (averaged) rating for this model, we call the rating method:

```
p.rating        #  4.0
```

Or to gather an array of all ratings for this model we can call the ratings method:

```
p.ratings
```

Using this knowledge, we can exit out of our console session and begin implementing this new functionality into our views and controllers.

Modifying our views

To support our new rating system, we need to address the issue of how to present that rating information to the user in the best possible way. One of the best solutions for this is to provide our users with a visual star rating system. One of the most popular is the solution that was provided by Komodo Media at http://www.komodomedia.com/blog/2007/01/css-star-rating-redux/; you can see a sample of this rating system in Figure 9-7.

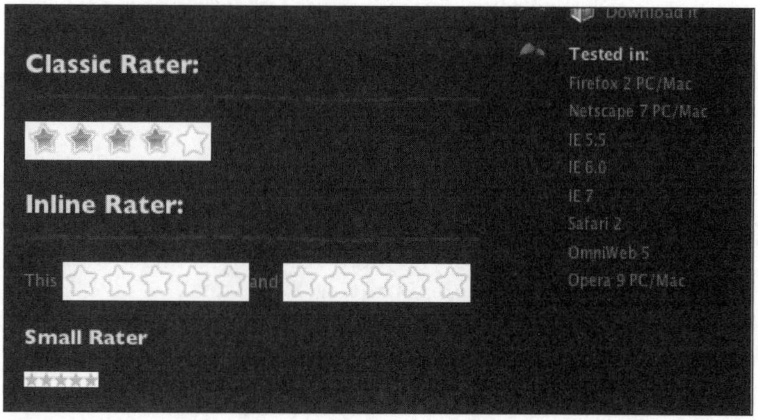

Figure 9-7. The CSS star rating system at Komodo Media

The Komodo rating system is a really nice, clean, all-around solution where our ratings are built with a standard unordered list and a few simple CSS rules. The markup for this rating system is clean too and looks like this within our template:

```
<ul class="star-rating">
  <li class="current-rating" style="width:60%;">
    Currently 3/5 Stars.
  </li>
  <li>
    <a href="#" title="1 star out of 5" class="one-star">1</a>
  </li>
  <li>
    <a href="#" title="2 stars out of 5" class="two-stars">2</a>
  </li>
  <li>
    <a href="#" title="3 stars out of 5" class="three-stars">3</a>
  </li>
  <li>
    <a href="#" title="4 stars out of 5" class="four-stars">4</a>
  </li>
  <li>
    <a href="#" title="5 stars out of 5" class="five-stars">5</a>
  </li>
</ul>
```

However, in order to make this system work for our application, you'll need to download the star images from this page and place them in the /public/images directory of our application. Once you have those added to your application, we can then add the necessary markup to our templates to display CSS star ratings.

Modifying the plug-in views

The first page that we'll want to clean up is our index template. Currently, it's displaying far too much information, as its shows all the fields in the plug-in table, which makes the page a bit ugly. Lets simplify this: we'll limit the fields to just those we are interested in and remove that ugly loop from the page and change it into a collection partial that we can use to iterate over our results instead.

Let's start by creating a new partial template named _plugin.html.erb in /app/views/plugins and placing the following display code in it:

```
<dl>
  <dt><%= link_to h(plugin.name), plugin %></dt>
  <dt>
  <ul class="star-rating small-star">
    <li class="current-rating" style="width:<%= plugin.rating*10 %>px">
              Currently <%= plugin.rating %>/5 Stars.
    </li>
  </ul>
```

```
        </dt>
        <dd><%= h truncate(plugin.description, 230) %></dd>
    </dl>
```

In this new partial, we're doing only a couple of things. First, we removed a large portion of the fields, leaving only name, description, and current rating for each plug-in. Within the partial, we're displaying the name of the plug-in and making it a link to the show template. We're also displaying the current rating of each plug-in using the small CSS star solution provided by the Komodo Media template, and finally, we're displaying a truncated version of the plug-in description.

We'll also have to modify the index.html.erb template to render our new collection partial like so:

```
<h1>Listing plugins</h1>
<%= render :partial => @plugins %>
<br />
<%= link_to 'New plugin', new_plugin_path %>
```

Once we've completed all that, if we open our web browser, we'll be treated to a nice clean listing as shown in Figure 9-8.

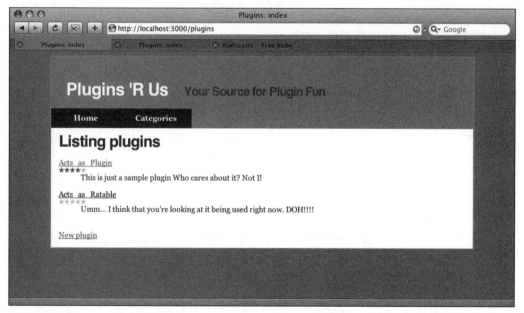

Figure 9-8. Our new plug-in listing page

Editing the show template

Now that our application's index page is set up, let's move our attention to the detail page (the show template). Currently, the page shows the fairly standard display illustrated in Figure 9-9.

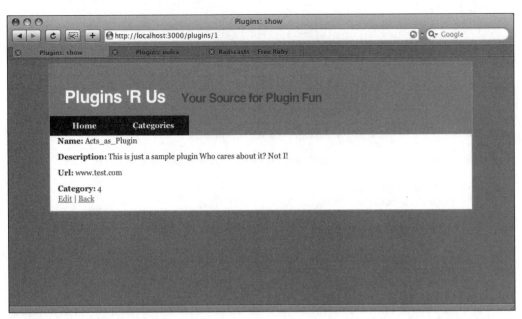

Figure 9-9. The default plug-in detail page

We're going to want to make a few changes to this template to clean it up. For example, instead of displaying the id of the associated category, we should change it to display the category's name. We should also add in the ability to display the current rating of the plug-in using our star rating system again. So open /app/views/plugin/show.html.erb, and modify the code to look like this:

```erb
<p>
  <b>Name:</b><br>
  <%=h @plugin.name %>
</p>

<p>
  <b>Description:</b><br>
  <%=h @plugin.description %>
</p>

<p>
  <b>Url:</b><br>
  <%=h @plugin.url %>
</p>

<p>
  <b>Category:</b><br>
  <%=h @plugin.category.name %>
</p>
<p>
  <b>Current Rating (<em><%= pluralize(@plugin.ratings.size, 'vote') ➥
```

```
%></em>):</b><br>
 <ul class="star-rating">
  <li class="current-rating" style="width:<%= @plugin.rating*25 %>px">
        Currently <%= @plugin.rating %>/5 Stars.
  </li>
 </ul>
</p>

<%= link_to 'Edit', edit_plugin_path(@plugin) %> |
<%= link_to 'Back', plugins_path %>
```

Viewing this page in our web browser, we can see that the display now looks like Figure 9-10.

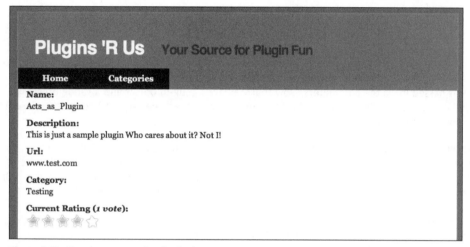

Figure 9-10. Cleaning up our plug-in display page

Things are coming along fairly nicely, but we still have an important task that we haven't addressed yet— how we're going to allow people to vote for a plug-in without giving them access to script/console. Let's solve that problem now.

Add a ratings controller

While we could certainly add a rate action to our plug-ins controller, doing so wouldn't gain us any advantage and might just complicate our application design. So in order to keep our controllers clean, it makes sense that we should probably create a new ratings controller that can be used to create new ratings. This new controller will only need a single action (create) that will be used to accept and create a new rating record. We can create our ratings controller like so:

ruby script/generate controller Ratings

```
exists  app/controllers/
exists  app/helpers/
create  app/views/ratings
exists  test/functional/
```

```
create  app/controllers/ratings_controller.rb
create  test/functional/ratings_controller_test.rb
create  app/helpers/ratings_helper.rb
```

Open that new ratings controller (/app/controllers/ratings_controller.rb), and let's add the same logic that we used previously in the console to add a new rating to a specified plug-in:

```ruby
class RatingsController < ApplicationController
  def create
    @plugin = Plugin.find(params[:plugin_id])
    rating = Rating.new(:rating => params[:rating])
    @plugin.ratings << rating
    redirect_to @plugin
  end
end
```

Our new create action does a few simple things. First, it expects that we'll be passing it the id of a plug-in as a parameter named plugin_id, and it uses this plugin_id parameter to do an ActiveRecord find and load the plug-in that we want to rate. Second, it creates a new Rating object using the rating that was passed in via the parameters. Now that we have a plug-in object and a rating object, we simply add our new rating to the ratings for the plug-in and redirect the request back to the show action of the plugins controller.

However, to make this work, we need to build a new route within our /config/routes.rb file so that we can send a request to the new controller and action. Since a rating will be required to be associated to a plug-in (and thus a plugin_id will always be mandatory), we should make the rating a nested route on top of our plug-ins route. So let's modify our routes to look like this:

```ruby
ActionController::Routing::Routes.draw do |map|
  map.resources :plugins, :has_many => :ratings
  map.resources :categories
  map.root :controller => 'plugins'
end
```

With this new route added, we now have a new named route, plugin_ratings_path, to access the create action of the ratings controller. Let's use that new named route to add the ability for users to rate a plug-in in our plugin show template.

Let's open that template again and add the following near the bottom:

```erb
      </ul>
    </p>
    <div id="rate_plugin">
      <h2>Rate this Plugin</h2>
      <ul class="star-rating">
        <li><%= link_to "1", plugin_ratings_path(@plugin, :rating => 1),
                        :method => :post, :title => "1 star out of 5",
                        :class => "one-star" %>
        </li>
        <li><%= link_to "2", plugin_ratings_path(@plugin, :rating => 2),
                        :method => :post, :title => "2 stars out of 5",
```

```
                          :class => "two-stars" %>
    </li>
    <li><%= link_to "3", plugin_ratings_path(@plugin, :rating => 3),
                        :method => :post, :title => "3 stars out of 5",
                        :class => "three-stars" %>
    </li>
    <li><%= link_to "4", plugin_ratings_path(@plugin, :rating => 4),
                        :method => :post,:title => "4 stars out of 5",
                        :class => "four-stars" %>
    </li>
    <li><%= link_to "5", plugin_ratings_path(@plugin, :rating => 5),
                        :method => :post, :title => "5 stars out of 5",
                        :class => "five-stars" %>
    </li>
  </ul>
</div>
<%= link_to 'Edit', edit_plugin_path(@plugin) %> |
<%= link_to 'Back', plugins_path %>
```

Here, we've added a second instance of our CSS star rating system to this template. Whereas in the first instance we simply displayed the current average rating for the specified plug-in, in this new instance, we're allowing people to vote. We do this by making each star a clickable link using this link_to method. Each link is using the named route plugins_rating_path to go to the create action in the ratings controller that we just built, and each link is passing the appropriate rating value. This gives us the result that you can see in Figure 9-11.

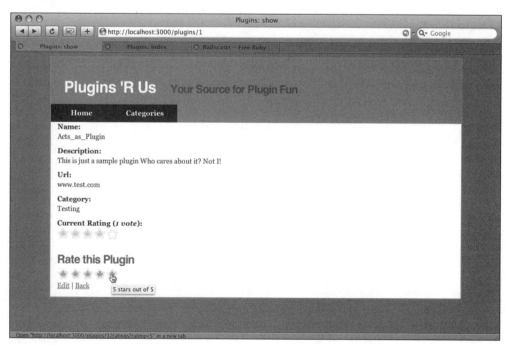

Figure 9-11. Added the ability to rate a plug-in

With that minor change, we now have the ability to click and rate any plug-in model—and we're at a good point to call it quits for this sample application. Not too shabby for just a few hours of work.

Summary

Within this short chapter, we explored how to use scaffolding and plug-ins to expedite application development. Along the way, we put together a pretty impressive prototype application in an incredibly short amount of time. We used scaffolding to get our basic application up and running with only a few lines of code, and then we added some advanced rating functionality through the use of the acts_as_rateable plug-in. You've also been able to see how all the lessons we've learned in the previous chapters can easily come together.

In the next chapter, we'll take a brief step back and look at how we can ensure that our application is working the way that we intended through the use of automated testing. You'll learn how to add tests using RSpec, and we'll revisit the application we built in this chapter as we learn how we can use RSpec to test the code that we used here.

Chapter 10

INTRODUCTION TO TESTING WITH RSPEC

Before we move into our main project for this book, we still have another very important topic to cover—testing.

There's no way to deny that testing your code is considered a core value of the Ruby and the Ruby on Rails communities. For example, in order to even file a bug report for the Rails source, it's required that you submit a test demonstrating the failure. Also if you ever attempt to obtain a full-time position developing in Ruby or Rails, you'd be hard-pressed to make it through a job interview without being asked about your commitment to testing, and finally there are even some extreme (and vocal) people within the community that claim that you're not a real programmer unless you're writing tests.

Yet even with such a solid emphasis on the importance of tests, many of the current books that teach Ruby or Rails forgo any discussion of the topic at all. Why? Well for one, testing can often be viewed as a more complex subject better suited to intermediate or advanced books than for beginning books. Second, covering tests typically takes up a lot more room (after all, each line of code may require several lines of test code) thus it can disrupt the process of learning a language to keep interrupting the code to introduce a test (plus it could turn a 500-page book into a 1,500-page book pretty quickly).

But testing your Rails code is extremely important, so I wanted at the very least to provide you with a good introduction to testing that can help you to both see the value of testing and understand the basics of how to do it yourself, as I steer you down what I believe is the best possible path for you to learn testing.

What is testing?

Obviously, if you're coming from a programming environment where testing wasn't emphasized, the first question that we need to answer is just what does it mean to test our code? Isn't it enough that it works once we type it in? Testing does sound like an awfully scary word, most likely bringing back memories from your educational days.

But would you be surprised to find out that you've already been doing a form of testing? In fact, every time we've booted up a web browser to see the effects of code that we've added or changed, we have in fact been testing our software. Yep, that would be considered testing our code, albeit in a purely manual and inefficient way. All a test does is provide some simple verification that our application yields the results that we expect. See? That's not so scary.

When we talk about creating tests for our code, what we're actually doing is working to automate that process for us. We write code that tests our application code. This test code pokes and prods at all the various levels of our application ensuring that it always provides us with the results that we expect.

Why should we test?

I'm sure at least some of you reading this are already thinking to yourself things like, "Why go through all that work when I can see that my application is working correctly?" Or, "I'm already on a deadline to get this code finished on time, wouldn't writing tests slow me down even further (after all, we're talking about potentially writing twice as much code)?"

At least I know those were the kinds of thoughts that I had in the past whenever I heard someone talk about writing test code. So let's talk about those thoughts.

Is it enough to see that your application is working correctly?

I bet you expected me to come right in here and say "No" didn't you? Well, a lot of Rails developers would say that and disagree with my next statement, but personally, I say, "It depends."

That's right; "it depends." I think that it depends on the scope of the application that you're creating, its complexity (or lack thereof), and it's potential to change over time. If all you're building is a simple web form that will be used only for a single event and will e-mail any data that's submitted to it to a single e-mail address, perhaps you don't need to go through the hassle of writing tests (of course, I would also add that using a full-featured web framework like Rails is a bit overkill for such a simple task).

However, if you're writing a web application that needs to perform anything more complex than that, I suggest that you probably should be writing tests.

As your application grows, it's going to become harder and harder for you to simply click around the application and be sure that you have verified every part of it is working. Writing automated tests allows you to ensure that all parts of your application are working correctly, which is very important because often the most annoying bugs are the ones that crop up after a small change was made in one place that ended up having unintended consequences in a completely separate part of the application.

Also, any application that's going to be used over a long period of time will almost certainly need to change and adapt at some point in its life cycle. I can't even begin to count the applications that I've written where I said, "There's no way that this application will ever need to change"—only to be on the receiving end of a series of change requests to it later down the road. People change; business needs change; and thus given a long enough period of time, even the simplest application will need to change as well. Writing tests for our applications not only helps protect us from unintended consequences as we implement new features and changes to the application later on, but they also serve as an ultimate form of documentation for the application. If you ever have to make changes to an application that you wrote three years earlier (or worse, that someone else wrote), you're not going to be stuck simply digging through their application code trying to figure out how it works, nor will you be stuck reading through some sloppy documentation manual that was written to appease a manager. instead, you'll have a complete set of concrete examples of how the application is supposed to function. You can see from the tests that when method X is called the application expects to get a result Y, and that is an incredibly powerful advantage to have.

Won't writing tests slow me down?

When you think about this question logically it makes perfect sense, doesn't it? I'm writing more code, therefore it must take me longer to finish the application. Strangely, however, that is often not the case. Don't get me wrong; as you first start learning, writing tests is going to take more effort and will slow you down. However, once you make it past that first hurdle and start to understand the syntax and the process of writing tests, you'll often find that your applications are being completed in less time. How is that possible?

Well, for one, writing tests allows you to write better code. The time you're spending writing tests allows you to reflect more about the quality of the code that you've written. Writing tests causes you to think more about your code and allows you to identify gaps in your logic that you might have missed otherwise. It also forces you to think more about catching invalid data in your application code that you might otherwise have missed.

Second, writing tests gives you a greater level of confidence about the code that you write. Because the code you write is known to pass the tests that define what the application is supposed to do, it removes lingering doubts about the code that you've written and allows you to move forward faster.

Finally, and most importantly, writing tests can speed up your development because you're able to spend far more time actually writing code and less time debugging errors. If by any chance, a change that we make breaks something in our code, we know about it instantly and even better, we have detailed information about what the exact issue is.

When do we need to write tests?

All those benefits sound good? Well, to gain all those benefits requires that we change our methodology for writing code. We'll have to adopt a popular methodology called test-first development. This means that rather than simply creating our Rails application and then (hopefully) writing a series of test code once the application is completed, we work in reverse. We start by first writing a test for the feature or functionality that we want, which of course will fail, as there is no code in our application to support it. It's only then that we write the code necessary to make that test pass.

According to test-first development, you should only write code that fixes a failing test.

An alternative expression that you'll hear to describe this method of coding is Red-Green-Refactor, which is simply an expression that describes the colors that most test suites will use to display tests. We start by writing a test that will fail (commonly displayed in red). Next, we write enough code to make our test pass (commonly displayed as green). From there, we can continue to refactor (or refine) our code to optimize it.

Writing tests first sounds a little crazy, doesn't it? Unfortunately, there's not a single argument or point I can provide to help make it sound better. It's one of those things that you have to do for a while yourself before it clicks. You'll begin to see the benefits of this approach as we move through the chapter.

Introducing testing

Rails makes getting started with automated testing incredibly easy, as it not only automatically creates a folder to hold your test suite (/test), but when you use the generators to create your components, Rails also creates empty test stubs within that /test directory for you. To see this in action, go ahead and reopen our plugins project from the last chapter, and let's look at what was created for us in /test, as shown in Figure 10-1.

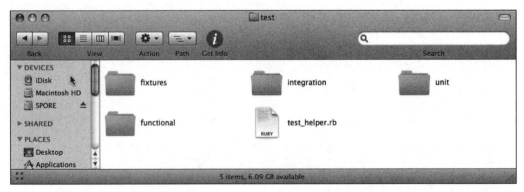

Figure 10-1. The contents of our test directory

Without us doing a single thing, Rails created a number of things for us.

First off, it created a folder named fixtures, which, surprisingly enough, holds our fixture data. If you're not familiar with that term, don't worry about it; "fixtures" is just a fancy way of saying "sample data." Looking within this directory, you'll see that it currently has two files: one for each model that we created for this project, each with a simple set of sample data in YAML format. The idea of fixtures in Rails is that you would edit these files with your own specific sample data, and then this data would be loaded into the test environment database before each test was executed.

Second, we were provided with a set of three folders for holding the three types of testing that Rails supports by default: unit, functional, and integration. Let's take a (very) brief look at each of these:

Unit tests are the most basic of the built-in tests and are used for testing the code in our models. Using unit tests, we create a series of methods that will be run to test our models' methods, validations, and other logic using a series of assertions. For example, to test that a new model is invalid if its attributes are empty, we might write a test that looks like this:

```
def test_invalid_with_empty_attributes
  plugin = Plugin.new
  assert !plugin.valid?
  assert plugin.errors.invalid?(:name)
  assert plugin.errors.invalid?(:description)
  assert plugin.errors.invalid?(:url)
  assert plugin.errors.invalid?(:category_id)
end
```

Functional tests are the next type of test that is included with Rails, and they are used for testing our controller actions and their associated views. For example, a functional test that could be used to ensure that an index action redirects to a special page if the user is not logged in might look like this:

```
def test_show_without_logged_in_user
  get :show
  assert_redirected_to :action => "signup"
  assert_equal "Must create an account to view this page", ➡
flash[:notice]
end
```

The final type of testing that's built into Rails is called integration testing and is a way of combining both unit tests and multiple functional tests into a single test that is used to test an entire process flow or story. In integration tests, we can follow the flow of a user experience across multiple controllers and actions, ensuring that an entire process works rather than just each individual component.

```
def test_signing_up _new_user
  User.delete_all
  get :show
  assert_redirected_to :action => "signup"
  assert_equal "Must create an account to view this page", ➡
flash[:notice]

  assert_template "signup"
  post_via_redirect "/user/create",
    :user => { :name => "Wall E",
               :address => "Earth",
               :email => "wall-e@bnl.com",
```

```
                            :password => "EVE" }
      assert_redirected_to :action => "index"
end
```

In this test, we ensure that the entire sign-up process is working the way that we would expect. We start by ensuring that our test database is completely empty of any previous users before making a request to view the show template. Because we shouldn't be able to see that page without a user account, we then verify that our request was redirected to the signup page instead and verify that a flash message was set for our redirect. Next, we test that when a sign-up form was submitted with valid attributes that our request was then redirected to the index action. So you can see that we were able to test the entire spectrum of a Rails request, and in essence, we built a test around a small user experience.

These testing tools are powerful and well worth your time to learn, however, they all suffer from a couple of key issues. For one, the tests you create tend to be very tightly coupled with the implementation code that you create—to the point that even a small change in your code will often also require a change to your test. A second issue is that these tests look and feel like code and are far removed from the way that our customers would write their requirements (at least, I've never met any customers that say things like "assert true"), so we're forced to do a lot of interpretation and translation of business requirements into test code, which means that our interpretation of the requirements into a test may not always be correct. These two issues mean that any tests that we create tend to be further removed from the business requirements of the application.

Wouldn't it be ideal if, instead of merely testing that our functions worked the way that we coded them, our tests were more focused on whether our application meets the business requirements? That way, how we implemented a solution would be less important than whether the implementation provided the correct results. And wouldn't it be even more ideal if our actual tests could be written using language that is similar to the language that's used to provide us with our project requirements?

It was for these exact reasons that Behavior-Driven Development (BDD) was created. BDD is designed not to be a replacement to the test-first development model but to be an evolution from it. However in BDD, one of the primary emphases is on *getting the words right*, so that everyone involved with the project (e.g., business owners, developers, and testers) are not only on the same page but are also using the same language to minimize miscommunications and misinterpretations.

This emphasis is a lot more than simple verbiage though; it's about getting the words right so that we can move the focus back onto what the application *should* be doing, not simply what's it's been coded to do. If you're interested in learning more of the philosophies behind BDD, you can read more about them at the official web site at http://behaviour-driven.org.

With BDD, we take all the best parts of test-driven development, yet enhance them with a cleaner syntax that's closer to the project requirements (or specifications as they're commonly called), and by doing so, we keep the tests that we create in BDD more focused on the requirements and not on the specific implementation. Thus we're able to bypass those issues that we discussed a few paragraphs ago. It's for reasons like these that we're going to focus our introduction to testing using the lessons gained from BDD, and using the number one BDD testing framework for Ruby—RSpec.

Introducing RSpec

RSpec is a BDD framework for Ruby that has taken the Ruby world by storm. Even though it's not built into Rails (yet), a large and ever-growing number of Rails developers have converted to using RSpec as their test framework of choice. You can find documentation and more information about RSpec at http://rspec.info/. Its current implementation (at the time of this writing) is composed of two different testing systems: a story runner framework that allows you to craft plain-text user stories as your tests as a form of integration testing (i.e., tests that cover the full gamut of the request/response cycle: routes, controllers, models, and views) and a spec (or specification) testing framework that's designed for testing each of the individual objects within our applications in isolation.

RSpec stories

RSpec stories tend to follow a narrative process of describing your desired actions. Let's take a quick look at one from the RSpec story runner documentation:

```
Story: transfer from savings to checking account
  As a savings account holder
  I want to transfer money from my savings account to my checking ➥
account
  So that I can get cash easily from an ATM

  Scenario: savings account has sufficient funds
    Given my savings account balance is $100
    And my checking account balance is $10
    When I transfer $20 from savings to checking
    Then my savings account balance should be $80
    And my checking account balance should be $30

  Scenario: savings account has insufficient funds
    Given my savings account balance is $50
    And my checking account balance is $10
    When I transfer $60 from savings to checking
    Then my savings account balance should be $50
    And my checking account balance should be $10
```

Believe it or not, that plain-text description right there is executed as a test within the story runner framework. Within these stories, we do a basic story set-up that always follows this format:

```
As a {ROLE}
I want {FEATURE or ACTION}
So that {GOAL}
```

After that, we create a series of scenarios that describe the test. Each scenario provides a given line that sets up the test. Next, we define a series of events (when) and the expected results (then). Pretty amazing stuff, right?

Well, the downside to all this power is that RSpec stories can be a bit complicated to set up correctly, and thus they are a topic that currently is intended for advanced developers. Setting up story runner tests is too complicated for our purposes in a foundation book, so we'll focus instead on the other set of tests within RSpec—the spec framework, which will actually be a far more useful tool for you. However, if after learning the spec framework, you want to keep going and learn the story framework, I highly recommend getting the Peepcode screencast on "Rpsec User Stories" that's available at http://peepcode.com/products/rspec-user-stories.

RSpec specs

As we discussed earlier, if we were using the default Test::Unit framework that's included with Rails, the natural flow of testing is that we tend to write tests for each method within our application. The downfall with this is that our tests then begin to simply represent our code and not the requirements of the application (i.e., our tests become focused on our implementation and not the purpose of our code).

Using RSpec, we move away from that temptation as our emphasis moves towards writing specifications (or specs) rather than simply writing tests. These specs serve to replace the implementation specific tests that we used to write and are much clearer, far more readable, and less coupled to our specific code. At its simplest definition, a spec can be thought of as merely a description of all the various behaviors that we can expect from an object given different conditions.

The best way to understand what I mean is to see some actual specs, so let's look at a few sample ones. Imagine that we wanted to write a Pirate spec from our pirates application a few chapters back.

We might specify on a piece of paper (or traditionally on a note card) the following specification for a pirate:

```
A new pirate
  should be required to provide a name
```

We could write that out as a pair of specs like so:

```
describe Pirate do
  it "should be valid with a name" do
    @pirate = Pirate.new(:name => 'Jack Sparrow')
    @pirate.should be_valid
  end

  it "should require a name" do
    @pirate = Pirate.new
    @pirate.should_not be_valid
    @pirate.should have(1).error_on(:name)
  end
end
```

Let's take a look at that specification's code. At its top level, we create a description block using the keyword describe. A description can be stated as an object (as we did here listing the Pirate object):

```
describe Pirate do
```

Alternatively, we could also have passed it a string like so:

```
describe "Captain Jack Sparrow" do
```

or even a combination of the two:

```
describe Pirate, "named Captain Jack Sparrow" do
```

Just for kicks and grins (and to show you pending specs), if I were to combine those three descriptions into a single spec, it would look like this:

```
describe Pirate do
  it "should be valid" do
    @pirate = Pirate.new(:name => 'Jack Sparrow')
    @pirate.should be_valid
  end

  it "should require a name" do
    @pirate = Pirate.new
    @pirate.should_not be_valid
    @pirate.should have(1).error_on(:name)
  end
end

describe "Captain Jack Sparrow" do
  it "should be valid"
end

describe Pirate, " named Captain Jack Sparrow" do
  it "should be valid"
end
```

We could then run our specs from the command line with a rake spec command, or if you're using TextMate, you can run the specs from your editor and see HTML output, as shown in Figure 10-2.

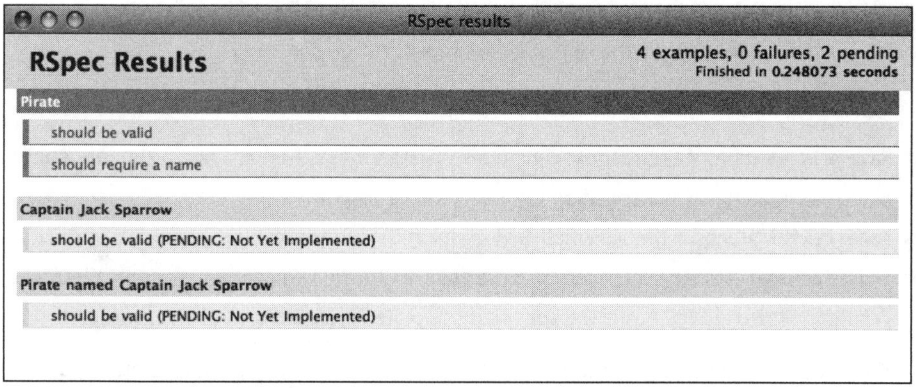

Figure 10-2. HTML output of a spec showing the different description blocks

You can see the various ways that those description blocks are displayed in that output. Now, once we're in a describe block, the tests that we write are called examples, each preceded with a special method named it (which simply represents the object we're testing). Each call to the it method takes a string as an object that represents what we're wanting to test in this example.

You saw in our earlier examples that we created a simple example to ensure that we were able to create a Pirate when we provided a name like so:

```
it "should be valid" do
  @pirate = Pirate.new(:name => 'Jack Sparrow')
  @pirate.should be_valid
end
```

But did you also notice the *uber* coolness that happened when we created an example yet didn't pass it a block in our extra describe examples? When those tests were executed, they came back as pending or not yet implemented examples! How cool is that? That means we can easily create a whole list of specifications into our test files and get immediate feedback as to our progress at implementing each of them as we add code to make each pass.

Matchers

You probably also noticed that in order for us to test our pirate in our previous spec example, we used lines like @pirate.should be_valid. In fact, when we're using RSpec, all of our expectations will typically fall into the pattern of saying that some object or attribute should or should_not and then have some form of a matcher afterward. In that example, we're using a matcher by the name of be_valid, which as the name implies, simply checks that our object is valid and has no errors. In addition to be_valid, RSpec includes a fairly significant number of premade matchers for our use in testing, including these:

- be_close: Matches if the actual value is within a specified range of the expected
- have_at_least, have_at_most, and have_exactly: Matches using expressions like >=, <=, or ==
- raise_error: Matches if any error is raised
- respond_to: Matches if the object responds to the methods passed to it
- be_true, be_false, be_nil: Matches on equality to true, false, or nil
- be_a_kind_of: Matches if the object class is equal to the specified class

We also have a nice set of matchers that are specific to Rails testing that includes these:

- have_rjs: Matches if the response includes RJS statements that replace or update content
- have_tag: Matches if the specified tag exists in the response
- have_text: Matches if the specified text exists in the response
- redirect_to: Matches if the response is a redirect to the URL, action, or controller/action
- render_template: Matches if the specified template is rendered by the response

More information about these and the rest of the matchers available with RSpec are available in the official API document at http://rspec.info/. It is also possible to create your own custom matchers in addition to the ones provided with the plug-ins.

All right, enough theory—let's move on to the basics of building a few specs of your own. The first step to doing that though is to install RSpec into your application.

As a simple example, let's reopen our plugins application from the previous chapter and add a few RSpec tests to it.

> *It will be a little more work for us to add RSpec specs to an existing application, rather than starting the application and building our specs and code together, but it'll be good enough for a simple introduction to how we can test our applications.*

Installing RSpec

RSpec is available in two flavors. There's a version that we can install systemwide as a Ruby gem using a simple sudo gem install rspec command, but this version is really intended for more general-use Ruby programming and not for Rails. To use RSpec with Rails, the preferred method is to install RSpec as a plug-in. To install the plug-in, we'll install both the RSpec plug-in (which provides our basic RSpec functionality, just like the gem) and the RSpec on Rails plug-in that adds a number of Rails-specific enhancements:

```
ruby script/plugin install http://rspec.rubyforge.org/svn/tags/➥
CURRENT/rspec
```

```
ruby script/plugin install http://rspec.rubyforge.org/svn/tags/➥
CURRENT/rspec_on_rails
```

Once these RSpec plug-ins are installed into our plugins application, we can use a generator that was added by the RSpec plug-ins to create our initial spec folders:

```
ruby script/generate rspec
        create  spec
        create  spec/spec_helper.rb
        create  spec/spec.opts
        create  previous_failures.txt
        create  script/spec_server
        create  script/spec
```

Besides this generator, those plug-ins also installed a number of other useful things into our application, including a number of other generators that we can use to create our models, controllers, and so forth, along with the necessary spec files for each of them. To view the installed generators, you can just run ruby script/generate without any additional parameters to see some help information and a list of all installed generators:

```
ruby script/generate
```

```
Usage: script/generate generator [options] [args]
```

```
Rails Info:
    -v, --version            Show the Rails version number and quit.
    -h, --help               Show this help message and quit.

General Options:
    -p, --pretend            Run but do not make any changes.
    -f, --force              Overwrite files that already exist.
    -s, --skip               Skip files that already exist.
    -q, --quiet              Suppress normal output.
    -t, --backtrace          Debugging: show backtrace on errors.
    -c, --svn                Modify files with subversion.

Installed Generators
  Plugins: rspec, rspec_controller, rspec_model, rspec_scaffold
  User: extjs
  Builtin: controller, integration_test, mailer, migration, model,
           observer, plugin, resource, scaffold, scaffold_resource,
           session_migration, web_service
```

You can see that in our list of installed generators, there are now generators installed by the plug-ins named rspec (which we just used) as well as rspec_controller, rspec_model, and rspec_scaffold. These new generators work the same as our normal model, controller, and scaffold generators with the addition that they also build some basic spec files for the resource that's being generated. When we're working in a test-first manner, we would always use these rspec_* generators instead of the normal ones.

The RSpec plug-ins also added a large number of new rake tasks to our plugins application; we can see just the RSpec tasks by running rake -T spec at the command line:

rake -T spec

```
rake spec                        # Run all specs in spec directory
rake spec:clobber_rcov           # Remove rcov products for rcov
rake spec:controllers            # Run the specs under spec/controllers
rake spec:db:fixtures:load       # Load fixtures (from spec/fixtures) into..
rake spec:doc                    # Print Specdoc for all specs (excl
rake spec:helpers                # Run the specs under spec/helpers
rake spec:lib                    # Run the specs under spec/lib
rake spec:models                 # Run the specs under spec/models
rake spec:plugin_doc             # Print Specdoc for all plugin specs
rake spec:plugins                # Run the specs under vendor/plugins
rake spec:plugins:rspec_on_rails # Run the examples for rspec_on_rai
rake spec:rcov                   # Run all specs in spec directory w
rake spec:server:restart         # reload spec_server.
rake spec:server:start           # start spec_server.
rake spec:server:stop            # stop spec_server.
rake spec:translate              # Translate/upgrade specs using the
rake spec:views                  # Run the specs under spec/views
```

The most important task in that list is the rake spec task, which we use to run all of our existing specs. If you go ahead and run that task now, you'll see that it reports, well, nothing because we haven't created any specs yet.

To fix that, we'll first need to manually create a few subdirectories within the /spec directory to hold our different specs. Normally, these directories would be created for us when we ran the rspec_* generators, but since we're trying to go back and add these specs onto an existing application, we'll need to create the folders manually. Within /spec, create three new directories named controllers, models, and views. Afterward, the content of your /spec directory should look like Figure 10-3.

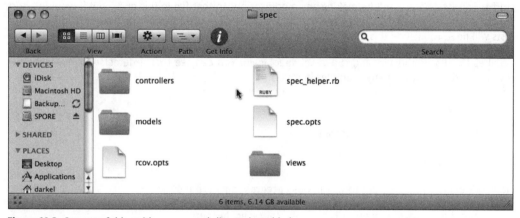

Figure 10-3. Our spec folder with our new subdirectories added

Now that we have RSpec installed into our application and we've created the appropriate places to add our specs, let's add a few to get a feel for it.

Adding model specs

As you recall, the first model we created in our plugins application was the Category model, which we used to build the categories that each plug-in could be associated to. Looking at /app/models/category.rb, we can see that the current implementation of our model looks like this:

```ruby
class Category < ActiveRecord::Base
  validates_presence_of :name
  validates_length_of :name, :within => 2..30
  has_many :plugins
end
```

If we were to try and put this into a specification, we might have written it out like this:

```
A category
  should have a name
  should have a name that's at least 2 characters
  should have a name that's less than 30 characters
  should have plugins associated with it
```

Let's go through the process of creating some specs for this model and to make it slightly more interesting (and to get a feel for the test first process)—go ahead and comment out or remove the validation and association methods from the Comment model—that way, we can actually see the Red-Green-Refactor process in action. To convert our specification into a test for RSpec, we'll first need to create a file to hold our examples. Create a new file named category_spec.rb in /spec/models, and place the following line of code in it:

```
require File.dirname(__FILE__) + '/../spec_helper'
```

This line simply includes the spec_helper.rb file from /spec, which contains some basic configuration stuff for our tests. We won't be making any modifications to that file in this book, but it wouldn't hurt for you to read through that file to see the defaults that have been set for you. In fact, all of our spec tests will need to include this file.

Go ahead and save this file, and run rake spec again. You can see that it detects our new spec file (even though there aren't any examples in it yet):

```
rake spec

Finished in 0.012287 seconds

0 examples, 0 failures
```

Now let's define what we want to test in our category_spec.rb file:

```
require File.dirname(__FILE__) + '/../spec_helper'

describe Category do
end
```

And then we'll go back and add some pending examples to the description:

```
require File.dirname(__FILE__) + '/../spec_helper'

describe Category do
  it "should have a name"

  it "should have a name that's at least 2 characters"

  it "should have a name that's less than 30 characters"

  it "should have plugins associated with it"

end
```

Now that we have some examples, if you go back and run our rake spec task again, you can see that our examples are there and listed as pending:

```
rake spec

PPPP

Pending:
Category should have plugins associated with it (Not Yet Implemented)
Category should have a name that's less than 30 characters (Not Yet ➥
Implemented)
Category should have a name that's at least 2 characters (Not Yet ➥
Implemented)
Category should have a name (Not Yet Implemented)

Finished in 0.229728 seconds

4 examples, 0 failures, 4 pending
```

Or if your text editor will run the specs, you can run your specs from there and get a nice HTML-formatted version like the one I get from TextMate on the Mac (see Figure 10-4).

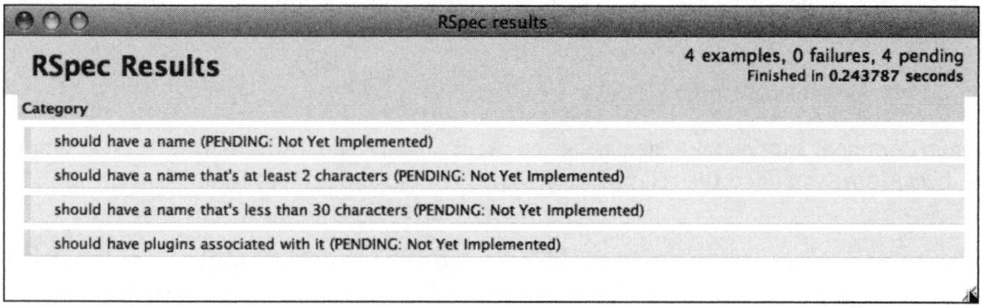

Figure 10-4. Pending examples for our Category model

For the rest of this chapter, I'll be displaying the HTML-formatted test results, but the information will be the same as the ones you're getting if you're simply running the rake spec command line task.

Let's go ahead and implement our first example for testing that a category must have a name. To do that, we simply need to create a new category without providing a name, and then test that the resulting object is not valid (i.e., an error was raised on it). Our example code should look like this:

```
it "should have a name" do
  @category = Category.new
  @category.should_not be_valid
end
```

Running our specs gives us the expected failure shown in Figure 10-5.

267

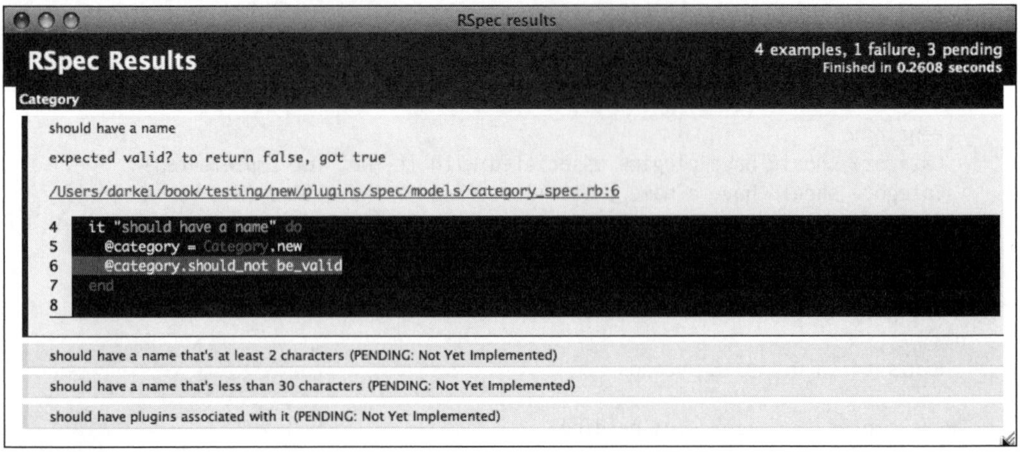

Figure 10-5. Our first spec has gone red to indicate a failure.

The easiest way to make this pass is to simply add some code to our Category model that will raise an error if a name is not provided. Therefore, go ahead and uncomment the following line from /app/models/category.rb:

```
validates_presence_of :name
```

Save your Comment model, and then rerun our specs again. You'll see that our first example now passes, because we've added the relevant code back into our model (see Figure 10-6).

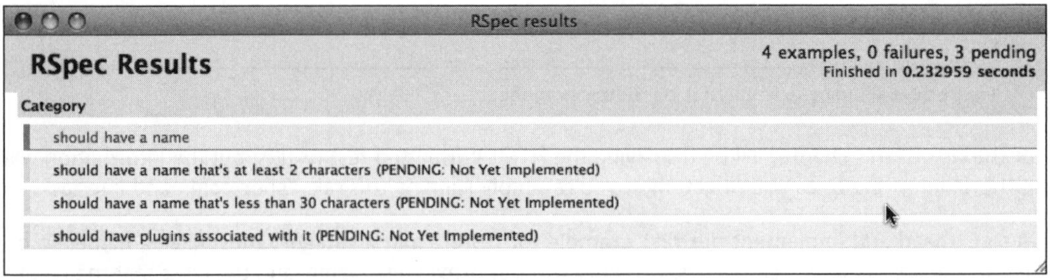

Figure 10-6. Our spec is back to green.

Now, let's go on to our second and third examples (since they are just flip-sides of the same coin). For these, we want to create some categories that have names that are too short and too long and ensure that they are invalid as well:

```
it "should have a name that's at least 2 characters" do
  @category = Category.new(:name => "a")
  @category.should_not be_valid
end
```

```
    it "should have a name that's less than 30 characters" do
      @category = Category.new(:name => "I am a crazy long name that ➥
  should fail")
      @category.should_not be_valid
    end
```

Once you add these two specs, our tests should once again fail until we go back to our Category model and uncomment the validates_length_of :name, :within => 2..30 line. Our model should now look like this:

```
    class Category < ActiveRecord::Base
      validates_presence_of :name
      validates_length_of :name, :within => 2..30
      # has_many :plugins
    end
```

Once you uncomment that line and rerun the tests, you'll see that we're back to green once again. See, I told you that writing specs is pretty easy, didn't I?

The last spec that we need to write for our Category model is the one to indicate that we have set up an association from this model to the Plugin model. The best approach for speccing this out is a subject that is often debated. Some even argue that we shouldn't write specs for association logic, since that's a core part of the Rails framework and thus we should be able to simply trust that it will work as advertised.

I personally fall a bit more into the middle of the road in the discussion, preferring to write a bare minimum spec of the functionality, merely to ensure that it is there but avoid testing the specifics of how it should work:

```
    it "should have plugins associated with it" do
      @category = Category.new(:name => 'Sample Category')
      @category.should have(:no).plugins
      @category.plugins.build(:name => 'Test', :description => 'Test', ➥
                                          :url => 'www.test.com')
      @category.should have(1).plugin
    end
```

For these purposes, I write a spec that first ensures that after we created a new Category, it had no plug-ins associated to it. Then I simply create a new plug-in on top of my new category with the build method and test again that I now have one plug-in associated. Running this test will currently fail, as you can see in Figure 10-7, due to the fact that the plugins method is undefined (you should recall that it's the association that adds that method).

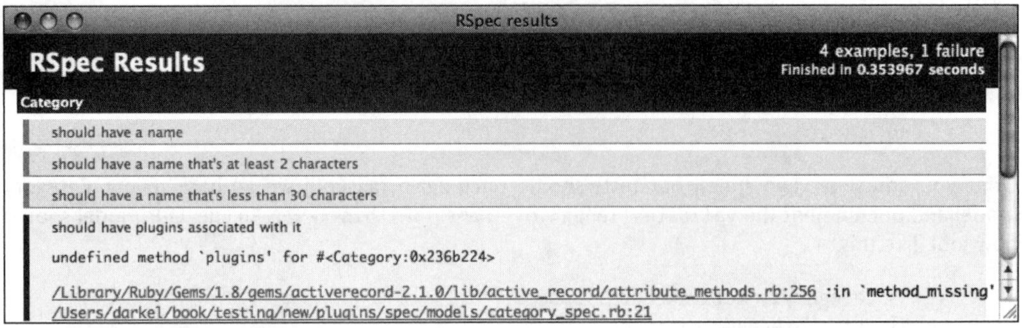

Figure 10-7. Testing for our association methods with a failing test

We make this test pass by simply adding our association logic back to the Category model. Afterward, our Category model should look like this:

```
class Category < ActiveRecord::Base
  validates_presence_of :name
  validates_length_of :name, :within => 2..30
  has_many :plugins
end
```

And running our tests again confirms that they are now passing once again (see Figure 10-8).

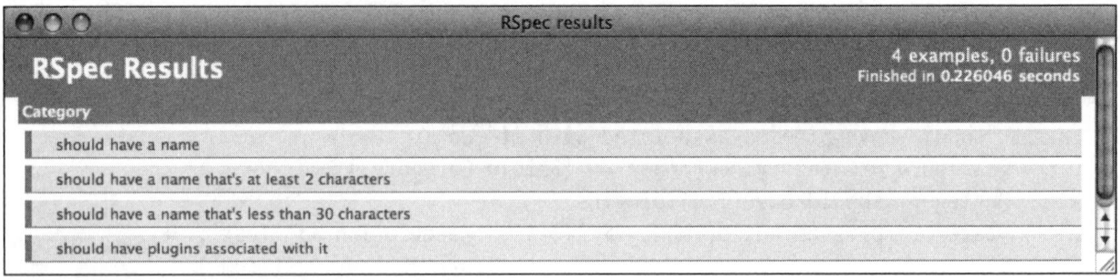

Figure 10-8. All our specs are passing.

We're at a good point for our model specs, as we've now tested each line of code in our Category model. Our final category_spec.rb looks like this:

```
require File.dirname(__FILE__) + '/../spec_helper'

describe Category do
  it "should have a name" do
    @category = Category.new
    @category.should_not be_valid
  end

  it "should have a name that's at least 2 characters" do
    @category = Category.new(:name => "a")
```

```
    @category.should_not be_valid
  end

  it "should have a name that's less than 30 characters" do
    @category = Category.new(:name => "I am a crazy long name that ➥
should fail")
    @category.should_not be_valid
  end

  it "should have plugins associated with it" do
    @category = Category.new(:name => 'Sample Category')
    @category.should have(:no).plugins
    @category.plugins.build(:name => 'Test', :description => 'Test',➥
                                    :url => 'www.test.com')
    @category.should have(1).plugins
  end
end
```

Things are good, but they could always be better. Before we move on to looking at how we can use RSpec to test our controllers and our views, let's look at a couple of ways that we can improve our current model spec.

Adding a before block to DRY up our specs

The first thing we can do to improve our specs is to eliminate duplication from each of our examples. The easiest way to do that is to take advantage of a feature within our specs of creating a before block that contains code that will be common to all tests. A before block in our specs is much like a before_filter in our controllers in that it allows us to define a block of code that will be executed before each example is run.

You'll notice that in our current spec examples, we start out each one by first creating a category. Let's add a before block that sets up a standard @category variable for all of our examples:

```
require File.dirname(__FILE__) + '/../spec_helper'

describe Category do

  before do
    @category = Category.new(:name => 'Sample Category')
  end

  it "should have a name" do
  (excerpted)
```

You can see that all we're doing is moving that simple @category create to a common section that will be used for each example within this description. Although we're not using it here, RSpec also supports the creation of an after block that can be used if we have a need to tear down an example as well.

If you're really observant, you might have noticed that the @category we've created in our before block is a valid Category, but many of the examples we created previously were dependent on having an invalid Category, such as having a Category with a name that was too long. To get around this, we'll obviously need to modify each of those examples slightly, so our category_spec.rb will look like this after our modifications:

```ruby
require File.dirname(__FILE__) + '/../spec_helper'

describe Category do

  before(:each) do
    @category = Category.new(:name => 'Sample Category')
  end

  it "should have a name" do
    @category.name = ''
    @category.should_not be_valid
  end

  it "should have a name that's at least 2 characters" do
    @category.name = "a"
    @category.should_not be_valid
  end

  it "should have a name that's less than 30 characters" do
    @category.name = "I am a crazy long name that should fail"
    @category.should_not be_valid
  end

  it "should have plugins associated with it" do
    @category.should have(:no).plugins
    @category.plugins.build(:name => 'Test', :description => 'Test',
                                    :url => 'www.test.com')
    @category.should have(1).plugin
  end
end
```

In our preceding examples, we create a single @category variable in the before block. Then in each of our examples, you can see that we can simply adjust the values associated with that @category to make them suitable.

You can see how using a before block can be a nice feature for keeping our tests DRY. In this example, we only moved a single line of code to the before block, but you can easily imagine a more complicated set-up for each test being extracted to this shared block.

Removing redundancy

The next enhancement we want to perform here is actually more of a cleanup of our model than a modification to our spec tests. If you notice our current validation logic in the Category model, you can see that we have two sets of validations on the name attribute. We ensure that the name attribute isn't blank and that it's length is between 2 and 30 characters. However, this introduces a minor problem to our validations in that it's possible for one error to trigger errors from two validation rules. To see that, let's add some more specs to our examples:

```
describe Category do

  before(:each) do
    @category = Category.new(:name => 'Sample Category')
  end

  it "should have a name" do
    @category.name = ''
    @category.should_not be_valid
    @category.should have(1).error_on(:name)
  end

  it "should have a name that's at least 2 characters" do
    @category.name = "a"
    @category.should_not be_valid
    @category.should have(1).error_on(:name)
  end

  it "should have a name that's less than 30 characters" do
    @category.name = "I am a crazy long name that should fail"
    @category.should_not be_valid
    @category.should have(1).error_on(:name)
  end

  it "should have plugins associated with it" do
    @category.should have(:no).plugins
    @category.plugins.build(:name => 'Test', :description => 'Test',
                                        :url => 'www.test.com')
    @category.should have(1).plugin
  end
end
```

For all of our validation examples, we simply added a test to ensure that only one error was raised on each. Running the specs gives us the result that you can see in Figure 10-9.

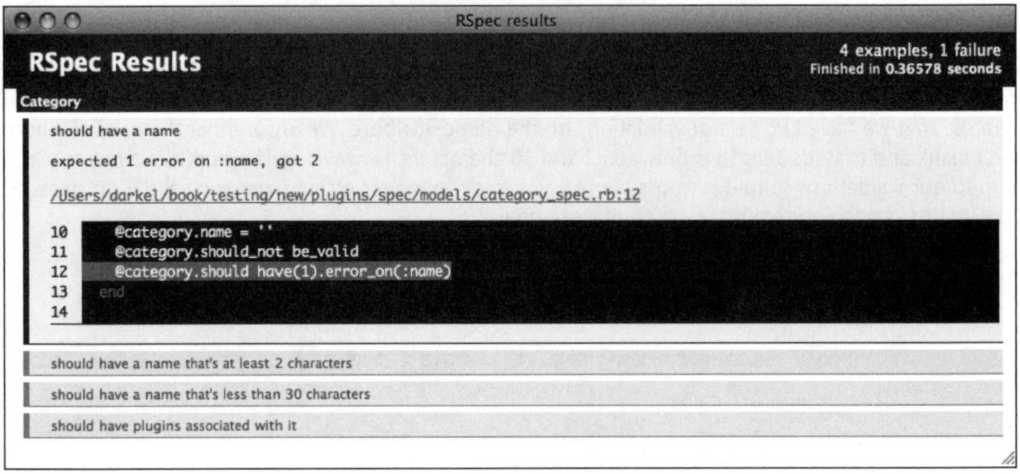

Figure 10-9. RSpec tests showing a problem with our validations

Here, our validation for the presence of a name attribute is actually getting two errors, which makes sense when you really think about it—if a plug-in is submitted without a name, it's also less than two characters. In fact, if we remove the validates_presence_of method call from our model, we leave our model looking like this:

```
class Category < ActiveRecord::Base
  # validates_presence_of :name
  validates_length_of :name, :within => 2..30
  has_many :plugins
end
```

You'll see that rerunning our tests gives us the passing result shown in Figure 10-10.

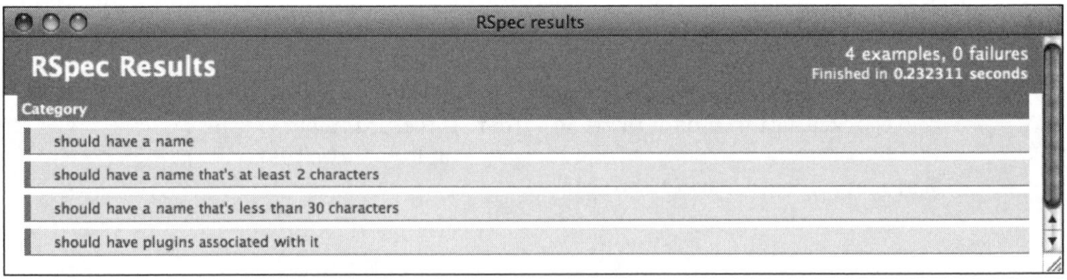

Figure 10-10. Specs pass after removing an unnecessary validation

Obviously, our other validation was unnecessary because if there was no name it would fail our length validation as well, and our specs have proven that we have lost no functionality with its removal. So we can feel confident that we've done the right thing.

Adding controller specs

The next area of testing with RSpec that we'll look at is how to build RSpec tests for the code in our controllers. You'll recall from our previous discussions of controllers and views that the two are very tightly bound together. So much so, in fact, that the standard Rails tests have no means for testing the two separately; instead, testing of both is done in the functional tests. However, using RSpec, the default is to test controllers in isolation from our views. Personally, I find it preferable to test controllers and views separately, so you don't have to worry about your controller tests failing just because you make minor changes to your views. However, if you want to override this feature, you can by adding the method integrate_views to your controller specs.

Mocking models

In addition to isolating our view tests from our controller tests, we also want to ensure that when we're writing specs for our controllers, we're focused solely on testing the code in the controllers. Maintaining this focus can be difficult at times, though, because of the fact that controllers are also going to be constantly touching our models. The challenge, of course, is figuring out how to test the controller code to find or create the Plugins model, without actually touching the data in the database. The answer is to utilize RSpec's mocking and stubbing features to bypass the need to touch the database.

Mocks are essentially imitation objects that we can use to simulate our models and validate what interactions they took part in. Anytime we want to test controller code that uses our Plugin or Category models, we create mocks of those models. Creating a mock is incredibly easy and is simply a matter of adding a method call to the mock method. So we could create a simple mock of our Plugin model like this:

```
@plugin = mock('Plugin')
```

Stubs are another form of imitation, but rather than imitating an object, they allow us to simulate methods by replacing them with canned responses. In the preceding example, we specified that the @plugin variable should be used to imitate the Plugin model. To use this mock within our application, we would need to stub the new method of the Plugin model so that when it's called, it returns our mock object instead of a real Plugin object. Doing so looks like this:

```
Plugin.stub!(:new).and_return(@plugin)
```

With this stub in place, any calls to Plugin.new would return our @plugin mock object instead of an ActiveRecord object.

> *One important note, though, is that creating a mock is, in essence, creating a form of contract with your tests: you're promising that this fake method will be called. In fact, creating a mock for a method that's never called in your spec will cause your spec to fail.*

Of course, since we're using RSpec with Rails, most of our mocks and stubs are going to be of ActiveRecord objects. This could be a little burdensome, as there are a standard set of internal methods in ActiveRecord objects that are often called implicitly as we interact with the object such as id (to return the ID of the object), new_record? (to determine if it's an existing record or a newly created one), and several others. In order for our mocks of an ActiveRecord object to work correctly, we would also need to stub out all these internal methods.

Or we could just use a specialized version of the mock that the RSpec on Rails plug-in gives us named mock_model, which wraps our standard mock method with a predefined set of default stubs configured for ActiveRecord objects. Converting our previous mock to a mock_model would be as simple as changing its code to use mock_model instead:

```
@plugin = mock_model(Plugin)
```

You'll be using the mock_model method extensively as we test controller actions. In fact, let's see how we use mocking as we build out some basic specs for our plugins controller.

To begin with, we'll first need to create a new spec file in /spec/controllers that has the same name as our controller and is appended with _spec.rb. Create a new file named plugins_controller_spec.rb in /spec/controllers, and within it, place our require to the spec_helper.rb (just as we did before with the model specs):

```
require File.dirname(__FILE__) + '/../spec_helper'
```

With this basic configuration in place, we can build specs for a pair of our controller actions.

Testing the index action

The first action we'll spec out for our examples is the index action, which as you should recall simply pulls a list of all available plug-ins from the database and then renders the index.html.erb template to display them (for our examples in this chapter, we'll ignore testing the XML-formatted responses of our controller actions). The code for this action lives in /app/controllers/plugins_controller.rb and looks like this:

```
def index
    @plugins = Plugin.find(:all)

    respond_to do |format|
      format.html # index.html.erb
      format.xml  { render :xml => @plugins }
    end
  end
```

To write a spec for this action, we'll first need to create a describe block that details what we're testing for:

```
describe PluginsController, " GET to /plugins" do
end
```

As you can see here, because we're dealing with RESTful routing for these actions, I prefer to write my descriptions listing the HTTP method that is used to access this action and the URL that would be accessed. However, it's important to remember that these descriptions are really for your own benefit, so if you prefer to describe the test as something like "testing index action," that's perfectly acceptable as well.

Now that we have our description block started, it's simply a matter of creating a few examples that describe what we expect from this controller action:

```
describe PluginsController, " GET to /plugins" do
  it "should be successful"

  it "should find a list of all plugins"

  it "should assign the list of plugins for the view"

  it "should render the index template"
end
```

For my examples, I broke down my expectations into a few key things that I want to test for. First, I expect that simply calling this action doesn't return an error, so I created an expectation that it "should be successful" to capture that. Next, I want to test that the code is going to gather a list of all plug-ins, so I created an expectation that it "should find a list of all plugins". Besides just gathering that collection of plug-ins, I want to ensure that the code has made that collection available to the view by assigning it to an instance variable, so I created an expectation that it "should assign the list of plugins for the view". Finally, I want to ensure that this code is rendering the correct display template, so I added an expectation that it "should render the index template". If you look through the code in our controller action, you should see that these expectations pretty much match up with what we can see the code doing.

Since we want to isolate these controller tests from touching our database, it makes sense that we'll need to mock our Plugin model, and since we're going to want this mocked object available to all of our examples, we'll place the creation of this mock in a before block. In addition, looking at the code in our controller, we can see that we're calling the find method on the Plugin model, so we'll also need to stub that method as well.

```
describe PluginsController, " GET to /plugins" do

  before do
    @plugin = mock_model(Plugin)
    Plugin.stub!(:find).and_return([@plugin])
  end

  it "should be successful"

  it "should find a list of all plugins"

  it "should assign the list of plugins for the view"

  it "should render the index template"
end
```

In the code we added, we used the mock_model method to mock out our Plugin ActiveRecord model, and we created a stub for the find method on the Plugin model and set it to return our Plugin mock instead. Running our specs now gives us the result that you can see in Figure 10-11.

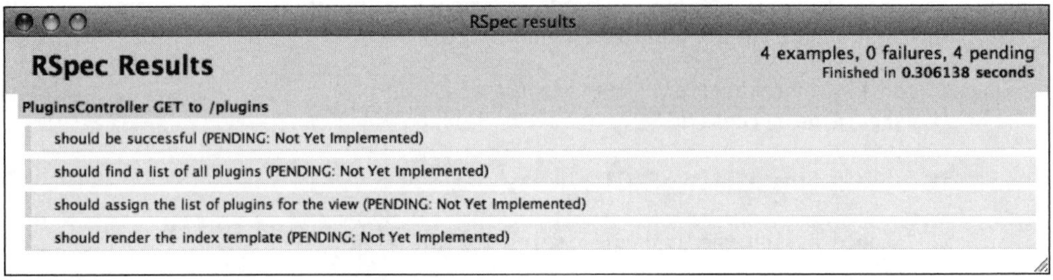

Figure 10-11. Pending specification for our index action

We'll start by fleshing out our most basic expectation—that calling our action should result in success and not error. To retrieve a controller action in RSpec, we have methods available to us named get and post that simulate an HTTP request. The get method is the one we want here, and we'd use it in this example like so:

```
it "should be successful" do
  get :index
  response.should be_success
end
```

Here, we simulated a GET request to the index action in our plugins controller and then set an expectation that the response of this action should return a success (technically, this equated to ensuring that the response returned an HTTP response of 200 OK). You can run our specs now and see that this example is now passing.

Our next expectation is to test that we are doing a database search for all available plug-ins within this action. In our before block, we created a stub for this find method, but here in our test is where we actually ensure that it was called. We can also ensure that our find method was called in the way that we expected (with the :all parameter) and that it returns the response that we want:

```
it "should find a list of all plugins" do
  Plugin.should_receive(:find).with(:all).and_return([@plugin])
  get :index
end
```

Pretty easy stuff, huh? Obviously, there is a small adjustment period as you pick up these various matches, but you should be able to see that once you do, the tests that we're writing are extremely clear, easy to read, and quite simply describe exactly what we expect in an almost natural language. Running our specs again at this point gives us the result shown in Figure 10-12.

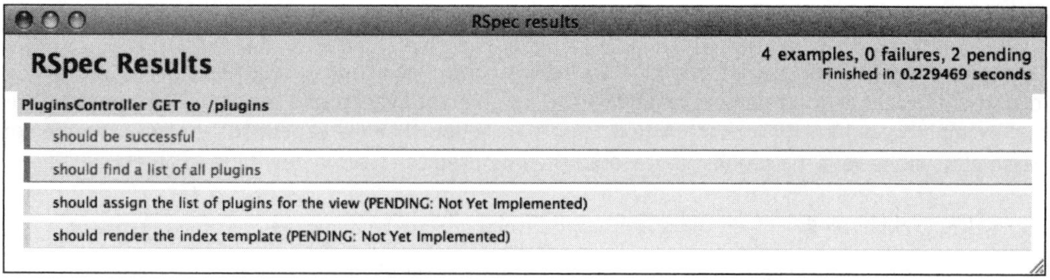

Figure 10-12. Halfway done with the specs for our index action

Let's see what it looks like to finish out the remainder of our examples for this action:

```
describe PluginsController, " GET to /plugins" do

  before do
    @plugin = mock_model(Plugin)
    Plugin.stub!(:find).and_return([@plugin])
  end

  it "should be successful" do
    get :index
    response.should be_success
  end

  it "should find a list of all plugins" do
    Plugin.should_receive(:find).with(:all).and_return(@plugin)
    get :index
  end

  it "should assign the list of plugins for the view" do
    get :index
    assigns[:plugins].should == [@plugin]
  end

  it "should render the index template" do
    get :index
    response.should render_template('index')
  end
end
```

Our final two examples followed the same pattern: in both we used our get method to once again retrieve the index action, and we set a simple expectation for each. For the first example, we checked that the @plugin object that was mocked earlier had been assigned to the @plugins instance variable. In the second example, we simply tested that our action rendered the index template using the render_template matcher.

Testing the create action

To round things out for our introduction to testing controller actions using RSpec, let's also take a look at a different action that uses an HTTP POST to access it instead of a simple GET. The most obvious example would be the create action, as it's an action that we expect to receive a number of parameters along with the request that would then be used to create a new plug-in object.

To do this we'll create a new describe block within our spec like so:

```
require File.dirname(__FILE__) + '/../spec_helper'

describe PluginsController, " GET to /plugins" do

  before do
    @plugin = mock_model(Plugin)
    Plugin.stub!(:find).and_return([@plugin])
  end

  it "should be successful" do
    get :index
    response.should be_success
  end

  it "should find a list of all plugins" do
    Plugin.should_receive(:find).with(:all).and_return(@plugin)
    get :index
  end

  it "should assign the list of plugins for the view" do
    get :index
    assigns[:plugins].should == [@plugin]
  end

  it "should render the index template" do
    get :index
    response.should render_template('index')
  end
end

describe PluginsController, " POST to /plugins " do
end
```

Here, I've added a new describe block that's intended to test what happens when we receive a POST request to the /plugins URL, which, of course, is routing to the create action in our controller. To move into writing our specific examples, let's first take another look at the code in our create action to get a better feel for what we want to test:

```ruby
def create
  @plugin = Plugin.new(params[:plugin])
  respond_to do |format|
    if @plugin.save
      flash[:notice] = 'Plugin was successfully created.'
      format.html { redirect_to(@plugin) }
      format.xml  { render :xml => @plugin, :status => :created,➥
                                            :location => @plugin }
    else
      format.html { render :action => "new" }
      format.xml  { render :xml => @plugin.errors,
                          :status => :unprocessable_entity }
    end
  end
end
```

Once again, we'll be concentrating only on the HTML format response for our introduction, yet even with that limitation, you can see that we have an interesting new problem with this action—multiple responses. In the action, we attempt to create a new plugin object based on the parameters that we receive in the request. If we successfully create the plugin object, we want to redirect the request to the show action. However if the save fails, we want to redisplay the new template. The way I like to handle this type of situation is to describe both paths as subdescriptions like so:

```ruby
describe PluginsController, " POST to /plugins " do
  describe "success path" do
  end

  describe "failure path" do
  end
end
```

This allows us to test both possible paths in a nice logical process. Let's use our understanding of what we expect to occur in each of these paths to add some pending expectations to each:

```ruby
describe PluginsController, " POST to /plugins " do
  describe "success path" do
    it "should create a new plugin"

    it "should redirect to the show template"

    it "should populate the flash message"
  end

  describe "failure path" do
    it "should redisplay the new template"

    it "should not populate the flash message"
  end
end
```

Running our controller specs at this point gives us the result that you can see in Figure 10-13.

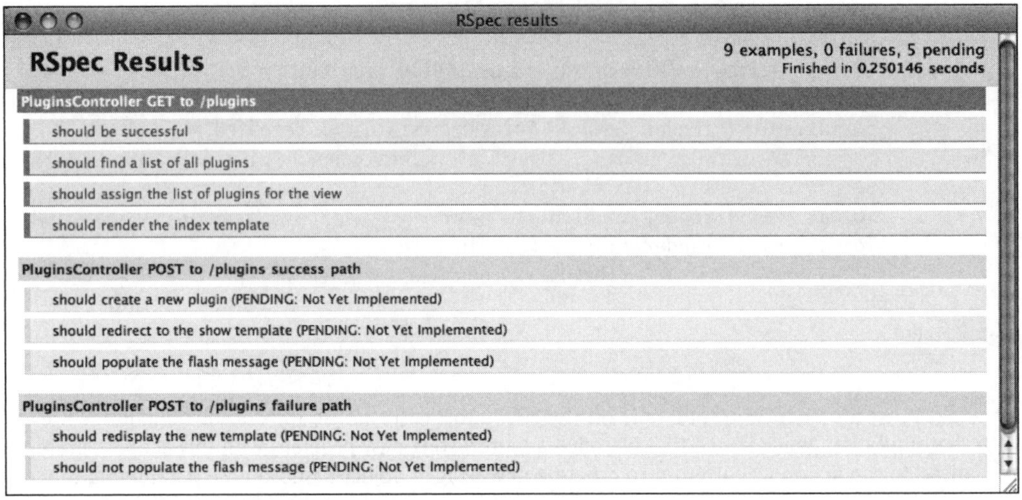

Figure 10-13. Added pending examples to our create action specs

We can see that whichever path we go down, we're going to need to have a mock of our Plugin model again, and since we're creating a new plug-in this time, we'll want to stub the new method this time. Let's add that mocking code into a before block that can be shared between both paths like so:

```
describe PluginsController, " POST to /plugins " do
  before do
    @plugin = mock_model(Plugin)
    Plugin.stub!(:new).and_return(@plugin)
  end

  describe "success path" do
    it "should create a new plugin"

    it "should redirect to the show template"

    it "should populate the flash message"
  end

  describe "failure path" do
    it "should redisplay the new template"

    it "should not populate the flash message"
  end
end
```

The next thing that we want to tackle is setting up each of our individual paths to return true or false for the save method when each of the examples is run. There are a few approaches we could take to do this. For one, we could explicitly set some valid or invalid parameters that would be received into the action like so:

```ruby
describe PluginsController, " POST to /plugins " do
  before do
    @plugin = mock_model(Plugin)
    Plugin.stub!(:new).and_return(@plugin)
    @params = {
      :name => 'Test',
      :description => 'My Test Plugin',
      :url => 'www.test.com',
      :category_id => '1'
    }
  end
```

In this way, we're able to explicitly test the controller action in exactly the same way that it would be used in real life. However, I don't like this approach, because it introduces more complexity into our tests and removes some of our isolation. Instead, I prefer to explicitly set the expectation for what should be returned in both paths. We can do that by adding an additional before block to each path:

```ruby
describe PluginsController, " POST to /plugins " do
  before do
    @plugin = mock_model(Plugin)
    Plugin.stub!(:new).and_return(@plugin)
  end

  describe "success path" do
    before do
      @plugin.should_receive(:save).and_return(true)
    end

    it "should create a new plugin"

    it "should redirect to the show template"

    it "should populate the flash message"
  end

  describe "failure path" do
    before do
      @plugin.should_receive(:save).and_return(false)
    end

    it "should redisplay the new template"

    it "should not populate the flash message"
  end
end
```

Here, we set the expectation for each of our paths to determine what the response should be when save is called. In this way, we're able to test each path easily, cleanly, and most importantly in isolation. Let's see what it looks like when we fill out our examples for the success path:

```ruby
describe "success path" do
  before do
    @plugin.should_receive(:save).and_return(true)
  end

  it "should create a new plugin" do
    Plugin.should_receive(:new).with(anything()).and_return(@plugin)
    post :create
  end

  it "should redirect to the show template" do
    post :create
    response.should redirect_to(plugin_url(@plugin))
  end

  it "should populate the flash message" do
    post :create
    flash[:notice].should == ('Plugin was successfully created.')
  end
end
```

After running our specs, you can see in Figure 10-14 that they are now passing.

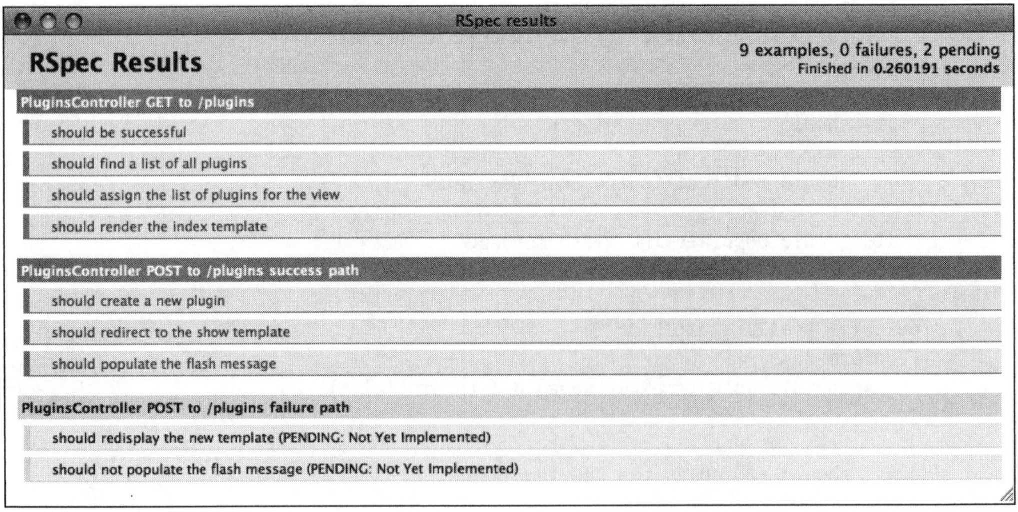

Figure 10-14. Our success path is now passing all specs.

To ensure in our example that our create action should create a new plugin object, we set the expectation on the new method to ensure that it would return our @plugin mock using the line Plugin.should_receive(:new).with(anything()).and_return(@plugin). Next, to simulate a request, we used the post method to the create action with the post :create method.

To test that we redirected to the show action, we set the expectation on our response that it would redirect to the named path plugin_url using the line response.should redirect_to(plugin_url(@plugin)).

Finally, we also set a quick test for our flash notice that it was populated with the correct message that we expected using the line flash[:notice].should eql('Plugin was successfully created.').

And with that, we've finished building our specs for the success path. From here, we can move onto testing the failure path, which should be just as easy. We'll simply make a call to post :create in each example and set some basic expectations using the predefined matchers to test the result.

In fact, it's so easy, we'll just skip ahead again to the finished result:

```
describe "failure path" do
    before do
      @plugin.should_receive(:save).and_return(false)
    end

    it "should redisplay the new template" do
      post :create
      response.should render_template(:new)
    end

    it "should not populate the flash message" do
      post :create
      flash[:notice].should be_nil
    end
  end
```

We simply test that the new template was redisplayed by using the render_template matcher in the line response.should render_template(:new). Our second example simply tested that the flash notice was never set by ensuring that it is equal to nil with a should be_nil matcher.

With these simple tests, we can run our controller specs one final time and see that all of our expectations have now been met (see Figure 10-15).

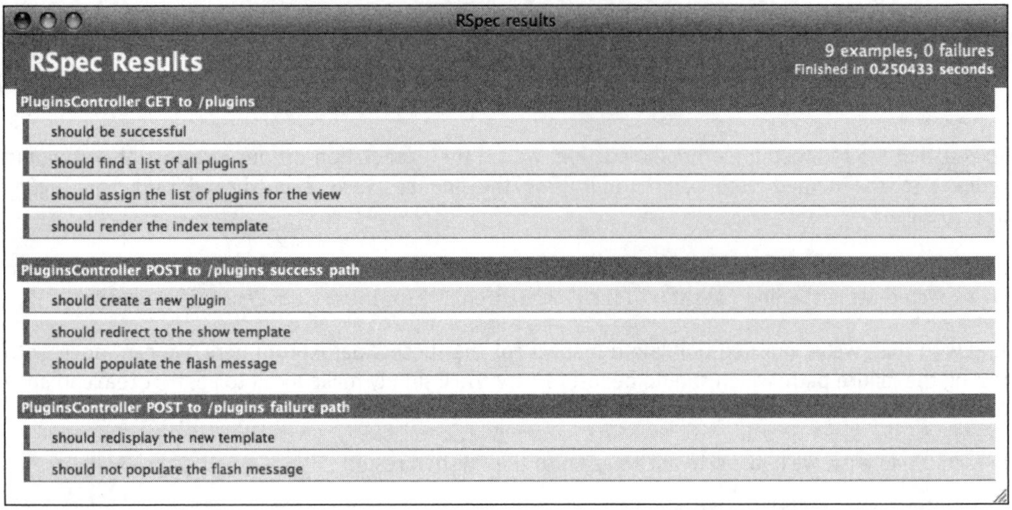

Figure 10-15. Our controller specs are completed.

Adding view specs

The final elements that we'll want to test from RSpec are our view templates themselves. Since we're testing our views completely separately from our controllers, we don't have to worry about things such as how the request was routed to the view or ensuring that the data was set properly. Instead, we can focus on view-specific items such as verifying that certain tags exist within the output.

In fact, our view specs will typically follow a common pattern of us setting up sample data elements for the template, calling the render method, and passing that method the specific template that we want rendered, which will look like this:

```
render "plugins/index"
```

Afterward, we'll set our view expectations, typically testing that the response from our render has certain tags using commands like this:

```
response.should have_tag("div#welcome")
```

Believe it or not, that's really all there is to testing your views. With view testing, focusing only on the most key elements in your layout that are critical to its success is usually best. If you try to get too granular and test every element in the page, you'll find that your tests become too brittle and have to be updated with every minor change to the templates.

Let's put together a simple test of the index action for our plug-ins as a good sample for testing views using RSpec. Our first step will be to create our spec file to hold our view specs. Within your /specs directory, you'll see that we currently have a views subdirectory. Here, we simply need to create a new subdirectory named plugins within this folder so that our path is /specs/views/plugins/ (you might note that this is similar to the layout we have in /app). Within this new plugins directory, we'll create a spec file for the index template and name it index.html.erb_spec.rb. And as you should expect, this file should start with a require statement for our spec_helper that looks like this: require File.dirname(__FILE__) + '/../../spec_helper'.

Now that we're within our spec, we can write a simple describe block for our spec:

```
require File.dirname(__FILE__) + '/../../spec_helper'

describe "/plugins/index.html.erb" do
end
```

Yeah, I know, it's not the most creative of descriptions, but it gets the message across of what I'm testing. Now, this template has a fairly simple task—just display a list of plug-ins. To test it, all we really need to do is build up some sample data with at least two plug-in objects and test that the template displayed both.

As you might expect, our first task to create the sample data will use a pair of mock_model calls within a before block:

```
before do
    plugin_1 = mock_model(Plugin)
    plugin_1.should_receive(:name).and_return("Test 1")
    plugin_1.should_receive(:rating).twice.and_return("5")
    plugin_1.should_receive(:description).and_return("MyText")

    plugin_2 = mock_model(Plugin)
    plugin_2.should_receive(:name).and_return("Test 2")
    plugin_2.should_receive(:rating).twice.and_return("5")
    plugin_2.should_receive(:description).and_return("MyText")

    assigns[:plugins] = [plugin_1, plugin_2]
end
```

You can see in this example that what we've done is create two mocks of the Plugin model, each with some sample expectations for what methods should be called and what they should return. You'll notice that I've indicated that the rating method should be called twice in the template. This is because, in the template, we call it once to set the CSS Star display value and once again to output the current rating as text. Other than possible confusion because that method is being called twice, you should be able to easily follow through the rest of the spec code—all the way down to the last line where we take our two mocks and use the assigns method to make them available in the examples as @plugins.

With our sample data set up, we can add a simple spec to test that our template is displaying our sample data:

```
require File.dirname(__FILE__) + '/../../spec_helper'

describe "/plugins/index.html.erb" do

  before do
    plugin_1 = mock_model(Plugin)
    plugin_1.should_receive(:name).and_return("Test 1")
```

```
            plugin_1.should_receive(:rating).twice.and_return("5")
            plugin_1.should_receive(:description).and_return("MyText")

            plugin_2 = mock_model(Plugin)
            plugin_2.should_receive(:name).and_return("Test 2")
            plugin_2.should_receive(:rating).twice.and_return("5")
            plugin_2.should_receive(:description).and_return("MyText")

            assigns[:plugins] = [plugin_1, plugin_2]
        end

    it "should dispay our plugin names" do
        render "/plugins/index.html.erb"
        response.should have_tag("dt", "Test 1")
        response.should have_tag("dt", "Test 2")
    end
  end
```

Our example simply renders the template and uses the have_tag matcher to verify that both of our plug-ins showed up in the response. Running this spec gives us the result shown in Figure 10-16.

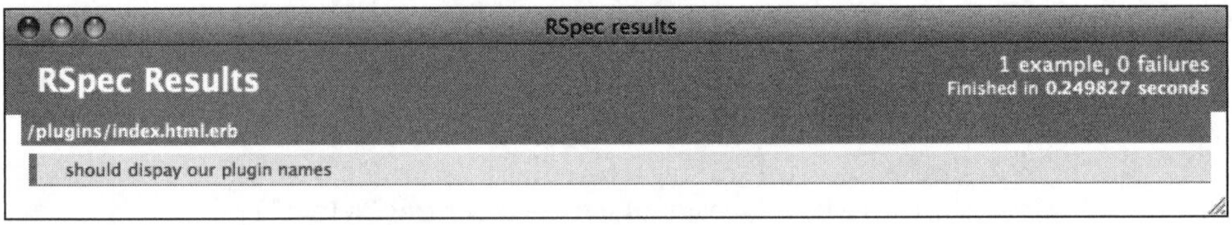

Figure 10-16. The results of our view specs

Summary

Even in our short little introduction to testing with RSpec, I trust that you've been able to get a taste for the power that automated testing can provide us for ensuring that our applications are working the way they should. Not only that, you've gained a deep appreciation for the power that RSpec provides in "getting the words right" for testing.

It's a powerful thing when you can provide your clients with very readable and nicely formatted HTML documentation (just like the page shown in Figure 10-17) that details the information about how the application is working.

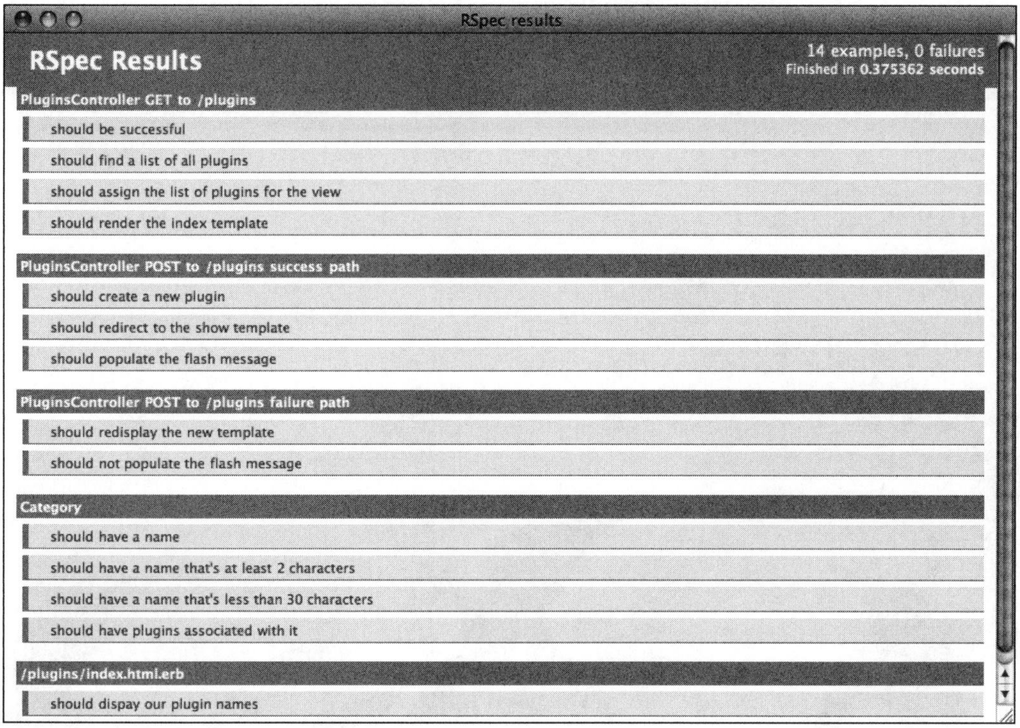

Figure 10-17. The complete output of all of our specs

Output like this helps us bridge the gap between our code and the business language of our clients: clients can read this and identify gaps in our specs or areas where we misunderstood the requirements.

In the next chapter, we're going to bring together everything that you've learned up to this point as we launch our first full application from scratch. You'll see how we take a project from initial idea to proof of concept and beyond into a full-fledged application. Buckle your seat belts—it's about to get even more fun than before.

Chapter 11

BUILDING A COMPLETE APPLICATION

Congratulations! We've completed our high-level tour of the basics of Rails applications. Over the course of the book so far you've learned how to use the following:

- The Rails command line generators to create Rails projects as well as to build your models, controllers, and so on
- ActiveRecord to connect your Rails application to your database
- Rails migrations to define and build your database structure over time
- ActiveRecord associations, named scopes, and custom methods to easily model complex relationships between your data structures
- Embedded Ruby to insert dynamic content into HTML templates
- Rails controllers to respond to your users' requests, interact with your models, and select the appropriate view
- The Rails routing system to build complex or friendly URL schemes for your application
- Code generation capabilities such as plug-ins and scaffolding that are available to you to jumpstart your applications or quickly add complex features.

We're now at a point where we can put all of that knowledge to work; you'll see how all those individual lessons work together as we build our own Rails application.

What we're going to build

For the sake of the book, I went back and forth as to what type of application we should build together. To be honest, I can often get frustrated by the many "beginner" books that are released that promise to teach you to build you own advanced web application like the next Twitter, Flickr, or Facebook. At surface level, those applications can seem to be very straightforward and simple, but they're just like an iceberg where only a mere one-tenth of the total volume is above water—and I felt that trivializing the complexity of those applications in a beginner's book is a disservice both to those applications and to you the reader.

Next, I considered pulling a sample application from the real-world client work that most of us do for our bread and butter. I looked at building web applications for many of the small businesses that I interact with for web development; however, those seemed to always either fall into the trap of being too boring due to mostly static pages, or they fell into the quagmire of requiring an e-commerce implementation (which would require a separate book of its own to cover correctly).

Of course, sometimes the best ideas come from real-life need, and thus we'll create a web application to meet a recent need that came up in my own life; our web application will combine enough functionality and dynamic content to tie together all the lessons you've learned thus far.

Here's what happened: I have a wonderful daughter who, since she was born, has had a special blanket and an extra special little teddy bear that she affectionately named Bear Bear. Well, sometime around the beginning of 2008, Bear Bear disappeared forever. We have no idea if he was left accidentally at a restaurant or store around town or if he was the victim of something more sinister, such as a bear-napping, but the end result was that we spent a lot of nights consoling a sad little girl who simply missed him. Even now, six months later, if she's reminded of him, her little eyes will well up with tears.

To help save other parents from having to endure such pain with their own children, we'll build a simple Rails application that can be used to help reunite children with missing toys that we'll name Lost Toys.

The sketch phase

Whenever I start a new application, I like to start first on a few blank sheets of paper. I jot down rough ideas, page layout sketches—anything I can to help me further define in my head of what I want to build before I start. So even though my sketches are going to look pretty horrible to you, I'll share them here so we can share in the process.

We're probably going to want some form of a static home page for this application, something simple that provides a little information about what the application is and the links necessary to navigate around the application. So I sketched out a series of ideas for how this might look, which you can see in Figure 11-1.

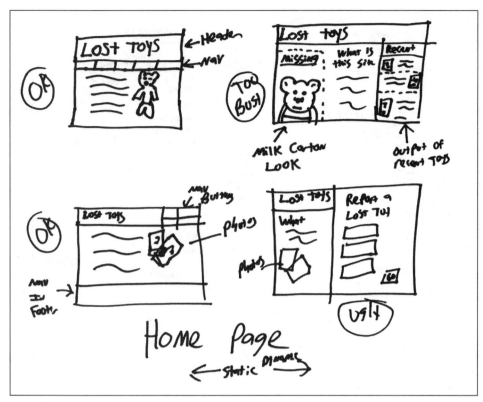

Figure 11-1. A rough sketch of our home page

Since the main focus of the application will be to allow parents to post about missing toys, including a description of the toy and a photograph, we'll need to have a form that they can use to do that. For extra good measure, we should also allow people to post about toys that they've found. In that way, businesses could post pictures online of the toys that were left in their establishments in the hopes of reuniting them with their owners. That changes the scope of our application a little bit, so it's good that we're thinking about these ideas now.

Finally, our application will need the ability to provide a list of the toys that are in the database and provide a detail page for each toy. These should be fairly standard fare for now, but we might want to think about providing some tools for our end users to allow them to search the lost toys directory a bit easier. So with those thoughts in my mind, I sketched the ideas that you can see in Figure 11-2.

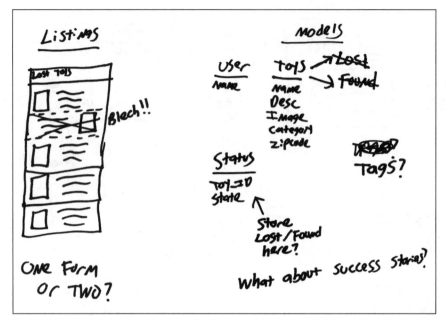

Figure 11-2. Rough sketches on the models and displaying our results

In that figure, you can see some of my ideas as I worked to determine what models would be needed and tried to see how they might relate to each other visually. In addition, I also sketched out a rough idea for how I would want the toy listing to display.

So with that simple premise in mind, let's get to the business of building this application in Rails.

Creating the Application

Our first step is to use the rails command to generate the application structure for our lost toys application in our project directory. Open a command line prompt wherever you want to create our new application, and create it like this:

```
rails lost_toys
      create
      create  app/controllers
      create  app/helpers
      create  app/models
      create  app/views/layouts
  --- output excerpted  ---
      create  doc/README_FOR_APP
      create  log/server.log
      create  log/production.log
      create  log/development.log
      create  log/test.log
```

Now that our application is created, we need to go ahead and change into this new directory:

```
cd lost_toys/
```

And I always like to start out by immediately removing the default index.html file from /public so it doesn't cause me any heartache later on, when it displays instead of the page I expected:

```
rm public/index.html
```

We'll go ahead and leave the database as a SQLite 3 database for now, so there's no need to modify the database.yml file in /config from its default settings.

A note about Git plug-ins

Remember way back in Chapter 1 where I talked about how one of the challenges of Rails development is in keeping up with the changes that can occur within the framework and the community? Well, we have a prime example of this occurrence right now.

You see, back when I first started writing this book, the majority of Rails developers were using a version control system by the name of Subversion. This meant that the majority of Rails plug-ins could be found across a wide variety of web sites around the Internet that were hosting Subversion repositories. Checking out the code from these repositories was a fairly trivial matter, since Mac and most Linux distributions automatically included a Subversion client, and Windows users could install one with very little fuss.

Subversion, however, was limited in that it was often quite difficult for developers to create experimental branches of their code to try out new ideas or to allow other developers the ability to merge their changes to the code into the main branch. For these reasons, many Rails developers began experimenting with some of the new distributed version control systems such as Bazaar, Mercurial, and Git.

> *What is a Distributed Version Control? According to Wikipedia, "distributed revision control takes a peer-to-peer approach, as opposed to the client-server approach of centralized systems. Rather than a single, central repository on which clients synchronize, each peer's working copy of the codebase is a bona-fide repository. Synchronization is conducted by exchanging patches (change-sets) from peer to peer."*

The Rails community expected to see developers migrate to one of these new distributed version control systems at some point, but it was the introduction of a new Git hosting solution named GitHub that really shook things up. See Figure 11-3.

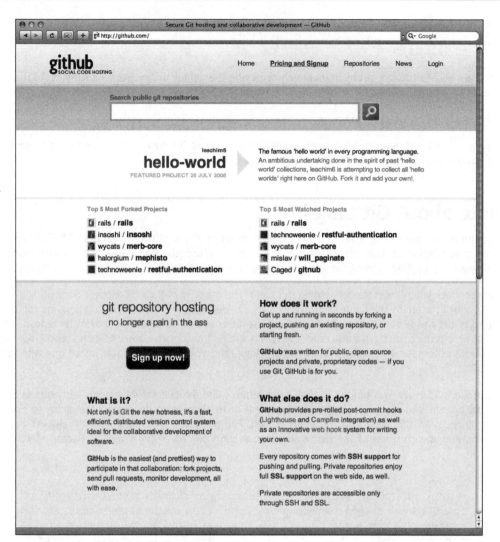

Figure 11-3. A screenshot of the GitHub homepage

GitHub changed the game by not only providing an easy system for developers to host the main branches of their Git repositories but by doing so in a way that added an almost social network feeling to the development community. Developers were hooked and quickly began moving many of their codebases to GitHub. Even the core team of Rails took notice and moved development of the Rails framework from their own Subversion repository out to GitHub.

This migration to Git has an unfortunate side effect for us: in order to easily obtain the most recent versions of most plug-ins that we would want to use, you'll need to have Git installed onto your development system. For our purposes, you won't need to learn how to use Git, merely have it installed.

The best resource I've found for Git can be found at http://git-scm.com/. On this site, you will not only find links to download the Git system onto each of the different operating system options, but you'll find a wealth of helpful information about Git: how to use it, as well as links to a number of excellent resources to gain more knowledge. Simply go to this web site, and use it to download and install the binary for your particular system.

Installing RSpec

Now that we have Git installed, we can use it to install the core RSpec plug-ins, so that we'll be able to test our application code as we're building it. Of course, writing out all the tests for an application like this while writing it would fill a whole book by itself, and you already have a number of examples from both the previous chapter and by using the rspec_scaffold command, so we'll be doing a simplified version of testing in this project.

While we will be doing some testing using RSpec in this project, we're not going to be very thorough at all, as our tests will be focused on the elements that are especially unique to our application. We'll trust that most standard Rails idioms and features are going to work without needing to be tested. So as we move through the project, when our code is the same as scaffold-generated code, we'll simply trust it. In the same manner, when we install a plug-in that already has a full test suite, we'll trust that it works as expected as well.

In this way, we'll be able to keep moving forward at a decent rate without getting bogged down in too much detail work; meanwhile, you'll still be gaining some benefit of additional knowledge of seeing RSpec applied to some custom situations.

Normally to install RSpec using Git, you would simply use the following commands:

```
script/plugin install git://github.com/dchelimsky/rspec.git
script/plugin install git://github.com/dchelimsky/rspec-rails.git
```

However, since those plug-ins are actively being developed, I didn't want to risk changes that occurred after this book's publication to cause you compatibility problems later, so I created forks of those projects under my own GitHub account that will be frozen to the versions that were used while I wrote this project. To install my forked version, you'll instead use the following commands from the root of our application:

```
ruby script/plugin install git://github.com/darkel/rspec.git
        removing: /Users/darkel/book/testing/lost_toys/vendor/plugins/➥
rspec/.git
        Initialized empty Git repository in /Users/darkel/book/testing/➥
lost_toys/vendor/plugins/rspec/.git/
    remote: Counting objects: 495, done.
    remote: Compressing objects: 100% (445/445), done.
    remote: Total 495 (delta 42), reused 301 (delta 17)
    Receiving objects: 100% (495/495), 311.17 KiB | 400 KiB/s, done.
    Resolving deltas: 100% (42/42), done.
```

```
ruby script/plugin install git://github.com/darkel/rspec-rails.git
        removing: /Users/darkel/book/testing/lost_toys/vendor/plugins/➥
rspec-rails/.git
        Initialized empty Git repository in /Users/darkel/book/testing➥
/lost_toys/vendor/plugins/rspec-rails/.git/
        remote: Counting objects: 197, done.
        remote: Compressing objects: 100% (153/153), done.
        remote: Total 197 (delta 11), reused 160 (delta 9)
        Receiving objects: 100% (197/197), 73.35 KiB, done.
        Resolving deltas: 100% (11/11), done.
```

With our RSpec plug-ins installed, we just need to use the included generator to build our initial spec directories with the following command:

```
ruby script/generate rspec
        create    lib/tasks/rspec.rake
        create    script/autospec
        create    script/spec
        create    script/spec_server
        create    spec
        create    spec/rcov.opts
        create    spec/spec.opts
        create    spec/spec_helper.rb
        create    stories
        create    stories/all.rb
        create    stories/helper.rb
```

With that, we're now ready to move onto building our application.

Installing a user registration system

One of the first challenges we have with our application is determining how we want to handle any sort of user registration and authentication. Obviously, we want to make the listings of lost and found toys accessible to the public without restriction, but what about the creation of new listings? On one hand, it would be ideal to not place any obstacles in front of our potential users and allow them to instantly post content into our application, but doing that would also open us up to a number of larger issues. For one, allowing anyone to post directly into our application would make us an easier target for spammers to use to post their own garbage into our application's listing. Now admittedly, spammers have gotten quite advanced in the tools that they use, and it's near impossible to block all of them. Even so, I'd rather not leave the door wide open for them to come in and set up shop. Second, leaving no restrictions on creating a post could cause us more support issues when a user contacts us wishing to update a listing that they created earlier.

For those reasons, we would be best served by adding at least some simple form of user authentication where we allow users to self-register into the application. Fortunately for us, we're not forced to build this system from scratch ourselves, the incredible Rails plug-in by the name of Restful Authentication makes it ridiculously easy to add a user registration and authentication system to an existing Rails application. The following sections provide a step-by-step guide to building our user registration system.

Step 1: Install the Restful Authentication plug-in

The Restful Authentication plug-in has also moved to GitHub, and to install it, we would normally run a simple install as follows:

```
ruby script/plugin install git://github.com/technoweenie/➥
restful-authentication.git
```

However, once again, to ensure that future changes don't break the instructions in this chapter, I've forked the current Restful Authentication plug-in, so our first step will be that you'll install my version into your application like so:

```
ruby script/plugin install git://github.com/darkel/➥
restful-authentication.git
```

Once the plug-in is installed, you'll see that it also outputs several pages of information about its use, and I highly recommend that you take the time to scroll back up and read through that (or if you want to be able to read it in a text editor or print it out, you'll find this same information in /vendor/plugins/restful-authentication/README). As you read through this document, there is some important information communicated inside it that I want to draw your attention to, such as the following section on installation:

```
Installation

This is a basic restful authentication generator for rails, taken from
acts as authenticated.  Currently it requires Rails 1.2.6 or above.
```

Step 2: Run the authenticated generator

Note that this plug-in hasn't actually enhanced our application yet. In fact, its purpose is simply to add a new generator to our application that we can now use to generate a user authentication system in our application. In addition, this plug-in is actually based on an older plug-in named Acts as Authenticated (both plug-ins were actually built by the same developer). The difference between the two, however, is that the Restful Authentication plug-in was built around the same REST principles that we've discussed throughout the book.

Immediately following the "Installation" quote is the usage information that we need to understand in order to use the generator command:

```
To use:

  ./script/generate authenticated user sessions \
    --include-activation \
    --stateful \
    --rspec \
    --skip-migration \
    --skip-routes \
    --old-passwords
```

299

* The first parameter specifies the model that gets created in signup
(typically a user or account model). A model with migration is
created, as well as a basic controller with the create method. You
probably want to say "User" here.

* The second parameter specifies the session controller name. This is
 the controller that handles the actual login/logout function on the
 site. (probably: "Session").

* --include-activation: Generates the code for a ActionMailer and its
 respective Activation Code through email.

* --stateful: Builds in support for acts_as_state_machine and generates
 activation code. (--stateful implies --include-activation). Based on
 the idea at http://www.vaporbase.com/postings/stateful_authentication.
 Passing --skip-migration will skip the user migration, and
 --skip-routes will skip resource generation -- both useful if you've
 already run this generator.

* --aasm: Works the same as stateful but uses the updated aasm gem

* --rspec: Generate RSpec tests and Stories in place of standard rails
 tests. This requires the "RSpec and RSpec-on-rails plugins":
 http://rspec.info/(make sure you "./script/generate rspec" after
 installing RSpec.) The rspec and story suite are much more thorough
 than the rails tests, and changes are unlikely to be backported.

* --old-passwords: Use the older password scheme
(see #COMPATIBILITY, above)

* --skip-migration: Don't generate a migration file for this model

* --skip-routes: Don't generate a resource line in config/routes.rb

As you can see, the generator is named authenticated and to this generator we need to pass the name of the model that we want to use for authentication (most likely, this will be named user) and the name of the controller that will be used to handle the login and logout functions (this should be called session). In addition to these two parameters, we also have a large pool of optional parameters that we can use to customize how the authentication system will work. For example, if we wanted the authentication system to send each of our users an e-mail with an activation code that they would use to verify and activate their accounts after signing up, we would add the --include-activation option onto our generator.

For our purposes though, we're going to keep our user authentication as simple as possible, so we won't be using any additional parameters except for the --rspec option. Using that option will ensure that the code that's created by the generator also includes a full suite of RSpec tests into our /spec directory. So we'll run the following command:

```
ruby script/generate authenticated user sessions --rspec
```

And you'll see that this one little command created quite a lot of stuff in our application. In fact, let's take a 50,000-foot view of everything that it created for us in the next section.

Step 3: Configure the database and models

We'll start by first looking at the default users database migration the previous command defined for us in /db/migrate that ends with create_users.rb:

```ruby
class CreateUsers < ActiveRecord::Migration
  def self.up
    create_table "users", :force => true do |t|
      t.column :login,                      :string, :limit => 40
      t.column :name,                       :string, :limit => 100,➡
 :default => '', :null => true
      t.column :email,                      :string, :limit => 100
      t.column :crypted_password,           :string, :limit => 40
      t.column :salt,                       :string, :limit => 40
      t.column :created_at,                 :datetime
      t.column :updated_at,                 :datetime
      t.column :remember_token,             :string, :limit => 40
      t.column :remember_token_expires_at,  :datetime


    end
    add_index :users, :login, :unique => true
  end

  def self.down
    drop_table "users"
  end
end
```

There you can see that it will create a "users" table that stores information about each user such as a login name, a full name, their email address, as well as a number of fields related to their password. If we wanted to customize this, we could simply add additional fields to this migration before we ran it; however, I think that these fields will be fine for now. So let's go ahead and close this file and create the "users" table in our database by running the migration.

```
rake db:migrate
== 20080719172723 CreateUsers: migrating ============================
-- create_table("users", {:force=>true})
   -> 0.0033s
-- add_index(:users, :login, {:unique=>true})
   -> 0.0020s
== 20080719172723 CreateUsers: migrated (0.0056s) ==================
```

But what good would a new table do if we didn't have a model to interact with it? If we look in /app/models, we'll find that the generator also created a User model for us in user.rb. The model currently looks like this:

```
require 'digest/sha1'

class User < ActiveRecord::Base
  include Authentication
  include Authentication::ByPassword
  include Authentication::ByCookieToken

  validates_presence_of     :login
  validates_length_of       :login,    :within => 3..40
  validates_uniqueness_of   :login,    :case_sensitive => false
  validates_format_of       :login,    :with => RE_LOGIN_OK,
                            :message => MSG_LOGIN_BAD

  validates_format_of       :name,     :with => RE_NAME_OK,
                            :message => MSG_NAME_BAD,
                            :allow_nil => true
  validates_length_of       :name,     :maximum => 100

  validates_presence_of     :email
  validates_length_of       :email,    :within => 6..100 #r@a.wk
  validates_uniqueness_of   :email,    :case_sensitive => false
  validates_format_of       :email,    :with => RE_EMAIL_OK,
                            :message => MSG_EMAIL_BAD


  # HACK HACK HACK -- how to do attr_accessible from here?
  # prevents a user from submitting a crafted form that bypasses
  # activation anything else you want your user to change should be
  # added here.
  attr_accessible :login, :email, :name, :password, ➥
:password_confirmation


  # Authenticates a user by their login name and unencrypted password.
  # Returns the user or nil.
  #
  # uff.  this is really an authorization, not authentication routine.
  # We really need a Dispatch Chain here or something.
  # This will also let us return a human error message.
  #
  def self.authenticate(login, password)
    u = find_by_login(login) # need to get the salt
    u && u.authenticated?(password) ? u : nil
  end

  protected

end
```

The User model seems fairly straightforward at first glance. It has a number of validations defined on the model data and has a large number of comments around a few custom methods. However, there's a lot more to this code than just what we see here—as you'll notice that the first few lines are include calls:

```
include Authentication
include Authentication::ByPassword
include Authentication::ByCookieToken
```

You see, to go along with this User model is a large set of Authentication code that is kept in separate modules. You can find these modules in the /vendor/plugins/restful-authentication/lib/. While reviewing all that authentication code would go beyond our purposes in this book, it won't hurt for you to poke around in those files sometime to get a better feel for how the plumbing of our authentication system works.

Step 4: Configure our controllers

Going back to our application code, the next thing we'll look at are the controllers and views that the generator created. If you look in /app/controllers, you'll see that we have two new controllers: sessions_controller.rb and users_controller.rb. The Users controller is used for the creation of new user accounts and currently has two actions: a new action, which will display the form that you can see in Figure 11-4, and a create action, which receives a submitted user sign-up form and creates the user.

Figure 11-4. The default sign-up form from Restful Authentication

We also have a sessions controller (/app/controllers/sessions_controller.rb) whose responsibility is for logging users in and out of our application (essentially creating and destroying their sessions, hence the name). This controller has three actions: a new action, which displays the form in Figure 11-5; a create action, which creates a new session on a successful form submission from the new action; and a destroy action, which logs out a user by removing the session.

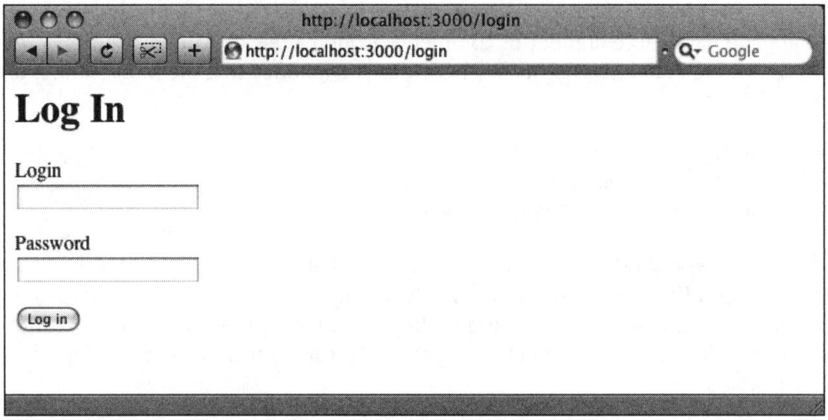

Figure 11-5. The default login form created by the Restful Authentication plug-in

We do need to make one change to our controllers though. If we look at the first few lines of our sessions and users controllers, we'll see these instructions:

```
# Be sure to include AuthenticationSystem in Application
# Controller instead
  include AuthenticatedSystem
```

Currently, our controllers are including a library from /lib named authenticated_system.rb. However, we want this functionality to be available to all controllers, so we need to remove these lines from the sessions and users controller and instead place the include AuthenticatedSystem call into the application controller (/app/controllers/application.rb). So afterward, our application controller should look like this:

```
class ApplicationController < ActionController::Base
  helper :all # include all helpers, all the time
  include AuthenticatedSystem
-- excerpt --
```

Step 5: Verify our routes

Finally, the RESTful Authentication generator also added a number of routes to our application that you can see in /config/routes.rb:

```
ActionController::Routing::Routes.draw do |map|
  map.logout '/logout', :controller => 'sessions', :action => 'destroy'
  map.login '/login', :controller => 'sessions', :action => 'new'
  map.register '/register', :controller => 'users', :action => 'create'
  map.signup '/signup', :controller => 'users', :action => 'new'
  map.resources :users
  map.resource :session
-- excerpt --
```

You can see that it added a pair of map.resources routes for our users and session controllers, as well as a number of custom named routes to make common actions like login, logout, and so on easier.

Step 6: Run specs to confirm everything is working correctly

Before we move on from here, for good measure, let's go ahead and run our specs to ensure that everything is working the way it's intended to up to this point. You can use rake spec at the command line. If your code editor supports running specs as Textmate does, you can see the HTML output in Figure 11-6.

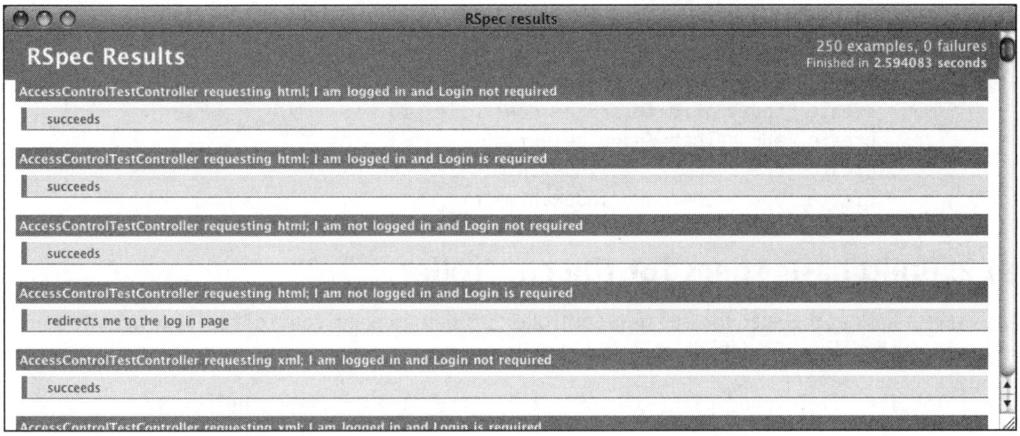

Figure 11-6. Running our RSpec shows that the Restful Authentication is working.

Seeing 250 passing examples is a beautiful thing, isn't it? Well, don't get too used to that, because we still have a lot of functionality to add to our application.

Creating a home page

One of the common challenges when building web applications is the need for static pages (i.e., pages that have no dynamic content) throughout the application. Examples of static pages we typically need are things such as home pages, "about us" pages, and "contact us" pages. For our application, we'd like to have a simple home page that basically explains what the site is and provides links to the dynamic content sections of the site.

At its simplest, your entire page (including layout code) could be generated as a single static HTML file and stored within the /public subdirectory of your Rails application. However, that can cause you heartaches later on if you need to make changes to the overall structure of the site as you would then have to go back and hand-edit all these files as well.

A more common approach is to generate a simple controller that lists each of these pages as actions, and that's the approach that we'll start with for our application. So let's create a controller for doing just that.

Step 1: Create a controller for our home page

We'll name this controller Page, and for good measure, we'll also have the generator create an empty index action and view template at the same time:

```
ruby script/generate rspec_controller Page index
        exists  app/controllers/
        exists  app/helpers/
        create  app/views/page
        exists  spec/controllers/
        exists  spec/helpers/
        create  spec/views/page
        create  spec/controllers/page_controller_spec.rb
        create  spec/helpers/page_helper_spec.rb
        create  app/controllers/page_controller.rb
        create  app/helpers/page_helper.rb
        create  spec/views/page/index.html.erb_spec.rb
        create  app/views/page/index.html.erb
```

Step 2: Build basic specs for the controller

Let's take a look at the spec for our new controller; it's named page_controller_spec.rb and found in /spec/controllers. By default, it looks like this:

```
require File.expand_path(File.dirname(__FILE__) + '/../spec_helper')

describe PageController do

  #Delete these examples and add some real ones
  it "should use PageController" do
    controller.should be_an_instance_of(PageController)
  end


  describe "GET 'index'" do
    it "should be successful" do
      get 'index'
      response.should be_success
    end
  end
end
```

Currently, it just has two default tests: it tests that the controller is named correctly (with should be_an_instance_of) and it tests that when we request the page that it's successful. Those are simple enough, but let's slightly enhance these to test that we're rendering the correct template and that this page is rendered as the home page of our application. So our modified spec should look like this:

```
require File.expand_path(File.dirname(__FILE__) + '/../spec_helper')

describe PageController do

  it "should use PageController" do
    controller.should be_an_instance_of(PageController)
  end

  describe "GET 'index'" do
    it "should be successful" do
      get 'index'
      response.should be_success
      response.should render_template(:index)
    end

    it "should be the home page" do
      route_for(:controller => "page", :action => "index").should == ➥
"/"
    end
  end
end
```

If you try to run the specs now, you should get a failure from the spec testing that this page should be our home page (since we haven't configured that in our routes yet). Let's fix that, so we can get back to glorious green. Open up routes.rb in /config, and add a route for the root of our application:

```
ActionController::Routing::Routes.draw do |map|
  map.logout '/logout', :controller => 'sessions', :action => 'destroy'
  map.login '/login', :controller => 'sessions', :action => 'new'
  map.register '/register', :controller => 'users', :action => 'create'
  map.signup '/signup', :controller => 'users', :action => 'new'
  map.resources :users
  map.resource :session
  map.root :controller => 'page'

  map.connect ':controller/:action/:id'
  map.connect ':controller/:action/:id.:format'
end
```

So we've just set up our application's home page. Let's next round it all out with some HTML content to populate it.

Step 3: Creating a common layout

Looking at our initial sketch again for the home page, I've put together some pretty rough HTML that we'll use for our application. However, in order to use it, you'll need to download and look in the source archive for this book where I've included a set of style sheets and images that you'll need to copy into the appropriate directories in /public. Once you have those resources installed, we'll start by creating a new layout file named application.html.erb in /app/views/layouts. In this new file, place the following content:

```
<!DOCTYPE html PUBLIC "-//W3C//DTD XHTML 1.0 Transitional//EN"
  "http://www.w3.org/TR/xhtml1/DTD/xhtml1-transitional.dtd">
<head>
  <title>Lost Toys - Reuniting Children with Toys</title>
  <%= stylesheet_link_tag 'application' %>
</head>
<body>
  <div id="container">
    <div id="header">
      <div id="nav_container">
        <ul id="navigation">
          <li><%= link_to image_tag('home.png'), root_path %></li>
          <li><%= link_to image_tag('browse_toys.png'), '#' %></li>
          <li><%= link_to image_tag('lost_toy.png'), '#' %></li>
          <li><%= link_to image_tag('found_toy.png'), '#' %></li>
        </ul>
      </div>
      <div id="logo"><%= image_tag "logo.png" %></div>
    </div>
    <div id="main">
      <%= yield %>
    </div>

    <div id="footer">
      <%= render :partial => 'users/user_bar' %>
      <h1>About Lost Toys</h1>
      <p>This is a where our footer text will go</p>
    </div>
  </div>
</body>
</html>
```

Let's take a closer look at some of the components of that layout file. The first thing you'll notice is that we're using one of our helper files to load a custom CSS style sheet named application:

```
<%= stylesheet_link_tag 'application' %>
```

A few lines after that, we're building our main navigation for the application using a combination of the link_to and image_tag helpers. Currently, several of the links don't have a destination (we haven't built them yet), so we're setting the links to '#':

```
<li><%= link_to image_tag('home.png'), root_path %></li>
<li><%= link_to image_tag('browse_toys.png'), '#' %></li>
<li><%= link_to image_tag('lost_toy.png'), '#' %></li>
<li><%= link_to image_tag('found_toy.png'), '#' %></li>
```

Next, we're setting a logo using another image_tag helper:

```
<div id="logo"><%= image_tag "logo.png" %></div>
```

And we're yielding to the template within a div named main:

```
<div id="main">
  <%= yield %>
</div>
```

Finally, we're rendering a partial named user_bar that was added by the Restful Authentication plug-in:

```
<%= render :partial => 'users/user_bar' %>
```

There's actually a small problem with the version of this user_bar partial in the version of the Restful Authentication plug-in that we're using, as it's currently attempting to call a method that doesn't exist. So we need to make a small edit to this partial in order for it to work. Open _user_bar.html.erb in /app/views/users, and remove a few lines so that in the end it will look like this:

```
<% if logged_in? -%>
  <div id="user-bar-action">
    (<%= link_to "log out", logout_path, {:title => "Log out"}%>)
  </div>
<% else -%>
  <div id="user-bar-action">
    <%= link_to "Log in",  login_path, {:title => "Log in" } %> /
    <%= link_to "Sign up", signup_path,
                                {:title => "Create an account"} %>
  </div>
<% end -%>
```

Once you've saved these changes, go ahead and fire up your server using the script/server command, and open the application in a browser to be rewarded with a page like the one shown in Figure 11-7.

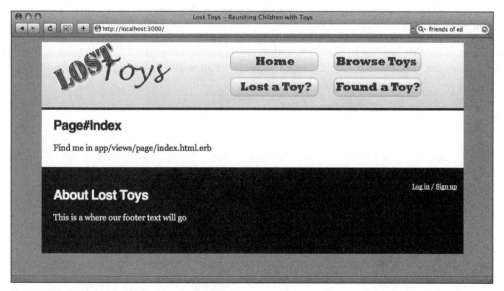

Figure 11-7. Our layout added to the application

Yeah, it's not the best-looking web site ever, but it'll do for an initial launch, and then I can bribe a more talented graphic designer to help me out.

Step 4: Create the home page

Currently, the home page is displaying the default text in the generated view template, but let's fix that now with some real content. Open /app/views/page/index.html.erb, and place the following content into it:

```
<h1>What is Lost Toys?</h1>
<div class="photo">
  <%= image_tag 'bear_bear.jpg', :id => 'bear_bear' %>
</div>
<p>Lost Toys is a web application that is designed to help reunite
    children with their most treasured bears, dolls, etc.</p>
<p>As with all great things - the idea for this site was born out of
 the pain of my own daughter losing her treasured teddy bear that
 had been with her from the time she was born until she was seven
years old.</p>
<p>As a parent, it's a horrible feeling to know that the one thing
   that would make your daughter happy is somewhere within your
   local area, possibly in the hands of someone who has no idea what
   to do with it.</p>
<p>It was because of this loss - that we came up with the idea of
   providing a simple web site that would allow people to post about
   lost and found toys in the hopes that at least one
   may be able to be reunited.</p>
<p>We provide this service completely free of charge.</p>
```

There's nothing special here that we need to pay special attention to—just some standard HTML content. After saving this content into the template, if we refresh our home page, you'll see the result shown in Figure 11-8.

With that simple change, we're complete with building the home page of our application. It's time now to turn our attention onto the dynamic needs of capturing and displaying lost toy information.

Figure 11-8. Our application's home page

Capturing lost toys

To capture information on lost toys, we'll obviously need to build a Toy model that we can use to store the data of our toy listings.

Step 1: Create a toy model

So what do we need to know about a lost (or found) toy? We'll start very simple by capturing some form of description of the toy and a status field that will be used to differentiate lost and found toys. In addition, since we want to enable one user to be able to post many toy listings, we should plan on there being a one-to-many relationship between users and toys and thus add a user_id field to our Toys model:

```
ruby script/generate rspec_model Toy description:text status:string ➥
user_id:integer
      exists  app/models/
      exists  spec/models/
      exists  spec/fixtures/
      create  app/models/toy.rb
      create  spec/models/toy_spec.rb
      create  spec/fixtures/toys.yml
      exists  db/migrate
      create  db/migrate/20080719221731_create_toys.rb
```

Let's go ahead and run our migration to add the toys table to our database, and then we'll start working on building the base specs for our Toy model:

```
rake db:migrate
== 20080719221731 CreateToys: migrating ===============================
-- create_table(:toys)
   -> 0.0035s
== 20080719221731 CreateToys: migrated (0.0037s) =====================
```

Now that we're dealing with database records, it's usually a good idea to go ahead and create the test database using the rake db:test:prepare command at the command line.

Step 2: Building the spec for our Toy model

Let's open the spec tests for our toys (/spec/models/toy_spec.rb), which currently looks like this:

```
require File.expand_path(File.dirname(__FILE__) + '/../spec_helper')

describe Toy do
  before(:each) do
    @valid_attributes = {
      :description => "value for description",
      :status => "value for status"
    }
  end

  it "should create a new instance given valid attributes" do
    Toy.create!(@valid_attributes)
  end
end
```

The sample spec that was provided builds a hash of valid attributes that it can then use in each of the specs. This approach can work and has the added benefit of also allowing you to create a hash of invalid attributes that you can also reuse. However, I'm not a big fan of simply building the hash and prefer instead to build my sample object in the before block and modify it in each of my examples (as we did in the last chapter). If you change this spec to that format instead, it should look like this instead:

```
require File.expand_path(File.dirname(__FILE__) + '/../spec_helper')

describe Toy do

  before(:each) do
    @toy = Toy.new(:description => "Lost Bear Bear", :status => "LOST")
  end

  it "should be valid with sample data" do
    @toy.should be_valid
  end
end
```

After we make these changes, we can run our spec again to ensure that we're still fine, as you can see in Figure 11-9.

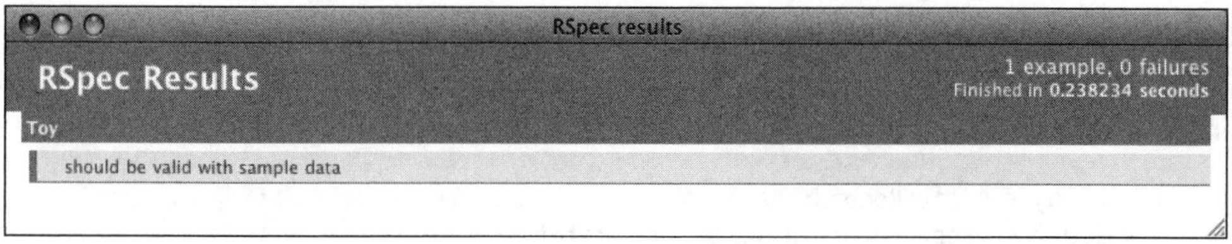

Figure 11-9. Our initial spec is good.

Everything's good so far, but let's add a few specs to further refine what sort of data we expect:

```
require File.expand_path(File.dirname(__FILE__) + '/../spec_helper')

describe Toy do

  before(:each) do
    @toy = Toy.new(:description => "Lost Bear Bear", :status => "LOST")
  end

  it "should be valid with sample data" do
    @toy.should be_valid
  end

  it "should require a description" do
    @toy.description = ''
    @toy.should_not be_valid
  end

  it "should require a status" do
    @toy.status = ''
    @toy.should_not be_valid
  end
```

```
    it "should require a status that's either LOST or FOUND" do
        @toy.status = 'Misc'
        @toy.should_not be_valid

        @toy.status = 'LOST'
        @toy.should be_valid

        @toy.status = 'FOUND'
        @toy.should be_valid
    end
end
```

Here, we've added three specs where we test that description and the status fields are not blank and that the status field contains the text either LOST or FOUND. Of course, all three of these specs are currently failing, as we haven't added any code yet to make them work. Let's fix that now.

Step 3: Adding validations

We can make the first couple specs pass with the simple addition of a validates_presence_of rule to our Toy model like so:

```
class Toy < ActiveRecord::Base
    validates_presence_of :description, :status
end
```

Sure enough, saving the changes to our model and rerunning our spec shows that we are on our way (see Figure 11-10).

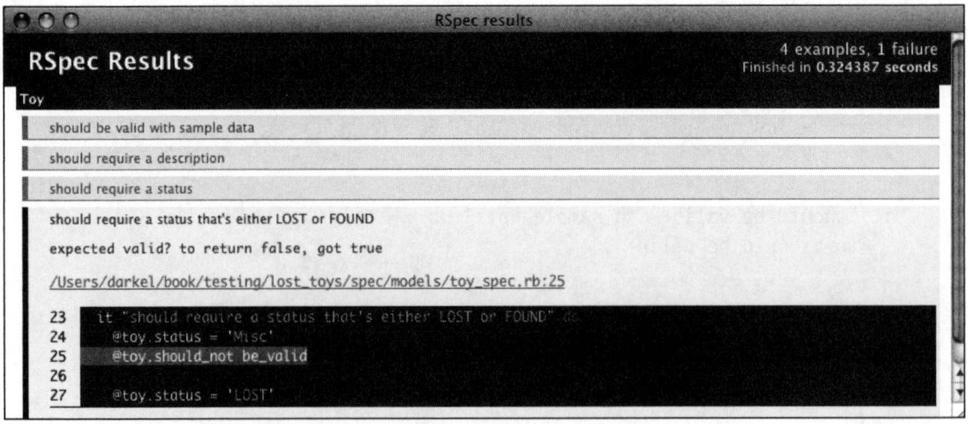

Figure 11-10. Only one spec left for our first pass at the Toy model

What we need to do is determine a way of ensuring that the allowable data in this field is always what we expect. An easy way to accomplish this would be to create a constant in our model that maintains the list of allowable statuses like so:

```
VALID_STATUSES = %w(LOST FOUND)
```

Next, we can use this constant in a validates_inclusion_of validation rule to ensure that the values are always right. Afterward, our Toy model (/app/models/toy.rb) will look like this:

```
class Toy < ActiveRecord::Base
  VALID_STATUSES = %w(LOST FOUND)

  validates_presence_of :description, :status
  validates_inclusion_of :status, :in => VALID_STATUSES
end
```

After saving our model, we can run our spec and see that we're back to all green (see Figure 11-11).

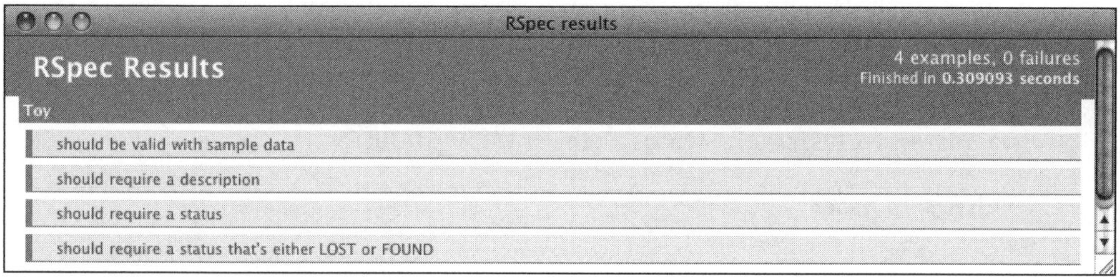

Figure 11-11. All of our specs are passing.

Step 4: Build associations

One thing we haven't done yet though is to add our relationships between the Toy and User models. We can do that easily through the addition of a simple has_many association to our User model (/app/models/user.rb):

```
require 'digest/sha1'

class User < ActiveRecord::Base
  include Authentication
  include Authentication::ByPassword
  include Authentication::ByCookieToken

  validates_presence_of    :login
  validates_length_of      :login,    :within => 3..40
  validates_uniqueness_of  :login,    :case_sensitive => false
  validates_format_of      :login,    :with => RE_LOGIN_OK,
                                      :message => MSG_LOGIN_BAD

  validates_format_of      :name,     :with => RE_NAME_OK,
                                      :message => MSG_NAME_BAD,
                                      :allow_nil => true
  validates_length_of      :name,     :maximum => 100
```

```
validates_presence_of      :email
validates_length_of        :email,    :within => 6..100
validates_uniqueness_of    :email,    :case_sensitive => false
validates_format_of        :email,    :with => RE_EMAIL_OK,
                                       :message => MSG_EMAIL_BAD
```

has_many :toys
-- excerpt --

We'll also set the reciprocal association from the Toy model (/app/models/toy.rb) back to the User model with a belongs_to association:

```
class Toy < ActiveRecord::Base
  VALID_STATUSES = %w(LOST FOUND)

  validates_presence_of :description, :status
  validates_inclusion_of :status, :in => VALID_STATUSES

  belongs_to :user
end
```

At this point, our Toy model is working about the way that we're expecting for this stage of development. However, it's not very useful without some controller actions and views to allow our users to be able to interact with it, so let's add those now.

Building the toys controller

We're going to build a toys controller to support the seven main CRUD actions that we've discussed previously, so in theory, we could simply build this as a scaffold. However, in my experience, the hassle of having to also modify the generated RSpec tests for a scaffold outweigh the benefits of speed gained. Instead, we'll build the code manually, starting with building the controller using our RSpec generator.

Step 1: Create the toys controller

```
ruby script/generate rspec_controller toys index show new edit
      exists  app/controllers/
      exists  app/helpers/
      create  app/views/toys
      exists  spec/controllers/
      exists  spec/helpers/
      create  spec/views/toys
      create  spec/controllers/toys_controller_spec.rb
      create  spec/helpers/toys_helper_spec.rb
      create  app/controllers/toys_controller.rb
      create  app/helpers/toys_helper.rb
      create  spec/views/toys/index.html.erb_spec.rb
      create  app/views/toys/index.html.erb
```

```
create   spec/views/toys/show.html.erb_spec.rb
create   app/views/toys/show.html.erb
create   spec/views/toys/new.html.erb_spec.rb
create   app/views/toys/new.html.erb
create   spec/views/toys/edit.html.erb_spec.rb
create   app/views/toys/edit.html.erb
```

You probably noticed that even though we said we were going to be building the seven CRUD actions, we only passed four actions into the generator. The reason why is actually fairly simple—the four that we passed into the generator are the only ones with associated view templates. The other three actions (create, update, and destroy) simply process the submitted data and either render an existing template or redirect to another action. So if we had passed them to the generator, we then would have had an extra step of deleting the associated templates the generator would have created for us. It's always preferred to be lazy and choose the steps that require us the least amount of additional work.

Step 2: Adding the toys route

Now that we have the controller added, our next step will be to add in the necessary routing support for it. Since we've already decided that we want this controller to support the standard CRUD actions, we can take advantage of that RESTful design and use the map.resources routing method to add our necessary routes. Open up /config/routes.rb, and add a map.resources :toys line like this:

```
ActionController::Routing::Routes.draw do |map|
  map.logout '/logout', :controller => 'sessions', :action => 'destroy'
  map.login '/login', :controller => 'sessions', :action => 'new'
  map.register '/register', :controller => 'users', :action => 'create'
  map.signup '/signup', :controller => 'users', :action => 'new'
  map.resources :users

  map.resource :session
  map.resources :toys

  map.root :controller => "page", :action => 'index'

  map.connect ':controller/:action/:id'
  map.connect ':controller/:action/:id.:format'
end
```

Adding that line to our routes configuration has provided us will a full suite of named routes to all seven CRUD actions that we'll build in this controller, plus support for additional formats at the same URL. So let's start building some of our views and their controller actions!

Building our toy forms

The most logical place to start is with the ability to capture data from the user, as we need to have added some data to the application before we can display it on any of the other actions. Now because we're going to be storing both the lost and the found toy reports in the same model (differentiating between the two through the status property), we have a few ways we could approach this.

For one, we could simply build a single form that users could use to submit and have them select in that form if this is a toy that was lost or a toy that was found. That would be the easiest approach for us as developers. However, I'm not a fan of the idea, because we wouldn't be able to customize the copy on the form to make it more specific to each user's need.

Alternatively, we could create the lost and found toy pages as separate pages and actions in our controller. However, considering that these are essentially exactly the same form except for a little body copy and the choice of one field, that wouldn't be a very DRY approach.

A third option would be to create a single controller action and form yet populate the form view with a lot of if/else conditionals to display one set of body copy if we're displaying a form for a lost toy and a different set of body copy if we're displaying the form for a found toy. This could work, but all of that extra code in the view template would be ugly and could make the template harder to maintain over time.

What I've chosen to do is yet another option - where we will build a single action (new) and use it to display one of two possible templates. Let's take a step-by-step look at how we'll build these forms in our application.

Step 1: Modify our routes

We'll start by first building two new named routes to point to the new action; each of these routes will populate a parameter specifying if the controller should display a lost toy form or a found toy form. Adding these to our routes will look like this:

```
ActionController::Routing::Routes.draw do |map|
  map.logout '/logout', :controller => 'sessions', :action => 'destroy'
  map.login '/login', :controller => 'sessions', :action => 'new'
  map.register '/register', :controller => 'users', :action => 'create'
  map.signup '/signup', :controller => 'users', :action => 'new'
  map.lost '/lost', :controller => 'toys', :action => 'new', ➥
:type => "LOST"
  map.found '/found', :controller => 'toys', :action => 'new', ➥
:type => "FOUND"

  map.resources :users
  map.resource :session
  map.resources :toys

  map.root :controller => "page", :action => 'index'

  map.connect ':controller/:action/:id'
  map.connect ':controller/:action/:id.:format'
end
```

Step 2: Create the new action and ensure that only logged in users can access it

Now we need to add the new action to our controller. In a standard controller, we would simply add it like this:

```
def new
  @toy = Toy.new
end
```

However, we have a couple of small snags that complicate things for us. For one, we said earlier that we wanted to be able to require a user to be logged in before posting any lost toys, so we need to somehow enforce user login before showing this form, and we should redirect a user who's not logged in to the login form. Fortunately, the Restful Authentication plug-in has us covered with a method named login_required that we can use in a before_filter to do just that. So we could just add the following line to our controller:

```
before_filter :login_required
```

However, earlier we also mentioned that we only wanted the actions that create or update data to require a login. To increase the chances of reuniting lost toys and children, we want everyone to be able to view the data without forcing them to log in. So we need to enhance that before filter to exclude our index and show actions. Therefore, our controller should look like this:

```
class ToysController < ApplicationController

  before_filter :login_required, :except => [:index, :show]

  def index
  end

  def show
  end

  def new
  end

  def edit
  end
end
```

Next, whenever we're dealing with associations where the model that we're creating "belongs to" another model, it's typically a good idea to scope the calls in our controller (i.e., to build it on top of the association). In our case, we want to build a toy but always have it associated to the user that created it. Restful Authentication always keeps a reference to the current logged in user in an attribute named current_user. Therefore, the easiest way to scope our action is to build the new toy used here through that current user's association to toys like so:

```
@toy = current_user.toys.build
```

In this way, we're still getting a new Toy object for our form, with the added benefit that the user_id attribute in the new toy object will already be set with the correct association back to the user.

Step 3: Modify the new action to render multiple templates

Our final challenge in building the new action is that we wanted to display two different forms based on the value of the :type parameter that we received from the route. We can do that by evaluating which type we received and using that data to render two different template files.

To keep the book moving at a decent pace, and because there hasn't been anything out of the ordinary yet, we haven't been creating specs for most of this controller's actions up to this point. However, this action is unique, so we should write a spec for it. By default, our toys_controller_spec.rb in /spec/controllers generated a simple set of example specs. However, we don't need those, so delete them from your spec file so that it looks like this:

```
require File.expand_path(File.dirname(__FILE__) + '/../spec_helper')

describe ToysController do
end
```

We said that we want to test that two different requests to the new action will render different forms based on what value is passed to it in the type parameter, so we can start out by writing a set of specs like this:

```
require File.expand_path(File.dirname(__FILE__) + '/../spec_helper')

describe ToysController do

  describe "GET 'new'" do
    describe "with request for LOST" do
      it "should render the lost template" do
        get 'new', {:type => "LOST"}
        response.should render_template("lost")
      end
    end

    describe "with request for FOUND" do
      it "should render the found template" do
        get 'new', {:type => "FOUND"}
        response.should render_template("found")
      end
    end
  end
end
```

Here, we've put an upper level describe block that specifies that we're testing a GET request to the new action. Within that block, we built two describe blocks. One tests that when we make a request to the new action with a type parameter of LOST, we render the lost template. We also have a second nested describe block that does the exact same thing except it's testing that we render the found template when we receive a FOUND in the type parameter.

That spec seems straightforward enough—except we're missing one thing. We need to set up a few basic mocks before we get down into these examples. In our last step, we specified that, in order to access this page, we were going to require that the user be logged in. Because of that we said that when we created a new Toy, we would do so using a scope of the user association like this:

```
@toy = current_user.toys.build
```

In order to get to these templates, we're going to need to mock the Toy model and stub its build method to return the Toy model mock, so we might need to put something together like this:

```
@toy = mock_model(Toy)
Toy.stub!(:build).and_return(@toy)
```

But there's an easier shortcut for doing this that we didn't cover in the RSpec chapter—we can add stubs and their return values directly onto a mock_model definition. So we can rewrite the preceding code as this single line:

```
@toy = mock_model(Toy, :build => @toy)
```

I don't know about you, but I like that a lot! OK, so we've mocked the calls to the Toy model, but we also need to mock the User model and stub a method call to current_user to return our User mock. Doing so will look like this:

```
@user = mock_model(User, :toys => @toy )
controller.stub!( :current_user ).and_return(@user)
```

Here, you can see that we defined a mock on the User model while also stubbing the toys method on that model to return our Toy mock. Afterward, we defined a stub at the controller level for the current_user method and told it to return our User mock.

In this way, we can call current_user and get a User mock. On that User mock, we can call toys to get our Toy mock, and finally on that Toy mock, we can call build to obtain the reference to a Toy mock. So we're able to follow the chained method calls of current_user.toys.build using these mocks. All that's left now is to place them in a before block in our specs so that these mocks will be available for all of our examples:

```
require File.expand_path(File.dirname(__FILE__) + '/../spec_helper')

describe ToysController do

  describe "GET 'new'" do
    before(:each) do
      @toy = mock_model(Toy, :build => @toy)
      @user = mock_model(User, :toys => @toy )
      controller.stub!( :current_user ).and_return(@user)
    end

    describe "with request for LOST" do
      it "should render the lost template" do
        get 'new', {:type => "LOST"}
        response.should render_template("lost")
```

```
        end
      end

    describe "with request for FOUND" do
      it "should render the found template" do
        get 'new', {:type => "FOUND"}
        response.should render_template("found")
      end
    end
  end
end
```

With that, our spec is complete, and we just need to put together our new action in the toys controller like this:

```ruby
class ToysController < ApplicationController

  before_filter :login_required, :except => [:index, :show]

  def index
  end

  def show
  end

  def new
    @toy = current_user.toys.build
    case params[:type]
      when "LOST" then render :file => 'toys/lost',
                                     :use_full_path => true,
                                     :layout => true
      when "FOUND" then render :file => 'toys/found',
                                     :use_full_path => true,
                                     :layout => true

    end
  end

  def edit
  end
end
```

Here, you can see that we've added the before_filter that we discussed; we've changed the scope of our @toy creation; and we're rendering two different template files (using the render :file) based on what :type we received in our parameters.

You should probably notice that we're also passing two additional parameters to the render :file call: use_full_path => true and :layout => true. The use_full_path parameter is just a shortcut to allow us to use relative paths to render the file rather than having to specify the full OS path (i.e., /users/home/code/lost_toys/app/views/toys), while the :layout => true parameter ensures that our application layout is also used when the template is rendered (by default, render :file does not include the layout).

With our controller action out of the way, we simply need to build those two templates.

> *With most things in programming, there is more than one way to solve a problem. In this example, I chose to use* render :file *so that I could display the correct template. However, an alternative and shorter approach might have been to use the* render :action *method like so:*
>
> ```
> when "LOST" then render :action => 'lost'
> when "FOUND" then render :action => 'found'
> ```
>
> *Both approaches work, but the question of which approach will cause me to do the least amount of research when I come back to the application a year from now is a valid one. If I see a* render :action *call, I'm going to immediately begin searching through my controller for an action with that name and will probably be momentarily confused when I don't find it. Using* render :template *is more verbose, but when I come back to this application in a year, there will be no question as to what's being rendered.*

Step 4: Build the lost toy form

We'll start by building the lost toy template. Create a new file in /app/views/toys named lost.html. erb, and in it, place the following form:

```erb
<h1>Report a lost toy</h1>
<% form_for @toy do |f| %>
  <%= f.error_messages %>
  <p>
    <%= f.label :title, "What kind of toy did you lose?" %>
    <%= f.text_field :title %>
  </p>
  <p>
    <%= f.label :description, "Describe the toy making sure to note➡
any distinguishing features and how someone could contact you if➡
it was found." %>
    <%= f.text_area :description %>
    <%= f.hidden_field :status, :value => "LOST" %>
  </p>
  <p>
    <%= f.submit "Create" %>
  </p>
<% end %>

<%= link_to 'Back', toys_path %>
```

There isn't anything too fancy in there—just our standard form helpers that, when rendered, will generate a form that looks like the one shown in Figure 11-12.

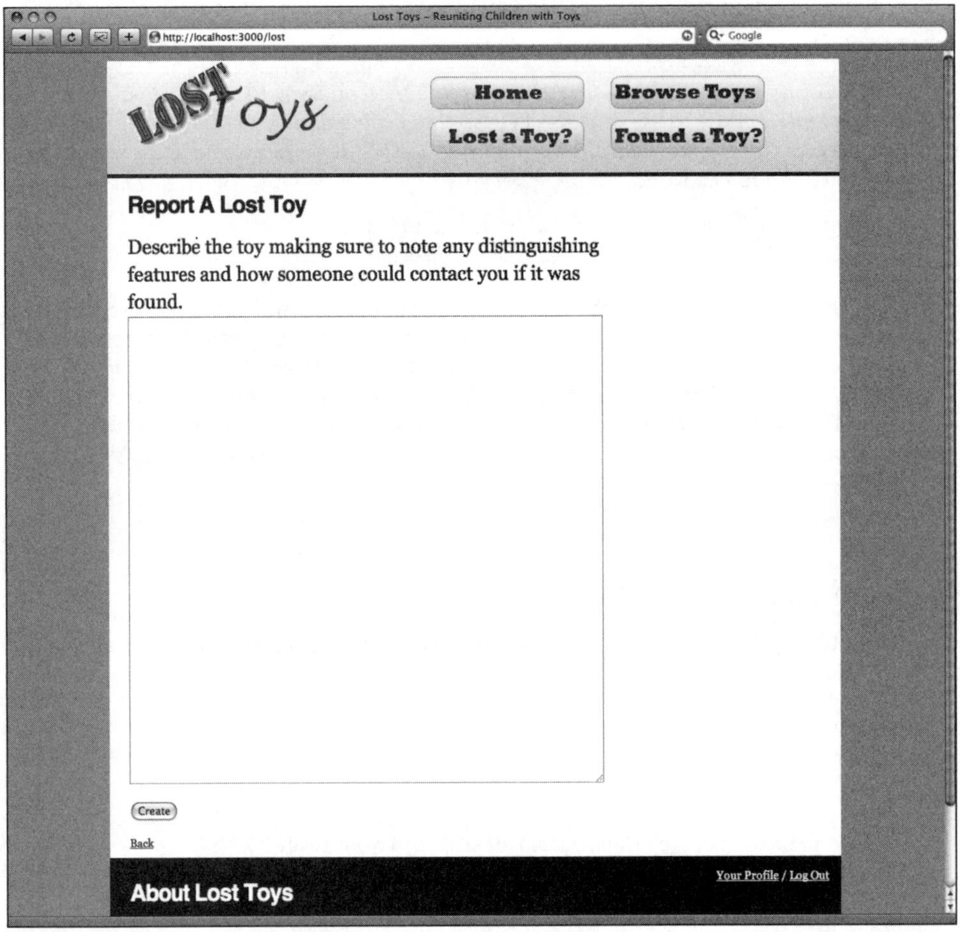

Figure 11-12. The form to report a lost toy

Of course, adding a link to this form will help users access it, so open our layout file again (/app/views/layouts/application.html.erb), and let's activate one of those navigation links to go to this form. We could change this:

```
<li><%= link_to image_tag('lost_toy.png'), '#' %></li>
```

to this:

```
<li><%= link_to image_tag('lost_toy.png'), lost_path %></li>
```

Of course, since we also already have our routes built to go to the index page of the toys and to go to a found form as well, we might as well edit all of our navigation links with the correct path. So let's modify them all to look like this:

```
-- excerpt --
<div id="nav_container">
  <ul id="navigation">
    <li><%= link_to image_tag('home.png'), root_path %></li>
    <li><%= link_to image_tag('browse_toys.png'), toys_path %></li>
    <li><%= link_to image_tag('lost_toy.png'), lost_path %></li>
    <li><%= link_to image_tag('found_toy.png'), found_path %></li>
  </ul>
</div>
-- excerpt --
```

Step 5: Build the found toy form

Our found form will be nearly identical, so create a new template in /app/views/toys named found.html.erb, and place the following content into it:

```
<h1>Report a toy that was found</h1>
<% form_for @toy do |f| %>
  <%= f.error_messages %>
  <p>
    <%= f.label :description, "Describe the toy and where you found➡
 it, and provide information on how the owner can reclaim it" %>
    <%= f.text_area :description %>
    <%= f.hidden_field :status, :value => "FOUND" %>
  </p>
  <p>
    <%= f.submit "Create" %>
  </p>
<% end %>

<%= link_to 'Back', toys_path %>
```

And with that last addition, our specs will now be passing, and our forms are now ready for users to start populating them—well, except for the fact that currently nothing will happen if someone filled out a form and submitted it!

Step 6: Build the create action

The problem is that both of these forms are going to submit to the create action in the toys controller, but we haven't built that action yet. The needs of a create action are typically pretty standard fare. They simply create a new Toy based on the parameters it received in the form submission and attempt to save that new toy. If the Toy saves successfully (i.e., it passes all validations and is inserted into the database), the action will redirect the request to the show action to view the toy that was just created. If, for some reason, the Toy could not be saved (most likely due to failing a validation rule), the action will simply redisplay the new form again.

Typically, you would see this written like so:

```
def create
  @toy = Toy.new(params[:toy])
  if @toy.save
    redirect_to(@toy)
  else
    render :action => "new"
  end
end
```

Of course, the real world is never quite as simple, and we need to modify that general design to accommodate a few of our special needs. First off, we want to scope the creation of the new toy to the currently logged in user:

```
@toy = current_user.toys.build(params[:toy])
```

Second, we're not actually using the new template, so rendering that template would be incorrect. We actually need to redetermine if the user was submitting a lost toy report or a found toy report and then redisplay the appropriate template. To do that, we'll need to look at the status attribute that's being submitted as one of the fields in the form. You've seen that, in order to access the entire form submission, we can simply access it in the parameters as params[:toy], but to get to one of the specific fields in that form, we simply need to access it as a sub-element like so: params[:toy][:status]. So with that knowledge in hand, we can build our create action in our controller like so:

```
class ToysController < ApplicationController

  before_filter :login_required, :except => [:index, :show]

  def index
  end

  def show
  end

  def new
    @toy = current_user.toys.build
    case params[:type]
      when "LOST" then render :file => 'toys/lost',
                                    :use_full_path => true,
                                    :layout => true
      when "FOUND" then render :file => 'toys/found',
                                    :use_full_path => true,
                                    :layout => true
    end
  end

  def create
    @toy = current_user.toys.build(params[:toy])
    if @toy.save
```

```
          redirect_to(@toy)
        else
          case params[:toy][:status]
            when "LOST" then render :file => 'toys/lost',
                                        :use_full_path => true,
                                        :layout => true
            when "FOUND" then render :file => 'toys/found',
                                        :use_full_path => true,
                                        :layout => true

          end
        end
      end

      def edit
      end
    end
```

At this point, our application is now configured to allow users to sign up and create reports of lost or found toys into the application. But honestly, I'm not happy with the result so far. While allowing users to create a report about a toy seems nice, it just feels lacking. Looking back at our original sketches, we can see there that when we were talking about displaying these reports, I tended to draw them with pictures as well as a description. No matter how good a description a user can write, it will never match the power to communicate that posting a picture of the toy would do. So let's go back and enhance our Toy objects to also allow users to upload a photo of the toy.

Enhance the reports with photos

There are actually several plug-ins available that we could use to add file uploading or image manipulation capabilities to our application. For the last few years, the most popular solution has been one named attachment_fu, which not only made it easy to upload files as attachments to a model but also provided advanced features such as automatic image resizing (which it did through calls to the ImageMagick graphics suite). The biggest downfall with attachment_fu, however, was that in order to obtain access to those image manipulation functions, you also had to install a Ruby Gem by the name of RMagick (which served as a Ruby interface to ImageMagick). Unfortunately, installing RMagick wasn't always an easy process and therefore caused quite a few developers a lot of headaches.

However, that pain inspired other developers to create new plug-ins that would provide similar functionality without requiring the installation of RMagick. One of the more popular plug-ins in this vein is one by the name of Paperclip created by the guys at thoughtbot (http://www.thoughtbot.com/projects/paperclip).

Paperclip is the plug-in that we'll be using to enhance our Toy model and allow it to easily associate an image upload to each toy. Outside of installing the plug-in (which we'll do in a moment), the only requirement for Paperclip to work is that we first install the ImageMagick graphics suite. Let's go through a step by step process of how we can install and configure the Paperclip plug-in in our lost toys application.

Step 1: Ensure you have ImageMagick installed

Installing ImageMagick is actually a pretty simple process. If you're on a Linux/Unix system, you can probably install it via apt, yum, or whatever package manager your system uses. Windows and Mac users can simply go to http://www.imagemagick.org/script/index.php, and there, they will find binary releases that they can download and install very easily.

Step 2: Install the Paperclip plug-in

Once ImageMagick is installed, we simply need to install the Paperclip plug-in. Normally, you would do that from the official GitHub repository like so:

```
ruby script/plugin install git://github.com/thoughtbot/paperclip.git
```

But once again, I've created my own fork of the plug-in so that you'll always have access to the version of the plug-in that was in use while the book was being written. You can install my version like so:

```
ruby script/plugin install git://github.com/darkel/paperclip.git
   Initialized empty Git repository in /Users/darkel/book/lost_toys/➥
vendor/plugins/paperclip/.git/
   remote: Counting objects: 45, done.
   remote: Compressing objects: 100% (36/36), done.
   remote: Total 45 (delta 2), reused 34 (delta 2)
   Receiving objects: 100% (45/45), 45.14 KiB, done.
   Resolving deltas: 100% (2/2), done.
```

Step 3: Enhance our toys table to support photo attachments

Now that the plug-in is installed, we simply need to add a few additional fields to our Toy model that will be used to store information about the photo that was uploaded. We'll create these new fields using a migration to modify our existing toys table like so:

```
ruby script/generate migration AddPhotosToToys photo_file_name:string➥
photo_content_type:string photo_file_size:integer
      exists  db/migrate
      create  db/migrate/20080727202944_add_photos_to_toys.rb
```

Opening up that new migration file in /db/migrate, we can see that it was created like this:

```
class AddPhotosToToys < ActiveRecord::Migration
  def self.up
    add_column :toys, :photo_file_name, :string
    add_column :toys, :photo_content_type, :string
    add_column :toys, :photo_file_size, :integer
  end

  def self.down
    remove_column :toys, :photo_file_size
    remove_column :toys, :photo_content_type
```

```
      remove_column :toys, :photo_file_name
    end
end
```

Step 4: Enhance the toys table in our database with a title

So far, things are looking good and we're at a point where we could run our migration now—except for one other thing. Looking back at our forms, I sort of feel like we should also require our users to create some sort of single-line name for the toy listing in addition to the description. Since we'll have to modify our forms in a moment anyway, let's go ahead and add that missing field to our toy model using an additional migration:

```
ruby script/generate migration AddTitleToToys title:string
      exists  db/migrate
      create  db/migrate/20080727203348_add_title_to_toys.rb
```

The preceding line created a new migration that looks like this:

```
class AddTitleToToys < ActiveRecord::Migration
  def self.up
    add_column :toys, :title, :string
  end

  def self.down
    remove_column :toys, :title
  end
end
```

That looks pretty good, so let's run our migrations and apply these changes to our database.

```
rake db:migrate
== 20080727202944 AddPhotosToToys: migrating ==========================
-- add_column(:toys, :photo_file_name, :string)
   -> 0.0250s
-- add_column(:toys, :photo_content_type, :string)
   -> 0.0127s
-- add_column(:toys, :photo_file_size, :integer)
   -> 0.0077s
== 20080727202944 AddPhotosToToys: migrated (0.0517s) ================

== 20080727203348 AddTitleToToys: migrating ===========================
-- add_column(:toys, :title, :string)
   -> 0.0060s
== 20080727203348 AddTitleToToys: migrated (0.0064s) ================
```

Sweet! Our next step will be to modify our toy model (/app/models/toy.rb) to be able to support photos and to handle this new field that we've added.

Step 5: Modify the Toy model

To add support for uploaded files, the Paperclip plug-in merely requires us to add a method call to our model named has_attached_file, passing in a reference name of the file that we want to attach. In our case, we're using the name photo (which is why we prefixed "photo" into all of the field names in our migration). In addition, we can pass in a hash of styles that will list the key names and dimensions for any resized copies of our uploaded image that we want the plug-in to create. In our case, we'll create two resized copies: one named medium that will feature a 300-pixel–wide scaled representation of our image and a thumbnail version, named thumb, that will be a 100-pixel–wide version. Once it's added to our model, the method will look like this:

```
has_attached_file :photo,
    :styles => { :medium => "300x300>", :thumb => "100x100>" }
```

In addition to this method, we also added that new title field to the toys model, and we should make that a required field. So we'll need to modify our validation logic to include this field. Afterward, our Toy model should look like this:

```
class Toy < ActiveRecord::Base
  VALID_STATUSES = %w(LOST FOUND)

  validates_presence_of :title, :description, :status
  validates_inclusion_of :status, :in => VALID_STATUSES

  belongs_to :user

  has_attached_file :photo,
      :styles => { :medium => "300x300>", :thumb => "100x100>" }
end
```

Step 6: Modify our forms to support file uploads

We're almost done; we simply need to modify our existing lost and found forms to accommodate the new fields. We'll need to change our /app/views/toys/lost.html.erb to look like this:

```
<h1>Report a lost toy</h1>
<% form_for @toy, :html => { :multipart => true } do |f| %>
  <%= f.error_messages %>
  <p>
    <%= f.label :title, "What kind of toy did you lose?" %>
    <%= f.text_field :title %>
  </p>
  <p>
    <%= f.label :description, "Describe the toy making sure to note➡
any distinguishing features and how someone could contact you➡
  if it was found." %>
    <%= f.text_area :description %>
```

```
    <%= f.hidden_field :status, :value => "LOST" %>
  </p>
  <p>
    <%= f.label :photo, "Please upload a photo of the toy." %>
    <%= f.file_field :photo %>  </p>
  </p>
  <p>
    <%= f.submit "Create" %>
  </p>
<% end %>

  <%= link_to 'Back', toys_path %>
```

And we'll change the found template (/app/views/toys/found.html.erb) to look like this:

```
<h1>Report a toy that was found</h1>
<% form_for @toy, :html => { :multipart => true } do |f| %>
  <%= f.error_messages %>
  <p>
    <%= f.label :title, "What kind of toy did you find?" %>
    <%= f.text_field :title %>
  </p>
  <p>
    <%= f.label :description, "Describe the toy and where you found ➥
it, and provide information on how the owner can reclaim it" %>
    <%= f.text_area :description %>
    <%= f.hidden_field :status, :value => "FOUND" %>
  </p>
  <p>
    <%= f.label :photo, "If possible, please upload a Photo of the ➥
toy." %>
    <%= f.file_field :photo %>  </p>
  </p>
  <p>
    <%= f.submit "Create" %>
  </p>
<% end %>

  <%= link_to 'Back', toys_path %>
```

In these two forms, we first modified the form to signify that it should be a multipart form so that it can handle uploading of data in addition to the normal form fields. Then we simply added our additional fields to the forms using the form helpers.

If we were to restart our application now and view these templates, we could look at our changes, as shown in Figure 11-13.

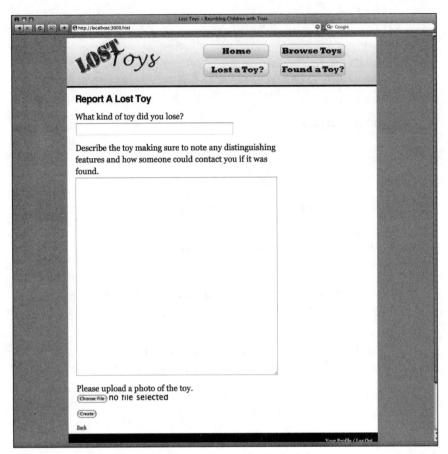

Figure 11-13. Added an image upload control to our form submission

I don't know about you, but I like the way things are shaping up a lot more now. In fact, now that we can add toys to the application, it's a good time to move on to building our index and view toy pages.

Build the toy listings

At this point, it would be a good idea for you to go ahead and create a user account in the system and create a few sample toys (both lost and found) so that we'll have some data to display in these coming pages.

Once you've done that, we can add a standard index action to our toys controller. Traditionally, an index action will look like this:

```
def index
  @toys = Toy.find(:all)
end
```

However, I like to include a clause to ensure that we're always returning these toys in the correct order of newest toys to oldest. So our index action in our toys controller should look like this:

```ruby
class ToysController < ApplicationController

  before_filter :login_required, :except => [:index, :show]

  def index
    @toys = Toy.find(:all, :order => 'created_at DESC')
  end

  def show
  end

  def new
    @toy = current_user.toys.build
    case params[:type]
      when "LOST" then render :file => 'toys/lost',
                                     :use_full_path => true,
                                     :layout => true
      when "FOUND" then render :file => 'toys/found',
                                     :use_full_path => true,
                                     :layout => true
    end
  end

  def create
    @toy = current_user.toys.build(params[:toy])
    if @toy.save
      redirect_to(@toy)
    else
      case params[:toy][:status]
        when "LOST" then render :file => 'toys/lost',
                                       :use_full_path => true,
                                       :layout => true
        when "FOUND" then render :file => 'toys/found',
                                       :use_full_path => true,
                                       :layout => true
      end
    end
  end

  def edit
  end
end
```

Now that we have a collection of our sample toys in the @toys instance variable, we can edit the index template at /app/views/toys/index.html.erb to display that collection:

```erb
<h1>Listing toys</h1>
<% for toy in @toys %>
  <h2 class="listing_title"><%= link_to(toy.title, toy) %></h2>
  <p class="thumb">
    <%= link_to(image_tag(toy.photo.url(:thumb)), toy) %>
  </p>
  <p>
    <%= simple_format(truncate(toy.description, 95) + link_to("More ➡
Info", toy)) %>
  </p>
<% end %>
<p class="closing">Thank you for your support</p>
```

This little bit of code will simply loop over our collection of toys displaying the thumbnail image of each along with a truncated version of the description text, and our page will look like the one shown in Figure 11-14.

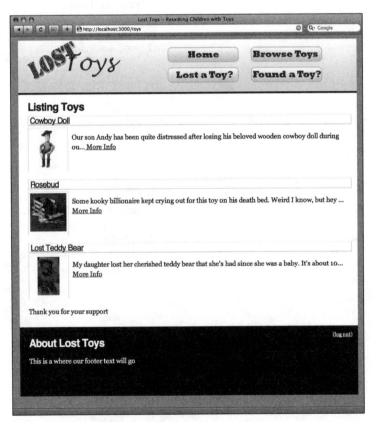

Figure 11-14. Our listing page for lost toys

Things are coming along nicely. Let's add the toy detail page (show template) to round things out for the front end.

Building the toy detail page

The last remaining page that's critical to the site is the toy detail page, which will show the full description and details about a toy. Fortunately for us though, adding it is also one of the easiest tasks left. We simply need to fill out our show action in the toys controller to load the @toy instance variable with the specific toy:

```ruby
class ToysController < ApplicationController

  before_filter :login_required, :except => [:index, :show]

  def index
    @toys = Toy.find(:all, :order => 'created_at DESC')
  end

  def show
    @toy = Toy.find(params[:id])
  end

  def new
    @toy = current_user.toys.build
    case params[:type]
      when "LOST" then render :file => 'toys/lost',
                                    :use_full_path => true,
                                    :layout => true
      when "FOUND" then render :file => 'toys/found',
                                    :use_full_path => true,
                                    :layout => true
    end
  end
-- excerpt --
```

Next, we populate our show template (/app/views/toys/show.html.erb) with some HTML and embedded Ruby to display the information about the toy:

```erb
<h1><%=h @toy.status %> TOY</h1>
<div class="photo">
  <%= image_tag @toy.photo.url(:medium) %>
</div>
  <%=simple_format(h @toy.description) %>
<p class="closing">
  <%= link_to 'Back', toys_path %>
</p>
```

Here, you can see that we're displaying the status of the toy (i.e., lost or found) in a header bar for the toy. Then we're going to display the larger 300-pixel–wide version of the uploaded photo (tagged with :medium), and finally, we'll display the description that the user submitted about the toy. To display that description though, we're wrapping it in a helper named simple_format, which will take the text that was submitted and transform it into standard HTML using a few simple rules. In this way, the text will have the same line breaks that the user submitted it with. When the template is saved, we can view a toy detail page by clicking one of the links on the index page, and we should be rewarded with a result like the pages shown in Figure 11-15.

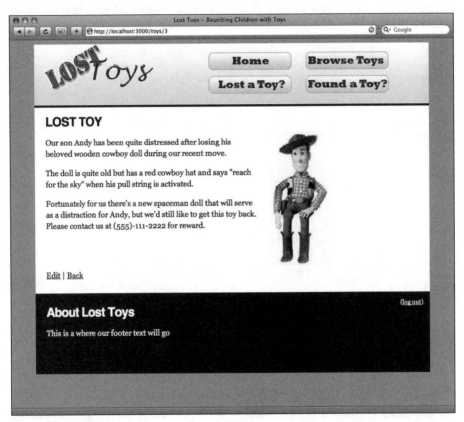

Figure 11-15. Displaying the detail page about a lost toy

With that change, all of our publicly accessible pages are now up and running, and we can send the site to a few friends to experiment with and send us some feedback. Meanwhile, we can take the rest of the evening off to eat hot wings and play Xbox Live.

Summary

I don't know about you, but I had a lot of fun in this chapter as we combined many of our previous lessons and began the process of building our own web application. We did a lot of exciting things, such as seeing firsthand how we use Rails database migrations to build our database over time and how to modify it as we discovered new needs. We got to explore building custom routes for our application in a way that not only gave us friendlier URLs but also allowed us to do some custom functionality in our controller actions. And we got to explore using a plug-in to add the advanced functionality of handling image uploads and automatic thumbnail creation for our application.

But probably most importantly, we were able to put together a working Rails application with a purpose in this chapter. It may not be the prettiest application out there (or the coolest), but it works and doesn't look too terribly bad.

Just because our application is functional doesn't mean it's finished though—far from it, as I know for a fact that our friends are almost certainly going to have some suggestions for additional features for our application. In our next chapter, we're going to pick up right where we left off and continue to refine and enhance our Lost Toys application.

Chapter 12

ENHANCING OUR APPLICATION

Being punctual and conscientious people, our friends were quick to write back with a small laundry list of changes, improvements, and additions to the application that we built in the previous chapter. Of course, we got a lot of feedback on subjects such as color choices and font-sizes, and while those are important, we'll disregard them for now.

For this iteration, what we're looking for is feedback that's focused on the core functionality of the application rather than the design choices. Fortunately, we did get some really good feedback as well. Some of the comments that we received follow:

- "I created a sample toy and then realized I had misspelled something; being able to go back and edit the record would be a nice feature."
- "I don't think I saw AJAX being used anywhere on that site. Are you feeling sick or something? What about an API?"
- "What's going to happen if it turns out the toy wasn't lost? Is there some way I can delete the post from the site?"
- "Seems like it would be more useful if I could list only the toys that were lost or only the toys that were found; having them intermixed isn't very useful."
- "Perhaps you should sort the records by state or county or something. If the site took off, I think it would be kind of a pain to have to deal with toys from too far away."

We have a few good ideas in there, and in this chapter, we're going to work on implementing as many of those as we can. To help turn this feedback into something workable, we'll break them down into stories; in software development terms, these are basically short descriptions of the desired features or functionality that's being written in straightforward and nontechnical language.

- **Story 1**: Provide a means for users to be able to go back and edit/update or remove any toy reports that they have added to the application.

- **Story 2**: Enhance the relevance of the toy reports by forcing users to provide some form of geographic information about where the toy was found or potentially lost.

- **Story 3**: Provide users with the ability to filter toy results. They should be allowed, at the most basic, to filter results based on the status of the toy (lost or found). But more importantly, we should add new functionality to the application that will allow them to filter results by geographic region.

- **Story 4**: Provide our users with an RSS feed so they can keep up to date on any new toys added to the application.

- **Story 5**: Enhance the coolness factor of our application by converting our filter capabilities with AJAX functionality.

- **Story 6**: Provide a simple XML API that would allow other clients to interact with our application's data.

That's certainly a lot of functionality that we're going to be adding in this chapter, and a few of those stories are going to require us to discover areas of Rails that we haven't worked with before. However, by the end of this chapter, not only will we have added quite a number of features to our application, but you'll have been exposed to some pretty exciting functionality that I believe should completely round out your introduction to Rails development.

So without further ado, let's get started on implementing our first story.

Story 1: Allow users to edit, update, or remove toy reports

Because we don't expect our users to be posting large amounts of records into our application, an easy approach to allowing users to edit posts would be to simply provide each user a detail page that provides them with a list of any toys that they have reported lost or found within the application.

From this page, we can then provide them with a link to a form they can use to edit each record or to remove it from the application completely.

Step 1: Build the controller action to display the user's toys

Since the emphasis of the page is on the user first and then providing a list of the toys that the user has created secondarily, we'll create this page with the show action (intended to display detail information about a user) in the users controller (/app/controllers/users_controller.rb). Within this controller, we'll add a show action that will generate a list of any toys that the current user has created like so:

```
def show
  @toys = current_user.toys
end
```

Step 2: Add the corresponding view template

Once we've added the show method to the users controller, we also need to build a corresponding view template for this action. Create a new file in /app/views/users/ named show.html.erb, and place the following HTML and ERb content into it:

```erb
<h1>Welcome <%= @user.name %></h1>

<p>Here are the toys that you have listed on the site.</p>

<ul>
  <% for toy in @toys %>
    <li><%= link_to toy.title, toy %> --
        <%= link_to 'Edit', edit_toy_path %> --
        <%= link_to 'Delete', toy, :method => :delete %>
    </li>
  <% end %>
</ul>
```

There's nothing too glamorous in this view. We display a welcome message with the user's name in the header. Then we create a simple loop over the @toys collection, displaying each toy's title and links to edit or delete each toy.

Step 3: Provide links to our user profile page

Now that we've added this user detail page to the application, we need to provide a way for our application's users to get to this page, so that means adding some form of link into our applications navigation. The logical place to add this link would be in the same user bar that we're displaying in the footer, which is also providing links to log in and log out.

Open /app/views/users/_user_bar.html.erb, and modify it so that, if a user is logged in, it will add the link to our user detail page:

```erb
<% if logged_in? -%>
  <div id="user-bar-action">
    <%= link_to "Your Profile", user_path(current_user), ➥
{ :title => "View Your Profile" } %> /
    <%= link_to "Log Out", logout_path, { :title => "Log out" }    %>
  </div>
<% else -%>
  <div id="user-bar-action">
    <%= link_to "Log in",  login_path, { :title => "Log in" } %> /
    <%= link_to "Sign up", signup_path, ➥
{ :title => "Create an account" } %>
  </div>
<% end -%>
```

Simple enough—once you've added that line of code to our file, if you were to view the application in a web browser, you would see that this change now gives us the output that you can see in Figure 12-1, where a link to the user profile has been added within the footer, and we're displaying the user profile template, which is displaying links to all of the toys that this user has created.

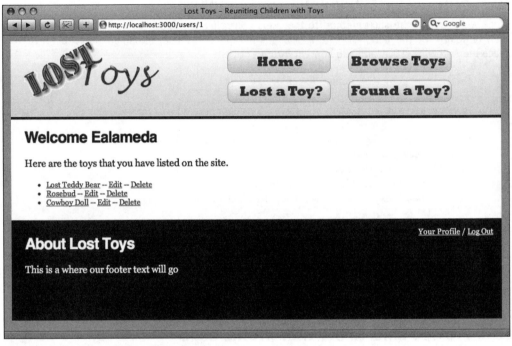

Figure 12-1. Displaying a user profile page

While that list of toys could stand to have some styles applied to it, and perhaps replace those edit and delete links with some nice pretty icons, we have some bigger fish to fry—namely that currently those edit and delete links aren't actually going to do anything when they're clicked.

Our number one goal is going to be to add that functionality. Let's start with the low-hanging fruit and add the code necessary for the delete function.

Step 4: Coding our destroy action

Because we're using RESTful routes, those delete links are being sent to a destroy action in the toys controller; unfortunately, that action doesn't exist. To add that missing destroy action, we'll edit the toys controller (/app/controllers/toys_controller.rb) again, so that our controller will now look like this:

```ruby
class ToysController < ApplicationController

  before_filter :login_required, :except => [:index, :show]

  def index
    @toys = Toy.find(:all, :order => 'created_at DESC')
  end

  def show
    @toy = Toy.find(params[:id])
  end

  def new
    @toy = current_user.toys.build
    case params[:type]
      when "LOST" then render :file => 'toys/lost',
                                     :use_full_path => true,
                                     :layout => true
      when "FOUND" then render :file => 'toys/found',
                                      :use_full_path => true,
                                      :layout => true
    end
  end

  def create
    @toy = current_user.toys.build(params[:toy])
    if @toy.save
      redirect_to(@toy)
    else
      case params[:toy][:status]
        when "LOST" then render :file => 'toys/lost',
                                       :use_full_path => true,
                                       :layout => true
        when "FOUND" then render :file => 'toys/found',
                                        :use_full_path => true,
                                        :layout => true
      end
    end
  end

  def edit
  end

  def destroy
    @toy = current_user.toys.find(params[:id])
    @toy.destroy
    redirect_to(toys_url)
  end
end
```

This new destroy action simply looks up the toy based on the ID that was submitted in the incoming parameters and uses it to find that toy within the currently logged in user's toys. If it finds one, it then calls the ActiveRecord destroy method on it (which you might recall will delete the record as well as execute any callbacks that have been set in the model). Afterward, it will redirect the request to the index action of the toys controller (using the toys_url named route).

Step 5: Add code to the edit action

Adding the code for a user to edit a toy is almost as easy as adding the delete functionality. We already have an empty edit action in the toys controller (that was added when we built the controller). We now just need to populate it with an ActiveRecord lookup of the specified toy like so:

```
def edit
  @toy = current_user.toys.find(params[:id])
end
```

Step 6: Build the view action template for the edit action

With the action built and populating an @toy instance variable with the specified record, we simply need to replace the sample content from the existing edit.html.erb in /app/views/toys to display an edit form for that object instead, like this:

```
<h1>Editing toy</h1>

<% form_for @toy, :html => { :multipart => true } do |f| %>

  <%= f.error_messages %>

  <p>
    <%= f.label :title, "Kind of toy" %><br>
    <%= f.text_field :title %>
  </p>
  <p>
    <%= f.label :description, "Description of toy" %><br />
    <%= f.text_area :description %>
  </p>
  <p>
    <%= f.label :photo, "update photo" %><br />
    <%= f.file_field :photo %>  </p>
  <p>
    <%= f.submit "Update" %>
  </p>
<% end %>

<%= link_to 'Show', @toy %> |
<%= link_to 'Back', toys_path %>
```

I don't believe there's anything in this form that you haven't seen before, and this form will display the existing data for a toy record, as shown in Figure 12-2.

Figure 12-2. The ability to edit an existing toy record.

Step 7: Build the update action

Our final step in this story will be to add the necessary code to our toys controller, so that when a user submits changes to a toy record, those changes will actually be saved (I've heard that this can make users happy).

Because we're dealing with RESTful routing, our edit form is sending its submission to the update action in the toys controller. So we simply need to add that update action to that controller with the standard update code that we've used in previous chapters:

```ruby
def update
  @toy = current_user.toys.find(params[:id])
  if @toy.update_attributes(params[:toy])
    redirect_to(@toy)
  else
    render :action => "edit"
  end
end
```

Easy as pie, huh? We load the specified toy into the @toy instance variable, and then we call the update_attributes method on that object (passing it all the values that were submitted by the edit form). If that update_attributes method call was successful, we'll redirect the request to the show action for the toy (so they can see their changes); otherwise, we'll redisplay that edit form again along with any error messages that were generated.

With that small addition, we just completed our first story (thus implementing two of the requests our friends submitted) and provided users of our application some much-needed missing tools. That was a fairly simple story to implement; now let's tackle a slightly more difficult one—the ability to filter our results set.

Story 2: Add geocoding to our application

Our second story is going to both be a bit more difficult and require a bit more coding, as it will mean making several core changes to our application. As you saw, two of our friends asked that we provide some form of solution for limiting the results that are displayed based on different criteria. One asked that we allow users to see only a particular type of toy result (lost or found), while another asked that we think about being able to limit the results to only those that are within the same state.

In this story, we are going to focus on enhancing our toy reports with some form of geographic information, and then, in the next story, we'll use that new geographic information and the type of report it is to provide a filter capability for our users. Now in a professional software development arena, this story would be considered too big and would be broken up into several substories (with stories such as obtain geographic information from users, convert existing records, add filter capabilities, and so on), but since it's all related to the same goal, we're going to perform them as a single story.

Limiting the results to only the records that are in the same state (California, Florida, etc.) as you is an interesting concept and wouldn't be too hard to implement with the addition of state drop-down menu in the forms. That drop-down could easily be added with the addition of a plug-in to our application that provides that functionality: state_select (http://agilewebdevelopment.com/plugins/state_select).

However, while that would meet the letter of the request, it doesn't entirely fulfill the spirit. Our friend was really hoping for a way to display only toy results that are close to him. His suggestion of doing it by state would be easy to implement, but in reality, we're still casting a pretty big net. After all, think about large states such as Texas or California. Would we really want to see all results from California when all we're really interested in are the results near a small mountain town in northern California? Probably not. So what we're really looking for here is a way to even further identify the location of our toy reports and a way to search for those that are close to us. Or in other words, we need a way to geocode an approximate geographic latitude and longitude for each toy and search within a specific radius.

Sounds pretty complicated, doesn't it? Normally, it would be—except for the fact that we have a powerful plug-in called GeoKit that provides exactly that functionality. We'll ask each user to provide some geographic information about where the toy was possibly lost or where it was found when creating each new toy listing in our application. Then when we add a filtered search result for our toy listings, we'll provide the option for a user to search for toys within a specific radius.

Sounds pretty cool to me—let's build that now.

Step 1: Install the GeoKit plug-in

The first step to using GeoKit in our developing application is to install the plug-in. However, GeoKit is one of the few that hasn't converted to Git yet, so we'll be doing an install from the web-based Subversion repository like this:

```
ruby script/plugin install svn://rubyforge.org/var/svn/geokit/trunk
```

Once the plug-in is installed, it outputs to the screen several pages worth of information about itself, which tells us quite a bit about the features of the plug-in and about how to use each of those features. For instance, GeoKit provides such features as the ability to calculate the distance between any two points on the earth, a set of ActiveRecord distance-based finders that allow us to do things like find all addresses in our database that are within a specific radius, and support for using multiple geocoders including ones from Google, Yahoo, Geocoder.us, and GeoCode. It even provides an interface to hostip.info, which can be used to convert an IP address into an approximate latitude and longitude.

Pretty fantastic stuff, huh? Well there's one downside that we'll need to address that shows up in that outputted information, and that's in the following excerpt:

```
Database Compatability
GeoKit does *not* work with SQLite, as it lacks the necessary geometry
   functions.
GeoKit works with MySQL (tested with version 5.0.41) or PostgreSQL
   (tested with version 8.2.6)
GeoKit is known to *not* work with Postgres <8.1 -- it uses the least()
   funciton.
```

D'oh! SQLite has served us well until now. Unfortunately, it's just not going to be quite good enough to allow us to add this functionality, so we're going to need to convert our database to MySQL.

Step 2: Install MySQL

As I'm sure you would guess, the first step to converting to MySQL is to make sure that you have it installed. Fortunately, installing MySQL is a fairly simple and straightforward process. If you're on a Linux-based OS, it's typically just a matter of installing the mysql-server package through your distributions package management system. If you're running another OS, you'll find the latest binary installation package for your operating system at http://dev.mysql.com/downloads. You can simply download your platform-specific version from there and run its installer application to quickly and easily install MySQL.

After the installation is complete, we should install the native MySQL bindings gem to gain a significant speed boost when using Ruby and MySQL together, which is typically done like this:

```
sudo gem install mysql
```

However, I have seen that with some Linux distributions (and occasionally on other operating systems with nondefault installations) that the gem install has failed, because it couldn't find the MySQL application. If this happens to you, you can solve it by manually specifying the path to the MySQL application like so:

```
sudo gem install mysql -- --with-mysql-dir=/usr/local/mysql
```

Step 3: Convert our application to use MySQL

Once you have MySQL installed, we can modify our database connection settings pretty simply by modifying our database.yml file in /config. In my own settings, I modified the development settings to match my local MySQL configuration like so:

```
development:
  adapter: mysql
  database: dev_toys
  username: root
  password:
  host: localhost
```

We've been spoiled by the fact that SQLite automatically creates our database for us if it doesn't exist. However, with a database solution like MySQL, we have to create the database ourselves before we can use it. Luckily, we have a rake task to make this process easier. To create the database defined in our development settings of database.yml, simply run the following from the command line:

```
rake db:create
```

And that rake task will create the database that we just defined in our database.yml file. Now that we've built our new database, we need to run our database migrations to build our schema in our new MySQL database:

```
rake db:migrate
== 20080726202915 CreateUsers: migrating ============================
-- create_table("users", {:force=>true})
   -> 0.0048s
-- add_index(:users, :login, {:unique=>true})
   -> 0.0349s
== 20080726202915 CreateUsers: migrated (0.0404s) ==================

== 20080727034712 CreateToys: migrating =============================
-- create_table(:toys)
   -> 0.0031s
== 20080727034712 CreateToys: migrated (0.0034s) ===================

== 20080727202944 AddPhotosToToys: migrating =======================
-- add_column(:toys, :photo_file_name, :string)
   -> 0.0060s
-- add_column(:toys, :photo_content_type, :string)
   -> 0.0172s
-- add_column(:toys, :photo_file_size, :integer)
   -> 0.0157s
== 20080727202944 AddPhotosToToys: migrated (0.0405s) ==============

== 20080727203348 AddTitleToToys: migrating ========================
-- add_column(:toys, :title, :string)
   -> 0.0221s
== 20080727203348 AddTitleToToys: migrated (0.0226s) ==============
```

With that, our application is now configured to use a MySQL database instead of a SQLite one. Of course, our database is also now empty, and we'll need to go back and add some records to our application, but before we do that, we'll need to make some additional changes to our application to support geocoding.

Step 4: Modify the schema to support geocode data

For our purposes of geocoding, I don't think that we need to get too specific about where a toy was lost or found, so we don't need to geocode down to a specific street address. Instead, we should pick something that's a bit more generic (and that people will be more willing to share). Using something like a city name might make sense except it might not be specific enough in larger metropolitan areas. Instead, I think we'll capture the ZIP code information.

We'll ask our users to provide a ZIP code for where they found a toy or an approximate ZIP code for where they might have lost the toy. We'll then use the geocoding capabilities of the GeoKit plug-in to convert that ZIP code into latitude and longitude coordinates (most likely the center of the ZIP code).

Later, we can use that latitude and longitude in distance-based searches. We could do something like allowing a user to limit toy results to within a 50-mile radius, which I think addresses the spirit of our story. So in order to support that functionality, we're going to need to add a few more fields to our toys database table. First off, we'll need to support capturing the ZIP code for the toy report, and we'll also need to store the latitude and longitude that we receive when geocoding that ZIP code. So let's add those fields to our database now with a new migration:

```
ruby script/generate migration AddGeoCodingToToys zipcode:string ➡
lat:float lng:float
       exists   db/migrate
       create   db/migrate/20080801155820_add_geo_coding_to_toys.rb
```

Next, we run our migration to add our new fields to the database:

```
rake db:migrate
== 20080801155820 AddGeoCodingToToys: migrating ========================
-- add_column(:toys, :zipcode, :string)
   -> 0.0732s
-- add_column(:toys, :lat, :float)
   -> 0.0394s
-- add_column(:toys, :lng, :float)
   -> 0.0060s
== 20080801155820 AddGeoCodingToToys: migrated (0.1232s) ==============
```

We're on our way. To use the GeoKit plug-in to give us a distance radius around one point, we'll need to convert the ZIP code we've received into latitude and longitude, and for that, we need to obtain a key to one of the online geocoding services.

Step 5: Obtain a geocoding key

To convert addresses (or in our case ZIP codes) into latitude and longitude coordinates, the GeoKit plug-in interfaces into several online geocoding services. However, in order for those to work, we need to create an account (which is free) on those services and provide our application key to the plug-in configuration.

To obtain your key, I recommend that you use either Google, Yahoo, or both. You can obtain a key from Google at http://www.google.com/apis/maps/signup.html or one from Yahoo at http://developer.yahoo.com/wsregapp.

Once you have your key, you'll need to add it to your configuration. At the time of this writing, the current version of the GeoKit plug-in was still appending its configuration elements onto the end of the environment.rb file in /config rather than creating a new configuration file in /config/initializers. I like to keep my configuration file clean, so let's tidy that up. Create a new file in /config/initializers named geokit.rb. Afterward, open your environment.rb file from /config. Somewhere around line 67, you should see an end statement and then the start of new items that look like these:

```
# These defaults are used in GeoKit::Mappable.distance_to and in
# acts_as_mappable
GeoKit::default_units = :miles
GeoKit::default_formula = :sphere
--excerpt--
```

You'll want to cut everything from below that end statement (including the excerpt shown previously) out of this file and paste it into our new geokit.rb config instead.

Now that our configuration is cleaned up a bit, we can get onto the task of configuring our geocoding. Within this configuration, you'll see some places where we are meant to paste our Yahoo and/or Google geocoding keys:

```
# This is your yahoo application key for the Yahoo Geocoder.
# See http://developer.yahoo.com/faq/index.html#appid
# and http://developer.yahoo.com/maps/rest/V1/geocode.html
GeoKit::Geocoders::yahoo = 'REPLACE_WITH_YOUR_YAHOO_KEY'

# This is your Google Maps geocoder key.
# See http://www.google.com/apis/maps/signup.html
# and http://www.google.com/apis/maps/documentation/#Geocoding_Examples
GeoKit::Geocoders::google = 'REPLACE_WITH_YOUR_GOOGLE_KEY'
```

Simply place your keys into those lines. At the very bottom of this configuration is a line for specifying our geocoding order; set the elements like so:

```
GeoKit::Geocoders::provider_order = [:google,:yahoo]
```

Obviously, if you're only using one geocoder, then you'll omit the other from this list. The advantage of having two, however, is that in the event that the first request fails or times out, the GeoKit plug-in will make a request to the second provider as a failover. Save this file, and restart your application (in order for these changes to the environment configuration to be loaded). Next, let's move on to enabling geocoding support in our Toy model.

Step 6: Add geocoding to the Toy model

Currently, our Toy model (/app/models/toy.rb) looks like this:

```
class Toy < ActiveRecord::Base
  VALID_STATUSES = %w(LOST FOUND)

  validates_presence_of :title, :description, :status
  validates_inclusion_of :status, :in => VALID_STATUSES

  belongs_to :user

  has_attached_file :photo,
      :styles => { :medium => "300x300>", :thumb => "100x100>" }

end
```

The first thing that we'll want to do is to add some extra validations to ensure that we don't save a toy that we wouldn't be able to do a geographic search for. To do that, we should validate that all three of our new fields are now present:

```
validates_presence_of :zipcode, :lat, :lng
```

Next, we simply need to configure our model to automatically geocode our ZIP code field. There are actually two ways that we can do this.

The longer way would require that we first tell the model to automatically mix in the GeoKit functionality through the use of the following method:

```
acts_as_mappable
```

Next, we would need to use a callback in the model to make the calls to the geocoders. Since we would only want this to occur before the validations are run (otherwise, our lat and lng fields would fail validation), we would use the before_validation callback method and pass it the name of a new method in our model:

```
before_validation :geocode_me
```

Finally, we would need to create the geocode_me method that we just specified in the previous line. So down at the bottom of your model, we would add a method that look like this:

```
def geocode_me
    geo=GeoKit::Geocoders::MultiGeocoder.geocode(zipcode)
    errors.add(:zipcode, "Could not geocode zip code") if !geo.success
    self.lat, self.lng = geo.lat,geo.lng if geo.success
end
```

What's going on here? Well, in the first line of this method, we're making a call out to the geocode method in the GeoKit plug-in and passing it our zipcode field; we're then assigning the returned values to a variable named geo. In the second line, we're checking to see if the previous line was successful (with !geo.success). If it wasn't, we're adding a validation error onto the zipcode field with a message to display to the user. Finally, in the last line, if the call was successful, we're assigning this object's lat and lng fields to the returned lat and lng fields from our geo response.

That process is pretty straightforward and simple I think, and this is the proper way to go if we needed to also add in any extra customizations or logic into our geocoding efforts. However, since our needs are fairly straightforward, we can skip much of that and add the same functionality like so:

```
acts_as_mappable :auto_geocode=>true
```

That one line will do all of the same geocoding that we would have just built, except for one small issue. By default, the plug-in will look for a field named "address" to use in the geocoding. Fortunately, we can override this default by setting our call like so:

```
acts_as_mappable :auto_geocode=>{:field=>:zipcode}
```

With that, our Toy model should look like this:

```
class Toy < ActiveRecord::Base
  VALID_STATUSES = %w(LOST FOUND)

  validates_presence_of :title, :description, :status
  validates_presence_of :zipcode, :lat, :lng
  validates_inclusion_of :status, :in => VALID_STATUSES

  belongs_to :user

  has_attached_file :photo,
      :styles => { :medium => "300x300>", :thumb => "100x100>" }

  acts_as_mappable :auto_geocode=>{:field=>:zipcode}
end
```

To see our geocoding in action, let's open a script/console window and play around with creating a few simple toys, so we can see the lat and lng get populated automatically.

Now for me, whenever I want to just experiment around with a model and not actually create new records in the database, I'll also pass the -s command line option to the script/console command to start up the console in sandbox mode like so:

```
ruby script/console -s
Loading development environment in sandbox (Rails 2.1.0)
Any modifications you make will be rolled back on exit
>>
```

The key feature of the sandbox is that anything we do in here isn't actually saved to the database, which means we can have a lot of fun! Let's create a new lost toy record:

```
toy1 = Toy.new(:title => "Boba Fett", :status => "LOST",
        :description => "lost my original boba fett action figure",
        :user_id => 1, :zipcode => "95926")
```

That's easy enough so far; you can even see in the returned object that the lat and lng fields are currently set to nil. However, that changes once we save the object:

```
toy1.save      #  true

toy1.lat       #  39.745667
toy1.lng       #  -121.845116
```

Success! Our geocoding is working, and we're converting ZIP codes into latitude and longitude coordinates. Of course, as long as we're in here, let's take a quick little peek at how easy it is now to search for a toy based on location. The GeoKit plug-in enhanced our regular ActiveRecord find method with some interesting new location-based method options such as :origin (for setting where to center our search) and :within (for setting how far away from the origin we should search). To test our existing record, we can do a find and set our origin to a neighboring ZIP code to see if it finds the lost toy that we just created:

```
Toy.find(:all, :origin=>"95951", :within => 25)
=> [#<Toy id: 1, description: "lost my original boba fett action....]
```

Just to verify that it wasn't a fluke, let's also test from a ZIP code that's much farther away to verify that we don't find a match:

```
Toy.find(:all, :origin=>"90210", :within => 25)
=> []
```

Looks like everything is good to go with our model's support for geocoding now.

Step 7: Modify the application's forms to capture ZIP codes

Of course, we still have one last set of changes to make in order for this to work for our users. We still need to add the ZIP code field to the forms in our view templates to allow users to populate it. This matter is trivial, so I'll just provide you with the relevant changes.

In /app/views/toys/lost.html.erb, you'll need to make the following changes:

```
<h1>Report a lost toy</h1>
<% form_for @toy, :html => { :multipart => true } do |f| %>
  <%= f.error_messages %>
  <p>
    <%= f.label :title, "What kind of toy did you lose?" %>
    <%= f.text_field :title %>
  </p>
  <p>
    <%= f.label :description, "Describe the toy, making sure to note ➡
any distinguishing features and how someone could contact you ➡
if it was found." %>
    <%= f.text_area :description %>
    <%= f.hidden_field :status, :value => "LOST" %>
  </p>
```

```
  <p>
    <%= f.label :zipcode,"Please provide an approximate zipcode ➥
  for where you might have lost the toy (for location based ➥
  searches)" %>
    <%= f.text_field :zipcode %>
  </p>
  <p>
    <%= f.label :photo, "Please upload a Photo of the toy" %>
    <%= f.file_field :photo %>  </p>
  </p>
  <p>
    <%= f.submit "Create" %>
  </p>
<% end %>

  <%= link_to 'Back', toys_path %>
```

In /app/views/toys/found.html.erb, you'll make the following changes:

```
<h1>Report a toy that was found</h1>
<% form_for @toy, :html => { :multipart => true } do |f| %>
  <%= f.error_messages %>
  <p>
    <%= f.label :title, "What kind of toy did you find?" %>
    <%= f.text_field :title %>
  </p>
  <p>
    <%= f.label :description, "Describe the toy and where you found ➥
  it and provide information on how the owner can reclaim it" %>
    <%= f.text_area :description %>
    <%= f.hidden_field :status, :value => "FOUND" %>
  </p>
  <p>
    <%= f.label :zipcode,"Please provide the approximate zipcode ➥
  for where you found the toy" %>
    <%= f.text_field :zipcode %>
  </p>
  <p>
    <%= f.label :photo, "If possible, please upload a Photo of the ➥
  toy" %>
    <%= f.file_field :photo %>  </p>
  </p>
  <p>
    <%= f.submit "Create" %>
  </p>
<% end %>

  <%= link_to 'Back', toys_path %>
```

Finally, within /app/views/toys/edit.html.erb, you'll also need to add your new ZIP code field like so:

```
<h1>Editing toy</h1>

<% form_for @toy, :html => { :multipart => true } do |f| %>

  <%= f.error_messages %>

  <p>
    <%= f.label :title, "Kind of toy" %><br>
    <%= f.text_field :title %>
  </p>
  <p>
    <%= f.label :description, "Description of toy" %><br />
    <%= f.text_area :description %>
  </p>
  <p>
    <%= f.label :zipcode,"Zipcode for where toy was lost / found" %>
    <%= f.text_field :zipcode %>
  </p>
  <p>
    <%= f.label :photo, "update photo" %><br />
    <%= f.file_field :photo %>  </p>
  <p>
    <%= f.submit "Update" %>
  </p>
<% end %>

<%= link_to 'Show', @toy %> |
<%= link_to 'Back', toys_path %>
```

At this point, it would be a good idea to go through the process of re-creating your user account and adding a number of sample toys into the database. When you create the new toys, you should create them with a variety of different ZIP codes (because if they're all the same, you won't be able to see them working when we add the filters in our next story).

Story 3: Enhance our toy listings with filters

Now that we can geocode our toys, we can add the ability for users to filter our listings to only the specific ones that they care about. For our simple purposes, we're going to allow our users to limit results based on whether the toy was reported as a lost toy or a found toy, and we're going to allow them to also limit the results based on proximity to a ZIP code that they provide. This should allow users to narrow down to a more specific set of toys that they might be looking for. In addition, we might have considered adding in the ability for users to search for key words in the descriptions. However, correctly implementing a full-text search can be a fairly complicated process, and I chose to bypass it for this book, rather than short-changing you by implementing a solution that you wouldn't want to put into production.

Step 1: Add named scopes to our Toy model

Since we're going to be searching based on the status of a toy, let's start out by adding some named scopes to our Toy model for some simple conditions that we'll most likely be using:

```ruby
class Toy < ActiveRecord::Base
  VALID_STATUSES = %w(LOST FOUND)

  validates_presence_of :title, :description, :status
  validates_presence_of :zipcode, :lat, :lng
  validates_inclusion_of :status, :in => VALID_STATUSES

  belongs_to :user

  has_attached_file :photo,
      :styles => { :medium => "300x300>", :thumb => "100x100>" }

  acts_as_mappable :auto_geocode=>{:field=>:zipcode}

  named_scope :lost, :conditions => "status = 'LOST'"
  named_scope :found, :conditions => "status = 'FOUND'"
  named_scope :recent, :order => "created_at DESC"

end
```

Here, I've added three simple named scopes: two that simply search based on the status of the toy (lost or found), and just for good measure, I've added a third that simply sets the order to ensure that we're always returning the results newest to oldest.

Step 2: Build the filter interface to our toys listing

Since we already know the fields that we want to filter on, we can go ahead and add a search form onto our browse toy listings page. So open /app/views/toys/index.html.erb and modify it like so:

```erb
<div id="adv_search">
  <h2>Filter Results By:</h2>
  <% form_tag({:action => 'index'}, :method => 'get') do %>
    <div class="search_element">
      <label>Zipcode:</label>
      <%= text_field_tag :zipcode, h(params[:zipcode]) %><br>
    </div>
    <div class="search_element">
```

```
    <label>Category:</label>
    <%= select_tag :status, options_for_select(Toy::VALID_STATUSES➥
+ [""], h(params[:status]) ) %>
  </div>
  <div class="search_element">
    <%= submit_tag 'Filter' %>
  </div>
 <% end %>
</div>

<h1>Listing toys</h1>
<% for toy in @toys %>
  <h2 class="listing_title"><%= link_to(toy.title, toy) %></h2>
  <p class="thumb"><%= link_to(image_tag(toy.photo.url(:thumb)), ➥
toy) %></p>
  <p><%= simple_format(truncate(toy.description, 95) + link_to(" ➥
More Info", toy)) %></p>
<% end %>
<p class="closing">Thank you for your support</p>
```

So what did we do there? Well, we added a new form to the top of our template. Because this form is not intended to edit a model, we didn't want to use our block of form_for helper methods. No, this is an independent form that is not associated to any models, so instead, we're using the _tag family for form helper methods, such as form_tag and, text_field_tag. We specified in the form_tag helper method that this form should be pointed to the index action. However, because this is a RESTful controller, we also had to specify explicitly that this form should use the GET HTTP method to access this action (if we had let the form do its default action of POST, RESTful routing would have sent the request to the create action instead).

> *Anytime you're writing a search or filter type of function, setting those requests to use GET instead of POST is typically a good idea. That way, your search parameters will be set within the URL, which makes it possible for your users to bookmark those search results or even share those results by sending that URL to a friend.*

Beyond the basic form setup, the form fields should seem straightforward. We're creating a text field to capture ZIP codes and a drop-down select box that has its values set from the VALID_STATUSES constant we created in the Toy model.

This simple addition causes our page to now look like Figure 12-3.

Figure 12-3. Our filter has been added to the page.

Step 3: Modify the index action in the Toys controller for filtered searches

As you probably noticed, our new filter form submits to the index action to get its results. In my experience, this is the perfect place for search and filter operations when dealing with a RESTful design, because it's the index action's purpose to display a collection of results. When we're dealing with search and filters, we're still dealing with displaying a collection—it's just a collection with some specific criteria.

In order to implement our filter functionality in the controller, we simply need to modify our index action to support searching with a number of additional (optional) criteria.

Currently, the index action in our toys controller looks like this:

```
def index
  @toys = Toy.find(:all, :order => 'created_at DESC')
end
```

And if we weren't already about to change it to support our filters, I would probably have simplified this using one of the named scopes we recently added to look something like this:

```
def index
  @toys = Toy.recent
end
```

Oh well, there's no use focusing on what could have been. What we need to do is to modify this index action to look at the values that are set in the params. If values such as zipcode or status are set, we know that this request is coming from the filter form, and thus we should dynamically build our search query using those values. If those values are not present in the params, we know that this is a normal request, and we can simply return our normal response.

However, I don't really like cluttering up my controllers with a bunch of additional logic. Controllers should stay as thin on code as possible, so instead, we'll modify our controller to call a new class method in the Toy model, which will evaluate those parameters, build the dynamic search, and return the appropriate results back to our controller. So let's modify our controller action to look like this:

```
def index
  @toys = Toy.find_with_search(params[:zipcode], params[:status])
end
```

Here, we've modified our action to call a find_with_search method instead, and we're passing into this new method the zipcode and status params. Now, we just need to build this new method in our Toy model.

Step 4: Build the find_with_search method in our Toy model

Back in our Toy model (/app/models/toy.rb), we'll need to define this new method as a class method like so:

```
def self.find_with_search(zipcode = nil, status = nil)
end
```

We've got the new class method defined, and it's set to accept our zipcode and status values as parameters (setting them with default values of nil if they're missing), but how will we handle the processing of this data?

Traditionally, I would probably have built a number of literal SQL queries and parsed them together into a string that would be used as the conditions parameter within a find query. Which would look something like this simplified example:

```
def self.find_with_search(zipcode = nil, status = nil)
  cond << "toys.status = 'LOST'" if status == "LOST"
  cond << "toys.status = 'FOUND'" if status == "FOUND"
```

```
      Toy.find :all, :conditions => cond
end
```

This solution is OK, but it forces us to move back down into writing raw SQL queries and doesn't take advantage of any of the named scope goodness that Rails 2.1 gave to us. Instead, what we'll do is build an array of all the scopes that we would want to call, join them together into a string, and then execute that string. Let's add these two methods to our Toy model and then we'll go over what they're doing for us:

```
def self.find_with_search(zipcode = nil, status = nil)
  search_scopes = %w(Toy recent)
  search_scopes << "lost" if status == "LOST"
  search_scopes << "found" if status == "FOUND"
  search_scopes << Toy.return_zipcode_search(zipcode)

  command_to_call = search_scopes.join(".")
  eval(command_to_call)
end

def self.return_zipcode_search(zipcode)
  if zipcode =~ /^[\d]{5}+$/
    return "find(:all, :origin => '#{zipcode}', :within => 50)"
  else
    return "find(:all)"
  end
end
```

The way this works is that we start out by defining a new array named search_scopes that initially contains two values (Toy and recent). At the end of this method, we're going to use the array method join to combine any values in this array, using a period to separate them and storing the result in a variable named command_to_call. So assuming that we never added anything additional to our search_scopes array, this command to call would contain a string with a value of "Toy.recent". We then take this string variable and pass it into the eval method, which will "evaluate" and essentially execute as code any string that's passed to it. So in this example, it would have called Toy.recent just as if it had been code that was typed into the source rather than a dynamic string that we generated. That's the overall outline of what we're doing. The remainder of the code is simply to add additional strings to our search_scopes array before it is joined and evaluated.

We add other items into our array by examining the values of status and zipcode that were passed to the method. We can append our lost or found named scopes into our array like so:

```
search_scopes << "lost" if status == "LOST"
search_scopes << "found" if status == "FOUND"
```

But our examination of the zipcode parameter is a little bit trickier. In this section, we actually call another method (return_zipcode_search) to do the work for us:

```
search_scopes << Toy.return_zipcode_search(zipcode)
```

The reason we're calling another method here is to reduce the complexity of our methods by making them focus on doing a single task instead of multiple tasks. In the return_zipcode_search method, we pass the zipcode variable through a regular expression to ensure that it is exactly five digits long and composed entirely of digits. If it passes that regular expression, we then add that value into a location-based find that we'll append onto the end of our array. If for any reason it fails that check, we'll simply append a find(:all) onto the end of the array.

> Technically, we could have converted our ZIP code search into a named scope as well using a dynamic feature of Ruby named lambda, but that's a slightly more advanced Ruby topic to understand than was necessary for a foundation book. However, a good resource to see how that could be implemented would be the RailsCasts episode on named scopes (http://railscasts.com/episodes/108-named-scope).

So when this is all put together, it will generate queries for us like this:

```
Toy.recent.lost.find(:all)
Toy.recent.found.find(:all, :origin => '66213', :within => 50)
```

Each of these queries will then be evaluated into an ActiveRecord query and the result returned back to our controller to be populated into the @toys instance variable that will then be displayed in our standard index template.

Pretty slick, huh?

> Using eval can often be considered a very bad thing because it introduces the risk of arbitrary code that we didn't supply being executed on the server. In this particular case, I think it would be OK as we're being very restrictive over what text could be in the string that eval is called on. In this example, the only place where user provided content could ever make it into the eval string is the ZIP code, and we're using a regular expression on that value to ensure that it is always only a five- digit number.

Story 4: Building an RSS feed for lost toys

Our next story is going to focus on providing one of those "must- have" features for any application that's launched these days—an RSS feed. While this story might sound a little intimidating at first glance, I think you'll be surprised at how quickly and easily we'll be able to complete it.

However, before we'll be able to implement this story, we need to take a deeper look at a subject that we've mentioned a few times throughout the book, that is, how Rails allows us to support sending different responses from the same actions based upon what type of data was requested.

Supporting multiple formats

You might recall that we've discussed in the book that one of the advantages of building our controllers RESTfully is that doing so also supports our need to return multiple formats from the same controller actions. Sending multiple formats from a single action is an incredibly powerful feature of

Rails, because it helps prevent us from having to clutter our controllers with multiple actions that perform the exact same functionality and differ only in how the response is formatted.

Thus we can simply add a small amount of code to a simple action (like our index action) and, from there, return any number of different responses. For example, from one controller action, we can define that it can support a JavaScript format to respond to AJAX request, an XML response for XML requests, as well as responses for special clients such as mobile phones or even a iPhone format.

Does that sound like it will be complicated to do? Well, it's not, and it takes only a few minor additions to our controller. Let's see it in action within our existing application.

Currently, the index action of our toys controller looks like this:

```
def index
  @toys = Toy.find_with_search(params[:zipcode], params[:status])
end
```

Nice and straightforward, isn't it? By default, this action will look for an HTML template in /app/views/toys named index.html.erb to render its response. What we need to do is modify the action to also support formats in addition to HTML, which we can do using the respond_to method like so:

```
def index
  @toys = Toy.find_with_search(params[:zipcode], params[:status])
  respond_to do |format|
    format.html
    format.js
    format.xml  { render :xml => @toys }
  end
end
```

Here, we're using the respond_to method to respond to a variety of formats. In this case, we've set this action to be able to respond to HTML requests (which will render the same index.html.erb template that it was using before). In addition, we've added a support to respond to a JavaScript request (format.js), which will look for a default JavaScript template (which we'll build in just a moment), and we've also added support for XML requests (format.xml), which will simply render out an XML representation of our @toys collection (render :xml => @toys).

> How does Rails know which response type to pick? It uses two methods for determining the desired response format. First, it will look within the request for an HTTP accept header and use its value to return the corresponding template. Therefore, if the request had a header that included Accept: text/xml, Rails would know to return the XML-formatted response. Second, Rails allows the requester to override what was set in the HTTP accept header by simply appending the requested response type at the end of the URL. In this way, we can use our web browser to view our various responses without having to hack the HTTP header. So to view the XML response for our index action, we could issue a request to URL http://localhost:3000/index.xml.

As you can probably imagine, building an RSS feed is simply going to be another formatted response that we'll add to the index action of our toys controller, so go ahead and change your index action in your toys controller to look like this:

```ruby
def index
  @toys = Toy.find_with_search(params[:zipcode], params[:status])
  respond_to do |format|
    format.html
    format.js
    format.xml  { render :xml => @toys }
    format.rss
  end
end
```

Unfortunately, at this time, Rails doesn't offer anything quite as simple as a render :rss => @toys feature, so we need to define our RSS feed manually.

While we could certainly build this as an ERB template, there's actually an easier method using the Ruby Builder library, which is included in standard Ruby and provides an incredibly easy interface for creating XML markup. While a full description of how to use the Builder library is a better subject for an intermediate Ruby book, the syntax is incredibly straightforward, and thus I don't believe that you'll have any problems reading how it's working for how we use it to build our RSS feed.

> You can also read more about the Ruby Builder library at http://builder.rubyforge.org/.

We've signaled to our index action that it should be able to respond to an RSS format request. So now we simply need to build a template file that will be used for RSS requests and use the Builder library to render its content. Create a new file in /app/views/toys named index.rss.builder, and in this file, place the following content:

```ruby
xml.instruct! :xml, :version => "1.0"
xml.rss :version => "2.0" do
  xml.channel do
    xml.title "Lost Toys"
    xml.description "Help Reunite children with lost toys"
    xml.link formatted_toys_url(:rss)

    for toy in @toys
      xml.item do
        xml.title toy.title
        xml.description toy.description
        xml.pubDate toy.created_at.to_s(:rfc822)
        xml.link formatted_toy_url(toy, :rss)
        xml.guid formatted_toy_url(toy, :rss)
      end
    end
  end
end
```

You can see here that the Builder library creates the feed with a quick series of method calls that match the fields that we need for an RSS feed and that we're able to loop over our @toys collection to output all of the items into the feed. From this point on, readers could subscribe to your RSS feed at http://localhost:3000/toys.rss. You can see the output of this feed in Figure 12-4.

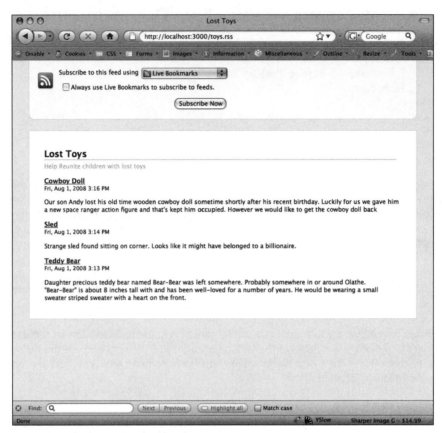

Figure 12-4. Viewing our RSS feed in a browser

I hope you agree that adding that extra response was pretty darn easy. In fact, we'll be using that ability to send multiple responses in our next several stories as we continue to enhance our application by exploring a few Rails feature that we haven't touched thus far in our application.

Story 5: AJAXifing our filter

I've mentioned a few times throughout the book that Rails includes support for AJAX functionality, but in this story, you'll have your first chance to dig into that support, as we implement a simple AJAX feature to our application.

Step 1: Include the necessary JavaScript files

The first step to doing that will be to include the necessary JavaScript files to our application. Rails includes the Prototype (http://www.prototypejs.org/) and script.aculo.us (http://script.aculo.us/) JavaScript libraries with every application in the /public/javascripts directory. To use them in our application, we simply need to include them into our view templates. Of course, Rails makes this process even easier with a simple helper method to include all the necessary JavaScript files that we'll use in our application's layout like this:

```
<!DOCTYPE html PUBLIC "-//W3C//DTD XHTML 1.0 Transitional//EN"
  "http://www.w3.org/TR/xhtml1/DTD/xhtml1-transitional.dtd">
<head>
  <title>Lost Toys - Reuniting Children with Toys</title>
  <%= stylesheet_link_tag 'application' %>
  <%= javascript_include_tag :defaults %>
</head>
<body>
--excerpt--
```

When viewing the rendered page, that one line of code (javascript_include_tag :defaults) may not look like it's done anything until we view the source and see that this one line has added five lines of code to include the necessary JavaScript libraries for us:

```
<!DOCTYPE html PUBLIC "-//W3C//DTD XHTML 1.0 Transitional//EN"
  "http://www.w3.org/TR/xhtml1/DTD/xhtml1-transitional.dtd">
<head>
  <title>Lost Toys - Reuniting Children with Toys</title>
  <link href="/stylesheets/application.css?1216782088"
                media="screen" rel="stylesheet" type="text/css" />
  <script src="/javascripts/prototype.js?1217103667"
            type="text/javascript"></script>
  <script src="/javascripts/effects.js?1217103667"
            type="text/javascript"></script>
  <script src="/javascripts/dragdrop.js?1217103667"
            type="text/javascript"></script>
  <script src="/javascripts/controls.js?1217103667"
            type="text/javascript"></script>
  <script src="/javascripts/application.js?1217103667"
            type="text/javascript"></script>
--excerpt--
```

Now that we have the necessary JavaScript libraries in our application, we can take advantage of a number of powerful helper methods that Rails provides to make adding AJAX a breeze.

Brief tour of AJAX helper methods

Before we convert our existing application template to use an AJAX helper, I thought it would be a good idea for us to pause for a moment and take a quick tour of a few of the more common AJAX helper methods that Rails provides for us to use in our view templates.

link_to_remote This is exactly what you think it is, a helper method exactly like our normal `link_to` helper, except this one will generate the link in a way that it will submit its request as an AJAX request. This allows us to instantly change any of our links to an AJAX request by simply replacing the helper method used to generate the link.

remote_form_for We can also instantly convert any of our forms into an AJAX based form by replacing the `form_for` helper with the `remote_form_for` call:

```
<% remote_form_for(@post) do |f| %>
```

Of course, just like with our normal form helpers, there's also a version for the instances when we're not editing a resource named `form_remote_tag`.

periodically_call_remote Have you ever wanted to have an element on the page refresh with server data on a regular basis? Well, that's exactly what the `periodically_call_remote` helper can do for you. Using it, we define a hidden AJAX request that will fire on a specified interval. For example, we can build a hidden AJAX call to the update action on the server every 10 seconds and use its response to update the content of comments div:

```
periodically_call_remote(:url => 'update', :frequency => '10', ➡
:update => 'comments')
```

observe_field Sometimes, you might have a need to do some sort of AJAX request in response to a user making changes to a form field. A good example is doing some sort of dynamic automatically complete or providing a live preview. We set the name of the field that we want to monitor, the URL that should be submitted to, and then a number of optional parameters, such as how often we should check for changes to the observed field (in seconds), and what field we should update based on the response:

```
<%= observe_field :auto_suggest, :url => { :action => :index },
      :frequency => 0.25,
      :update => :suggestions,
      :with => 'query'
%>
```

Step 2: Convert the filter form to use AJAX

For the purposes of our application, we can save a little bandwidth and increase the cool factor of our toy listings by changing the filtered results from a request and full page reload into an AJAX request that simply updates the page with the updated list of filtered results.

Let's convert our filtering search feature into an AJAX request. To do that, we'll use one of our AJAX helper methods to convert our existing search form into an AJAX form. Looking in our `index.html.erb` template, you can see that currently we start the definition of our filter form like this:

```
<% form_tag({:action => 'index'}, :method => 'get') do %>
```

To convert this to an AJAX request, we can change this to use the `form_remote_tag` helper method like this instead:

```
<% form_remote_tag :url => toys_path, :method => "get" do %>
```

So if you haven't already, go ahead and make this change to our advanced filter form in `index.html.erb`.

This one simple change has completely modified our existing form to now use AJAX (if available) for submitting its data to the server. From this point on, any submissions from this form will now be transmitted via JavaScript, and thus they will follow the `format.js` response path in our controller action.

It's time now to take a look at how we can use that response path to send back changes to our existing page using dynamic JavaScript that was written in Ruby.

Brief tour of RJS

RJS is Rails's solution for generating JavaScript code using Ruby. This incredibly powerful feature is a server-side solution for generating dynamic responses to AJAX requests without having to resort to writing raw JavaScript. Typically, the RJS code that we will write will reside in specially named RJS templates that can be found in the same directories as our traditional HTML views. However, whereas our standard view template would be named something like `index.html.erb`, the RJS template for the same action would be named `index.js.rjs`. So you can see it continues the same naming convention with the first word representing the name of the template (usually the same as the action it's associated to), the second name representing the type of content that we're returning (`js` for JavaScript in this instance), and the final name representing the rendering engine that is used to parse the template (RJS for this).

Within an RJS template, we have access to an object named page that represents our current web page. Using this object, we can do some pretty amazing things to the contents of the page using a variety of methods defined on that page object.

For example, the way that we interact with the elements on the page is through the DOM (short for Document Object Model), which isn't that different than the way that you would use CSS to style an element within the page. We simply have to specify the element on the page that we want to affect and the easiest way to do that is to lock onto the ID of the element using a special method that uses our array brackets [ ].

Imagine that we wanted to use RJS to do some manipulation of our filter form that we added recently, which looks like this:

```
<div id="adv_search">
  <h2>Filter Results By:</h2>
  -- excerpted --
</div>
```

Using RJS, we could do things to this form such as hide the entire form using a `page['adv_search'].hide` and then cause that form to reappear using `page['adv_search'].show`. We could even change the contents of that form using something like this:

```
page.replace_html "adv_search", "You're semi-evil.
                                 You're quasi-evil.
                                 You're the margarine of evil.
                                 You're the Diet Coke of evil.
                                 Just one calorie, not evil enough."
```

Or we could trigger an advanced visual effect, such as having the entire element momentarily flash as the color yellow and then transition back to normal with a page.visual_effect :highlight, "adv_search". Now tell me that's not cool!

Let's do a quick tour of some of the methods that you'll be using most often when writing RJS templates.

[] As we just discussed, this method is useful for obtaining a reference to an element on the page via its ID such as page['adv_search'].

hide As we discussed, this method is useful for hiding elements on the page. The element still exists within the source, but its CSS styles are essentially set to display: none.

We can call it either as part of a chain like this

```
page['adv_search'].hide
```

or we call it directly on the page object, passing in any number of element IDs to hide like this:

```
page.hide 'adv_search', 'comments', 'toy_12'
```

show This method will un-hide a hidden element on the page, causing it to suddenly appear on the rendered page. In essence, it can be considered the opposite of the hide method.

We can call it either as part of a chain like this

```
page['adv_search'].show
```

or we call it directly on the page object, passing in any number of element IDs to show like this:

```
page.show 'adv_search', 'comments', 'toy_12'
```

remove This method removes the element completely from the page and the source. There is no way to undo this outside of manually re-adding the element:

```
page.remove 'adv_search', 'comments', 'toy_12'
```

insert_html This inserts an HTML element at a specified position within the specified element. Possible positions are:

- :top: HTML is inserted inside the element, before the element's existing content.
- :bottom: HTML is inserted inside the element, after the element's existing content.
- :before: HTML is inserted immediately preceding the element.
- :after: HTML is inserted immediately following the element.

In practice, we can pass in a literal element like so:

```
page.insert_html :bottom, 'my_list', '<li>One more item</li>'
```

Or if we are using a partial, we can call it to render the new element:

```
page.insert_html :before, 'content', :partial => 'search_form'
```

replace_html This method is similar to insert_html but is used to replace the content of the given ID. You saw earlier that we talked about using it to replace the content of our search form with yet another movie quote:

```
page.replace_html "adv_search", "You're semi-evil.
                                  You're quasi-evil.
                                  You're the margarine of evil.
                                  You're the Diet Coke of evil.
                                  Just one calorie, not evil enough."
```

But we can also use it to render partials and instance variables similar to the way that we render the partials in the view templates:

```
page.replace_html "toy_listing", :partial => @toys
```

alert Though not quite as useful for production use as some others, this method will cause a JavaScript alert box with a given message:

```
page.alert('I can haz cheeseburger!')
```

call This method allows you to call other JavaScript functions that are defined within the page. It's useful if you're using a third- party JavaScript library and want to be able to interact with it from your RJS templates:

```
page.call 'alert', 'All your base are belong to us!'
```

delay The delay method allows you to insert a pause before executing another RJS action (specified in a block to the delay method). This can be really useful when you want to display some form of temporary message to the user and then remove it from the page after a few moments:

```
page['adv_search'].show
page.delay(10) do
  page['adv_search'].hide
end
```

toggle The effect of hiding and showing the same element again and again is so common that the toggle helper method was added simply to iterate between the states. In other words, if the element is hidden and toggle is called on it, the element will be shown, and vice versa.

```
page.toggle 'adv_search'
```

visual_effect This method is pure fun, as it allows you to call any of the visual effects that are defined by the script.aculo.us library such as highlight, appear, fade, slidedown, or slideup. It also features a few predefined toggle visual effects such as toggle_appear, toggle_slide, and toggle_blind that can be called to toggle an element's visibility with style.

```
page.visual_effect :highlight, "adv_search"
```

369

Step 3: Build an RJS response

With that brief understanding, you're ready to build a simple RJS template to respond to the AJAX request that our filter form is now going to be sending. We've already configured our controller by adding the format.js line in our respond_to block, and we've already converted the form, so all that's left is to build the RJS template itself.

Create a new file in /app/views/toys named index.js.rjs, and within this template, we'll place our RJS command to replace the toy results. However, to make that easier, we should clean up our view a bit. Currently, the section of our index template that displays our toy listings looks like this:

```
-- excerpt --
<h1>Listing toys</h1>
<% for toy in @toys %>
  <h2 class="listing_title"><%= link_to(toy.title, toy) %></h2>
  <p class="thumb"><%= link_to(image_tag(toy.photo.url(:thumb)), ➥
  toy) %></p>
  <p><%= simple_format(truncate(toy.description, 95) + link_to(" ➥
  More Info", toy)) %></p>
<% end %>
-- excerpt --
```

That's OK, except for the fact that it would be a lot easier for us if we could add some sort of wrapper div with a unique ID that we could use to target the specific section that we want to replace. In addition, we could simplify this code (and the code in our RJS template) if we were using a collection partial instead of simply looping over the result set within the view template. So let's make those changes.

First off, we'll create a new partial in /app/views/toys named _toy.html.erb, in which we'll place the code that was previously in our loop.

```
<h2 class="listing_title"><%= link_to(toy.title, toy) %></h2>
  <p class="thumb"><%= link_to(image_tag(toy.photo.url(:thumb)), ➥
  toy) %></p>
<p><%= simple_format(truncate(toy.description, 95) + link_to(" ➥
  More Info", toy)) %></p>
```

Next, back in the index.html.erb template, we'll add a wrapper div with an ID of toy_listing and replace our code that was moved with a call to render the partial:

```
<h1>Listing toys</h1>
<div id="toy_listing">
  <%= render :partial => @toys %>
</div>
```

Simple enough. Now, we can populate our index.js.rjs template with a call to replace the contents of our toy_listing div with the results of rendering that same partial again with the new results like so:

```
page.replace_html "toy_listing", :partial => @toys
```

That certainly works, but it can happen fairly fast, and the user may not even realize that the content has changed. Therefore, it's usually a good idea that anytime we change the content of the page in response to an AJAX request that we also add some form of visual effect to signal the user that the content has changed. In our case, the simple "highlight" visual effect should work just fine. So our final index.js.rjs template should look like this:

```
page.replace_html "toy_listing", :partial => @toys
page.visual_effect :highlight, "toy_listing"
```

After making this change, you should start up your application so you can see the effect in action (it's not exactly something that I can show you in a screenshot).

That's all there is to adding some AJAX sweetness to our simple little application. In my experience, a little bit of AJAX goes a long way. So it's always best to avoid overdoing it.

Story 6: A simple XML API

For our final story that we'll implement in this project, we're also going to take a quick look at how we can use the XML format to provide our users with some additional ways to access our data. You've already seen that we added an XML response to our index action with the format.xml { render :xml => @toys } line, but have you ever wondered how we could access it?

Well, in this final story we're not only going to build a full XML API for our application, but we're also going to explore a library in Rails that you haven't seen yet by the name of ActiveResource, and we'll use this library to build a complete external interface to our lost toys application.

We can most easily access the XML version of our toys list page by simply appending .xml to the end of the URL. So rather than viewing http://localhost:3000/toys, we will visit http://localhost:3000/toys.xml. You can see the results of viewing that URL in the Firefox web browser in Figure 12-5.

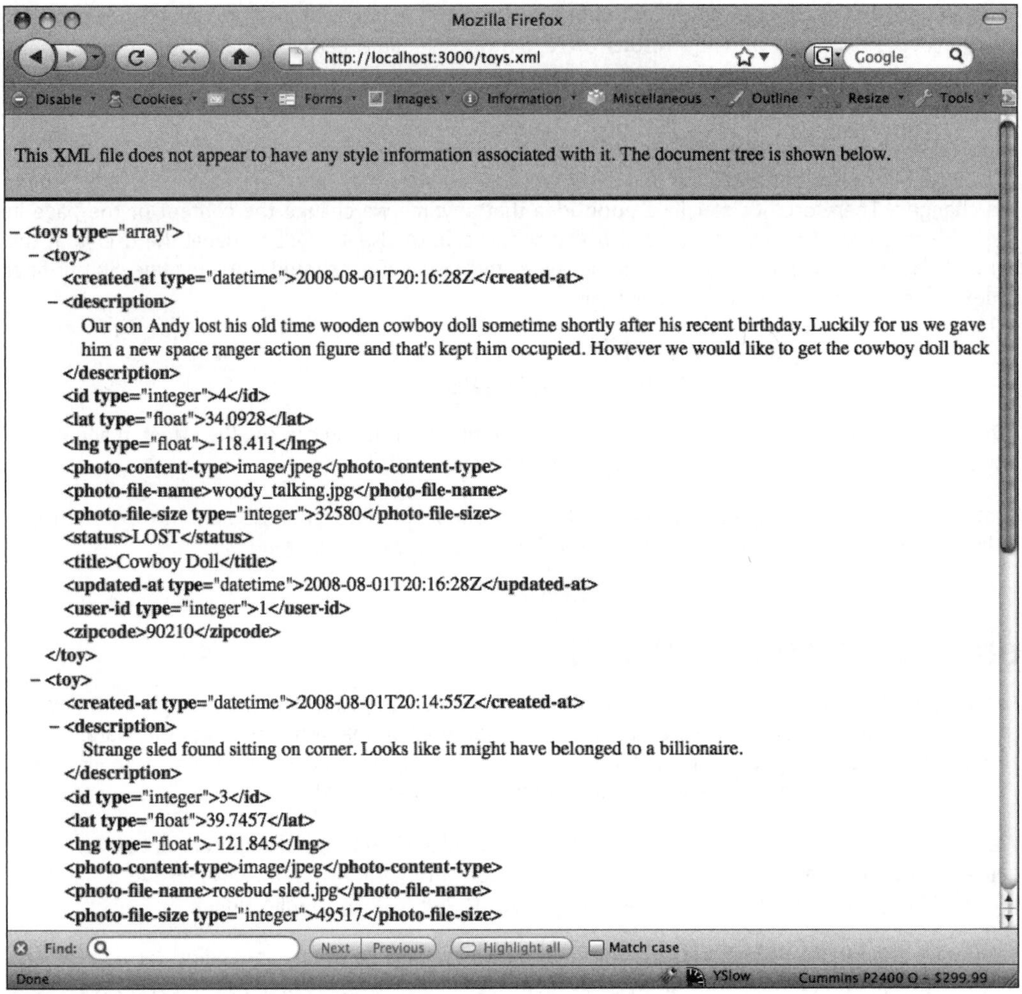

Figure 12-5. Viewing the XML version of our toy listings

Of course, reading the XML through a web browser, while kind of neat, isn't exactly very useful. To see a more practical use of our XML interface, let's also add an XML response to the show action and then explore a powerful REST client library that's included with Rails named ActiveResource.

In your toys controller, modify your show action to look like this:

```
def show
  @toy = Toy.find(params[:id])
  respond_to do |format|
    format.html
    format.xml  { render :xml => @toy }
  end
end
```

With that change, we can also append a .xml to the end of any toy detail page to view the XML representation of it (i.e., http://localhost:3000/toys/4.xml).

Building an ActiveResource client

A major feature that Rails added into its 2.0 release was a powerful client library that makes interfacing to RESTful web services as simple as making a call to an ActiveRecord table. Sound too good to be true? Well, let me prove it to you with a very simplified implementation of an ActiveResource client.

To do that, let's create a new Rails application that we can use to interface to our Lost Toys application. In your project's directory, let's create a new Rails application named toy_client:

```
rails toy_client
```

Then change into that directory and remove the index.html from /public.

```
cd toy_client
rm public/index.html
```

Now, to link up to our application's RESTful interface, we simply need to create a model that will inherit from ActiveResource instead of ActiveRecord. So create a new file in /app/models named toy.rb, and place the following class definition in it:

```
class Toy < ActiveResource::Base
end
```

Now within this new ActiveResource model, we need to define where the resource data will be found. We can do that by setting the model's site attribute like so:

```
class Toy < ActiveResource::Base
  self.site = 'http://localhost:3000'
end
```

That's all that's needed for the simplest implementation. Save this file, and open a script/console session to see our ActiveResource model in action.

Within the script/console session, we can obtain a list of all the records from our Lost Toys application with a find :all call:

```
Toy.find :all
```

We can also interact with a single record and interact with its individual attributes just as we could with ActiveRecord:

```
woody = Toy.find 4
woody.title      # "Cowboy Doll"
woody.status     # "LOST"
woody.zipcode    # "90210"
```

That's well and good, and while you could certainly have some fun just with this, simply reading data from a remote application isn't exactly a very exciting API, is it? What we really want to have is the

ability to create and destroy content remotely. Enhancing our toys controller to support that functionality is simply a matter of adding a few more respond_to blocks to our other actions.

So going back into the toys controller in our lost toys application, we'll need to modify the new action
like so:

```
def new
  @toy = current_user.toys.build

  respond_to do |format|
    format.html {
      case params[:type]
        when "LOST" then render :file => 'toys/lost',
                                    :use_full_path => true,
                                    :layout => true
        when "FOUND" then render :file => 'toys/found',
                                    :use_full_path => true,
                                    :layout => true

      end
    }
    format.xml  { render :xml => @toy }
  end
end
```

Here, you can see that when we added our respond_to, we moved our existing template rendering
case statement into the html response (as that logic is only relevant for HTML requests). For XML
requests, we're simply going to render out an empty Toy object.

Next, we'll modify the create action (which is what will be executed when our ActiveResource client
attempts to save a new Toy resource) like so:

```
def create
  @toy = current_user.toys.build(params[:toy])

  respond_to do |format|
    if @toy.save
      format.html { redirect_to(@toy) }
      format.xml { render :xml => @toy, :status => :created,
                                    :location => @toy}
    else
      format.html {
        case params[:toy][:status]
          when "LOST" then render :file => 'toys/lost',
                                      :use_full_path => true,
                                      :layout => true
          when "FOUND" then render :file => 'toys/found',
                                      :use_full_path => true,
                                      :layout => true

        end
      }
```

```
      format.xml  { render :xml => @toy.errors,
                               :status => :unprocessable_entity }
    end
  end
end
```

This should seem fairly similar to the previous requests with a couple new additions. We have our normal addition of a respond_to block and the addition of the HTML and XML responses. However within our XML response, we're sending back more than just some rendered XML; we're also sending back a status and, in the case of the success, a location.

Those status and location options are important bits of information that are bundled up into the response headers and sent back along with the data. The status of created shows up as an HTTP status code of 201, which signals to the client that the resource was created. Meanwhile, according to conventions, anytime an item is created, the URI of that new item needs to be sent back in the location response header, and thus that's what we're doing with the location option providing the client with the URL it would need to access the resource directly now.

> *Rails supports many HTTP status codes. For a full list of the available integer codes and a mapping to corresponding default message texts, see the online Rails source code at:* http://dev.rubyonrails.org/browser/trunk/actionpack/lib/action_controller/status_codes.rb.

In order to allow a remote user to update a record, we'll next need to change the update action like so:

```
def update
  @toy = current_user.toys.find(params[:id])
  respond_to do |format|
    if @toy.update_attributes(params[:toy])
      format.html { redirect_to(@toy) }
      format.xml { head :ok}
    else
      format.html { render :action => "edit" }
      format.xml  { render :xml => @toy.errors,
                               :status => :unprocessable_entity }
    end
  end
end
```

Once again, this should seem the same as our previous discussions with the addition of the head :ok response if the update is successful. That method is used to return a response to the requester that has no content (merely headers with an HTTP status code of 200). It's used in instances like this—where we don't need to return any data back to the client other than just the simple notification that the request was successful.

375

Finally, we'll modify the destroy action so that when it receives a request to delete, it will simply send back an acknowledgement that everything processed successfully:

```
def destroy
  @toy = current_user.toys.find(params[:id])
  @toy.destroy
  respond_to do |format|
    format.html { redirect_to(toys_url) }
    format.xml { head :ok}
  end
end
```

Nice and simple—it merely returns an :ok response if the object was deleted. With that, our toys controller is now completely ready to serve as a RESTful XML API for our external application.

Let's go back to our toys_client application and start up a new script/console session, so we can experiment with our new API. We'll start by creating a new Toy:

```
ruby script/console
Loading development environment (Rails 2.1.0)

t = Toy.new(:title => "test", :description => "test", ➥
:status => "LOST", :zipcode => "95926")

t.save
ActiveResource::UnauthorizedAccess: Failed with 401 Unauthorized
```

It failed with an Unauthorized Access error message! What's up with that?

Well the answer is simple: if you recall that in our Lost Toys application, we decided that it would be best if we required that only logged in users could create, edit, or destroy toy records. So we added that before filter on everything but the index and show actions:

```
before_filter :login_required, :except => [:index, :show]
```

To get around this, we need to have a way to pass our authentication credentials with the request to create a new toy. We can do this by modifying our ActiveResource Toy model here in our toys_client application to set the username and password to working values like so:

```
class Toy < ActiveResource::Base
  self.site = 'http://localhost:3000'

  self.user = "ealameda"
  self.password = "password"
end
```

Save your model, and let's reload our environment into the script/console (or simply quit the current console session and restart) and try that request again:

```
reload!
Reloading...
=> true
```

```
t = Toy.new(:title => "test", :description => "test", ➥
:status => "LOST", :zipcode => "95926")

t.save
=> true
```

We got a success message this time. In fact, our t reference has now been populated with the full object as well, so we can ask it for its ID now:

```
t.id    # 7
```

My request came back with an ID of 7, and in fact, we were to view the toy listings in the Lost Toys application, we would see that our new toy should be displaying there (as Figure 12-6 shows).

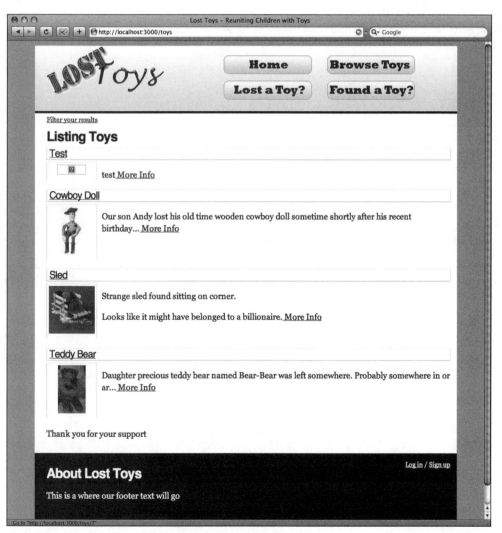

Figure 12-6. You can see our remotely added lost toy record.

To delete that record, we can simply call the destroy method on our reference like so:

```
t.destroy
=> #<Net::HTTPOK 200 OK readbody=true>
```

Alternatively, if we didn't have a reference to the record already loaded and we wanted to delete it directly, we could have just called the delete method on the Toy model and passed in the ID of the record we wanted to delete like so:

```
Toy.delete 6
=> #<Net::HTTPOK 200 OK readbody=true>
```

As you can see, using ActiveResource makes interacting with a remote application as simple as ActiveRecord makes interacting with a local database. So this example should give you a nice taste of what's possible with ActiveResource. You should be able to imagine that it would be very easy to use these exact same method calls to display data from an external Rails application and display its data in your own application.

Summary

Wow! Even I'm amazed at how much we've covered in this short chapter. We've taken the simple application that we started in the previous chapter and really expanded it greatly. Along with adding some additional templates to our site, we added both geocoding and location-based searching to the application as we converted the database from SQLite to MySQL. We then tackled the often tricky subject of adding search and filtering capabilities while maintaining a RESTful approach, and we did it in a way that took advantage of the named scope goodness that was recently added to Rails. Finally, we looked at supporting multiple formats from our RESTful controller as we added some AJAX love to the application and explored not only adding a RESTful XML service to the application but also how it could be consumed using the ActiveResource library.

In the next chapter, we'll close out our discussions of this sample project as we talk about some important considerations that you need to keep in mind regarding performance optimizations and security for Rails applications.

Chapter 13

SECURITY AND PERFORMANCE ENHANCEMENTS

Now that we have our first basic web application completed and ready to deploy into the wild, we have a few important topics left to discuss concerning any applications that we build.

To start off, we need to talk about the issues surrounding keeping our applications and their data safe from malicious hands by reviewing some proper security measures.

Second, as our applications grow and become more popular over time, their performance could suffer due to poor design decisions that we made early on that don't show up until the application is under stress. So we'll need to talk about building our applications with a mind for performance as well. Rails applications can perform very well and have immense scalability to boot; it's just a matter of ensuring that we as the developers haven't shot ourselves in the foot by our designs.

Security

Anytime that you even think of putting a web application on the public Internet, the security of the application and its data needs to be given serious consideration. Web applications are constantly under attack by hackers and script kiddies, and every day uncounted numbers of web applications are hacked, and their content is defaced or their data compromised.

Web application security is a huge topic and experts in the field make a substantial amount of money for their knowledge, so while I can't make you an expert in web security in this short section, I can cover the most common attacks that hackers will use and discuss the methods and approaches that you need to use to build a defense and plug any holes in your application before it's too late.

Of course, most discussions on security tend to break down to a single golden rule—never trust anything submitted by a user. Let's see how that rule is applied to the most common attacks.

Cross-Site Scripting (XSS)

Cross-site scripting (XSS) is a web application vulnerability where malicious users are able to inject code into a web page that will be viewed by other users of the application. In doing so, an attacker can create scripts that can exploit browser holes while the user is on a trusted site or trick users into providing sensitive information (such as passwords) back to the attacker.

In fact, according to research done by Symantec in 2007, cross-site scripting attacks composed nearly 80 percent of all documented security vulnerabilities on web sites. This type of exploit is particularly of concern for us when building database-driven web applications in Rails. Fortunately, it's also an easy one to fix.

This exploitation can occur anytime that we allow any data that was provided by users of our application to be directly displayed in the pages of our application. Instead, we need to convert the output of any user-submitted content so that any HTML metacharacters are converted to their equivalent HTML entities (a process called escaping). When we escape data that was submitted by a user, HTML characters such as < and > will be replaced with entities such as < and >, which will effectively prevent any XSS attacks from being executed on the page.

Of course, Rails makes this process easy to do with the addition of a helper method named h() that we can use to escape any output. In fact, we've already used this method a number of times even though I never drew attention to it. Look back in our Lost Toys application, and check out the show template at /app/views/toys/show.html.erb; you'll see that we used the method there to escape two fields:

```
<h1><%=h @toy.status %> TOY</h1>
<div class="photo">
   <%= image_tag @toy.photo.url(:medium) %>
</div>
   <%=simple_format(h @toy.description) %>
```

In that template, we're using the h() helper method to escape whatever value was placed in the database in the show and description fields, so that we can prevent any malicious content from being executed on the web page when this page is viewed.

Of course, the question might come up as to why we didn't use the h() helper on our @toy.photo.url as well, and the truth is that we could have done that, in which case that line would have looked like this:

```
<%= image_tag h(@toy.photo.url(:medium)) %>
```

I chose not to escape that value simply because I didn't feel it was necessary: that value was generated not by a user but by the system. However, I know that some developers would feel that it's always best to be safe and escape all values, not just the user-provided ones. It's certainly a safe practice to always use the h() helper on any data that will be displayed in your view templates, but at a bare minimum, you must always use it on any user-provided data.

> *Some people might ask, "But what if you want to allow users to use simple HTML code (e.g., emboldening words or adding links) to their posts?"*
>
> *The short answer is that it depends. If you're dealing with a controlled set of users that you feel you can trust not to do anything malicious, allowing users to write raw HTML that could then be displayed on a page might be considered OK.*
>
> *There are, however, a number of safer alternatives. Many Rails developers prefer to provide their users a pure text markup language such as Textile or Markdown (similar to what many wikis, blogs, and forums use for markup) that is then converted to safe HTML on the server. In fact, Rails even provides helper methods for automatically converting Textile (textilize) or Markdown (markdown) into HTML if the proper Ruby gems are installed on the server (textilize requires the RedCloth gem, and markdown requires the BlueCloth gem).*

Another option for securing your view templates is to install a Rails plug-in by the name of XSS-Shield (http://code.google.com/p/xss-shield/), which modifies how our view templates work so that they will automatically escape any output without requiring you to explicitly call the h() helper. This approach to the problem is certainly good, and I know a few developers who prefer it. Personally, though, I prefer to use the h() helper simply because I consider the issue of XSS important enough that I don't want to trust that an external plug-in hasn't been accidentally deleted, thus leaving my views unprotected. Using h() each time means more work and less DRY code for me, but that's just my personal preference.

SQL injection

A second very common attack on web applications is the SQL injection attack. When we were talking about XSS, we were concerned about what data could be submitted to our application and viewed on a page. With SQL injection, we're concerned with what data could be submitted and sent to our database. Once again, we're concerned with what data a user is providing us.

The risk here is that if we accept any string that a user submits and then pass that string directly in a SQL statement, a user could submit SQL commands that compromise the data in our database.

> *For a great laugh on SQL injection, check out the xkcd comic at http://xkcd.com/327/. I actually have this one printed out and on my desk at work (along with many other xkcd comics).*

So how do we protect our Rails applications from SQL injection attacks?

Believe it or not, in most circumstances we don't have to, as Rails provides built-in protection against SQL injection; it automatically sanitizes our database inputs and ensures that nothing nasty sneaks by.

It does this by ensuring that any input is properly quoted and escaped (by prepending backslashes in front of certain characters), which effectively makes the data safe to send to the database. So when you issue a call to Toy.find(params[:id]), you can feel comfortable in the knowledge that this query is safe from SQL injection attacks.

You're safe, that is, assuming that you're not manually introducing issues yourself. Unfortunately, going off the beaten path and risking introducing opportunities for SQL injection attacks is not difficult; all it really takes is for us to pass any unsanitized string directly into an ActiveRecord find calls. The easiest way to fall into this trap is to attempt to use simple string interpolation to place strings directly into our queries like in these examples:

```
Toy.find(:all, :limit => "#{params}")
User.find(:first, ➡
                :conditions => "last_name like '%#{params[:lname]}%' "
```

You can see that, in these examples, any string that was in those variables is now inserted directly into our queries. The way around these is to use a bind variable (similar to other languages such as Java and .NET), in which we put a placeholder into the query and allow Rails to replace that placeholder with our string (after it has been sanitized). So we could rewrite our previous example like this:

```
User.find(:first, ➡
                :conditions => ["last_name like ?", params[:lname]]
```

What we've done here is change the argument to our conditions clause from a string to an array. By doing so, ActiveRecord will automatically bind the value in our params[:lname] element into the ? placeholder. However, when it does that, it will also automatically escape any special characters it encounters and place quotes around the string when it is inserted into our query.

> It should go without saying that if you're using methods like find_by_sql, which allow you to pass in your own raw SQL statements, that you'll also need to give extra special attention to this process to ensure that you're not creating SQL injection opportunities

Of course, going the extra mile never hurts, so you might also want to validate that the inputs that you're receiving are within a specific list of values that you would expect or within the specific format that you want, such as we did in the Lost Toys application.

For example, when we wanted to ensure that we didn't allow a toy to be created without a status, we also ensured that it had a status that we expected:

```
VALID_STATUSES = %w(LOST FOUND)
validates_inclusion_of :status, :in => VALID_STATUSES
```

In this way, we would reject any submissions with a status that we didn't recognize. Another example came later on when we were building our filter query dynamically. In it, we wanted to ensure that our ZIP code query could only ever contain a ZIP code that was composed of five digits, so we first tested the ZIP code that was submitted with a regular expression:

```
if zipcode =~ /^[\d]{5}+$/
  return "find(:all, :origin => '#{zipcode}', :within => 50)"
else
  return "find(:all)"
end
```

By explicitly testing our inputs, we're ensuring that if there were any values that weren't digits in that parameter, it would never be allowed into a query that could reach our database.

An alternative approach that you can use is to take advantage of base methods in ActiveRecord to quote the column value directly. One such method is quote, which could be used in a custom finder method like this:

```
def Toy.find_with_limit(limit)
  find(:all, :limit => connection.quote(limit))
end
```

The keys, however, are once again ensuring that you're not trusting that any input from the user is safe and ensuring that you go the extra mile to protect your database from any malicious input.

Using attr_protected and attr_accessible to secure your models

Another common security hole in Rails applications is the liberal use of creating records directly from form parameters that were submitted. We've done this together a number of times:

```
@toy = Toy.new(params[:toy])
@toy = Toy.update_attributes(params[:toy])
```

In both of those examples, we simply accepted any value that was passed to us from the toy form and created or updated our toy record with those values. That's an incredibly convenient process, but it can be risky if we have sensitive attributes that we don't want to risk being updated willy-nilly.

For example, imagine that we were building a forum application and had a user model with a table that looked like this:

```
create_table "users", :force => true do |t|
    t.string   "login", :limit => 40
    t.string   "name", :limit => 100, :default => ""
    t.string   "email",  :limit => 100
    t.boolean  "administrator",  :default => false
  end
```

They key attribute to notice here is the Boolean field that is being used to determine whether or not the user should be considered an administrator in the application. Obviously, we're not going to allow just any user to make themselves an administrator, and thus we'd have a protected interface to promote a normal user to an administrator that only authorized users could access.

However, if we provided a form that allowed normal users to update their names, e-mail addresses, and so on, a tricky user might be able to simply hack the form to also send the necessary administrator values with something like <input name="user[administrator]" type="hidden" value="1" />

and our User.update_attributes(params[:user]) would dumbly allow that field to be updated as well—thereby making this user an administrator. D'oh!

Does this mean that our convenience approach is trashed in this instance? Nope, it just means that we need to think a little more carefully about which fields we want to allow to be bulk updated/created and which ones we want to only be assigned explicitly.

We could solve this problem of protecting sensitive attributes from being updated by malicious users through the use of a method named attr_protected to list the attributes that we want to protect. Using this method, any attributes tagged as protected can not be updated using the bulk assignment methods. So in our User model, we could declare administrator as protected like so:

```
class User < ActiveRecord::Base
  attr_protected :administrator
  --excerpt--
```

Alternatively, we could approach the problem in reverse by using a method named attr_accessible to list the attributes that *can* be bulk assigned and any other attributes in our model will be automatically protected:

```
class User < ActiveRecord::Base
  attr_accessible :login, :name, :email
  --excerpt--
```

In either approach, in order to modify a protected value, you would need to access it directly:

```
@user.administrator = params[:user][:administrator]
```

Which approach should you use? It really depends on the number of fields that you need to protect. Personally, I always choose the approach that means less typing for me (typically attr_protected).

Unscoped finds

Incorrectly scoped finds can occur when we allow access to a resource based solely on the resource's ID. The issue comes in when we code our applications to ensure that a user must be logged in to view a page, but we don't go the extra step to ensure that they should be able to view the specific data that they're requesting.

Imagine that we had just built a new online store application where users could purchase downloadable widgets from us. On this site, we wanted to give our customers a receipt page that they could go to in order to download their customized widget at a URL that looked like www.mydomain.com/receipt/125. If we assume that we have a receipt controller that is following the basic CRUD principles and has a RESTful design, this request would go to the show action, which might look like this:

```
def show
  @receipt = Reciept.find(params[:id])
end
```

Do you see the problem here? The security issue is that any user could load up another user's receipt simply by changing the ID in the URL. So a malicious user could simply go to URLs like www.mydomain.com/receipt/126 and www.mydomain.com/receipt/127 to gain access to the download links to another user's widget. Not exactly the kind of system that builds confidence from our user base, is it?

The way around this vulnerability is to modify the query that we send to the database so that it's querying not only for the primary key but also that the currently logged in user matches the user_id that owns this receipt. You could attempt to do this manually in ActiveRecord by passing an extra condition to the find method:

```
@receipt = Receipt.find(params[:id], :conditions => ["user_id = ?",➥
  current_user])
```

But the preferred approach would be to use our method chaining to dynamically build the find with the proper scope. Rather than issuing the query directly against the Receipt class, we should issue the query through the model that owns the record (i.e., the User model) like this:

```
@receipt = current_user.receipts.find(params[:id])
```

By changing this find to be scoped on the current_user, we've changed the query that will be generated to also search based on the user's ID, that is, SELECT * FROM `receipts` WHERE (`receipts`.`id` = 14 AND (`receipts`.user_id = 101)) .

In fact, we discussed adding the scope to our ActiveRecord finds a bit in the last chapter, when we created an edit page that would allow users to edit the toys that they had added. In there, we created the edit action in the toys controller to load the toy like so:

```
def edit
  @toy = current_user.toys.find(params[:id])
end
```

This action would issue a query against our database that looked like SELECT * FROM `toys` WHERE (`toys`.`id` = 124 AND (`toys`.user_id = 1)). So while properly scoping our finds is more of a programming practice than an actual security issue, you can see that it's an important step to preventing unauthorized access to our users' data.

Cross-site request forgery (CSRF)

Cross-site request forgery (CSRF) attacks are in some ways similar to XSS attacks, except that rather than injecting unauthorized code to be displayed, the purpose is to use another user's authorization token to interact with a web application as the trusted user in a malicious way.

In fact, CSRF attacks typically will have the following characteristics:

- They will use sites that rely on a user's identity.
- They will exploit the site's trust in a user's identity.
- They will trick the user's browser into sending unauthorized HTTP requests to the target site.

A common attack would be to post images on a site where, when a user views them, the image tag will actually send a command to the site on behalf of the user:

```
<img src="http://mytasks.com/delete?all">
```

A user who attempts to load a page with this image tag on it will unknowingly send a request to the mytasks.com site to delete all of their tasks. The problem escalates and becomes a serious threat if the user is currently logged into that site or has an authentication cookie stored in their browser that would allow this command to be executed.

So how do we protect against these types of attacks? The good news is that we don't have to, as Rails provides us with solid CSRF protection solution by default. Rails automatically checks a session token on every request to the application so that this form of hijacking is prevented from occurring.

You can see this protection enabled in the application controller (/app/controllers/application.rb), where around line 8 you should see something like the following:

```
# See ActionController::RequestForgeryProtection for details
# Uncomment the :secret if you're not using the cookie session store
protect_from_forgery # :secret => '60155b7e5b5d4765bc256d4e5e81dbf1'
```

You'll notice that the secret hash is commented out; that's because it's not needed for the default cookie session store, which already encrypts its data. For other session stores, you would need to uncomment that secret hash. By default, the secret will be encrypted using an SHA1 encryption digest method, but you can modify it manually like so:

```
protect_from_forgery # :secret => '60155b7e55d4765bc256d4e5e81dbf1',➡
   :digest => 'MD5'
```

As long as the CSRF protection is enabled, any requests that don't match the request forgery protection token for the current session will result in an `ActionController::InvalidAuthenticityToken` exception being thrown, thereby preventing the unauthorized action from occurring.

Performance

Of course, the most secure and coolest web application in the world won't be worth diddly-squat to the users if they get frustrated from long page loads and an all-around slow performing application. Because of that, I want to close out this chapter with some high-level discussions of some best practice advice and tips that you can use to ensure that your Rails application will be able to handle a reasonable amount of users before you need to consider upgrading the hardware. Along the way, we'll talk about some common mistakes that beginning Rails programmers can make, as well as approaches we can use to identify problems in our application.

Don't loop all around SQL

The first performance issue that we can encounter in our Rails applications is an entirely self-inflicted one. Rails makes it so incredibly easy for us to build code that retrieves data from associated objects in just a few lines of Ruby code that it's possible to lose site of what's really happening in the generated SQL and end up hurting our own performance.

For example, what if we wanted to print out a quick report of all of the toys in our Lost Toys application along with the name of the user who submitted them?

```
@toys = Toy.find(:all)
@toys.each do |toy|
  puts toy.title
  puts toy.user.name
end
```

Looks innocuous enough, doesn't it? Unfortunately, a simple report like this can kill your application's performance as the amount of data in the application grows over time. That's because if you look in the logs, you would see that this simple set of commands is generating a lot.

There's one query to get the orders:

```
Toy Load (0.217965)   SELECT * FROM `toys`
```

And it's followed by a new query for each record in the toys database to retrieve the associated user information:

```
User Load (0.056665)   SELECT * FROM `users` WHERE (`users`.`id` = 1)
User Load (0.013239)   SELECT * FROM `users` WHERE (`users`.`id` = 2)
User Load (0.000265)   SELECT * FROM `users` WHERE (`users`.`id` = 1)
```

So to display only three toy records, our simple little Ruby code issued at least four queries against our database. This might not sound so bad when we're only talking about three extra queries, but imagine the impact all those extra queries would have on our database when we're pulling back a million records. Not only is that hugely inefficient but the extra time it takes for each and every one of those individual queries to be sent to the database and the response sent back can really add up to affect your application's performance.

We can solve this performance problem by using a more intelligent approach to building our query. You might recall from our earlier discussions of ActiveRecord that one of our options that we can pass to the find method is named :include, which is used to perform an eager loading of an association as well. In more human terms, this means that we can load the data from both tables with fewer queries.

By simply changing our initial find method to this:

```
@toys = Toy.find(:all, :include => :user)
```

we're able to reduce the queries that are issued to either a single query that looks something like this:

```
SELECT toys.*, users.* FROM orders
  LEFT JOIN users ON ( users.id = toys.user_id )
```

Recently, Rails added some further optimization of these types of includes; it will pull the results in two smaller queries instead of one large query. In doing so, Rails was able to gain a speed boost for these types of queries and thus your logs may show a result set like this:

```
SELECT * FROM `toys`
SELECT * FROM `users` WHERE (`users`.id IN ('1','2','3'))
```

So by using the :include option, we've eliminated all those extra hits on the database and retrieved the same results in either one or two queries.

An important note to remember when using includes, however, is that the plurality of your include statement needs to match the plurality of the association that you're using as well. So when coming from a has_many association (such as a user, which has many toys), you would use the User.find(:all, :include => :toys). Yet when coming from a singular association (such as a toy, which belongs to a user), you would use something like Toy.find(:all, :include => :user).

Use select to limit what you retrieve

Another way that we can be smarter about what we do in our ActiveRecord finds is to limit our results into only the data that we're interested in using. You see, whenever we perform a query to load a record like Toy.find(3), ActiveRecord performs a query against the database which loads all columns using SQL like SELECT * FROM `toys` WHERE (`toys`.`id` = 3).

While nothing there is too alarming, the performance issue that we can encounter is if we only need a small subset of the fields. In those instances, we can use the :select clause to limit our find to only the fields that we want:

```
Toy.find(:all, :select => "id, title, zipcode, updated_at")
```

This type of optimization becomes much more important anytime our database table stores BLOB data types such as binary or text data, which not only increase the amount of data that needs to be loaded from the database but are typically stored external to the rest of the row data and thus are slower for the database to return.

Use counter cache

Many times when we're dealing with has_many associations, we want to be able to quickly provide a summary count of the associated objects. For example, if we had a blog post that has_many comments, being able to list the number of comments that each post has on a summary screen could be a useful feature.

In our own Lost Toys application, if we wanted to pull back a count of the number of toys associated to the current user, we might use a query like current_user.toys.count, which of course would submit a query to the database like SELECT count(*) AS count_all FROM `toys` WHERE (`toys`.user_id = 1).

Once again, this type of query isn't so bad in isolation, but once we start dynamically counting thousands of rows for 50 different users, we immediately hit some performance pain. Fortunately it's a pain that we can avoid using an ActiveRecord technique called counter caching. Using counter caching, Rails maintains a count of the number of associated records as an attribute in the parent record, so we can simply display that value rather than having to dynamically generate it by counting the associated rows.

Enabling this feature is a fairly simple matter. First, we need to add a database attribute to our parent model to store this cached count. We name it with the same name as our child table with _count added at the end. This new field must be declared as an integer with a default value of 0. To create it in our Lost Toys application, we might use a migration like this:

```
script/generate migration Add_Toys_count_to_User toys_count:integer
```

We then need to modify the migration to set the default value for our new field to 0; otherwise, our counter cache will not work at all:

```
class AddToysCountToUser < ActiveRecord::Migration
  def self.up
    add_column :users, :toys_count, :integer, :default => 0
  end

  def self.down
    remove_column :users, :toys_count
  end
end
```

After running our migration to add this column to our database schema, our next step is to enable the counter cache in our application by declaring it on the has_many association in the users table.

```
has_many :toys, :counter_cache => true
```

With those simple changes made, a count of toy records associated to this user will now be automatically maintained. Anytime we add a new toy record to a user, the count in the users table will be incremented, and the count will be decremented anytime we delete an associated toy.

> *These instructions are intended for setting up a counter cache in a table that doesn't already have data loaded. If we were adding a counter cache to the system after it has already had a set of users and toys added, we would also need to go through the process of setting the initial value of each counter cache to its current count.*

Thus when we issue a query such as current_user.toys.size, our response will be returned from the cached count and not by having the database do a full table scan to count all the records.

Indexes

If you've noticed a theme that the majority of our optimization techniques are involving the database, you're spot on. In my experiences (outside of just sheer programmer error), the majority of slow web requests are going to be an issue of connecting to an external resource such as the file system or the database in an inefficient manner. Since Rails is designed for building database-driven web applications, obviously most of our attention will be focused on looking at how we're interacting with the database.

Huge collections of books have been written within the realm of database performance and optimization, and we can certainly do tons of things within the configuration of our database to optimize it for faster performance with our Rails application. However, the one topic that I did want to take a moment to address in this book is indexing.

I'm not sure if it's because Rails migrations separate developers from having to interact with the database or if it's just the sheer speed with which we're able to build Rails applications, but I'm always amazed at the number of applications that I've encountered that have had poor or even no indexes defined in the applications database.

What are indexes? Within a database, an index provides a solution for speeding up queries by providing a catalog of the values in the database. A simple analogy is similar to how you might interact with this book: if you wanted look up every place in this book where we talked about ActiveRecord validations, you could be thorough and go through every single page of the book, or you could save yourself some time and simply flip to the index in the back of the book and use that to open directly to the relevant pages. Database indexes are very similar in that the database maintains a catalog listing all of the values in the field that we've indexed and where they can be found in the table. By doing so, when we issue a query against that field, the database engine doesn't have to scan every row in the table. It can simply use the index to quickly load the matching rows. That's a simplified description, but it should be enough to help you understand the importance of indexes.

Without proper indexes built, your Rails application will constantly be doing more work than necessary to load the records for any queries that you perform. While in development or during the initial launch these types of problems won't be noticeable at all, since the database size will be fairly small. But over time, as more and more data is added to the tables and your database needs to sort through more and more rows of data to find the relevant ones, a lack of indexes will bring your applications performance to a standstill.

So how do we add indexes? Well, each relational database engine is going to have its own unique quirks about how indexes are defined, used, and so on, but ActiveRecord provides a simple abstraction that we can use to add indexes in our migrations. It looks like this:

```
add_index :table_name, :column_name
```

How do you know which tables you should index? That's a little harder question to answer without going too deep into database optimization theory. The simplest answer for Rails applications is to look for fields that we're using in find operations (besides the id). Those fields are typically, but not always, likely candidates for an index.

For example, looking at our Toys model from our main project, you can see that one of the key fields that we're searching for is the status of the toy. So you might think that it would make sense to build an index onto this field like so:

```
class AddStatusIndexToToys < ActiveRecord::Migration
  def self.up
    add_index :toys, :status
  end

  def self.down
    remove_index :toys, :status
  end
end
```

But whether that will be a good thing or not is debatable. The issue with that field is that we currently have the status field configured to only allow two possible fields (LOST or FOUND). Therefore, the most that an index might be able to do is remove half of the entries in the table from our search.

Depending on the amount of data and how the database is configured to optimize queries, the database engine might very well decide that only removing half the records does not provide it with enough exclusivity in the results to actually speed up the results. In other words, the database engine may decide that it's quicker for it to simply check every record in the table looking for matches, rather than going through the extra work of loading the index and using it to generate a list of results, only then to have to still scan through a large portion of the records. To save time, the database might choose to not use the index.

You can see, then, that choosing what indexes to build can be a bit more complex than simply building indexes on any field we query.

One field that would probably benefit from indexing is the created_at field, which we're using to sort our records from newest to oldest in the recent named scope. In that way, the database could use our index to help sort the rows faster.

Of course, those are just ideas on how we might add indexes to make our database faster. To really understand how different indexes will affect our application, we need to test the application with real data and real indexes defined to see what improves and what doesn't.

One of the tricks that I picked up this last year for helping to determine where indexes are needed is to load up my database with a ton of sample data and use that as a baseline to find where the slow-performing pages are. There's nothing like suddenly having several hundred thousand records that your database has to sort to identify bad performing queries and missing indexes.

Ben Curtis has written an excellent Ruby gem for generating fake data. It's called faker, and you can read about it at http://faker.rubyforge.org/. Installing it is a simple process of running

```
sudo gem install faker
```

Once you have the gem installed, you can either use it in a script/console session to load a large amount of data into your application via your models, or you can create a rake task that you can run from the command line. In fact, if you look in /lib/tasks of several of our earlier projects, you'll see that I had created some fairly simple tasks to do just that. For example, in our demoblog application, you'll find the following rake task:

```
namespace :eldon do
  desc "Load Sample Data"
  task :load_fake_data => :environment do
    require 'Faker'
    1..100.times do
      p = Post.new
      p.headline = Faker::Company.bs
      p.body = Faker::Lorem.paragraphs
      p.save
    end
  end
end
```

In that task, you can see that after I require the faker gem, I created a loop from 1 to 100 in which I added a new Post object using the faker methods to generate dummy content into some of the fields.

To use this task to load my database, I would simply open a command prompt in the root of my application and run this:

```
rake eldon:load_fake_data
```

For your own applications, you could easily set up something similar and modify the count to generate 500,000 or more records. Then, simply start the task before you leave work for the evening so that it can run overnight and provide you with a massively loaded database the next morning.

From there, you can use your application as normal and immediately see the areas that aren't performing correctly, and you can see the impact of adding indexes.

If you want to get more advanced (or automated), you can also use tools such as the Rails Analyzer tools (`http://rails-analyzer.rubyforge.org/`) that can be useful for helping determine slow spots in your application by analyzing your log files.

Use caching

Of course, the best way to reduce load on our database and web servers is to avoid generating content as much as possible and use caching instead.

> In case you're not familiar with the term "caching," Wikipedia defines it as follows (`http://en.wikipedia.org/wiki/Cache`):
>
> A collection of data duplicating original values stored elsewhere or computed earlier, where the original data is expensive to fetch (owing to longer access time) or to compute, compared to the cost of reading the cache. In other words, a cache is a temporary storage area where frequently accessed data can be stored for rapid access. Once the data is stored in the cache, future use can be made by accessing the cached copy rather than re-fetching or recomputing the original data, so that the average access time is shorter. Cache, therefore, helps expedite data access that the CPU would otherwise need to fetch from main memory.

In essence, caching is a way that we can save the results of some expensive action that Rails performs and use that saved result for all future requests, rather than regenerating the results again and again and again. Using a cache thus reduces load off our application. When you consider how much time is wasted by many web applications generating and regenerating the exact same results, it's easy to see how an intelligent caching solution can dramatically improve performance.

Rails provides support for three powerful types of caching to avoid the expensive process of generating dynamic HTML from database results. However, each of these caching systems has key differences—not only in how they work but in what situations they were designed to be used—that are important to understand.

Page caching

The simplest and fastest performing type of caching that Rails supports is page caching. In page caching, the results of the first request for a page are simply stored on the file system as a static HTML file. So all future requests to that specific URL would be served the stored HTML file by the web server and never even hit our Rails application—no hits to the database and no hits to any of our controllers or views. You just can't get any faster than having a web server return a static HTML file.

The downfall with this method, of course, is the fact that we can't display any form of dynamic personalized content that would be unique to each request, as each request is going to get the same static file. So if we're doing things such as displaying the user's name, displaying the current date or time on the server, or even aging information such as created 3 minutes ago, then page caching might not be for us.

However, if our application has pages that don't display personalized content, such as home pages or about us pages, or if we have pages that aren't updated too frequently (such as blog posts), page caching can be an excellent solution.

Enabling page caching is an incredibly easy process. In fact, it only requires adding a single line to our controller. Back in our Lost Toys application, imagine that we had a home page that wasn't displaying any type of dynamic data so that it would make a great fit for page caching (unfortunately, our current home page does have dynamic data—the user's profile links in the footer). To enable page caching, we would simply modify our page controller like so:

```
class PageController < ApplicationController
  caches_page :index

  def index
  end
end
```

We just add the caches_page method to our controller followed by a list of actions that we want to cache. After that, if we were to start our application and open a browser to view the home page, we would see that the page loaded normally, except that in the background, Rails would have saved a copy of the rendered HTML that it sent back to the browser in the /public directory.

> Note that, by default, caching is disabled while you're working in the development environment. If you want to see your application performing the caching, you'll either need to start your Rails application in production mode or edit the development.rb in /config/environments to set perform_caching to true.
>
> ```
> config.action_controller.perform_caching         = true
> ```

You can even see the initial cache in the logs for your page request:

```
Processing PageController#index (for 127.0.0.1 at 2008-08-10 ➥
  14:32:10) [GET]
Parameters: {"action"=>"index", "controller"=>"page"}
Rendering template within layouts/application
Rendering page/index
Rendered users/_user_bar (0.00015)
Cached page: /index.html (0.00048)
Completed in 0.00472 (212 reqs/sec) | Rendering: 0.00200 (42%) |➥
  DB: 0.00000 (0%) | 200 OK [http://localhost/]
```

After that initial request, all subsequent requests to our home page will not show up in the log, as those requests are no longer being served by Rails. Pretty sweet, huh?

Action caching

The next level of caching that Rails supports, action caching, is similar to page caching in that it stores the entire rendered HTML file, so once again, our cached pages need to be free of any personalized content. However, action caching differs from page caching in that the request is sent through our Rails application before the cached page is returned to the user. The advantage of this is that it allows any controller filters to be run before the cached page is returned, which is extremely helpful if you wanted to verify that the user should be able to see this page before displaying it to them (as we did with the login_required filter in our toys controller).

To enable action caching, we simply add the following line to the controller:

```
caches_action :index, :show
```

You can see that using action caching is just as easy as using page caching; we simply add a caches_action method to our controller passing it the names of any actions that we want cached.

Action caching adds a bit more flexibility in that we can use our controller filters again, but that flexibility does cause us to take a hit in performance when compared against the raw speed of page caching.

Fragment caching

The final level of caching that Rails provides out of the box is the slowest performing of the three but also the most flexible option. While page and action caching were focused on caching results from the controller level, fragment caching is all about caching elements within a page. Using fragment caching, we can selectively cache portions of a page (such as the header, navigation, or body text), while allowing other sections of the page to remain completely dynamic.

Because this level of caching is performed in the view, we must set it up in the view template for it to be used. Assuming that we don't already have page or action caching enabled in the controller for our home page in the Lost Toys application, we could enable fragment caching in the index template by wrapping any content that we want to cache in a cache block like so:

```
<% cache do %>
  <h1>What is Lost Toys?</h1>
  <div class="photo">
    <%= image_tag 'bear_bear.jpg', :id => 'bear_bear' %>
  </div>
  <p>Lost Toys is a web application that is designed to help ➥
reunite children with their most treasured bears, dolls, etc.</p>
  <p>As with all great things - the idea for this site was born ➥
out of the pain of my own daughter losing her treasured teddy bear ➥
that had been with her from the time she was born until she was ➥
seven years old</p>
  <p>As a parent, it's a horrible feeling to know that the one ➥
thing that would make your daughter happy is somewhere within your ➥
local area, possibly in the hands of someone who has no idea what ➥
```

```
to do with it.</p>
  <p>It was because of this loss - that we came up with the idea of➡
  providing a simple web site that would allow people to post about➡
  lost and found toys on this site in the hopes that at least one➡
  may be able to be reunited.</p>
  <p>We provide this service completely free of charge.</p>
<% end %>
```

By simply wrapping anything in our view template that we want to be cached, we've now implemented a caching system that allows for sections of our page to remain dynamic while caching the sections that rarely change.

Cache expiration

Caching our content is a powerful tool, but what do we do if our underlying content changes? Any of the preceding caching systems would currently just continue to serve the original cached content indefinitely, blissfully unaware of the fact that they should have updated their content. What we need is to implement a system for expiring our caches as well.

The easiest approach for dealing with expiring the cache is to simply delete them manually. For page caching, that would mean going into our /public directory and removing any static HTML files from that folder and any subdirectories that match our controller names that hold static HTML in them as well.

To manually remove our action and fragment caches, we could simply run a rake task designed for removing them named rake tmp:cache:clear. That solution is simple and clean but not very auto-mated. So if we have pages that frequently will need to have the caches expired, we'll need a better solution that won't require us to log into the server.

We can automate cache expiration through the intelligent implementation of methods named expire_page, expire_action, and expire_fragment within our controller actions that would be used to update the underlying content. As you might expect by their names, which method you use is dependent on which type of caching you're doing.

Imagine that, in our Lost Toys application, we had enabled page caching in our toys controller for our public-facing pages of index and show (even though we wouldn't do this due to the dynamic nature of those pages).

Since our index template is displaying a list of all the most recent toys that were added to the application, anytime we add a new toy to the application, the cache for the index action would need to be expired so that the next time it was rendered it would display the most recent entries. To do that, we would modify our create action (the action that actually adds the new record) to expire the cache for the index action when it creates a new record:

```
def create
  @toy = current_user.toys.build(params[:toy])
  if @toy.save
    expire_page(:controller => 'toys', :action => 'index')
    redirect_to(@toy)
  else
    case params[:toy][:status]
```

```
          when "LOST" then render :file => 'toys/lost',
                                    :use_full_path => true,
                                    :layout => true
          when "FOUND" then render :file => 'toys/found',
                                    :use_full_path => true,
                                    :layout => true
      end
    end
  end
```

In addition, in the previous chapter, we provided a way for users to go back and edit toy records that they created, so we would need to add an expiration option in the update action as well. However, in this action, we would want to expire both the listing page (index action) and the detail page (show action) to be sure that the changes were reflected in both places. So that update action might look like this:

```
def update
  @toy = current_user.toys.find(params[:id])
  if @toy.update_attributes(params[:toy])
    expire_page(:controller => 'toys', :action => 'index')
    expire_page(:controller => 'toys', :action => 'show', ➥
:id => @toy.id)
    redirect_to(@toy)
  else
    render :action => "edit"
  end
end
```

Here, you can see that we're not limited to doing only a single expiration call per controller. In addition, even though we're not showing it here, we'd probably also want to expire our caches upon deleting a record from the database as well.

If you were using action or fragment caching instead, you could simply change the expire_page methods listed previously with the appropriate expire_action or expire_fragment methods instead.

When implementing an explicit cache expiration system like this, look for any actions that could affect your output and ensure that they are expiring all the appropriate cached areas where the content might be displayed. Most applications that implement caching would only need a simple implementation as we've done in this section. However, for more complicated needs, there is another solution: you could implement a more advanced Rails class called a sweeper, which is half observer and half filter. A sweeper's purpose in life is to monitor events that occur on a specific model and allow the developer to override the standard before/after filter methods with cache expiration methods. Setting up a sweeper is a bit too complicated for this book, but if you would like to learn more about when, why, and how to use sweepers for cache expiration, see the excellent tutorial available online at http://railsenvy.com/2007/2/28/rails-caching-tutorial.

Summary

In this chapter, we took a quick tour of the methods and practices that are important to follow if you want to keep your application up and running over the long term. First, we talked about how to protect your application against the malicious users who might want to bring your application down—or worse, exploit holes in our application to affect our users. Along the way, you learned about the most common types of attacks that you need to guard against and discussed the ways that Rails makes protecting your data easy.

Second, we discussed some high-level approaches for ensuring that our Rails applications won't buckle under the pressure as both our user base and our database size increases over time. I exposed some common programming mistakes that can severely hurt applications' performance, and we took a brief tour of the Rails caching systems that are available to further increase scalability.

In the next chapter, we'll tackle our final important task: deploying our Rails application into the wild.

Chapter 14

DEPLOYING YOUR RAILS APPLICATION

Here we are, near the end of our journey together, and at this point, you should now be ready to begin experimenting and building Rails applications on your own. Perhaps (and hopefully) you've already started building one now. Letting the rubber meet the road, so to speak, is how you're going to grow the most as a Rails developer and how you'll come across those new and interesting challenges that will shape you as a developer.

However, before we say goodbye, we have one final critical subject to discuss—deployment, or the processes by which you might move your new application off of your development system and out into the wild for real users to interact with.

Setting up a production server

While I certainly don't want to bore you with stories about how much the early adopters of Rails suffered when it came time to deploy their applications (walking 8 miles uphill in the snow, both ways), the truth is that the early days of deploying Rails applications were fairly painful. Fortunately for you, Rails has evolved in this area, and now, a number of options are available to you that won't inflict a fraction of the pain and frustration that we early adopters once went through. In this chapter, we're going to discuss several of the options available to you that I believe are fairly painless for deploying your Rails application onto a production server.

A brief history of Rails deployment

In the beginning was WEBrick (the Ruby based web server that's included with Ruby), and while it was certainly a convenient and easy-to-use solution for development, it was far too slow and couldn't scale for production use (some people tried though!).

Instead, Rails developers looked to running Rails as a CGI application. This meant loading up a web server so that the server would simply proxy the requests to processes that were running their Rails application. Those processes would run our Rails application for the request and return the response back to the web server to be delivered to the end user. Simple enough; however, the nature of CGI was not without massive problems. You see, with a CGI process, each and every request would have to both load a new Ruby interpreter session and load the Rails framework. So, while deploying a Rails application as a CGI application wasn't too difficult to set up, it was also incredibly slow and was most often only used as a last resort.

Instead, Rails developers preferred to run their applications using a modified version of CGI named FastCGI. In FastCGI, the processes were long running and created only once to load the Ruby interpreter and Rails framework. After a FastCGI process was spun up, it would keep running and be available to respond to a large number of requests. This meant that we no longer had to suffer the extra time of waiting for the processes to spin up with each request. At this point, Rails applications were sitting fairly pretty in terms of acceptable performance. Unfortunately though, setting up a Rails server with FastCGI was a nightmare of configuration, and larger applications were constantly fighting FastCGI processes that had gone zombie (they looked alive but would no longer respond to requests). Still, with limited alternatives available to us, FastCGI became the preferred deployment method for the time.

All that changed rather quickly in the spring of 2006, when Zed Shaw released the Mongrel Ruby web server. Mongrel was a web server designed and optimized for serving Ruby web applications such as Ruby on Rails. In some ways, it was like FastCGI in that each Mongrel process would be spun up running a copy of our Rails application and then stick around to respond to multiple requests. However, it was faster than FastCGI and didn't have the nightmare configuration or zombie process issues. Suddenly, Rails developers had a fast and reliable process that they could use to run their web applications.

Before long, many best practices developed for deploying Rails applications using a cluster of Mongrel processes that used a proxy web server such as Pound, Pen, or even Apache 2.2 (using mod_proxy_balancer) as a means of load balancing requests between the mongrel processes. In fact, this solution became the unofficial standard for the last few years and is how most Rails applications are configured today—with the footnote that the majority of Rails developers today are currently using Apache or Nginx in front of their Mongrel clusters. Therefore, it makes sense that we'll need to discuss how to deploy our Rails applications to a cluster of Mongrel servers in this manner.

However, in early 2008, several new challengers to the Rails deployment throne were introduced. In fact, a couple of these options are so promising that I would feel like I was doing you a disservice if I didn't cover them as well, so in our discussions we're also going to do a high-level tour of deployment using the new Phusion Passenger (mod_rails) project as well as the exciting new option of developing and deploying Rails applications to a cloud-based server solution named Heroku.

Option one: Mongrel cluster

At the time of this writing, the most common deployment method is still to deploy your Rails application to a server that is running a Mongrel cluster front-ended by a proxy web server. It's a proven solution, even if installing and configuring it can be a slightly involved process.

Covering the full gamut of system administration tasks for installing this option onto all the possible operating systems, for all web servers, with all potential configuration options falls far outside the scope of this book. However, on the support web site for this book (www.foundationrails.com), I'll be providing links to a number of online tutorials and resources that should help you. But for good measure, we'll cover the primary steps involved with setting up a Mongrel cluster on an Ubuntu Linux server in this section.

Installing the necessary software

Once you have a new Ubuntu Linux server created with a basic configuration, the first step we'll have to do is to install the necessary Ruby, MySQL, and web server applications using the Advanced Packaging Tool (or apt for short). To install software in Debian-based systems such as Ubuntu, we use the apt-get command.

To install a common set of applications would require the following command:

```
sudo apt-get install ruby mysql-server rubygems ruby1.8-dev ➥
build-essential libmysql-ruby irb
```

Once all these applications are installed, we next need to make sure we've got an updated version of RubyGems before we can install Rails. Fortunately, RubyGems provides some commands to self-update:

```
sudo gem update
sudo gem update --system
```

Installing Rails

With RubyGems updated, we can use it to install our Rails framework. This is a very simple procedure and consists of only one short command:

```
sudo gem install rails
```

You'll notice that with this command RubyGems pulls down all of the necessary libraries that make up Rails.

Installing Mongrel

At this point, it makes sense to go ahead and install the mongrel_cluster gems to our server. Again, this is just a simple one-line command:

```
sudo gem install mongrel_cluster
```

We use the mongrel_cluster gem to control multiple Mongrel processes and thus simplify our administration of them. You can read more about mongrel_cluster at http://mongrel.rubyforge.org/wiki/MongrelCluster.

403

Configuring our web server

Installing the web server will typically come down to a choice between Apache or Nginx. If Apache is not already installed on your server, you can usually install it easily using the following command:

```
sudo aptitude install apache2 apache2.2-common apache2-mpm-prefork ➡
apache2-utils libexpat1 ssl-cert
```

Otherwise, if you're interested in going the Nginx route, you'll most likely be building it from source, as you'll want to have the most current version. You'll find links to step-by-step instructions for how to build Nginx from source at the support web site for this book.

Once you have a basic web server installed, the next major decision you have to make is to determine the number of Mongrel processes that you're going to run. Since each Mongrel process that you activate will be sitting idle, waiting for any incoming requests, yet consuming server resources, you definitely don't want to spin up too many. However, if your traffic load exceeds the number of Mongrel processes that can respond to it, your users will perceive your site as painfully slow (as each request has to wait for an available Mongrel process to service it).

We need to decide on the number of Mongrel processes now, so we can use that count as we build our proxy configuration. A big portion of this decision is going to depend on the system resources you have available on the server. Most applications will start out with somewhere between two and four Mongrel processes (personally, I recommend starting small and adding more later). For example, let's assume that we're setting up a domain named foundationrails.com, and we've decided that we will be running our Rails application on three Mongrel processes.

If we were running Nginx as our web server, our Nginx configuration might look like this:

```
upstream mongrel {
  server 127.0.0.1:3000;
  server 127.0.0.1:3001;
  server 127.0.0.1:3002;
}
server {
  listen 80;
  server_name .foundationrails.com;
  root /var/www/foundationrails/current/public;

  location / {
    if (-f $request_filename/index.html) {
      rewrite (.*) $1/index.html break;
    }

    if (!-f $request_filename) {
      proxy_pass http://mongrel;
    }
  }
}
```

> For those of you not familiar with Nginx, it's an alternative web server and reverse proxy that was created by a Russian developer named Igor Sysoev. It's lightweight, fast, and easy to configure, which has caused it to make huge gains in popularity over the last few years. In fact, several high-profile and large-scale web sites are using Nginx to serve their content, including Wordpress.com, Penny-arcade.com, and Hulu.com. You can read more about Nginx at http://www.nginx.net/.

Of course, some people are much more comfortable using Apache, so if you were running Apache 2.2 with mod_proxy installed, your httpd.conf file might have a virtual host configuration that looked like this:

```
<VirtualHost *:80>
  ServerName foundationrails.com

    ServerAlias www.foundationrails.com

  DocumentRoot /var/www/apps/foundationrails/current/public

  <Directory /var/www/apps/foundationrails/current/public>
    Options FollowSymLinks
    AllowOverride None
    Order allow,deny
    Allow from all
  </Directory>

  # Configure mongrel_cluster
  <Proxy balancer://foundationrails_cluster>
    BalancerMember http://127.0.0.1:3000
    BalancerMember http://127.0.0.1:3001
    BalancerMember http://127.0.0.1:3002
</Proxy>

  RewriteEngine On

  # Prevent access to .svn directories
  RewriteRule ^(.*/)?\.svn/ - [F,L]
  ErrorDocument 403 "Access Forbidden"

  # Check for maintenance file and redirect all requests
  RewriteCond %{DOCUMENT_ROOT}/system/maintenance.html -f
  RewriteCond %{SCRIPT_FILENAME} !maintenance.html
  RewriteRule ^.*$ /system/maintenance.html [L]

  # Rewrite index to check for static
  RewriteRule ^/$ /index.html [QSA]

  # Rewrite to check for Rails cached page
  RewriteRule ^([^.]+)$ $1.html [QSA]
```

```
        # Redirect all non-static requests to cluster
        RewriteCond %{DOCUMENT_ROOT}/%{REQUEST_FILENAME} !-f
        RewriteRule ^/(.*)$ balancer://foundationrails_cluster% ➥
    {REQUEST_URI} [P,QSA,L]

        # Deflate
        AddOutputFilterByType DEFLATE text/html text/plain text/xml ➥
      text/css application/x-javascript
        BrowserMatch ^Mozilla/4 gzip-only-text/html
        BrowserMatch ^Mozilla/4\.0[678] no-gzip
        BrowserMatch \bMSIE !no-gzip !gzip-only-text/html

        ErrorLog logs/www.foundationrails.com-error_log
        CustomLog logs/www.foundationrails.com-access_log combined
    </VirtualHost>
```

Whether you choose to use Apache or Nginx is really a matter of personal preference. Both are valid options, and both are going to require more configuration than I've shown here. I've just highlighted the important bits that are specific to using them to proxy to your mongrel processes.

Wrapping up option one

All that's left to do now is to simply copy our code to the server and start up our Mongrel cluster to make it accessible from the web. We'll talk about making that process easier using a tool named Capistrano later in this chapter.

Finally, configuring your server to restart the Mongrel cluster whenever your server restarts would be a good idea (otherwise, a random reboot would take your site offline until you had time to log back in and manually restart it). You can do this by switching to the root user on the server and editing the crontab using this command:

```
crontab -e
```

Once you're in the editing screen, you would want to add a line like this to restart the Mongrel cluster after a reboot:

```
@reboot mongrel_rails cluster::start -C /var/www/myapp/current/➥
config/mongrel_cluster.yml
```

As you can see, configuring a web server to serve Rails applications this way does require a fair amount of system administration knowledge, and we didn't even talk about any of the more advanced subjects, such as server security, performance optimization, or disabling unwanted processes.

If setting up a server like this sounds a little intimidating to you, you're not alone. Fortunately a growing number of service providers have stepped in to help offset this intimidation by offering complete prebuilt Rails stacks that they will install and even manage for you. Some examples include RailsMachine.com, Joyent.com, and EngineYard.com.

Granted, these full-service providers are going to cost substantially more than a do-it-yourself solution, but for that additional charge, they are also providing you with a considerable amount of peace of mind and guaranteed scalability. In fact, a fairly significant number of popular Rails applications are hosted on providers such as these.

Option two: Apache with mod_rails (Passenger)

One of the newest and easiest solutions for deploying your Rails application these days is to utilize a new Apache module developed by a company in the Netherlands named Phusion. The module is named Passenger, but it's quickly become more commonly known as mod_rails. As the name implies, it allows you to simply run your Rails application as an Apache module. This makes the deployment and configuration issues surrounding building a production Rails server considerably easier.

In fact, once you have your basic server built with the necessary Ruby, Rails, and Apache web server applications and libraries installed, adding Passenger to the system is a pretty simple process. First, we install the gem:

```
sudo gem install passenger
```

After the gem is installed, we can run a step-by-step installation program that will automatically configure Passenger into our Apache configuration using the following command:

```
passenger-install-apache2-module
```

And here's the output of one of my run-throughs of installing Passenger:

```
Welcome to the Passenger Apache 2 module installer.

This installer will guide you through the entire installation process.
It shouldn't take more than 3 minutes in total.

Here's what you can expect from the installation process:

 1. The Apache 2 module will be installed for you.
 2. You'll learn how to configure Apache.
 3. You'll learn how to deploy a Ruby on Rails application.

Don't worry if anything goes wrong. This installer will advise you ➥
 on how to solve any problems.

Checking for required software...

 * GNU C++ compiler... found at /usr/bin/g++
 * Ruby development headers... found
 * OpenSSL support for Ruby... found
 * RubyGems... found
 * Rake... found at /usr/bin/rake
 * Apache 2... found at /usr/sbin/httpd
 * Apache 2 development headers... not found
 * Apache Portable Runtime (APR) development headers... found at ➥
 /usr/bin/apr-1-config
 * fastthread... found
```

```
Some required software is not installed.
But don't worry, this installer will tell you how to install them.
-------------------------------------------
Installation instructions for required software

 * To install Apache 2 development headers:
   Please run yum install httpd-devel as root.
```

I've got to admit, I was pretty impressed with that configuration. Not only did it detect that I was missing something, but it went the extra mile to give me the exact command I needed to correct the issue in my Linux distribution (this was installed on a server running Red Hat Enterprise Server). How cool is that?

Once I installed the Apache development headers using the yum install httpd-devel command it recommended, I started the installation process again and was shortly greeted by this:

```
The Apache 2 module was successfully installed.

Please edit your Apache configuration file, and add these lines:

    LoadModule passenger_module /usr/lib/ruby/gems/1.8/gems/➡
passenger-1.0.4/ext/apache2/mod_passenger.so
    RailsSpawnServer /usr/lib/ruby/gems/1.8/gems/passenger-1.0.4/➡
bin/passenger-spawn-server
    RailsRuby /usr/bin/ruby

After you restart Apache, you are ready to deploy any number of Ruby
on Rails applications on Apache, without any further Ruby on Rails
specific configuration!

Deploying a Ruby on Rails application: an example

Suppose you have a Ruby on Rails application in /somewhere. Add
 a virtual host to your Apache configuration file, and set its
DocumentRoot to /somewhere/public, like this:

    <VirtualHost *:80>
       ServerName www.yourhost.com
       DocumentRoot /somewhere/public
    </VirtualHost>

And that's it! You may also want to check the Users Guide for security
and optimization tips and other useful information:

  /usr/lib/ruby/gems/1.8/gems/passenger-1.0.4/doc/Users guide.html

Enjoy Passenger, a product of Phusion (www.phusion.nl) :-)
http://www.modrails.com/
```

Amazingly easy, huh? Passenger also supports a pretty significant amount of configuration options that you'll want to read about in its *User Guide* so you can get the most of out of it. However, one item that's probably most important to you is the information on how you can restart your Rails application (such as when you deploy new code).

Obviously, you can always go the sledgehammer route and simply do a restart of Apache, but fortunately, there's an easier way. If you create or modify a file in /tmp named `restart.txt`, Passenger will detect this and automatically reload and restart your Rails application.

In practice, the easiest way to do this on a Unix-based system (such as Linux or OS X) is to use the touch command like so:

```
touch /tmp/restart.txt
```

This useful command simply updates the file modification time of the specified file to the current timestamp (or creates the file if it doesn't exist), thus it would quickly cause the Passenger system to detect that the file has changed and signal Passenger to restart your application processes.

Option three: new services

The final deployment option we'll discuss in this chapter is a radical departure from our previous solutions. As an alternative to the traditional model of building your own web server, a new breed of services has begun to appear that aims to remove all of the pain of deploying your Rails applications. One such service, even though it's still in beta at the time of this writing, is getting the most attention in the community lately—Heroku (www.heroku.com).

Heroku aims to completely remove the pain of building and deploying Rails applications by providing you the convenience of a completely web-based development solution, as you can see in Figure 14-1.

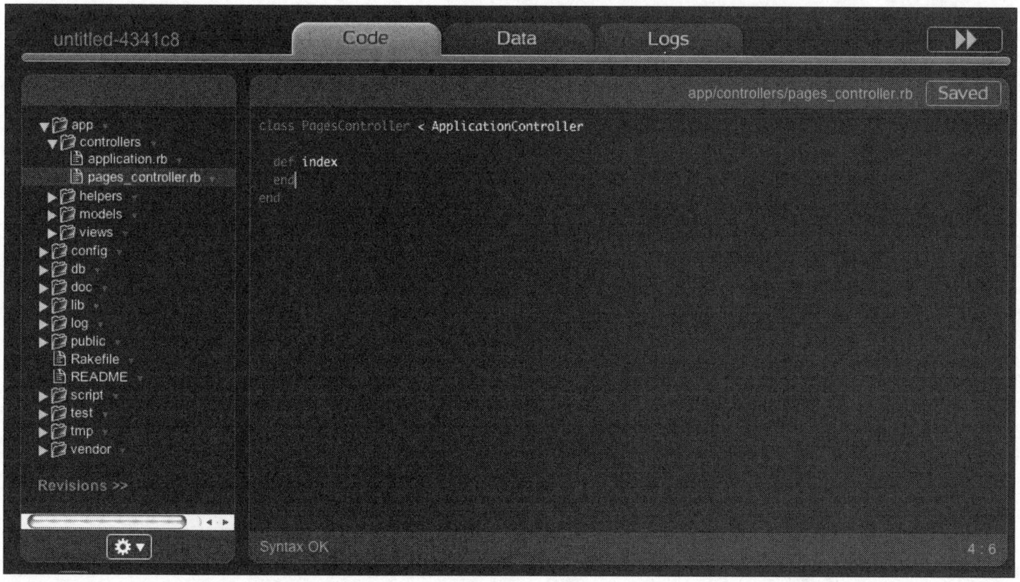

Figure 14-1. Heroku's web-based code editor

> *If you prefer to develop on their own local machine, Heroku recently launched a new feature that allows you to write your Rails code on your local system and publish it to their servers using a new* heroku *gem. You can install the gem using a simple* gem install heroku *command and find more information about how to use it at* www.heroku.com

The Heroku editor is impressively full featured and, in my tests, provides easy access to pretty much everything that you would need for Rails development, including some tasks I didn't expect such as installing custom gems.

Of course, creating Rails applications in a web browser (while cool) isn't the end of the story for Heroku. Their service gets even more interesting when you look at the easy conversion of your development application into a full production application through the click of a single button. Once you click that deploy button, your Rails application will be available running on a complete Rails stack using Nginx, Mongrel, and PostgreSQL. The solution is fully load balanced and it is deployed onto an elastic computing cloud network provided by Amazon's Elastic Compute Cloud (Amazon EC2) service.

That elastic cloud is one of the most impressive features of Heroku's service, as it means that additional horsepower can be added dynamically as demand for your application increases. So with a complete Rails stack and access to near unlimited amount of computing power, your fears of your application being able to immediately scale should be allayed.

The other key advantage of the Heroku service is its price. Paying for a traditional hosting solution is sort of like paying for cell phone service. You pay for a specific amount of CPU, memory, and bandwidth a month. Things are fine as long as you stay under that limit, but once you go over that limit, you have to pay more. It doesn't matter if your application has only used a quarter of the available resources for the previous six months; once you go over, you have to pay.

With Heroku, however, you're quite literally paying only for what you use. If your application gets an extremely low amount of traffic, you'll be paying a low amount for the service. In the event of a sudden spike, Heroku can automatically spin up additional processes to handle the spike in traffic, and you only have to pay for the resources that you use for the duration of the spike.

All in all, Heroku represents a pretty exciting trend for Rails deployment, and I recommend that you do take the time to consider it as an option.

Deploying your application

While you could certainly push your code to your new production web server using manual methods such as FTP or manually exporting from your version control system, you'll find, as your application continues to grow, that doing things manually will eventually lead to madness. Fortunately, there's no reason to do that, as most Rails developers utilize an automated deployment using a tool named Capistrano. We'll wrap up our chapter with a quick tour of how to set up our application for automated deployment.

Our first step is get our Rails application into a version control system such as Subversion or Git.

> *Subversion is a highly popular version control system where you maintain a single repository that holds all revisions of your application code. Developers check out this code locally, make changes, and commit those changes back to the main repository.*
>
> *Git is part of a new breed of version control called distributed version control, where instead of having a single central repository, each developer maintains his or her own personal repository that can be easily shared and merged with other developers.*

Getting your project into Subversion

Up until early 2008, the most commonly used version control system for Rails applications was Subversion, and while many of the big-name applications have begun moving to Git (including Ruby on Rails itself), you'll find that Subversion is still a popular alternative and fairly easy to set up. In this section, we'll walk through the necessary steps involved with getting your Rails project into a Subversion repository.

Obviously, the first step will be to install and configure your new Subversion server and create a new repository for your application. For the purposes of this walkthrough, we'll assume that we're importing a new Rails project named myapp into a Subversion repository named myapp that exists at https://my.subversion.com/repos/myapp. With that information, we would open a command prompt and import the current application using the following command:

```
svn import /projects/myapp https://my.subversion.com/repos/myapp/trunk➥
 -m "initial import" --username ealameda
```

Once we have the application imported, we can remove our existing version and check out a fresh version from our repository:

```
rm -rf myapp
svn co https://my.subversion.com/repos/myapp/trunk myapp
cd myapp
```

Checking out a new version is important, as this new version contains the necessary Subversion files that we can use to make modifications to the repository. To start with, let's clean up our repository by removing some of the files that will be generated locally anytime the application is run and thus don't need to be managed with version control (such as logs and temporary files).

We'll start by removing all log files out of the subversion repository:

```
svn remove log/*
svn commit -m 'removing all log files from subversion'
svn propset svn:ignore "*.log" log/
svn update log/
svn commit -m 'Ignoring all files in /log/ ending in .log'
```

Next, we'll remove all of our temporary files:

```
svn propset svn:ignore "*" tmp/sessions tmp/cache tmp/sockets
svn commit -m "Ignoring all files in /tmp/"
svn update tmp/
svn commit -m 'Ignore the whole tmp/ directory'
```

At this point, our code is now managed by Subversion, and we can use all of the standard Subversion commands to commit changes, compare differences, and keep a solid track of our source code.

A good resource for learning subversion is the free online book *Version Control with Subversion* that is available at http://svnbook.red-bean.com/.

Getting your project into Git

Of course, the new hotness for version control for Rails applications these days is the Git version control system. Git is an open source distributed version control system that was originally written by Linus Torvalds (the creator of Linux) as a tool to help manage the development of the Linux kernel. You can find out more about Git at http://git.or.cz.

Assuming that you've already installed Git, using it to manage our Rails projects is a fairly simple and uninvolved process (especially when compared to Subversion).

Once your project is created and you're ready to make it a Git repository, you simply open a command shell into the root of your application and run the command:

```
git init
```

And that's it. Our application is now a Git-enabled repository. All that's left to do is to specify which files we don't want to be under version control. We do that by creating a new text file in the root of our application named .gitignore and listing out the files and directories that we want Git to ignore within this file. Some of the common elements we'll want to ignore include our log files and anything in our /tmp directory. So an example of a .gitignore file might look like:

```
log/*.log
tmp/**/*
```

Now, it's simply time to add our files to our Git repository and commit the changes:

```
git add .
git commit -a -m "initial import"
```

If you want to gain a deeper understanding of what Git is, how it works, and how to use it, I would highly recommend checking out some of the resources that are available at www.peepcode.com; there are also a growing number of free screencasts about Git at www.gitcasts.com.

And if you haven't already done so, you need to check out www.github.com, a Rails application that serves as a centralized Git repository host and adds a number of social features that encourages developers to contribute to one another's projects.

Configuring Capistrano

Now that we have our application in version control, we simply need to install the Capistrano gem like so:

```
sudo gem install capistrano
```

Once the gem is installed, we can set up our application to use Capistrano for deployment by opening a command prompt into the root of the application and running this command:

```
capify .
```

This command created a couple of new files within our application: a file in the root named Capfile used to configure where Capistrano should look for deployment recipes and a file in /config named deploy.rb that is a default recipe file containing the configuration for deploying your Rails application. You'll want to edit this recipe file to match your deployment settings such as the name of your application, the location of your version control, and the IP addresses of your production servers. The official Capistrano site (http://capify.org/) provides a wealth of information on how to configure this recipe.

Once we have our deployment recipe configured, it's a simple matter to set up our production servers to be prepared for automated deployment; we simply need to run the following command:

```
cap deploy:setup
```

This command will log in to each of our production servers and configure the necessary directory structure for Capistrano deployment. Once that's completed, we can deploy our application for the first time by running:

```
cap deploy:cold
```

At this point (assuming you didn't receive any errors), your application should now be configured and running on your production web servers. Anytime you need to deploy changes to your application code, you can do so quickly by simply running the cap:deploy command, which will deploy the latest version of your code out of your version control system and automatically restart all your web servers to run the latest version of the code.

Summary

In this chapter, we explored several of the common options and technologies for Rails deployment. Of course, as Rails deployment is a constantly evolving art, this information is simply a snapshot in time for how Rails applications are deployed today. For the most current information, be sure to check out the support web site for this book where I'll be providing links to various tutorials and step-by-step guides.

Appendix A

WHERE TO GO FROM HERE

Learning how to program applications in Rails is not a single destination but an ongoing journey, one that I hope that this book in some small way has inspired you to continue. Even though building web applications in Rails is easy, Rails itself is a large and complex framework with lots of rewards for those who choose to go beyond the basics and dig deeper into all the framework has to offer. It's a path that I've been on now since early September of 2005 and one that I don't see ending anytime soon.

As we come to an end of this book, I wanted to take a few moments to share with you some of my favorite resources along this path to help you with your ongoing journey as well.

News sites

The ever-changing nature of the Internet means that web sites will come and go without any warning, and thus some of my favorite Rails-related sites of last year are no longer in existence (or at least no longer being updated). However, this section offers a list of some of the sites that I currently track on a regular basis to help continue my learning and to stay informed of what's happening in the community.

Official Rails blog

The official blog of Ruby on Rails (http://weblog.rubyonrails.org/) is always a good source for new releases, upcoming changes to Rails, and general information relevant to the community. Traditionally, it hasn't been updated very regularly, but that seems to be changing with the recent addition of some new bloggers who are posting weekly updates.

Ruby Inside

Ruby Inside (http://www.rubyinside.com/) is by far the most popular Ruby-related blog and features highly relevant and well-filtered content on a regular basis. It was created and is maintained by Peter Cooper, who is also the author of *Beginning Ruby* (Apress 2007).

Ruby Flow

Peter Cooper also launched Ruby Flow (http://www.rubyflow.com/) in 2008. Whereas Ruby Inside is more of a filtered news site, Ruby Flow serves as a community-driven link blog that is open to the public to submit interesting news and tidbits relevant to the Ruby and Rails community. Due to the nature of the system, you'd expect to find a large pool of people posting links to material that they've written that's not very good. I have to admit that I've often been surprised by quite the opposite; I've found a high number of quality writings from people that I hadn't read before.

Rails Inside

A sister site to the Ruby Inside blog, Rails Inside (http://www.railsinside.com/) is focused squarely on Rails-related news. Although the blog is very new at the time of this writing, it looks extremely promising, and this is why I'm recommending it.

Rails Envy podcast

The guys at Rails Envy (http://railsenvy.com/) have put out some really great tutorials and some absolutely hilarious videos on their site that you should take the time to check out. However, it's their weekly podcast that really takes the cake. Each week, they publish a short (5- to 15-minute) podcast where they review anything new or noteworthy within the Rails community over the last week. You'll often find pure gold in some of the links they mention, and they're always entertaining to listen to.

Planet Ruby on Rails

If you follow RSS feeds, the Planet Ruby on Rails (http://www.planetrubyonrails.org/) RSS feed is extremely excellent, as it serves as an aggregator to a large pool of Ruby- and Rails-related blogs.

Documentation sites

In this section, you'll find a number of sites that I recommend that you use as references for understanding how Rails works.

Official documents

The official API documentation for Rails is at http://api.rubyonrails.org/. The material here can often be a little outdated from the most current developments, but there's a wealth of information available. This site's biggest fault is that the interface can be a bit unwieldy at times, but a number of new sites have launched that attempt to provide the same documentation in a better package, my favorite of which is Rails Docs.

Rails Docs

Rails Docs (http://rails-doc.org/) is a brand new documentation site that launched in 2008. It features all of the Rails documentation in a cleaner, more attractive interface, and it's further enhanced with the ability for users to contribute to the documentation in the form of notes.

This is the site I've been going to on a regular basis when I wanted to double-check the available parameters for a method or verify that my understanding of the way a Rails feature works is correct.

Ryan Daigle's What's New in Edge Rails

I contemplated placing the What's New in Edge Rails site (http://ryandaigle.com/) in one of the other categories, but it seemed to fit best here. Ryan Daigle performs an incredible service to the Rails community by constantly evaluating new changes that have been committed to the edge version of the Rails core and providing detailed write-ups on what those changes are, what they will mean to developers in the future, and most importantly, how to use those new features. You don't want to miss this site if you want to keep current.

Official Rails code and ticketing

In 2008, the Rails core moved the development of Rails off of their own Subversion server and onto GitHub (http://github.com/rails). This move makes it easy for you to not only view the source but create your own fork of Rails that you can modify to your heart's content.

In addition, the ticketing and bug-tracking system was also moved from a trac instance to an account on a Rails application named Lighthouse that was created by Rick Olsen and Justin Palmer. Within that system, you can view and report bugs for Rails at http://rails.lighthouseapp.com/dashboard.

Personal Blogs

Of course, some of the best experiences you can have are from learning directly from other Rails developers who are willing to share the lessons that they've learned along the way. There is certainly no lack of those out there, and by subscribing to the RSS feed of the Planet Ruby on Rails site or by checking out the links that the Rails Envy guys share every week, you'll be led to a wealth of the best content available.

That being said, I do have a few favorite blogs that will cause me to drop whatever I'm doing and see what they've posted whenever I see a new post from them in my RSS reader. I list them for you in the following sections, in no particular order.

Jim Neath's blog

A fairly new addition to my favorites list, Jim Neath (http://jimneath.org/) has posted some truly incredible tutorials on things such as integrating jQuery and Rails and using Rails to convert videos.

John Nunemaker's Rails Tips blog

John Nunemaker is one of those guys that I need to make a point to meet one day. His blog (http://railstips.org/) is a steady and sure resource for making advanced concepts seem simple. He posts lots of code with just the right amount of explanation interspersed.

Ilya Grigorik's Igvita site

When you're reading a post on the Igvita site (http://www.igvita.com/) written by Ilya Grigorik, you'll be amazed at the quality of each and every post. His content is excellent, as he tackles some of the more advanced concepts such as database and web application performance. And he does it with such style, providing professional-level illustrations to highlight key points.

Rails Spikes

The Rails Spikes site (http://railspikes.com/) is another fast and fun site to read. Posts tend to be a bit shorter than on the other sites I listed and occasionally aren't always code specific, but that doesn't mean that they're any less rich in quality content.

Screencasts

Of course, sometimes seeing is better than reading. In those cases, these two screencast sites are the best of the best.

Peepcode screencasts

First off, we have Peepcode screencasts (http://peepcode.com/) from Geoffrey Grosenbach. These always-excellent hour-long training videos are on a variety of subjects that are Rails related, and each costs around $9. If you really want to dig into a specific subject such as REST, RSpec, or benchmarking, I can't recommend a better resource than Peepcode.

RailsCasts

The other resource that I must insist that you use is RailsCasts (http://railscasts.com/). Ryan Bates puts out an excellent (and free) screencast at RailsCasts every Monday. Each of the screencasts is short, typically in the 2- to 12-minute range, but each packs a huge wallop of best practice advice and timely information. In fact, stop reading this book now and go watch a few of them.

Books

I hate to admit it, but I'm sure that I'm one of Amazon.com's favorite customers. I seem to have developed quite the addiction to Ruby- and Rails-related books and can honestly say that I believe that I own (and have read) all of the currently available ones (I also have a lot preordered). All this is leading up to the fact that I'd also like to recommend a few books for you to consider purchasing and working your way through, as I found all of these books to be the absolute cream of the crop.

Going deeper in Ruby

Certainly, a number of books out there promise to give you a deeper understanding of the Ruby language, and most of them are good. However, for someone first starting out, these three are the ones that I would most highly recommend:

- *Why's Poignant Guide to Ruby* by Why the Lucky Stiff is a free book available online at http://poignantguide.net/ruby/ that is weird and quirky yet fun. I remember reading it on the bus going to and from work when I first started learning Ruby and thinking to myself that I couldn't believe what I was reading. This book may not be for everyone, but the price is right for you to at least give it a try and see what you think.

- *Beginning Ruby: From Novice to Professional* by Peter Cooper (Apress 2007) is an excellent beginner's tutorial through the Ruby language with interesting examples.

- *Design Patterns in Ruby* by Russ Olsen (Addison-Wesley 2007) is by far my favorite Ruby book. While the subject matter of design patterns might seem a bit more advanced, Olsen presents it in such a fun and engaging way that I believe he makes it accessible to beginners as well. I highly recommended it.

Going deeper in Rails

To be honest, one of the problems I have with the current state of Rails books is that there really don't seem to be many good books available for the intermediate Rails developer (i.e., someone who has finished a beginner's book like this one and is now ready to learn more about implementing those concepts). I wrote one book to fit in that gap, *Practical Rails Projects* (Apress 2007), but the book was written for Rails 1.2.6, as Rails 2.0 wasn't yet available. However, if you're willing to go back and build applications in the Rails 1.2.6 way, I think it's an excellent book (of course, I'm biased though).

Outside of that, there are a pair of recently released Rails books that I've found to be well above average and would recommend for you to read:

- *Advanced Rails Recipes* by Mike Clark (Pragmatic Bookshelf 2008) is an incredible collection of small solutions to common problems that we can encounter as Rails developers. Most of the recipes in the book were contributed by other developers within the community, so you'll get a wide spectrum of insight and information on a variety of topics.

- *Practical REST on Rails 2 Projects* by Ben Scofield (Apress 2008) is a new book that focuses solely on how we use the REST principles that we've discussed in this book. While you won't gain a lot more detail on REST than we discussed here, you will gain insight into how other applications can interface to your application using a variety of technologies, such as PHP and JavaScript. It's definitely a good follow-up book if you want to refresh on what REST is or how to interface to it.

General programming

Finally, large numbers of books have motivated or inspired me over the years. However, I feel these two books introduced some of the ideas that influenced me the most and thus I'd like to share them with you:

- *My Job Went to India* by Chad Fowler (Pragmatic Bookshelf 2005) is a book that both Chad and his publisher have admitted was poorly named. Inside the book, however, are powerful ideas on what you need to do to build a successful career as a developer, make yourself invaluable to your company, and generally be the best programmer you can be.

- *Practices of an Agile Developer* by Venkat Subramaniam and Andy Hunt (Pragmatic Bookshelf 2006) is another one of those life-changing books. In this book, the authors expose common problems that we allow in our approaches to development and introduce best practice advice on how to correct them—all while being fun and engaging. In fact, I've often thought that it would make a great book for a development team to read together.

Appendix B

RAILS INSTALLATION

To be able to follow along with the examples in this book's application (and later to build your own applications), you will need to install a number of software packages onto your development machine. At a bare minimum, we'll just need to install the packages explained in the following sections.

Ruby

Rails is a framework that was written in Ruby. When we create Rails applications, we are coding in Ruby; therefore, you need to ensure that you have a working installation of Ruby. Once you have that, you can use Ruby tools to install the Ruby on Rails framework.

Rails

Once you have Ruby installed, you'll also ensure that you have a package manager system named RubyGems and use it to add the Rails framework to your system.

Database

Rails was designed for easily creating database-driven web applications. Therefore, you need to have a database available to your applications. For the purposes of this book, we'll focus on SQLite, which became the default database for Rails applications in 2008. SQLite is a fast and lightweight file-based database engine—perfect for development but less ideal for production use.

> There are currently two different version of SQLite available: SQLite and SQLite 3. The Rails default is SQLite 3.

The processes you have for each of these items is going to depend somewhat on your operating system. However, no matter what operating system you're running on your development system, these are the core packages that you'll need to make sure you have:

- Ruby
- RubyGems
- Ruby on Rails
- SQLite database

Let's see the most common approaches to getting each of these installed by operating system.

Windows

I'll be honest and let you know right from the start that developing Ruby on Rails applications is going to be a source of some unique challenges for you. The blessing of open source software is that any number of developers are constantly looking at and improving the code over the course of time. Unfortunately, the curse of open source projects is that, since these developers are investing their own time freely into the development, they tend to favor the systems that they themselves are using rather than ensuring that all operating systems are covered equally.

Glance through the flickr photos of any Ruby or Rails conference, and there's no denying that Ruby developers using Windows are in the minority.

That's not to imply that Ruby or Rails is in any way less stable or feature-rich on the Windows OS. I'm merely letting you know that occasionally you might face an additional challenge in getting some Ruby packages (called gems) installed. With that warning out of the way, let's discuss the most common options for getting your Windows system configured for Ruby on Rails development.

Instant Rails

For a number of years, the most popular configuration option for Rails developers on Windows has been to use a completely self-contained Ruby on Rails environment by the name of Instant Rails. With Instant Rails, you simply download the latest version in a zip package from the official web site at http://instantrails.rubyforge.org/wiki/wiki.pl?Instant_Rails and unzip it into the directory of your choice. Within this package is an executable that includes Ruby, RubyGems, Rails, Apache, SQlite3, MySQL, Mongrel, and a large number of common RubyGems.

Once Instant Rails is installed, you'll manage your Rails applications from a console application like the one shown in Figure B-1.

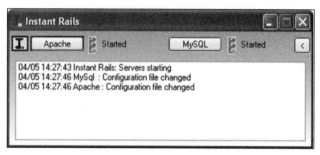

Figure B-1. The Instant Rails management console

It doesn't get much easier than this for an installation process. However, the downfall with this is that you are at the mercy of the release cycle for the Instant Rails application (which will naturally lag a bit behind the normal Ruby and Rails release cycles).

> *It's important to remember that because Instant Rails doesn't modify any of your Windows environment configurations, your normal command line prompt doesn't have access to your Ruby files. In order to run any of the command line generation tools in Rails, you need to use the console window provided in the management console application. To open its special command line window, select the* Rails Applications ➤ Open Ruby Console Window *menu option.*

Cygwin

Another option is Cygwin (several developers in my local Ruby users group have stated that they've had success with this). You can install Cygwin and use it as the baseline for setting up a Ruby on Rails development environment by following the guidelines contained in a blog post from developer Matt Polito at http://www.mattpolito.info/2008/04/07/rails-development-on-windows/. If you're not familiar with Cygwin, it's an emulated UNIX shell that runs under Windows, thereby giving you much of the same command line tools and power that Mac and Linux developers have.

You can download Cygwin from its official site at http://www.cygwin.com/.

Once you have it downloaded, you'll run its installer application and accept most of the default settings. The exceptions being that you'll want to ensure that the install setting is set for Just Me and that the Default Text File Type gets set to Unix/Binary.

Once you get to the Select Packages screen, you'll want to choose a number of additional packages. According to Matt's original blog post, he recommended that you install the following:

- curl
- gcc
- git
- grep
- keychain
- make
- ruby
- rsync
- sqlite3
- subversion
- subversion-ruby
- wget
- which

Now that you have Cygwin installed with a number of the packages that you need, you just need to install RubyGems and use that to install Ruby on Rails.

You can download the latest version of RubyGems from http://rubyforge.org/frs/?group_id=126. Once you have it downloaded and unzipped, simply open a new Cygwin window, and run the following command to install RubyGems:

```
ruby setup.rb
```

From this point on, you can follow standard instructions for installing the remaining gems that you need:

```
gem install rails --include-dependencies
gem install sqlite3-ruby
gem install mysql
gem install mongrel
```

Afterward, just start up a Cygwin shell anytime you want to follow along with this book or build your own Rails applications.

> Another option that I had far less success with in the past—but others (including my technical reviewer) have favored—is to use Ruby One-Click Installer for Windows, a prepackaged Windows installer for Ruby and RubyGems. You can download the application at http://rubyforge.org/projects/rubyinstaller/.

Mac (Leopard)

Congratulations—OS X Leopard (10.5) comes with a full Ruby and Ruby on Rails development stack already preinstalled. In fact, all you need to do is simply update Rails to the latest version, and you are ready to go:

```
sudo gem update rails
```

Although not required for a baseline Rails installation, it's also a good idea to install the XCode development tools from your installation disc as well, because many popular Ruby gems (such as Mongrel) will be unable to install without the compiler that's included in XCode.

Mac (Tiger)

If you're still running the previous edition of OS X (10.4 Tiger), you'll be pleasantly surprised to find that you do have many of the necessary tools already installed. Unfortunately, though, Tiger shipped with a broken installation of Ruby.

To get around this, most Rails developers have followed Dan Benjamin's excellent step-by-step instructions at http://hivelogic.com/articles/2007/02/ruby-rails-mongrel-mysql-osx to install a complete development system from source.

After following these instructions, you'll be set up with a clean development system for Rails development. However, I would recommend enhancing the installation with the addition of the SQLite database.

Starting with Tiger, Mac OS X began including SQLite along with the operating system, so there's no need to worry about installing SQLite. The necessary SQLite Ruby gem to interface to a SQLite database is a bit more complicated, however. Before you can install the Ruby gem, you will need to install an application named SWIG (Simplified Wrapper and Interface Generator). Otherwise, the SQLite gem will not use the correct SQLite library and will default to using a pure Ruby version of SQLite that doesn't work as well.

The easiest way to install SWIG is to first install the MacPorts tool. MacPorts is a free and open source application that simplifies installation of many open source tools that otherwise would require compiling from source manually. You can install the latest version of MacPorts from http://www.macports.org.

Once you have MacPorts installed, you can install the SWIG library from the command line with this simple command:

```
sudo port install swig
```

Next, you'll open a command prompt and use RubyGems to install the SQLite Ruby gem:

```
sudo gem install sqlite3-ruby
```

You'll see a list of possible install versions. You should choose the highest numbered version for your operating system (choose the Ruby version).

Linux

Unfortunately, because of the large number of different Linux distributions, attempting to document a single installation method would be an exercise in futility.

The good news, however, is that if you've installed any of the development packages with your distribution, there's a good chance that Ruby may already be installed. If it's not, it's typically just a matter of using whichever package manager your Linux distribution requires to add it, and doing so is generally fairly painless. If you're a bit more daring, you could even build from source.

A great resource to find step-by-step instructions for your specific Linux distribution is the official Ruby on Rails wiki (http://wiki.rubyonrails.org).

Installing SQLite 3 on Linux/UNIX

Most distributions offer a package manager that makes installing SQLite as simple as asking it to install. You could also install from source by checking out the latest build from the SQLite home page at http://www.sqlite.org.

Once your have SQLite 3 installed, you need to install the SQLite Ruby gem:

```
sudo gem install sqlite3-ruby
```

You should choose the highest numbered version for your operating system (choose the Ruby version).

Choosing a Code Editor

After getting these software packages installed to build a Rails software development system, the last important step is to choose a code editor that you'll use to edit your Rails code. Choosing the correct code editor is typically a matter of personal preference (and the source of Holy Wars within some circles).

We'll close out this section with a few links to the official sites of some code editors that I recommend; you download and try them to determine the right fit for yourself.

Mac OS X

Hands down, the most popular code editor for Mac users is TextMate (http://macromates.com/), which is made by Macromates. This is the editor that the entire Rails core development team uses and the one that you see in all of the Ruby on Rails screencasts. It's also the one that I use, and I can honestly say that it was the best software purchase I have ever made.

I do have a few friends that use NetBeans (http://www.netbeans.org/features/ruby/index.html) and really love it as well. Whereas TextMate is designed to be a text editor, NetBeans is designed to be a full-featured IDE (integrated development environment) with support for things such as code completion and a debugger.

Windows

In addition to the many cross-platform choices, many Windows developers prefer to use a fairly new text editor by the name of "E the text editor" (`http://www.e-texteditor.com/`), which has done a rather amazing amount of work to ensure that it was compatible with many of the bundles that have been created for TextMate on OS X.

Linux

Linux users tend to be a more varied bunch, and many of my Linux developer friends still swear by using the command line editors that they're accustomed to using on a daily basis such as VI or Emacs. However, I have also seen many developers customize the Gedit or Kedit text editors that came with their window manager to make them more like TextMate. Personally, when I used to develop on a Linux system as my primary system, I tended to use the cross-platform development solutions.

Cross-Platform

Finally, we have the list of solutions that are available across all operating systems. We already talked about NetBeans, which is cross-platform, but other choices to consider follow:

- Vim (`http://www.vim.org/`)
- RadRails (`http://www.aptana.com/rails/`)
- JEdit (`http://jedit.org`)

Whichever code editor you choose, I highly recommend you invest the time to truly learn its shortcuts and power tools. As with any craft, you're only as good as your tools, and learning how to really use your code editor will pay immense dividends to your future as a developer.

Appendix C

DATABASE DESIGN 101

As you've seen in Chapters 4 and 5, Rails makes building our databases amazingly easy. However, the danger is that Rails also makes it easy for you to implement a poorly designed database.

While discussing proper database design might be too academic for the main flow of our foundation book, I thought it was an important enough topic that I should at least give you a little guidance. So as an added bonus for you, I've put together this short introduction to basic database design theory where we'll talk about what database design is, why it's important, and the three normal forms that we typically care about.

An easy mistake

Take, for example, a database design for an auto dealership where we want to store records of every car that is currently or has ever been available on the site. Of course, if the car has been sold, we might also want to be able to capture information about the customer who bought that car, in which case we could design a table like Figure C-1.

Figure C-1.
An example of an unoptimized database design

At first glance, this table might make sense, but it has some problems. For example, suppose the same customer buys two cars. In this table design, her information would have to be entered into our database twice. That not only wastes space in our database but also could cause issues if we send out mailers from this database—this one customer would get multiple mailers.

Even worse, though, is the issue of maintaining this customer information over the long term. What would we do if we found out that this customer had moved? We'd have to go back to our database and update her address in multiple places, or our data would not be consistent. A better design would be to separate the customer information from the vehicle information, as shown in Figure C-2.

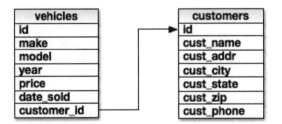

Figure C-2. Separating customer information from vehicle information

In this design, we've moved all of our customer information into a single table, and the vehicles table just maintains a reference to the appropriate customer record. By entering each customer's information only once in a customers table and linking that record to any car purchase, we have eliminated redundant (and sometimes conflicting) data. Not only that, but if we ever need to update the customer's information, we only have to make the change in a single location, and it will be updated for all vehicles that the customer has purchased.

In essence, what we've done here is a simplified version of the process referred to as normalization. Normalization can be thought of as the system of organizing data into related tables with the goal of eliminating (or at least reducing) redundant data across our database.

The normal forms

To help database designers with the process of normalization, sets of criteria were created that are called the normal forms. We use these forms not only to describe our database design but also as a means of measurement for how normalized a database design is. These normal forms are used to determine the degree of vulnerability that a specific table design has to inconsistencies caused by redundant data. The higher the normal form that's been applied to a table, the less vulnerable that table is. While a larger pool of normal forms exists, really only the first three normal forms are going to be applicable to traditional database design.

First Normal Form (FNF)

For a database design to meet the criteria of First Normal Form, each column within the tables must not contain multiple values. The common example that is bandied about to understand First Normal Form is a design that stores a person's name and address in single columns, like the one shown in Figure C-3.

users	
id	1
name	John Doe
address	123 Test Lane Los Angeles, CA 95926

Figure C-3. A table design that breaks First Normal Form

Instead, we should break up each of these columns into multiple columns so that we can more easily access the data that exists in each of the individual fields. For example, rather than having a single name field, we should break down the name into multiple columns (i.e., last name, middle name, and first name). The table design shown in Figure C-4 illustrates First Normal Form.

users
id
first_name
middle_name
last_name
address_1
address_2
city
state

Figure C-4.
A table design that is a valid First Normal Form

Second Normal Form (SNF)

For a database design to meet the criteria of Second Normal Form, each column within a table (besides the primary key) must depend on the entire primary key and not just a part of it. This is primarily an issue for database designs where we have a composite primary key (i.e., the primary key is composed of two keys). Figure C-5 shows a table with composite primary keys that violates the Second Normal Form.

memberships
user_id
group_id
user_name
group_name
last_login
date_joined

Figure C-5. A table design that violates Second Normal Form

What is a primary key? In relational database design, a primary key is used to uniquely identify each row in a table. The primary key comprises a single column or set of columns and must have a unique value (i.e., no two rows can have the same primary key). Within a Rails database, primary keys will by convention be single column integer values that are automatically incremented.

In the example in Figure C-5, the potential issue is that, because there are two primary keys, it's possible to add columns such as the group_name column that are really relevant to only one of the keys (in this case the group_id key).

The use of composite primary keys is a somewhat controversial subject within the topic of database design with a large set of proponents for and opponents to their use. As a framework, Rails has taken the stance that it will not support composite primary keys, and thus it is not possible to design a database table that uses composite primary keys with the default Rails framework (however, a few plug-ins are available that can add that capability to your Rails application if you absolutely can't live without it). The good news of all of this is that if your database design is following the Rails defaults (i.e., a single-ID primary key) and you've already ensured that it met the criteria for First Normal Form, your design is automatically a valid Second Normal Form database.

In fact, any table that uses an artificially generated primary key and does not use composite primary keys is in Second Normal Form.

Third Normal Form (TNF)

Third Normal Form is a bit harder to achieve in real-world usage and thus is frequently posited as an ideal that is often violated to maintain speed. The main idea in Third Normal Form is that all nonkey columns must not depend on each other. In other words, changing a single column should not also require that you have to change another. A simple example is the case of storing addresses within a table. You might have a database design that looks like the one shown in Figure C-6.

addresses
id
line_1
line_2
city
state
zip

Figure C-6. A table design that violates Third Normal Form

The Third Normal Form violation in this table is that if we change the state column, we almost certainly also need to change the city and ZIP code columns as well. To make the table meet the criteria for Third Normal Form would mean maintaining a separate table of just city, state, and ZIP code information, which might look like the design shown in Figure C-7.

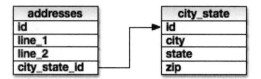

Figure C-7. It passes Third normal form, but is it practical?

Implementing Third Normal Form sounds great in theory, but in practice, it can make fetching our relevant data a much more complex process than necessary and thus is often bypassed for the sake of speed. In fact, most texts on database design advise new designers to design to Third Normal Form in their initial design and then denormalize elements for speed.

Of course, database design is a much bigger subject than just these basic steps of normalization and denormalization. However, if you understand these simplified concepts, they will carry you a long way in ensuring that your databases will remain flexible enough to be used for a long, long time.

INDEX

Symbols

! (exclamation mark) in method names, 38
! = operator, 27
&& (AND) operators, 27
<%# %> Tags (ERb), 145
<% %> tags (ERb), 143–144
<%- -%> tags (ERb), 144–145
<%= %> tags (ERb), 141–142
%w operator, 31, 35
$ (dollar sign) for naming global variables, 24
( ) parentheses in multiple comparisons, 27
? (question mark) in method names, 37
@ (at symbol) for naming instance variables, 23
@@ (at symbols) for naming class variables, 23
[ ] method (RJS), 368
[ ] (square brackets) for arrays, 29
{ } (curly braces) for hashes, 31
| | (OR) operators, 27
= (equals sign) assignment operator, 27
= = (double equals sign) comparison operator, 27

A

accessor methods (Ruby), 36–37
actions
  action caching, 396
  Action Mailer library, 57
  Action Pack libraries, 57
  Action View library, 139
  ActionController library, 173
  defining (controllers), 173–180
  redirection of, 188
Active Resource library, 57
Active Support library, 58
ActiveRecord
  ActiveRecord-based sessions, 183–184
  belongs_to method, 119–121
  building associations, 117–118
  callbacks, 116–117
  collection associations, 121–122
  custom associations, 128–130
  dirty objects, 136–137
  has_and_belongs_to_many method, 123–126
  has_many method, 122–123
  has_many :through association, 126–128
  has_one method, 121
  library, 57, 233
  named scopes, 135–136
  objects, 157, 276
  recursive relationships (self-referential joins), 130–132
  single-table inheritance, 132–134
  singular associations (one-to-one), 118–119
ActiveRecord library
  building first model, 71–74
  clients sample project, 70–71
  create method, 76–77
  CRUD operations and, 74
  delete method, 87
  find method, 77–79
  find method in Rails application, 83–84
  find_by method, 79–81
  find_by_sql method, 83
  legacy database schemas, 111–112
  migrations. *See* migrations (Rails)
  moving finds to model, 84
  new records, creating, 76
  optional parameters for find methods, 81–83

W

Windows, Microsoft
    E-the text editor for, 429
    installing Rails development software on,
        424–426
    Ruby One-Click Installer for, 426
with_options method, 212
writing tests, 255–256

X

XML API (Lost Toys), 371–373
.xml.builder extension, 140
XSS-Shield Rails plug-in, 383

Y

YAML (Yet Another Markup Language) format, 52
yield method, 147–148

Z

zip codes, converting to coordinates (geocoding),
    349